W9-AEK-922

The Renewal of Buddhism in China:
Chu-hung and the Late Ming Synthesis

BUDDHIST STUDIES AND TRANSLATIONS
SPONSORED BY THE
COLUMBIA UNIVERSITY SEMINAR IN ORIENTAL THOUGHT
AND RELIGION WITH THE COOPERATION OF
THE INSTITUTE FOR ADVANCED STUDIES OF WORLD RELIGIONS

1. Portrait of Chu-hung *(YCFH* 34, p. 1a–b)

THE RENEWAL
OF
BUDDHISM
IN CHINA

*Chu-hung
and the
Late Ming Synthesis*

Chün-fang Yü

New York   Columbia University Press   1981

Library of Congress Cataloging in Publication Data

Yü, Chün-fang.
    The renewal of Buddhism in China.

    (Buddhist studies and translations) (IASWR
series)
    Bibliography: p.
    Includes index.
    1. Chu-hung, 1535–1615.   2. Priests, Buddhist—
China—Biography.   3. Buddhism—China—History.
I. Title.   II. Series.   III. Series: Institute
for Advanced Studies of World Religions. IASWR series
BQ946.U2Y8   294.3′657′0924   79-28073
ISBN 0-231-04972-2

Columbia University Press
New York   Guildford, Surrey

This book is dedicated to the memory of *Nai-nai,*
my maternal grandmother,
who first introduced me to Buddhism through her
simple piety,

and to the memory of my father, Chi-meng Yü,
who instilled in me the Confucian love for learning.

Committee on Buddhist Studies and Translations

IASWR Series

Buddhist Monastic Discipline: The Sanskrit Prātimokṣa Sūtras of the Mahā-sāṃghikas and Mūlasarvāstivādins, by Charles S. Prebish (The Pennsylvania State University Press).

Sūtra of the Past Vows of Earth Store Bodhisattva, tr. Heng Ching.

Avatāra: The Humanization of Philosophy Through the Bhagavad Gītā, by Antonio T. deNicolás (Nicolas Hays Ltd.).

The Holy Teaching of Vimalakīrti: A Mahāyāna Scripture, tr. Robert A. F. Thurman (The Pennsylvania State University Press).

Scripture of the Lotus Blossom of the Fine Dharma (The Lotus Sūtra), tr. Leon Hurvitz (Columbia University Press).

Hua-yen Buddhism: The Jewel Net of Indra, by Francis H. Cook (The Pennsylvania State University Press).

A Buddhist Leader in Ming China: The Life and Thought of Han-shan Te-ch'ing, by Sung-peng Hsu (The Pennsylvania State University Press).

The Syncretic Religion of Lin Chao-en, by Judith A. Berling (Columbia University Press).

The Renewal of Buddhism in China: Chu-hung and the Late Ming Synthesis, by Chün-fang Yü (Columbia University Press).

CONTENTS

PREFACE

IN THE COURSE of my research on Chu-hung and Ming Buddhism, I have benefited from the advice, suggestions, and criticisms of many teachers, scholars, colleagues, and friends. It has not always been possible for me to express my great appreciation and gratitude to these people. I would like, therefore, to record my formal acknowledgment and indebtedness to them now.

Professor Wm. Theodore de Bary, my teacher for many years, has been unfailingly helpful in his patient guidance and creative suggestions. Despite his demanding schedule of scholarly and administrative duties, I have never been deprived of his counsel and advice whenever these were needed. It was he who introduced me to the field of Ming thought and led me to develop an abiding interest in it. It would be difficult to imagine the completion of this study without his constant help and encouragement.

During my stay in Taiwan from October 1967 to May 1968, the Reverend Nan-t'ing, abbot of Hua-yen Lien-she of Taipei, acted both as my instructor in Buddhist philosophy and my informant on monastic life. He went through the entire text of Chu-hung's commentary on the *A-mi-t'o ching* (Smaller Sukhāvatīvyūha Sutra) with me and also clarified many points that were unclear to me about monastic rules and practices. Most important of all, by his personal example he made me realize that even in this age of *mo-fa*—the decay of the Law—it is still possible to find a Buddhist monk of wisdom and compassion.

Professor Makita Tairyō, formerly of the Institute of Humanistic Studies, Kyoto University, was most gracious in consenting to direct my research while I was at the institute from October 1968 to May 1969. He was generous with his time and readily made available from his personal collections books relating to my topic whenever they could not be found in the various libraries in Kyoto. Aside from offering many helpful suggestions, he was also a most amiable host. It is due to his kindness and hospitality that my stay in Kyoto will always remain a memorable event in my life.

I also want to express my indebtedness to Professors Philip Yampolsky, Alex Wayman, and John Meskill of Columbia University. Since I was a student in Professor Yampolsky's seminars, I have benefited from his constructive criticisms. Professors Yampolsky, Wayman, and Meskill helped me a great deal, either by pointing out weaknesses in my argument or alerting me to other important sources relating to the subject.

When I revised the manuscript for publication, I benefited from suggestions of colleagues and friends. Irene Bloom, Sung-peng Hsu, Anna K. Seidel, and Holmes H. Welch read the manuscript either in part or in its entirety and offered me much-needed improvement in the various stages of the seemingly endless process of revision. Karen Mitchell of Columbia University Press deserves a word of special thanks for her editorial assistance. Grace Ahmed of Rutgers University, with her characteristic good humor and patience, typed the manuscript several times as it was revised. Olive Holmes, formerly of Harvard University, came to my rescue and helped me with the preparation of the glossary and index.

I would like to thank Sidney Leonard Greenblatt for giving me invaluable help when I struggled with the writing of my dissertation, the early incarnation of this study. Through our long and interminable discussions I was challenged to address myself to an audience wider than my fellow Buddhologists and historians of Ming China.

I would also like to acknowledge my gratitude to the Research Council of Rutgers University, which provided me with two research grants to cover the expenses connected with preparation of the manuscript for publication.

Although my debt to these people and institutions is considerable, I alone am responsible for any imperfections in this book.

Princeton, N.J.   Chün-fang Yü

ON THE ILLUSTRATIONS

THERE ARE eight illustrations interspersed in the text of this book. Seven are wood-cut prints made in the late Ming, and one is a lithographic print made in the late Ch'ing. These prints come from four sources and in different ways touch upon Chu-hung and Ming Buddhism.

The portrait of Chu-hung (figure 1, frontispiece) and the panoramic view of the Yün-ch'i monastery (figure 8 and jacket) are found in the complete work of Chu-hung, *Yün-ch'i fa-hui*. He wrote four poems commenting on his portraits, and this one was probably written for the portrait we see here.

[I am] As thin as dried-up firewood,
As feeble as fallen leaves;
As stupid as a blind tortoise, and
As awkward as a crippled turtle.
There is no Way [for me] to venerate,
No Dharma [for me] to speak about.
If you ask me why I am sitting thus cross-legged,
I am only calling *A-mi-t'o-fo*.[1]

The panoramic view of the monastery shows all the major buildings of the Yün-ch'i Ssu, as well as the scenic spots on the mountain, most of which Chu-hung had written about in his poems. Following the steps leading from Fan Village on the extreme right, one comes to the place for releasing life (*fang-sheng-so*) at the lower center of the left side of the picture. Going further up, on the right one sees the stupa of Chu-hung and on the left, that of the nun Chu-chin, who was Chu-hung's wife, surnamed T'ang, before both left the household life. The winding path goes through a thicket of bamboos, and then one comes to the front gate of the monastery. The Meditation

Hall *(ch'an-t'ang)* is in the middle, the Dharma Hall *(fa-t'ang)* is be-hind it, and the Western Hall *(hsi-t'ang)* where monks lived is to the left. On the extreme left, there is finally the hall for storing the scriptures *(tsang-ching-t'ang)*.

The next four prints (figure 2–5) depict significant events in Chu-hung's life, and they come from a most unusual book entitled *Ching-tu ch'uan-teng kuei-yüan-ching* (Transmission of the Lamp in the Pure Land Tradition: Mirror of the Return to the Origin). This work was written by a monk named Chih-ta who lived in the Pao-kuo Monastery of Hangchow at the end of the Ming and the begin-ning of the Ch'ing. It is an account of the lives of Hui-yüan, Yen-shou, and Chu-hung, the "three patriarchs" of the Pure Land tradi-tion, written in the dramatic form called *ch'uan-ch'i*, which was very popular in the Ming.[2] This was one of a few plays that used ex-plicitly Buddhist themes for the edification of the audience. Accord-ing to the author's preface,[3] though the form is that of a play, he prefers to call his work a *shih-lu*, "actual record," because he wants the audience to take seriously the events that take place in it. The theatre-goer should imitate the actions of the three patriarchs by practicing *nien-fo* (calling the name of the Buddha), adopting a veg-etarian diet, refraining from killing sentient beings, and, above all, seeking rebirth in the Pure Land. The language of the drama is plain, so that even young children can understand it. The author asks that the donor who sponsors the performance be sincere and serious. The performance of the play is similar to the preaching of the Dharma. Hence no meat or wine should be served, but the donor should offer candles, incense, and tea. Similarly, the actors who perform the play should consider themselves to be preaching the Dharma. Maintaining correct thought after fasting, they ought to feel that the performance is spiritual almsgiving *(fa-shih)*, in no way different from material almsgiving *(ts'ai-shih)*.

The play is in four *chüan*. Even though it is about the three patriarchs, the sections on each are not evenly distributed. The sec-tion on Chu-hung occupies 47 out of 123 pages and is almost half the length of the play. Moreover, in the play, the second patriarch, Yen-shou, predicts just before he dies that the Pure Land teaching would become greatly glorified by Chu-hung in the Ming. It is obvi-ous that the author regards Chu-hung as the culminator of the Pure Land tradition.

Figure 2 depicts the incident that triggers Chu-hung's decision to leave home. It is New Year's Eve, and Chu-hung and his wife T'ang are in the study. The maid is about to serve tea to Chu-hung in his favorite teacup. A guardian spirit *(hu-shen)* suddenly appears and the maid, taking him for a ghost, stumbles in her fright and drops the cup. T'ang consoles her husband, saying, "Everything is impermanent. All things that gather must also disperse."

Figure 3 depicts Chu-hung's enlightenment at Tun-ch'ang. Chu-hung is here sitting in deep concentration. In the state of samadhi he sees the Buddha burning incense and Māra holding a halberd. But a moment later he would see the Buddha and Māra change places, and this experience leads to his enlightenment.

Figure 4 shows Chu-hung standing by a rice field with a lay follower who is a first-degree licentiate with the unusual but highly appropriate surname Shui, "water." Chu-hung calls the name of the Buddha, and as a result, rain pours down to the relief and delight of anxious farmers.

Figure 5 depicts the ritual of "plenary mass" *(shui-lu),* which lasts for seven days and nights. Souls in torment (one is headless) come to Yün-ch'i monastery to listen to Chu-hung, who is seated on the platform dressed in the full ritual regalia. In the lower left-hand corner, some hungry ghosts are receiving food from the offerings left near the temple gate. Kuan-yin, holding a vase in her left hand and a willow branch in her right, is looking on from mid-air with approval.

The last two illustrations (figure 6 and 7) do not directly concern Chu-hung, but they serve as vivid illustrations of popular Buddhist practices in which Chu-hung was keenly interested. Figure 6 shows a tortoise being released at Chiao-shan monastery. This lithographic print comes from a very interesting book entitled *Hung-hsüeh yin-yüan* (Causes and Conditions of Bright Snow), which contains 240 pictures accompanied by short essays recording important events in the life of the author, Lin Ch'ing. The first volume was published in 1838 and contains entries ranging from the author's childhood to age forty. The second volume was published in 1841 and covers the decade from his fortieth to his fiftieth year. The last volume was published in 1849 and covers the next five years of the author's life. The illustration used here appears in the second volume and records an event that took place in the summer of 1836. In late July of that year, the author was visiting the monastery Chiao-

shan in the middle of the Yangtze River. Facing Chin-shan monastery, which was about fifteen miles away, Chiao-shan had been famous ever since the K'ang-hsi emperor visited it in 1703. According to
the author, he had paid about ten cash for the tortoise at the market
a few days earlier. Then he took the tortoise to Chiao-shan and set it
free in the river. However, instead of swimming away, the tortoise
came back and climbed ashore, as it is doing in the picture. Perhaps
this was because the current was too strong for the tortoise, who had
become weak from captivity. But the author rather suspected that it
wanted to stay on the temple grounds. In the end, he had it put in
the pond for releasing life *(fang-sheng-ch'ih)* at Chiao-shan, and the
tortoise swam in contentment.[4]

The last illustration (figure 8) comes from a Ming edition of the
Hsi-hsiang chi (Romance of the Western Chamber).[5] It is a scene depicting a typical Buddhist service. Madame Ts'ui has asked the
monks to read the sutra for the benefit of her dead husband. In
order to be near her daughter Ying-ying, Chang Chün-jui has also
asked the monks to do the same for his parents. On the fifteenth day
of the second month, the day the Buddha entered Nirvana, a
memorial service is duly conducted at the temple. In this picture,
while monks are reading the sutra, Chang is lighting a candle and
Ying-ying is helping her mother offer the incense. Services of this
kind were very much a part of popular Buddhist practice in the
Ming. Chu-hung referred to them as *ching-ch'an* (reading sutras and
saying penance) and felt that the practice contributed to the commercialization and worldliness of the sangha.

The Renewal of Buddhism in China:
Chu-hung and the Late Ming Synthesis

CHAPTER ONE

Introduction

THE LIFE, work, and teachings of Yün-ch'i Chu-hung (1535–1615), a prominent Buddhist monk of the late Ming dynasty, are the subject of this study. I came to Chu-hung as a result of a general interest in Ming thought, an interest that has had some bearing on my research methodology and the framework within which the data are interpreted. I have sought to examine Chu-hung not simply as a Buddhist thinker within a self-contained tradition of Chinese Buddhism, but as one who contributed to the broader intellectual and social life of his times. As I hope the following pages will illustrate, this approach should illuminate some aspects of Ming Buddhism, and at the same time broaden understanding of the intellectual milieu of the late Ming period.

I would further argue that such an approach is necessary because of the nature of Chinese thought since the Sung. Neo-Confucianism inaugurated an era of intense intellectual creativity, manifested in new developments in Confucianism, Buddhism, and Taoism throughout the Sung, Yüan, Ming, and early Ch'ing dynasties. There are, of course, many features of Neo-Confucianism that distinguish it from the Confucianism of the Ch'in and Han periods, one of these being a creative interaction with Buddhism and Taoism. Individual Neo-Confucians might approve or reject particular doctrines and practices, but they could not ignore the existence of Buddhism and Taoism. Long before the trend of combining three teachings in one (san-chiao ho-i) became prevalent in the late Ming, it was already true that no one in any of these three traditions could work without being influenced by the other two. An adequate understanding of Neo-Confucianism therefore presupposes some knowledge of Buddhism and Taoism. A similar and perhaps equally compelling case can be made for the importance of a knowledge of how developments in Neo-Confucianism affected Buddhism and Taoism. Furthermore, since Buddhism and Taoism were in a subordinate position vis-à-vis Neo-Confucianism, which was more highly esteemed, Buddhists and Taoists usually had to justify their causes by attempting some kind of reconciliation with the Neo-Confucian "orthodoxy." Familiarity with Neo-Confucian ideas and the ability to engage in discourse with Neo-Confucians frequently were among the important qualifications of an eminent monk. This was clearly the case with Chu-hung and his contemporaries. In order to understand Chu-hung, it is therefore necessary to consider him not only as a Ming Buddhist thinker, but also as a Ming thinker.

The late sixteenth and the early seventeenth centuries have emerged through recent studies as among the most active and creative periods in Chinese intellectual history. To appreciate this vitality and diversity, one need only recall that this was the period of such diverse individuals as the utopian activist Ho Hsin-yin (1517–1579), the Tung-lin reformer Kao P'an-lung (1562–1625), the historian-scholar Chiao Hung (1540–1620), and the brilliant eccentric Li Chih (1527–1602).[1] It was the period that witnessed the beginning of a new emphasis on empiricism—the pursuit of "practical learning." Chinese thinkers came into contact, if not to terms, with Catholicism and the Western scientific learning brought to China by the Jesuit missionaries. It was an age of critical reassessment of the past, intense awareness of the present, and lively expectations for the future. Despite the multifarious interests, preoccupations, and causes that impelled these late Ming Neo-Confucian thinkers, many of them shared certain similar attitudes. As de Bary has observed, these can be characterized as Confucian forms of "liberalism and pragmatism."[2] Late Ming thinkers showed moral earnestness in the reformation of society. They were interested in practical methods of spiritual cultivation, and they valued solid, serious scholarship. Theoretical discourse unrelated to practice was generally considered impractical and unbeneficial. Yet, since each person was accorded equal recognition as an autonomous being, the Neo-Confucians of the late Ming were tolerant of the opinions of others. While adherence to an orthodoxy was not entirely absent, the prevailing attitude was open-mindedness in regard to other teachings. "Combining three teachings in one" became a motto of the day.

Late Ming Buddhism also reflected the spirit of the age. After two hundred years of relative obscurity, Buddhism received new energy through four monks of outstanding learning and charisma who suddenly appeared on the scene almost contemporaneously. In addition to Chu-hung, they were Tzu-po Chen-k'o (1543–1603), Han-shan Te-ch'ing (1546–1623), and Ou-i Chih-hsü (1599–1655). Their influence permeated the monastic and lay Buddhist communities of their times and charted the course for the development of Buddhism in later generations. Both monastic and lay Buddhism of the Ch'ing and Republican periods derived their doctrinal formulations and practical methods of cultivation from Ming precedents. Traces of the dual cultivation of Ch'an and Pure Land (ch'an-ching shuang-hsiu) Buddhism in the monasteries may be detected as early as the Sung (960–1279).[3] The significance of lay Buddhism had already been demonstrated in the fourth century.[4] Yet the Ming models claimed attention because of their proximity in time and the impact of their success, if not the originality of their ideas. It is for this reason that one might consider what happened in the last hundred years of the Ming a renewal of Buddhism.

Chu-hung, Chen-k'o, Te-ch'ing, and Chih-hsü were very different individuals, in both temperament and accomplishments, but they too showed a remarkable consensus in their general attitudes and beliefs. They all saw the need for reviving Buddhism. They all felt that the most effective way to achieve this goal was to transcend sectarian rivalries, to stress religious cultivation over doctrinal specialization, to arrive at an understanding of Confucianism, while seeking no confrontation with it. "Liberalism" and "pragmatism," then, could characterize their guiding philosophy equally well.

Buddhist leadership in the late Ming faced similar problems, exhibited similar vitality, and offered similar answers to those proffered by other intellectual elites of the society at large. Thus, the converse of the argument made earlier also applies: To understand the total intellectual climate of the late Ming, one must know the condition of Buddhism, because it was an integral part of the general intellectual and spiritual revitalization of the period. The study of Ming Buddhism takes on added importance because it helps us understand the later development of Chinese Buddhism and sheds light on the perennial problem of religious and philosophical syncretism in China.

Despite the multitude of reasons that can be adduced for the study of Ming Buddhism, relatively little work has yet been done in this field.[5] A survey of Chinese works on Chinese Buddhism shows that they concentrate heavily on pre-T'ang and T'ang (618–907) times.[6] There are a number of works in English dealing with the T'ang and early Sung, a result of the great popularity of the Ch'an (Zen) school in the West. But the general neglect of more recent developments in Chinese Buddhism is apparent in Western scholarship as well.[7] Japanese scholars are almost alone in having paid serious attention to this underdeveloped area. As the references in this study testify, I owe much to the efforts of these scholars. The works of Takao Giken and Makita Tairyō deserve special mention in this regard.

The tendency to underrepresent post-T'ang Buddhism is not fortuitous, for it has been generally agreed by scholars and the sangha alike that Chinese Buddhism reached its full glory during the T'ang and that after the T'ang, except for the Ch'an school during the Sung, Buddhism went into a steady decline. Post-T'ang Buddhism is regarded as having been in a state of decline because no new sutras were being translated, no new doctrines were being formulated, and the sangha as a whole was of a qualitatively low caliber. Chu-hung himself used these same criteria to justify his claim that he was living in the epoch of *mo-fa,* or the decay of the Dharma. The present study does not, perhaps, question these judgments, but it does question whether these are the only criteria for examining and evaluating post-T'ang Buddhism. By taking Chu-hung as the subject of my study, I do not thereby claim that he should be accorded the same prestige as such early masters as Chih-i or Hsüan-tsang. Ming Buddhism ought to be studied not because it was better or worse than its predecessors, but because it differed from them.

My research into Ming Buddhism leads me to believe that its tendency toward syncretism, its stronger emphasis on practice, and its relatively slight interest in doctrine most strikingly differentiated it from its predecessors. Syncretism in Ming Buddhism is evidenced in both the internal combination of Buddhist schools and the external rapprochement with Confucianism and Taoism. To make such an observation is not to deny that such tendencies may already have existed in the T'ang and pre-T'ang periods or that both tendencies were manifest from at least the Sung onward. The very fact that among all Buddhist schools only Ch'an and Pure Land continued to

flourish after the persecution of A.D. 845 is a clear indication of the
general emphasis on religious cultivation, for both Ch'an and Pure
Land Buddhists were basically uninterested in formulating doctrine
or carrying on philosophical discourse. Each school offered its own
practical method of salvation. As for syncretism, Yung-ming Yen-
shou (904–975) was perhaps best known for his efforts to bring
about a synthesis among various Buddhist schools, including T'ien-
t'ai, Ch'an, Pure Land (Ching-t'u), Vinaya (Lü), and esoteric Buddhism or Tantrism (Chen-yen). His advocacy of the dual practice of
Ch'an and Pure Land exerted considerable influence on later Buddhists, Chu-hung included. Another Sung master, Ch'i-sung (d.
1072), who was famous for his defense of Buddhism against its Confucian critics, was also a syncretist who argued most forcefully for
the compatibility of the three teachings.

Chu-hung, as we shall see, pursued these same tendencies with
striking single-mindedness. He was energetic in advocating practical
and methodical approaches to religious cultivation, and he was genuinely hopeful of a dialogue with Confucianism. Though he was a
faithful Pure Land believer all his life and was posthumously revered as a Pure Land patriarch, he did not restrict himself solely to
Pure Land practices. He stressed the observance of Vinaya, the importance of sutra study and Ch'an meditation, as well as the correct
performance of Tantric rituals. This is an important fact. However,
he neither compartmentalized these pursuits nor regarded them as
unrelated, in contrast, perhaps, to some Buddhist leaders in Japan.
He considered all of them as different aspects of *ching-yeh* (pure
deeds) and incorporated Ch'an, Vinaya, and Tantrism in a broadly
defined path of Pure Land. Borrowing from Hua-yen terminology,
Chu-hung distinguished two levels of "one mind" resulting from
Buddha invocation *(nien-fo)*: the one mind of particularity *(shih i-
hsin)* and the one mind of universality *(li i-hsin)*. While the first might
be shallow, the second was profound, for it was not different from
absolute reality *(shih-hsiang)* itself. Chu-hung used this concept to justify his syncretic approach to Buddhism in general and to prove the
identity between Pure Land *nien-fo* and Ch'an meditation in particular. Although its origins may be traced to an earlier period, the characteristic development of syncretism in the Ming was such as to
suggest a qualitative distinction between Ming Buddhism and Buddhism in the T'ang and pre-T'ang periods.

Syncretism is not the only process that distinguishes Ming Buddhism from its predecessors. Like syncretism, sinicization—the process of the incorporation of Buddhism into Chinese society—is evident in an earlier period, but its effects were particularly marked during the Ming. This suggests another, closely related way of looking at this period. One aspect of the sinicization of Buddhism in the post-T'ang period was that monasteries gradually ceased to be the sole centers for Buddhist study and practice. Another was the interrelated fact that it was no longer necessary to renounce societal and familial ties to become a Buddhist. Lay Buddhist associations grew increasingly popular, while the monastic order lost both prestige and vitality because of lack of discipline and the effects of secularization. Chu-hung's career reflected these trends. He was most successful in promoting lay Buddhism. The form of Buddhism he presented to his lay followers, many of whom came from the gentry-official class, put as much emphasis on civic virtue and filial piety as it did on compassion and wisdom. It was really a sinicized Buddhism. Chu-hung was also severe in his criticism of the sangha, and he tried to institute monastic reform using his own monastery, Yünch'i Ssu, as a base. A great many factors were involved in the discrediting of the monastic order during the Ming. Some of them will be discussed in the pages that follow.

Having observed that the Buddhism of the post-T'ang differed from the Buddhism of earlier periods and that even more pronounced changes were evident in Ming Buddhism, it is appropriate to inquire into the reasons for the differences. What external and internal factors were responsible for the changes that must have occurred? What were their manifestations? Did this later form of Buddhism offer any new interpretation of doctrine? Did it produce new forms of spirituality? Did it have any effect on the society at large? And finally, was there any lasting contribution to the religious life of the sangha and the Chinese people?

These are large and complex questions, and answers to them would require a thorough study of the entire history of post-T'ang Chinese Buddhism. This book is intended as a first step in that direction. It is divided into two main parts, corresponding to Chu-hung's two major activities: as a proselytizer of the lay Buddhist movement and as a leader of monastic reform. Chapter II deals with Chu-hung's life, summarizing his major writings and his most important activities. Chapter III discusses the tradition of the joint practice of Ch'an and Pure Land. The views of Chu-hung and his spiritual predecessors on the meaning and function of *nien-fo* are treated in detail. The nature of Pure Land as a Buddhist school and Chu-hung's relationship to it are also dealt with at some length. Chapter IV offers a detailed analysis of Chu-hung's role in the lay Buddhist movement. His theory of lay Buddhism is explored, and his methodology of lay practice receives more detailed scrutiny. Chapter V analyzes Chu-hung's *Record of Self-knowledge (Tzu-chih Lu)*, a work written for his disciples and a general audience. Since the significance of this work can be understood only within a larger context, the analysis includes a historical treatment of the development of morality books *(shan-shu)*. In particular, two morality books that served as prototypes for this genre, the *T'ai-shang kan-ying p'ien* (Treatise of the Exalted One on Response and Retribution) and the *Kung-kuo ko* (The Ledger of Merits and Demerits), are analyzed thematically and compared to Chu-hung's *Record*. As a morality book, the *Record of Self-knowledge* has a special value. It is interesting both as an example of the ideology of the three teachings in one, a trend so prevalent in the Ming, and as the only morality book written by a leading Buddhist with the conscious intention of injecting Buddhist views and values into popular morality. A work of this nature serves as an excellent specimen for the study of syncretism in China. Since few morality books are available in English, a complete translation of the *Record of Self-knowledge* appears as Appendix I of this book.

Chapters VI through VIII deal with the condition of the sangha and Chu-hung's attempts at reform. Chapter VI seeks to relate the causes of monastic decline to the external factors of long-standing governmental control (limitation of monasteries, manipulation of ordination certificates, institution of monk officials) and concludes that these measures were often ineffective. Chapter VII is devoted to an analysis of internal causes of the monastic decline. These include the degeneration of Ch'an practice, the neglect of discipline, and secularization. Chu-hung's response to the monastic crisis was to emphasize strict observance of the Vinaya rules, and he made the revival of monastic discipline one of his lifelong commitments. Chapter VIII presents both his opinions on monastic discipline and the actual measures applied at the monastery Chu-hung founded and served for over forty years. A list of the monastic personnel of Yün-ch'i,

together with a description of their duties, is provided in Appendix
II. Appendix III contains a translation of some sample rules Chu-
hung instituted for his fellow monks at Yün-ch'i. These are useful
documents, for they reveal Chu-hung's administrative ability and tell
us about the daily routines and problems of managing a monastery
in sixteenth century China. Chapter IX provides an assessment of
Chu-hung's life and work, along with some observations concerning
Ming Buddhism in general.

CHAPTER TWO

Chu-hung's
Life and Major Works

THE SOURCES for Chu-hung's biography are extensive. The primary sources include inscriptions and biographies written by Chu-hung's friends, disciples, and lay followers; his own essays commemorating his parents and first wife; and incidental reminiscences scattered through his writings.

The inscriptions and biographies include the following: (1) Te-ch'ing, "Ku Hang Yün-ch'i Lien-ch'ih ta-shih t'a-ming" (Stupa Inscription of Master Lien-ch'ih of Yün-ch'i in Old Hangchow); (2) Wu Ying-pin, "Lien-tsung pa-tsu Hang-chou ku Yün-ch'i ssu chung-hsing tsun-su Lien-ch'ih ta-shih t'a-ming ping hsü" (Stupa Inscription with Preface of Master Lien-ch'ih, the Eighth Patriarch of the Pure Land School and the Restorer of the Ancient Yün-ch'i Monastery in Hangchow); (3) Kuang-yün, "Yün-ch'i pen-shih hsing-lüeh" (A Brief Biography of My Master Yün-ch'i); (4) Yü Ch'un-hsi, "Yün-ch'i Lien-ch'ih ta-shih chuan" (Biography of Master Lien-ch'ih of Yün-ch'i). Except for the one by Yü Ch'un-hsi, all are included in Chu-hung's collected works, *Yün-ch'i fa-hui*.[1] The most important of Chu-hung's own essays that make reference to his family background and early life are these: "Tzu-shang pu-hsiao wen" (Self-lamentation on My Lack of Filial Piety), "Hsien k'ao-pi yi-hsing chi" (A Record of My Dead Parents' Deeds), and "Chang nei-jen chih-ming" (A Memorial Inscription for My Wife, Chang). These too are included in *Yün-ch'i fa-hui*.[2]

There are also a considerable number of secondary sources, compiled during the early Ch'ing dynasty.[3] They are often quite brief entries, some one or two pages in length and some just a few lines. Without exception, these sources are summaries or excerpts of

materials listed among the primary sources, especially the inscriptions written by Te-ch'ing and the biography of Kuang-yün. *Wu-teng
yen-t'ung* (Strict Genealogy of the Five Lamps), *Wu-teng ch'üan-shu*
(The Complete Works of the Five Lamps), and *Hsü-teng ts'un-kao*
(Remaining Documents of the Continuation of the Lamps), are collections of biographies of Ch'an monks and not simply of monks in
general. It is interesting to note that in all three Chu-hung, together
with Ta-kuan (Tzu-po Chen-k'o) and Te-ch'ing, is listed in the section entitled "lineage unknown" *(wei-hsiang fa-ssu)*. In the following
discussion of Chu-hung's life, activities, and writings, all references
are to primary sources unless otherwise indicated.

Chu-hung was born on the twenty-second of the first month in
the fourteenth year of Chia-ch'ing (February 23, 1535) in Jen-ho
hsien of Hangchow in present-day Chekiang, for centuries one of
the most important Buddhist provinces. The boy, named Fo-hui,
was the eldest son of the old and locally prominent Shen family. His
parents were both forty-five when Chu-hung was born. His father,
Te-chien, never served in any official capacity, but according to Chu-
hung, he was well read, skilled in calligraphy, and familiar with yin-
yang philosophy, medicine, and divination.[4] In his advice to Chu-
hung, he often stressed the necessity for lifelong study, tolerance,
and the ability to forgive others. He also cautioned his son against
having anything to do with officialdom. One should not take government money, weave cloth for the government, or serve as a guaran-
tor or even a low-class copyist of government documents. Currying
favors from officials or acting as a go-between on matters between
the government and the common people was even more suspect.
This advice left a deep impression on him. Years later, after Chu-
hung became a monk, he said:

I took this instruction with deep respect. Afterward, when I looked around
at my relatives and friends, I saw that of those who suffered misfortunes,
seven or eight out of ten suffered them because of their involvement with
officials. Reflecting upon this, I decided that to become an official myself
was not something I would be willing to do. After I became a monk, I extended this admonition even further and dared not go near officials. I told
my disciples that they should not go into the households of officials to ask
for donations, nor engage in any lawsuit with others relying upon their relationship with officials as support. Satisfied with poverty and keeping myself
intact, I was fortunate to escape disaster. Although this prohibition is also
found in Buddhist precepts, I really received it from my father.[5]

Yet despite this negative attitude toward officialdom, Chu-hung lived the first thirty-two years of his life as a conventional Confucian literatus. He studied diligently and was quite outstanding among his classmates for his understanding of Confucian and Taoist classics. His father was interested in his studies, but told him that fame and prestige should be considered of secondary importance. When he was sixteen and studying very hard for the local examination away from home, his father wrote him a letter saying: "Fame and wealth are ordained by Heaven and you should not get too attached to them." Chu-hung was moved to tears and replied: "I know that I am not as diligent as the others, but as far as my literary ability is concerned, there is no cause for anxiety."[6] The following year, at the age of seventeen, he passed the examination and became a *chu-sheng* or student of the government school.

Aside from preparing for the higher examinations, he also began to study Buddhism and Taoism. He first became interested in Buddhism through an old woman living next door. Noticing that she would chant the name of the Buddha several thousand times a day, he asked why she did so. She answered that her late husband used to practice *nien-fo* (Buddha invocation) and that when he died there was no illness. He simply bade farewell to members of the family and passed away peacefully.[7] Chu-hung was so impressed by the story that he began to practice *nien-fo* and put the motto "Birth and death are the Great Matter," a favorite phrase used by students of Ch'an Buddhism, on his desk as a reminder. It was also around this time, if not earlier, that he discovered the *Record of Merits and Demerits,* a famous morality book written in the Sung dynasty. He reprinted and distributed copies free of charge. Later in life he used this book as the basis for writing the *Record of Self-knowledge.* We do not know the exact date of his becoming a lay Buddhist devotee *(chü-shih),* but by the age of twenty, when he got married, he already referred to himself as Lien-ch'ih Chü-shih. Lien-ch'ih (lotus pond) implied his desire for rebirth in the Western Paradise of the Pure Land. His wife bore him a son five years after the marriage, but the child died in infancy and she herself died five years later. Evidently she was a devoted wife, and Chu-hung remembered her with much fondness. In an essay dedicated to her memory, there is this passage:

I was by nature lazy and uninterested in worldly affairs. You did everything yourself and never troubled me with it. Thus I could freely engage in philosophical discussions or spiritual cultivation with classmates and friends and was never aware of any worries of this world. I worshipped the Buddha daily, and you made ceremonial banners yourself. You used the money from your dowry to buy offerings to the Buddha and never showed any sign of grudging. I followed a vegetarian diet in my daily life, so you were always careful to choose the vegetables for each meal and to serve the food without tasting it first yourself. I loved to buy Buddhist scriptures, so whenever anyone came with them, you would buy them without letting me know and give them to me, saying: "I know this is what you value."[8]

Besides keeping to a vegetarian diet and practicing *nien-fo,* he also forbade the killing of animals for sacrificial purposes; he used fruits and vegetables as substitutes.

Yet for all his inclination toward Buddhism, Chu-hung might have remained only a lay believer. In Ming times it was quite common for an educated Confucian to be familiar with Buddhist teachings and at some time during his lifetime to engage in one form of Buddhist practice or another. That Chu-hung cut his ties with the secular world completely and became a monk seems in all likelihood to have been bound up with his continued failures in the higher examinations and the repeated loss through death of the members of his family. Within a short span of six years, he lost his son, his wife, and both parents. His father died when he was twenty-seven. At that time Chu-hung resolved that if he did not pass the provincial examination by the age of thirty and the metropolitan examination by the age of forty, he would give up the ambition of pursuing an official career.[9] His wife died when he was twenty-nine. His mother insisted that he remarry, and so he married a girl from a poor family named T'ang. She was also a vegetarian and a believer in Buddhism. When he was thirty-one, his mother died. Success had also eluded him.

The final break occurred because of a trivial incident. There are three different versions of the story. In one version,[10] he was reading *Hui-teng chi* (Collection of the Lamp of Wisdom),[11] when he accidentally dropped a teacup and suddenly realized the futility of transient existence. In another version,[12] the incident occurred on New Year's Eve, when his wife served him tea. The cup suddenly broke as he was about to take it from her, and Chu-hung said smiling: "There is no existence without separation." According to the third version,[13] it was also New Year's Eve and it was the maid who broke a piece of blue-glazed china. When Chu-hung reprimanded

2. Leaving the Household Life (*Ching-t'u ch'uan-teng kuei-yüan ching, chüan* 1, p. 7b)

her, his wife said: "There is a fixed destiny for everything in the world, and this china also has its destiny." Her words touched him to the quick, and he was said to have made up his mind to leave the world.

Whatever the details, it is clear that the incident was important only in a symbolic sense. He had no doubt been frustrated for a long time by his repeated academic failures. Frequent losses of his loved ones had further deepened his sense of the futility and of the transience of life. The breaking of the cup, though trivial in itself, was the culmination of a long, unconscious psychological process. Perhaps the following poem, which he wrote for his wife on that occasion, best expresses his feelings:

Did you not see the woman of our neighbor to the east?
    Healthy as a tigress, punctuating her days with frequent child-
        births.
    Only last evening she was leaning against the door,
    But this morning has already returned to dust.
Did you also not see the lad of our neighbor to the west?
    Fierce as a dragon, sleeping soundly after a full evening meal.
    His soul left without ever returning;
    At dawn he entered the domain of Lord Yama [hell].
If people near us are like this,
    How much more uncertain are those distant and far away.
Just search at your leisure among our relatives and friends.
    So many deaths year in and year out
I now believe in the poems of Tzu-yang [Chang Po-tuan, a Sung
      Taoist]
    What he said is really true.
Someone galloped in the streets only yesterday, but today his body
      rests in the coffin.
If someone is clever, then he does not sleep;
Others are the same as myself.
The fox and the hare look at each other, and neither is more
      secure than the other.
    Around us similar examples abound—
Entering the wombs of horses and cows,
    It is truly pitiable: the travails of hell.
To return to the world as a man again
    will be more difficult than fishing for a needle in the ocean.

As I sing this sad song, my heart is full of sorrow;
 Tears, like blood, flow drop by drop from my eyes.
I offer you these words as a memento of the life we shared
    together;
 Whether you accept them or not is for you to decide.[14]

In 1566, when he was thirty-two, he asked the monk Hsing-t'ien
Li of Hsi-shan (west of present day Lin-an, Chekiang) to shave his
head. Then he received the complete precepts for a monk as well as
those for a bodhisattva from the Vinaya master Wu-ch'en Yü at the
ordination platform of the Chao-ch'ing Monastery in Hangchow.[15]

Chu-hung's second wife took the vow of an *upāsikā* (a Buddhist
laywoman who observes the first five precepts) at the same time he
received his tonsure from Hsing-t'ien Li.[16] She was then nineteen
years old. After her own mother died, at the age of forty-seven, she
became a nun and received the name Chu-chin. Some of Chu-hung's
prominent lay disciples, Sung Ying-ch'ang and Chu Chung-ch'un
among others, contributed money, bought a house in the city, and
rebuilt it as a nunnery. When she was fifty-nine, she was installed in
it as the abbess. The nunnery was called Hsiao-i An (Abbey of Filial
Piety and Righteousness) to commemorate her filial piety and the
generosity of the lay donors.[17]

Chu-hung's relationship with his second wife was rather unusual
and he later recalled her unselfish support with gratitude.[18] Before
he became a monk he wrote a letter, according to the required state
procedure, requesting permission from the educational commissioner to enter the monastic order. His older brother tried to inter-
cept the letter and thus thwart his aim, but when Chu-hung's wife
learned about it, she told Chu-hung. On the evening Chu-hung was
to receive the tonsure, his relatives and friends tried to prevent him
from doing so. They urged her to join them, but she answered that
she had known for a long time about her husband's desire for salvation and could not be expected to alter his resolve. Eventually she
succeeded in persuading the others to give up the attempt. Several
years later, when he was staying in the Wa-kuan Monastery in Nanking, he became critically ill. When his wife heard about it, she immediately prayed to the Dipper in the Taoist fashion for Chu-hung's
recovery. It is an interesting footnote to the religious life of this time

that her Buddhist faith did not preclude her engaging in Taoist practices.

Her devotion apparently was regarded as exemplary. Chu-hung's aunt, who was then the matriarch of the family, was moved to praise her conduct in front of all the women, saying: "Have you ever seen such a thing? She was deserted by her husband when he became a monk. But instead of feeling resentment she prays, even now, for his well-being. Such conduct is really rare. You ought to model yourselves after her." Chu-hung felt that it was largely due to her understanding and sympathy that he could leave the world so resolutely. She died a year before Chu-hung and was later buried near her husband.

After Chu-hung became a monk, following the mendicant tradition he spent the next six years traveling throughout the country to seek instruction from prominent teachers. In the capital he visited the Ch'an masters Pien-jung and Hsiao-yen.[19] According to Chu-hung both monks passed away the year after he visited them.[20] We are not given the year of his visit, but since he went back to Hang-chow in 1571, it must have been before that time. Although he did not study under them long, he was apparently deeply impressed by what he learned, especially from Pien-jung. Hsiao-yen was a recluse who seldom received visitors.[21] Pien-jung emphasized practice and left no writings behind. Chu-hung tells us about his first meeting with Pien-jung:

After I came to the capital, I went, along with twenty other monks, to pay my respects to Master Pien-jung. When we asked him for instruction, the master told us we should neither seek profit and fame nor should we try to curry favor with the high and mighty. Rather, we should devote all our efforts to the Way. After we came out, some youths laughed, saying that they had expected to hear something unusual and questioning what good these platitudes could do. I felt differently and thought that it was precisely this point that made the old man deserve respect. Even though he was reticent in speech, he could have quoted some clever sayings of former masters in order to impress people. That he did not do so was because he wanted to teach only what he himself practiced. This is a true, practicing Ch'an monk. We ought not to look down upon him.[22]

It was said that Chu-hung had his first enlightenment on his way to Tung-ch'ang (present-day Liao-ch'eng in Shantung). He wrote the following verse on this occasion:

東昌發悟

3. Enlightenment at Tung-ch'ang (*Ching-t'u ch'uan-teng kuei-yüan ching,*
chüan 1, p. 8a)

Things of twenty years ago may be held in doubt.
It is no wonder that I encounter my enlightenment three thou-
    sand *li* away.
Burning incense and throwing the halberd are idle dreams,
Māra and Buddha argue the right and the wrong in vain.

During these years of wandering, characteristically he did not forget
his duty as a son. During the three years of mourning for his
mother, he carried the wooden spirit tablet with him wherever he
went and offered sacrifices at each meal.

Chu-hung took part in five sessions of Ch'an meditation held in
different monasteries in the Chekiang area, but he was so single-
minded that not once did he bother to find out the names of monks
sitting next to him. In 1571 Chu-hung came to a village called Fan-
tsun on Mount Yün-ch'i in his native Hangchow. He found the quiet
surroundings much to his liking and decided to remain there for the
rest of his life. Two natives of the place, Ch'en Ju-yü and Li Hsiu,
who were students at the national university, built a hut for him. He
continued his efforts at meditation, eating but once a day and fasting, at one time, for as long as seven days. It is said that he hung an
iron plaque around his neck on which was written the words: "I will
talk to people only when flowers bloom on the iron tree."

On Mount Yün-ch'i were the remains of a monastery built in
967 for a Ch'an master known as the Tamer of Tigers (Fu-hu Ch'an-
shih).[23] This monk's name was Chih-feng. He lived during the Five
Dynasties (907–960), the year of his death being the second year of
Yung-hsi (985) of the Northern Sung. He was known for his strict
observance of Vinaya. Once during his meditation he was visited by
a god who called himself the Guardian of Discipline (Hu-chieh
Shen). The god told him that he was almost perfect in his conduct
except for occasional small breaches. Chih-feng immediately asked
what his shortcomings were. The god answered that since even the
water used in washing the begging bowl was a gift from donors, he
should not throw it away as he usually did. From then on Chih-feng
always drank the water. Another anecdote told of his compassion for
tigers near his monastery in the mountains. He would beg for
money in order to buy meat for the hungry tigers. It was said that
the tigers would often wait for him to return and carry him back
into the mountain.[24]

The Yün-ch'i monastery was destroyed by a flood in the seventh year of Hung-chih (1494) and had been left in ruins for the last seventy-odd years. When Chu-hung first came there, he was greatly attracted by the serenity and seclusion of the place, but he had no intention of building a monastic center. In fact, he had quite negative feelings about establishing new monasteries, as this reflection shows:

Public monasteries are for the masses [to live in as monks], and they are, of course, a good thing. But one should take charge of them only after one has taken care of one's own business. Otherwise, one will end up either wasting all one's spirit and energy or becoming attached to worldly things. Thus it will cause one who has not attained the Truth never to get there, and one who has attained it to falter midway. In the case of restoring the Yün-ch'i, each step was taken only after it was forced upon me by circumstances. I never tried to take any initiative in its restoration. Even so, I felt that I had suffered considerable harm [in my own religious cultivation].[25]

Despite his reluctance, Chu-hung consented to head the monastery. But his ambivalence about assuming the role of a religious leader seemed to persist. Later on in life, he expressed similar reservations about lay associations, yet he also consented to head at least one of them.

Of the circumstances that precipitated the subsequent restoration of Yün-ch'i Monastery, two events were most important: Chu-hung's success in bringing sorely needed rain to relieve a serious drought, and his success in driving out tigers infesting the neighborhood. As a result of these feats, the local people volunteered to rebuild the monastery in order to show Chu-hung their gratitude.

The area around the mountain on which the monastery stood was said to be endangered by the presence of tigers. Each year more than twenty people and many more domestic animals were killed. To correct the situation Chu-hung recited some sutras and performed the Tantric ritual of "bestowing food on hungry ghosts" (shih-shih). In the end, he claimed that the tigers were pacified and no longer harmed people.[26] But apparently this was not quite the case, for in the twenty-fourth year of Wan-li (1596) Chu-hung performed another service to pacify the tigers. The text of the prayer used in the service, which has been preserved, throws some light on the procedure:

In the tenth month of the twenty-fourth year of Wan-li, Ting-pei, Wu-tu, and some other villages in Ch'ien-t'ang *hsien* of our prefecture suffered from the harm caused by tigers. Many people and domestic animals were killed. So-and-so from our village came to me and asked me to pray for relief. I believe that human beings and tigers originally possess the same nature, and the cause for the destruction lies in hatred inherited from the past. If we capture the tigers, then we harm one other. If we drive them away, then what is the difference between us and other people? Thus we must perform fasting and create merit so that we may hope to transform them silently and the harm will quietly disappear. Therefore in the Miao-ching Monastery of Huang-shan in this realm I assembled the sangha and set up the *bodhimaṇḍa* [a place for religious offerings] to pray for relief and ward off this calamity. The service lasted five days and nights. It was satisfactorily concluded on such-and-such a date. During the ceremony, incense, candles, fruits, and refreshments were respectfully offered and the monks were asked sincerely to prostrate themselves in front of the twelve scriptures containing the penitential rites which originated with Emperor Wu of Liang (*Liang-huang ch'an-fa*). Throughout the night, the Tantric ritual of feeding the flaming mouth [i.e., of the hungry ghosts, *yü-chia yen-k'ou*] was performed. With the merit accrued thereby, I further prayed to all the saints who had tamed tigers since ancient times, asking them to carry this prayer to the gods of the mountains and the earth in all directions. I beseeched those who had harmed the lives of tigers in their previous lives to renounce their anger and resentment, so that the tigers would not seek retribution. I hope those who are attacked by tigers today can all be soon reborn into one of the good realms of rebirth for sentient beings, and that they will not fall into the evil ones. Man does not intend to harm tigers, so if he but cultivate the heart of compassion, he will forever relinquish killing; neither do tigers want to injure men on purpose, and we hope that they will speedily live out their present incarnations and depart from the wheel of suffering. The efficacy of this service will extend protection even to the smallest species of sentient beings and enable the lost souls who have wandered in limbo for many generations to achieve early release. May everyone plant the seed of enlightenment; may the whole world become the land of bliss.[27]

According to the story handed down,[28] in the same year (fifth year of Lung-ch'ing, 1571) there was a serious drought. The villagers begged Chu-hung to pray for rain. At first he refused, saying, "I only know how to recite the name of the Buddha; I have no other magical skills." Yet they insisted and in the end prevailed upon him to perform the ritual. He went out to the rice fields and, while beating on a wooden fish (a small drum) and walking around the fields, recited the name of the Buddha. It rained in the area he covered. The villagers, amazed by his ability and deeply grateful, came for-

4. Sprinkling Rain of Dharma (*Ching-t'u ch'uan-teng kuei-yüan ching, chüan* 1, p. 9b)

ward with wood and tools and offered to rebuild the abandoned temple. They said: "Since the Ch'an master has benefited our village, we want to build a new temple on the old site, so that the burning of incense will last forever in our midst." The temple was finished in a short time. There was no elaborate outer gate, nor main hall in the middle. The only buildings were the Meditation Hall, where the monks worked, and the Dharma Hall, where the scriptures and statues were kept. Despite Chu-hung's initial hesitation, the Yün-ch'i monastery gradually became a center of Buddhist training. He made the practice of Pure Land the primary goal for the monastic community. During the winter, sitting in meditation *(tso-ch'an)* was the main pursuit, while lecturing on the scriptures was secondary.

A general problem in interpreting the biographies of monks is that of distinguishing history from hagiography. In this case, the only available sources include the testimony of Chu-hung and his followers concerning the miraculous feats of taming the tigers and producing rain. Yet whether these miracles actually took place may be less important than what people made of them. Functionally speaking, it was the performance of these rites and their assumed validity that served to bind the villagers and Chu-hung together. Temple building by private citizens had, after all, always been one of the three common means for the building of temples since the T'ang dynasty; the other two had been their construction by monks and by official patronage.[29] According to Eberhard, who made a study of temple-building activities in post-T'ang times, "of all temples the percentage of those built by private persons remained between 20 and 40% of the total, but in those periods in which government building was strong, building by monks was weak and vice versa."[30] The periods when temple building by the government was strongest were around A.D. 950 (61 percent), A.D. 1150 (47 percent), and A.D. 1500 (48 percent). Those periods when temple building by monks was strongest were around A.D. 850 (70 percent), A.D. 1050 (56 percent), and A.D. 1400 (56 percent); private citizens were most active around A.D. 1200 (39 percent), A.D. 1300 (36 percent), and A.D. 1800 (40 percent). The interesting thing to note about the period of roughly a century when Chu-hung was active (1550–1650), which happened to be the second highest peak of temple-building activities since 900, is that government-sponsored building dropped from 43 to 33 percent. The lowest point, 28 percent, was reached in 1600, by which time monk-initiated temple building had increased from 27 to 43 percent. Temple building by private citizens, however, remained constant at 31 percent until 1600, and then dropped to 24 percent around 1650. The trend during this period was clearly the rise of temple building by monks.

Thus, although the revival of Yün-ch'i did not follow the general trend, it does afford us some insight into the origins and characteristics of a temple built by voluntary contributions from local citizenry. When a monastery was eatablished by the local people, the effort usually but not invariably involved the approval and encouragement of a revered monk by the gentry-official class in return for deeds beneficial to the community in the past and for future spiritual guidance. As to the monk, once installed he felt responsibility for and a sense of obligation to the community. One can speculate that this kind of relationship between monastery and community might, because of mutual loyalty, ensure a long existence for the monastery. As a matter of fact, Yün-ch'i was reported to be still alive and active at least up to World War II, as evidenced by the publication of a history of the monastery in 1934.[31] The monastery is also mentioned in *Shina Bukkyō shiseki* (Historical Monuments of Chinese Buddhism) by Sekino Tadashi and Tokiwa Daijō, who saw it during their study tour of Chinese monasteries and monuments in the 1920s.[32]

Chu-hung showed his sensitivity to the needs of the community on many other occasions. In the sixteenth year of Wan-li (1588), the neighborhood was ravaged by a plague that resulted from continual drought and natural disasters. The price of grain rose sharply; those who did not die of the plague succumbed to starvation. At the request of prefect Yü Liang-shu, Chu-hung performed the Tantric ritual of relieving the "flaming mouths" at the Ling-chih monastery in order to avert disaster, secure blessing for the country, and safeguard the people. It lasted for seven days and nights. Assembled monks recited the Diamond Sutra, the chapter called "The Ground of Mind of Bodhisattva Precepts" (*P'u-sa-chieh hsin-ti p'in*) of the Sutra of Brahma's Net, the Sutra of the Virtue of the Original Vow of Bhaiṣajya-guru-vaiḍūryaprabhāṣa, the Buddha of Medicine (*Yao-shih liu-li-kuang ju-lai pen-yüan kung-te ching*), the Lotus Sutra, and the chapter called "The Vows of Bodhisattva Samantabhadra" (*P'u-hsien hsing-yüan p'in*) of the Avataṁsaka Sutra.[33] It was re-

普濟幽魂

5. Universal Relief of Wandering Souls (*Ching-t'u ch'uan-teng kuei-yüan ching,* *chüan* 1, p. 10a)

ported that at the end of the ritual, the plague abated. On another occasion, Prefect Yü asked Chu-hung to head a fund-raising campaign to rebuild the bridge called Chu-ch'iao (Vermilion Bridge), which had been washed away by tides. Transportation was interrupted and travelers complained of hardships. Chu-hung asked every resident, no matter whether rich or poor, to contribute one eight-hundredth of a tael of silver. The reason for choosing the "eight" in the eight-hundredth was that it symbolized *k'un* or "earth" and therefore could curb "water." Before long the needed fund was gathered. It was said that because Chu-hung recited spells (*chou,* mantras) on the site when the foundation was ready to be laid, the tide did not come for several days and thus it was possible to finish the bridge in time.[34]

It is an intriguing question to what extent Chu-hung's social and community activities were motivated by his concern for the welfare of the common people and to what extent they were motivated by a sense of obligation toward his lay supporters. We know that Yün-ch'i relied entirely on popular contributions:

For fifty years since the establishment of the monastery . . . more than a few thousand people often resided in the temple. He [Chu-hung] did not seek out permanent donors, but allowed them to come forward of their own accord. As soon as there was surplus income, he distributed it to other temples. He did not let it accumulate in the treasury. If there were people who offered fruits or money to the master aside from the usual vegetarian feasts, he would accept them and then immediately exchange them for clothing and medicine to give to the poor and sick.[35]

Recognizing the economic dependence of Yün-ch'i, some Japanese scholars have suggested that Chu-hung may have accommodated himself and his teaching to a lay following which came to consist largely of the official-literati class. Oura Masahiro[36] further suggests that, despite the fact that Chu-hung received a great deal of help from the common people in reviving Yün-ch'i, loyalty to him later lay more in the prestigious and influential official-literati class from which he himself came than in the common people. But the evidence for this is not convincing, and the implied dichotomy between genuine compassion and opportunistic accommodation in Chu-hung's motives seems artificial and arbitrary. Chu-hung's interest in the common people cannot be doubted simply because he was also interested in gaining adherents among the official-literati class. There was a tacit understanding that by accepting lay support, he was also accepting responsibility for the community's welfare when the occasion arose. The local government was responsible for famine relief and repair of bridges, but the leading priests and monks of the community were usually expected to lend support and blessing to these enterprises. In fact, the active participation of monasteries in community activities had been a Buddhist tradition since the T'ang. Monasteries then not only served as hostels for travelers, but also managed the Inexhaustible Treasuries (wu-chin-tsang), so that they functioned as safe-deposit vaults, pawnbrokers, and loan associations for the entire community.[37] There was also the institution of pei-t'ien (fields of compassion), tracts of land set aside by monasteries for the purpose of social relief. The proceeds from this land were used to establish hospitals and dispensaries for the sick, feeding stations for the hungry, and sanctuaries for the aged and the ill. Other examples were the establishment of bathhouses within the temple precincts and rest houses along the roads to famous shrines, or such projects as road building, bridge construction, well digging, and the planting of trees along the highways.[38] Although Chu-hung did not mention these historical precedents, it seems certain that both he and his followers were aware of their existence.

After the restoration of Yün-ch'i, Chu-hung stayed there as its abbot until his death in 1615. He succeeded in making Yün-ch'i a model of Pure Land practice, strict observance of monastic discipline, and active lay following. In spite of his early training in the Ch'an school, he emphasized the Pure Land approach to salvation more and more. In one year, the twelfth year of Wan-li (1584), he completed two works. They were A-mi-t'o-ching shu-ch'ao (YCFH 6–9), a commentary on the Smaller Sukhāvatīvyūha Sutra (the most fundamental sutra of the Pure Land school), and a collection of biographies of Pure Land practitioners who were believed to have achieved rebirth in the Western Paradise, Wang-sheng chi (YCFH 16). These were Chu-hung's earliest written works, and they pointed in the direction his teachings subsequently took.

Most latter-day adherents and scholars of Buddhism have regarded Chu-hung as the last influential thinker in the tradition of syncretism between the Pure Land and Ch'an schools.[39] If syncretism implies the combination of two equally significant elements, then it cannot be said that Chu-hung syncretized Pure Land and Ch'an. Rather, as will be shown in subsequent chapters, Chu-hung tried to advocate the Pure Land doctrine, and specifically the recitation of the Buddha's name, as the all-inclusive approach to Buddhism. To facilitate its acceptance, he also accepted Ch'an, Hua-yen, T'ien-t'ai, and even Tantric tenets as valid. However, his acceptance of them was always accompanied by the realization that the Pure Land approach was most effective and suitable for his era. In other words, according to Chu-hung, one could achieve salvation as well as enlightenment by *nien-fo* (recitation of the Buddha's name) alone, even if one did not engage in the other forms of cultivation, but the converse would not be true.

Chu-hung's second preoccupation was the revitalization of the Buddhist Vinaya. This can also be seen in the order and quantity of his writing. After the works concerning Pure Land, the next two were about Vinaya. *Tzu-men ch'ung-hsing lu (YCFH* 15), a collection of accounts of the exemplary conduct of monks noted for their strict observation of Buddhist precepts, came out in the thirteenth year of Wan-li (1585). Two years later, he wrote *Chieh-shu fa-yin (YCFH* 1–4), which was an explanation of Chih-i's commentary on the section of bodhisattva precepts contained in the Sutra of Brahma's Net. This work was especially significant because it provided a theoretical rationale for monastic discipline and also had considerable impact on lay Buddhism. In his comments throughout the text, he tried to complement the Buddhist concept of compassion with the Confucian concept of filial piety. He also suggested not killing, release of animals, and a vegetarian diet as essential to fulfilling the demands of compassion and filial piety. His essay on the same theme, entitled "To Refrain from Killing and to Release Sentient Beings,"[40] became a classic in its genre. It also started a vogue in lay circles to organize societies for releasing life *(fang-sheng hui)*, organizations that tried to raise funds to build "ponds of released life" *(fang-sheng-ch'ih)* and to get together at definite intervals to set free captured birds, fish, and other animals.

In the administration of Yün-ch'i, Chu-hung's ability both as a Vinaya master and as a competent abbot shone forth. He instituted detailed rules and regulations governing every aspect of the monastic life, *Yün-ch'i kung-chu kuei-yüeh* (Rules and Agreements for Communal Living at Yün-ch'i, *YCFH* 32). He selected, condensed, and compiled various texts about Vinaya rules for the education of monks, nuns, and novices. He also reinstated the *poṣadha* ceremony, the ritual of recitation of the *prātimokṣa* precepts which had fallen into disuse since the T'ang dynasty. At this ritual the five precepts, the ten precepts, the complete set of 250 precepts for a monk, and finally the ten grave and forty-eight light precepts for a bodhisattva were recited in front of an assembly of all the monks of the temple. Offenses were then to be confessed and the precepts received anew. This was still the practice three centuries later in China.

Chu-hung died on the fourth day of the seventh month in the forty-third year of Wan-li (1615), at the age of eighty-one *sui*.[41] Shortly before he died, he went into the city to bid farewell to his disciples. He went first to the lay believer Sung Shou-i, and then to everyone he knew. He told them that he was going to another place soon. The night before he died he went into his room, closed his eyes, and did not say a word. When the monks at Yün-ch'i realized he was going to die, they sent for the lay disciples in the city, and all gathered around him. His last words were, "You should recite the name of the Buddha with a sincere heart. Do not try other tricks, and do not violate my rules." He did not appoint a successor, but specified that the person must be perfect in his understanding and morality and that seniority in ordination should be taken as the criterion.[42] After Chu-hung's death, two of his lay disciples, Tsou K'uang-ming and Wang Yü-ch'un, spent ten days gathering together all his writings. But the actual printing of the collected works did not take place until ten years later, in the fourth year of T'ien-ch'i (1624), as a collective endeavor of eighteen monks and thirty-eight lay devotees, all of whom were Chu-hung's disciples. The complete works, named *Yün-ch'i fa-hui* by Sung Shou-i, were divided into three main divisions and consisted of thirty-four *chüan* in all.[43]

CHAPTER THREE

Chu-hung and the Joint Practice of Pure Land and Ch'an

HAKUIN (1686–1769), the famous Japanese Zen master, was Chu-hung's most vehement critic. In one of his works, the *Orategama Zokushū,* he made the following comment:

Toward the end of the Ming dynasty there appeared a man known as Chu-hung from Yün-ch'i. His talents were not sufficient to tackle the mysteries of Zen, nor had he the eye to see into the Way. As he studied onward he could not gain the delights of Nirvana; as he retrogressed, he suffered from the terrors of the cycle of birth and death. Finally, unable to stand his distress, he was attracted to the memory of Hui-yüan's Lotus Society. He abandoned the "steepness" technique of the founders of Zen, and calling himself the "Great Master of the Lotus Pond," he wrote a commentary on the *Amitāyus Sūtra,* advocated strongly the teaching relating to the calling of the Buddha's name, and displayed an incredibly shallow understanding of Zen.[1]

In his indignation, Hakuin somewhat misstated the facts. It is true, as we have seen, that Chu-hung was attracted by Pure Land practice—specifically by *nien-fo* or the calling of the Buddha's name—even before he became a monk. It is also true that he wrote a commentary on a sutra—not, incidentally, on the Amitāyus Sutra, but on the Smaller Sukhāvatīvyūha Sutra, and not late and after his failure to progress in Ch'an meditation, but early in his career. Nevertheless, Hakuin's main point was valid, for throughout his career Chu-hung had sought to combine Pure Land recitation of the Buddha's name with Ch'an meditation on *kung-an (kōan)*. It was precisely with respect to this issue that Hakuin found fault with Chu-hung.

Hakuin set forth his objections to the mixing of Pure Land and Ch'an in these words:

How sad indeed! The great teachings withered and vulgar concepts arose; the old songs died out and banalities flourished. A hundred years ago the true style changed, and Zen followers adopted an obnoxious teaching. Those who would combine Pure Land with Zen are [as common] as hemp and millet. In olden times outward appearance was the *śrāvaka* practice, the internal mystery was the bodhisattva Way. Nowadays outward appearance is the Zen teaching, and the inner mystery is the Pure Land practice. It is just like mixing milk and water in one vessel.[2]

Hakuin, a defender of the purity of the Zen tradition, attacked Chu-hung because the latter introduced Pure Land elements into Ch'an and thereby corrupted the "steepness" method of the Ch'an practice. A close reading of these passages and others gives the impression that Hakuin regarded Chu-hung as the initiator of the dual practice of Pure Land and Ch'an. While he was certainly not its initiator, Chu-hung did play an important role in its popularization. Ou-i Chih-hsü, another famous late Ming Buddhist master, was deeply influenced by Chu-hung and in his early career continued the effort to popularize the combination of Pure Land and Ch'an. Most Buddhist monks recognized the validity of this approach during the Ming, and it is probable that Ch'an monks continued to practice *nien-fo* during the Ch'ing as well. In his description of Buddhism during the Republican period, Holmes Welch notes that most monasteries, especially the most famous ones, maintained the joint practice of Ch'an and Pure Land, either through the establishment of both a meditation hall and a hall for reciting the Buddha's name, or by the incorporation of the two practices in a single hall as was the case at Chiao-shan.[3] According to Ogasawara, it was Emperor Yung-cheng of the Ch'ing who adopted Chu-hung's idea by decreeing the establishment of both a meditation hall *(ch'an t'ang)* and a hall for the recitation of the Buddha's name *(nien-fo t'ang)* in the same monastery.[4] The practice at Chiao-shan, moreover, appears to have been copied from that carried out at Chu-hung's Yün-ch'i monastery.[5] Hakuin was quite right to trace the prevalence of the joint practice of Pure Land and Ch'an to Chu-hung's ideas and activities.

As we have seen, Chu-hung was not included in the lineages of any of the Ch'an schools. He was, however, posthumously named the eighth patriarch of the Pure Land school.[6] Could this imply that the joint practice of Pure Land and Ch'an was advocated only by the Pure Land school? Could it reflect the effort of Pure Land Buddhists to change the image of their school as the simple faith of the unsophisticated? Can one assume that this kind of syncretic practice was endorsed by Pure Land practitioners because it was more popular in orientation and hence more suited to nonsectarian accommodation?

An examination of the available evidence suggests that such questions are really inappropriate. In the context of Ming Buddhism it is hardly valid to make a clear-cut distinction between an orthodox Ch'an tradition of "steepness" and a popular Pure Land school with syncretic tendencies. We cannot even be certain that there was a Pure Land school in the same sense that there was a T'ien-t'ai school or a Ch'an school. To be sure, there were several Pure Land traditions, but there was no single Pure Land school with a genuine patriarchal transmission. The list of Pure Land patriarchs is more likely to have been a creation of certain pious latter-day Buddhists. The question of the authenticity of a Pure Land school and Chu-hung's place in it will be reserved for later discussion; here it will be useful to review briefly the situation of Ch'an Buddhism during the Ming dynasty.

Ch'an Buddhism in the Late Ming

In Chu-hung's time, there were definitely Ch'an monks and Ch'an schools. To be specific, there were two Ch'an sects, the Lin-chi and the Ts'ao-tung. In the history of Chinese Buddhism, the persecution of the Hui-ch'ang era (842–845) marked a watershed. After this time, only Ch'an and Pure Land teachings continued to exert any influence. By the middle of the ninth century, the Southern School of Ch'an had won the day. This school regarded Hui-neng as the Sixth Patriarch and the legitimate heir to the Ch'an teachings brought to China by Bodhidharma. The Northern School, which acclaimed the famous priest Shen-hsiu as its leader, had come to prominence before the Southern School, but had been unable to hold out against the latter.[7] It was from the Southern School that all later Ch'an sects were to trace their line of descent. The exact date when the five Ch'an sects or the Five Houses came to be generally recognized cannot be ascertained. This term, however, appears to have been in use during the period of the Five Dynasties (907–960) not long after the death of Fa-yen (885–985), the founder of the last of the Five Houses.[8] Although all of them traced their lineages directly to Hui-neng, Hui-neng's disciples Nan-yüeh Huai-jang (677–744) and Ch'ing-yüan Hsing-ssu (d. 740), and especially their famous heirs, Ma-tsu Tao-i (709–788) and Shih-t'ou Hsi-ch'ien (700–790), were the real founders of the later sects.[9]

Many legends grew up around Ma-tsu and Shih-t'ou. Both produced many disciples, and their schools developed into flourishing establishments; indeed, all the famous Masters of the late T'ang dynasty derived from them. An often-quoted passage describes their fame: "In Kiangsi the Master was Ta-chi [Ma-tsu]; in Hunan the Master was Shih-t'ou. People went back and forth between them all the time, and those who never met these two great Masters were completely ignorant." Their connection with the Sixth Patriarch is obscure; but there is no doubt that they adopted him as their Patriarch.[10]

The Lin-chi and Kuei-yang sects can be traced to Ma-tsu, while the Ts'ao-tung, Yün-men, and Fa-yen sects are traced to Shih-t'ou. Although these five branches were still active by the beginning of the twelfth century, the Lin-chi and Yün-men sects occupied a dominant position. Emperor Hui-tsung of the Northern Sung (r. 1101–1125) summarized the situation of the Ch'an sects of his time in a preface he wrote for a work on Ch'an history:

After Nan-yüeh and Ch'ing-yüan, [Ch'an Buddhism] has been divided into five sects (*wu-tsung*). Each developed its own tradition and taught according to the differences in the learners' talents. Although they differ in particular emphases, their goals are still the same. . . . These sects have benefited sentient beings and enabled many people to reach enlightenment. Each has spread wide in influence and put forth luxuriant foliage, but the two sects of Yün-men and Lin-chi now dominate the whole world.[11]

The Lin-chi sect continued to play a dominant role during the Southern Sung, but the Yün-men sect was supplanted by Ts'ao-tung, which first emerged in importance during the Southern Sung and achieved a position of prominence by the end of the dynasty.[12] During the Yüan dynasty, famous monks who had influence at court belonged either to the Lin-chi or to the Ts'ao-tung sect.[13]

Both the Lin-chi and Ts'ao-tung sects were still active during the Ming dynasty, and one might ask why Chu-hung was not affiliated with either of them. But Chu-hung was not the only case. As mentioned earlier, Chen-k'o, Te-ch'ing, and Chih-hsü were also listed in the "lineage unknown" section of the biographies of Ch'an monks. Was their absence from the rolls of the Lin-chi and Ts'ao-tung sects due, as Hakuin would have put it, to their "incredibly shallow understanding of Zen"? Or was their exclusion due to a deliberate choice? Rather than being barred from the Ch'an sects, these monks may have decided not to affiliate with either because they saw little significance in such an affiliation. It appeared that by the end of the Ming, the Ch'an tradition had become so bankrupt that to be associated with it may have been more of a liability than an asset.

The decline of Ch'an certainly did not begin in Chu-hung's time. K'ung-ku Ching-lung (b. 1393), a twentieth-generation Lin-chi Ch'an master during the early years of the Ming dynasty,[14] had this to say about the condition of Ch'an:

Since the end of the Sung dynasty, the method of Ch'an instruction has been substandard, and the quality of students has also been very inferior. Thus the mysterious art has been corrupted, and what is now transmitted is just a dead technique (ssu-fa). Originally there was neither string nor bondage, but when you bind yourself with a nonexistent string, you are no longer a living person. Nowadays, people cling to artificial rules and mechanical, lifeless kung-an. Consequently they become attached to a one-sided view and have no way of gaining awakening.[15]

The kind of lifeless Ch'an he was condemning was one that rejected nien-fo and sutra recitation. According to Ching-lung, this purist approach to Ch'an meditation was a misunderstanding of the true spirit of Ch'an. He explained it this way:

Those who hold fast to Ch'an meditation and work on some critical phrase (hua-t'ou) regard themselves as carrying out the true cultivation of quiescence. They do not believe that they ought to do anything else. Thus they never practice nien-fo, nor do they engage in daily worship and sutra recitation. For them, there is "only Ch'an, but no Pure Land." This kind of Ch'an meditation, however, is not the correct way, for to hold on to a dead hua-t'ou is to be no different from a clod of earth or a piece of tile. Of those persons who fall into this sickness, nine out of ten will have no way out. Ch'an is alive. It is like a gourd on top of water. It turns around whenever it is touched. Therefore, it has been said that one should meditate on the living meanings of the patriarchs, not on some dead phrases. If one carries out Ch'an meditation in this way, he will not neglect either rebirth in the Pure Land through nien-fo, nor morning and evening worship, nor sutra recitation; for whether one turns left or right, one will always encounter the Way.[16]

Signs of spiritual stagnation were even more pronounced by Chu-hung's time. Chapter VII will take up Chu-hung's detailed criticisms of the monastic order in general and Ch'an practice in particular. Here, however, we will turn our attention to observations concerning Ch'an cultivation made by two of Chu-hung's contemporaries.

In his autobiography, Te-ch'ing made this entry under the forty-fourth year of Chia-ch'ing (1565).

Master Yün-ku set up a Ch'an semester at T'ien-chieh [monastery], and used the *kung-an,* "Who is the one reciting the Buddha's name?" Before this time, Ch'an was not known south of the Yang-tzu. Master Yün-ku was the first one to advocate the practice of Ch'an. I am the only one among the young monks who practiced Ch'an. At that time, the monks living in the monastery all wore ordinary clothes of various colors. I threw away all my old clothes and was alone in wearing a monk's robe. Those who saw me thought that I was strange.[17]

Te-ch'ing's claim that Ch'an was not practiced in the south until Yün-ku initiated it through the use of *nien-fo kung-an* is probably an exaggeration. That Yün-ku used the *nien-fo kung-an* and was then regarded as the leader in reviving a defunct Ch'an tradition does, however, reveal much about the religious climate of the time. For it was precisely this *nien-fo kung-an* containing the question "Who is the one reciting the Buddha's name?" that consistently marked the tradition of the dual practice of Pure Land and Ch'an. Whether Yün-ku was really the first monk to introduce Ch'an meditation to the area south of the Yangtze is not really the important point. Of far greater significance to the argument presented here is the fact that Te-ch'ing, who regarded himself as a Ch'an monk and spent a good deal of his energy advocating Ch'an cultivation, equated the dual practice of Ch'an and Pure Land with Ch'an meditation proper. Indeed, it is doubtful that Te-ch'ing would have made any clear-cut distinction between the dual practice and an orthodox Ch'an practice. In his discussion of what passed for Ch'an cultivation in his day, he had only harsh words to offer:

When well-intentioned men nowadays become lay Buddhists, they pride themselves on their worldly knowledge and secular wit. Slighting the precious precepts and the ten virtues, they leave themselves open for Māra. They think that to delight in the way of Ch'an is most superior. So they look up a few ready-made *kung-an* of the patriarchs, memorize them, and, taking advantage of their quick wit and clever eloquence, believe that they have gained awakening. They are fully satisfied, and they have no idea where they have gone wrong.[18]

Chih-hsü also agreed that Ch'an practice during the late Ming was in a deplorable state. He questioned the significance of the patriarchal transmission among the Ch'an sects of his time. Since the true spirit of Ch'an was no longer there, exclusion or inclusion in the lineage of a Ch'an sect had lost all meaning for him:

Since the great Master Ch'u-shih Chi [1296–1370], no one else has achieved renown in the Ch'an sects. [If one must single out someone] old man Tzu-po [Tzu-po Chen-k'o] might be another. Master Shou-ch'ang Wu-ming also has the manner of the ancients. Nowadays people who fight over lineage qualifications are like secular princes. If a ruler does not have virtue, he is no better than a commoner. Chieh and Chou were examples. [These were famous villains in Chinese history, the last emperors of the Hsia and Shang, the first two dynasties.] If a monk receives the line of transmission from his teacher but corrupts the Buddhist teaching and discipline, he is no different from these evil rulers. [On the other hand] if one has gained the Way, even if he is a commoner, he can establish a great tradition. Kao-tsu of Han and T'ai-tsu of Ming were examples of this kind. Similarly, if a monk never receives the line of transmission from any teacher, but achieves a natural accord with the essential spirit of the Buddhas and the patriarchs, isn't that the same as it was for these great rulers? [19]

Both Tzu-po Chen-k'o and Shou-ch'ang Wu-ming are located in the "lineage unknown" section of important biographical works on Ch'an monks, such as the *Wu-teng yen-t'ung* (The Strict Genealogy of the Five Lamps). It is no wonder, then, that Ch'en Yüan, a modern historian of Chinese Buddhism, was impressed by the fact that Chih-hsü did not even mention the name of Mi-yün Yüan-wu, a Ch'an monk of considerable prestige who lived around this time.[20] By the end of the Ming, the Ch'an sects had declined so much that the kind of training they offered was no longer deemed spiritually viable. Serious Buddhists had to find other alternatives. In the case of Chu-hung and others like him, this included a rejection of rigid sectarian affiliation and a free, creative synthesis of the best features of the Ch'an, Pure Land, and Vinaya schools.

Chu-hung and the Pure Land School

After Chu-hung died, he was recognized as the eighth patriarch of the Pure Land school. At least this seems to have been the consensus during the Ch'ing dynasty.[21] It was not the only tradition, however, for according to another method of reckoning, Chu-hung was the ninth patriarch.[22]

The discrepancy is connected with two separate attempts to create a tradition of patriarchal transmission for Pure Land Buddhism and thus establish it as an independent school. Shih-chih Tsung-hsiao of Ssu-ming (d. 1214), a T'ien-t'ai monk of the Sung dynasty, was the first to make such an attempt. In his work *Lo-pang wen-lei* (Various Writings on the Country of Bliss), which was published in 1200, he established Hui-yüan (334–416) as the first patriarch *(shih-tsu)* of the Pure Land school and named Shan-tao (613–681), Fa-chao (d. 822), Shao-k'ang (d. 805), Sheng-ch'ang (fl. 990), and Tsung-tse (fl. 1086) as the five successive patriarchs *(chi-tsu).*[23]

Chih-p'an (fl. 1258–1269), another T'ien-t'ai monk active approximately fifty years after Tsung-hsiao, undertook the second attempt to create a patriarchal tradition for Pure Land. His list of seven patriarchs appears in his *Fo-tsu-t'ung chi* (Record of the Lineage of the Buddha and Patriarchs) in the section entitled "A Record on the Establishment of the Teaching of Pure Land" *(Ching-t'u li-chiao chih).*[24] His list includes Hui-yüan, Shan-tao, Ch'eng-yüan (711–802), Fa-chao, Shao-k'ang, Yen-shou (903–975), and Sheng-ch'ang. Although it resembles Tsung-hsiao's list, there are some significant differences. Chih-p'an included Ch'eng-yüan, who was Fa-chao's teacher, as well as Yen-shou, possibly the most famous Ch'an monk actively to advocate the joint practice of Ch'an and Pure Land. On the other hand, he omitted Tsung-tse. P'eng-an Ta-yu, yet another T'ien-t'ai monk who lived during the early years of the Ming dynasty, combined the two lists noted above and came up with a list of eight patriarchs in which Tsung-tse was listed as the eighth.[25] Since that time, although some writers were to preserve this tradition and make Chu-hung the ninth patriarch, others put Chu-hung in Tsung-tse's place and thus made him the eighth patriarch.

What conclusions can be drawn from these divergent lists of Pure Land patriarchs? Do they, in fact, represent a lineage? All the lists begin with Hui-yüan. Yet Hui-yüan and Shan-tao, the second patriarch, were separated by nearly two hundred years, and although Ch'eng-yüan was Fa-chao's teacher, there was no discernible relationship between Shan-tao and Ch'eng-yüan. Nor was there any actual connection between Shan-tao and Fa-chao. Shao-k'ang, the fifth patriarch according to Chih-p'an, lived one hundred years before his successor, Yen-shou. The chronological gap between Sheng-ch'ang and Tsung-tse is equally great. More interesting, however, is the attempt to add Chu-hung to the patriarchal tradition. Since he lived five to six hundred years after Sheng-ch'ang and Tsung-tse, what possible relationship, except for the most tenuous, symbolic one, could there have been between Chu-hung and the other two?

The Pure Land patriarchal tradition obviously meant something quite different from that of the Ch'an schools; it did not denote a lineage relationship between the patriarchs as it does in the case of Ch'an. Indeed, the Pure Land patriarchal tradition was really a construction of the T'ien-t'ai monks of the Sung dynasty. Pure Land teachings and practices had been in existence for centuries, but before the publication of *Lo-pang wen-lei*, we find neither mention of a patriarchal tradition nor treatment of Pure Land as a separate, independent school. What we do find is the sudden emergence during the Southern Sung of Pure Land as a school, complete with a carefully constructed patriarchal line. There was one compelling reason for its emergence at that time: the challenge posed by the patriarchal traditions of the Ch'an schools felt by the T'ien-t'ai monks. With the appearance of *Ching-te ch'uan-teng lu* (The Transmissions of the Lamp), dated 1004, in which the patriarchal transmission of the Ch'an sects was set forth, other schools of Buddhism felt threatened and sought to establish similar traditions of their own. The T'ien-t'ai school formulated its own patriarchal tradition in such works as Tsung-chien's *Shih-men cheng-t'ung* (The Orthodox Tradition of Buddhism) and Chih-p'an's *Fo-tsu-t'ung chi* (Record of the Lineage of the Buddha and Patriarchs). It is interesting to note that the three monks who tried at various times to establish a Pure Land patriarchal tradition, Tsung-hsiao and Chih-p'an of the Sung and Ta-yu of the Ming, all belonged to the T'ien-t'ai school. From the time when the T'ien-t'ai master Chih-i (538–597) incorporated meditation on the Amitābha Buddha as one method for achieving samadhi (concentration; *san-mei*), T'ien-t'ai monks developed a continuous tradition of professing Pure Land faith. Thus it is not accidental that the three monks who showed an active interest in establishing Pure Land as a school were T'ien-t'ai monks. It is also not without good reason that several of the patriarchs they named—Shao-k'ang and Yen-shou, for example—had strong leanings toward T'ien-t'ai teachings.

It has been customary to discuss Chinese Buddhism in terms of the schools it inspired, and Pure Land has been treated as a major one. This can be very misleading, however, for unlike Ch'an, Pure Land does not have a lineage based on patriarchal transmission.[26] Unlike T'ien-t'ai and Hua-yen practitioners, those who practice Pure Land do not agree on the absolute authority of either one scripture or a group of scriptures. There were actually two distinct traditions within Pure Land. Hui-yüan represented one tradition, in which the *Pan-chou san-mei ching* was regarded as the authoritative scripture. In this tradition, practice focused on meditation upon the Amitābha Buddha, stressing the mental visualization of Amitābha and the resultant state of samadhi as the supreme goal. Shan-tao, on the other hand, represented a different tradition that can be traced further back to T'an-luan (476–542) and Tao-ch'o (562–645). The authoritative scriptures in this tradition were the so-called Three Scriptures of the Pure Land—The Larger Sukhāvatīvyūha Sutra *(Wu-liang-shou ching)*, the *Kuan-wu-liang-shou ching* (Amitāyurdhyāna Sutra), and the Smaller Sukhāvatīvyūha Sutra *(A-mi-t'o ching)*. In contrast to the first tradition, this one emphasized the oral invocation of the name of Amitābha. Rebirth in the Western Paradise (Sukhāvatī) was regarded as the final goal by both groups, but the former stressed the importance of "seeing Buddha" during samadhi in this life—a concern that was not shared by the latter.

An examination of the careers of the eight Pure Land patriarchs makes clear that some followed Hui-yüan's tradition more closely, while others followed that of Shan-tao. The claim that all these people belonged to a single Pure Land tradition thus appears to be without substance. It has been suggested that Tsung-hsiao was the first person who attempted to set up Pure Land as a separate school, in the same way as the T'ien-t'ai, Ch'an, and Vinaya schools.[27] The sources provided by Tsung-hsiao and Chih-p'an[28] may be culled to discover how the eight patriarchs were viewed by those who sought to establish a Pure Land lineage. The picture that emerges from these accounts, though not always historically accurate, does represent a kind of consensus that can be considered the "orthodox line" from the twelfth century onward.

The Pure Land Patriarchs

Hui-yüan[29] was a native of Yen-men in what is now Shansi province, and his secular name was Chia. In 346, Hui-yüan traveled with his maternal uncle to Hsü-ch'ang and Lo-yang, where he studied Confucian and Taoist classics for a period of seven years. He was a good scholar and excelled in the study of Lao Tzu and Chuang Tzu. He met Tao-an (312–385) when he was twenty-one years of age. After listening to Tao-an's exposition of the Prajñāpāramitā Sutra he awakened to the truth of Buddhism. When he had his hair shaved off and joined the monastic order, he said that all other philosophies were as worthless as chaff. In 381, Yüan went to Mt. Lu in Kiangsi and, delighted with the beauty of the surrounding area, decided to remain there. The governor had a monastery built for him and named it the Eastern Grove. For the next thirty years Yüan never left Mt. Lu. When he saw guests off, he would go only as far as the bank of Tiger Brook. In 402, Yüan organized the Lotus Society to practice the samadhi of Buddha contemplation (*nien-fo san-mei*). The membership consisted of both monks and laymen and is said to have numbered 123. The whole congregation stood in front of the images of Buddha Amitābha and his two attendant bodhisattvas, Kuan-yin (Avalokiteśvara) and Ta-shih-chih (Mahāsthāmaprāpta), offered incense, and made a collective vow to be reborn in the Western Paradise. Some followers wrote poems extolling the excellence of *nien-fo san-mei,* and Hui-yüan himself wrote a preface to that collection saying that even though there were various methods for achieving samadhi, Buddha contemplation was the easiest and the most effective.

Hui-yüan was a lifelong practitioner of Buddha contemplation. He saw Amitābha three times during his first eleven years of practicing this form of meditation. Just seven days before he died, he received another vision. This time the body of the Amitābha Buddha filled all space and various Buddhas of transformation *(hua-fo)* issued forth from his halo. Fourteen streams of water, flowing upward and downward, shone brilliantly. The sound of the water expounded the teachings of suffering, impermanence, and the nonexistence of self. Amitābha said to Hui-yüan, "I have come to comfort you by the power of my original vow. Seven days hence you will be reborn in my country." Yüan also saw some of his disciples who had passed away earlier. They stood beside Amitābha and said to him: "Master, you made up your mind [to be reborn in the Pure Land] before all of us. Why are you coming so late?" After receiving this vision, Yüan told his disciples: "Since I came to live here, I have been fortunate in obtaining the holy vision of the Pure Land three times. Now I have seen it again. My rebirth there is assured. I will become sick tomorrow, and seven days from now I shall leave you. Work hard and do not become entangled in sorrow." When the predicted date arrived, Hui-yüan passed away. He was eighty-three years old.

Shan-tao[30] met Master Tao-ch'o (d. 645) during the Chen-kuan era (627–649) of the T'ang dynasty. When he heard Tao-ch'o lecture on the *Kuan-ching* (Amitāyurdhyāna Sutra), he was overjoyed and declared that this was really the shortcut to entry into Buddhism. Compared to all the other paths of cultivation, which he felt to be both difficult and obscure, the path advocated in the *Kuan-ching* could indeed lead one speedily out of samsara, the cycle of rebirth. From then on, Tao practiced *nien-fo*[31] with extreme urgency. Then he went to the capital and promoted the four sutras of the Pure Land (the Three Scriptures plus the *Ku-yin-sheng t'o-lo-ni ching*). He kept a statue of Amitābha in his room and, whenever he was there, would kneel down and invoke the name of Amitābha with all his might, stopping only when he was exhausted. Even on extremely cold days, he would perspire as a result of his effort. For thirty years he preached Pure Land teachings without a moment's relaxation. He encouraged both Buddha contemplation as outlined in *Pan-chou san-mei ching* and other meritorious acts such as the worship and adoration of Buddha mentioned in other Mahāyāna scriptures. With the income he received from lay donations, he made a hundred thousand copies of the *A-mi-t'o ching* and painted frescoes depicting the scene of the Pure Land on two or three hundred walls.

Because of his work, an incalculable number of monks and lay people in the capital were converted to the Pure Land faith. Some of his followers recited the *A-mi-t'o ching* one hundred to five thousand times. Other followers invoked Buddha's name as many as a hundred thousand times daily; still others obtained samadhi through Buddha contemplation. Once someone asked Shan-tao if one could achieve rebirth in the Pure Land by calling the Buddha's name. He answered: "As soon as you call the name, your wish will be fulfilled." Shan-tao then called the name and immediately a ray of light shone forth from his mouth. He tried it ten to a hundred times; each time the light shone forth. Shan-tao wrote the following verse to encourage people to practice Buddha invocation:

Gradually your skin becomes puckered and your hair turns white;
Slowly, your steps become infirm.
Even if you have a roomful of gold and jade,
How can you escape from disease and old age?
Despite much enjoyment and happiness,
Death will eventually come upon you.
There is only one shortcut in cultivation.
That is to recite *A-mi-t'o fo.*

Late in his life, Shan-tao told people he was tired of his body and desired to return to the West. He climbed to the top of a willow tree and, calling to the West, asked Amitābha and the bodhisattvas to help him persevere in his right-mindfulness. Then he jumped down and killed himself.

Ch'eng-yüan[32] achieved his fame primarily through his disciple, Fa-chao. Fa-chao was the national teacher during T'ai-tsung's reign. He recommended his teacher as a person of miraculous attainments. As a result, the emperor offered his respects to Ch'eng-yüan and named his temple The Bodhimanda of Pan-chou or Sustained Meditation *(Pan-chou tao-ch'ang).* According to Liu Tsung-yüan's biography of Ch'eng-yüan, Fa-chao became Ch'eng-yüan's disciple under rather peculiar circumstances. When Fa-chao was residing at Mt. Lu, he ascended to the Western Paradise during a trance and saw a monk in rags serving the Buddha. When Fa-chao asked who this monk was, the Buddha answered that it was Ch'eng-yüan of Mt. Heng. Afterward, Fa-chao found Ch'eng-yüan, who closely resembled the monk he had seen in his trance, and became the latter's disciple.

According to his biographers,[33] Fa-chao had several visions of the Pure Land during his lifetime. In the second year of Ta-li (767) during the T'ang dynasty, he was living at the Yün-feng monastery at Heng-chou (Heng-yang in present-day Hunan) and was widely known for his discipline, meditation, and compassionate acts. One day, while he was eating a meal in the refectory, he saw in his rice bowl scenes of some celestial monasteries. When he described what he had seen to two of his fellow monks, they told him that the scenes resembled Mt. Wu-t'ai. In 769 Fa-chao established the practice of Five Assembly Buddha Invocation (wu-hui nien-fo)[34] at the Hu-tung monastery. While he was leading collective Buddha invocation there, the monastery is said to have become enveloped in five-colored clouds, and Fa-chao had a vision of the Amitābha Buddha and his two attendant bodhisattvas. Reminded by an old man of his earlier desire to make a pilgrimage to Mt. Wu-t'ai, Fa-chao now went there and received a decisive revelation. This occurred while he was visiting Ta-sheng-hsien-chu-ling monastery on Mt. Wu-t'ai. As Fa-chao entered the lecture hall, he saw Mañjuśrī standing in the east and P'u-hsien (Samantabhadra) in the west, each preaching the Dharma. Right away, he paid the two bodhisattvas his respects and asked them what would be the best path to pursue for one living in the degenerate age of the Law. Mañjuśrī told him that Buddha invocation was the superior path and that he himself had achieved supreme knowledge precisely because he had practiced it in the past. After this vision, Fa-chao continued to advocate the Five Assembly Buddha Invocation in Ping-chou (T'ai-yüan in present-day Shansi). It is said that Emperor Te-tsung, from within his palace, often heard voices reciting the Buddha's name coming from a northeasterly direction. The emperor therefore sent messengers to seek out Fa-chao and invite him to teach members of the imperial family how to practice the Five Assembly Buddha Invocation.

Shao-k'ang[35] was a native of Hsien-tu of Chin-yün (in present-day Chekiang). At the beginning of the Chen-yüan era (785–804), he went to the White Horse monastery in Lo-yang. While he was in the main hall, he saw a brilliant light shining forth from a volume of writings. This turned out to be Shan-tao's "Hsi-fang hua-tao wen" (Essay on Teaching People about the West). In order to make sure that this was not some fluke, he said: "If I am predestined to carry out Pure Land teaching, let the writing shine once more." Even before he had finished speaking, light filled the room. Shao-k'ang then went to the Kuang-ming monastery in Ch'ang-an and made offerings to Shan-tao's portrait there. He said that he saw the likeness of Shan-tao ascend into the air and declare to him: "If you carry out my teaching and benefit sentient beings, you will definitely be reborn in the Land of Bliss." Later he met a monk who told him that he ought to go to Hsin-ting (in present-day Chekiang) to work. When Shao-k'ang first went there, no one knew him. By giving money to children he persuaded them to invoke the Buddha's name. At first, he gave them one coin for each invocation of *A-mi-t'o-fo*. After a month had passed, many people started doing it, so he now gave them one coin for every ten invocations. A year later, people who recited the Buddha's name were said to be very numerous, and they came from all walks of life. Subsequently, he erected a Pure Land Bodhimanda *(Ching-t'u tao-ch'ang)* on Mt. Wu-lung. He assembled the congregation at midnight around an altar of three steps to practice Buddha invocation. Shao-k'ang would call out the Amitābha's name in a loud voice, and the congregation would follow his lead. Every time he called out the Buddha's name, some among the assembly would see a Buddha issue forth from his mouth. When he called out the name ten consecutive times, they saw ten Buddhas come forth one after another, like beads on a string. Shao-k'ang said to the congregation, which numbered several thousand, "Those among you who see the Buddha [Amitābha] will surely be reborn in the West." Not everyone in the congregation saw this miracle. In later generations, Shao-k'ang came to be regarded as a reincarnation of Shan-tao.

Yen-shou[36] served as a tax official under the king of Wu-yüeh. He used government money to buy fish and shrimp to set them free. When this was discovered, the king, instead of having him executed, which was the designated punishment, ordered his subordinates to test Yen-shou. He said that if Yen-shou became frightened and changed his expression, he should be executed. If not, he should be pardoned. Yen-shou showed no fear and was forgiven. After this, he became a monk and practiced the meditation of the T'ien-t'ai school. His conversion to Pure Land took place during a midnight vision. One night, while he was performing the penitential rituals[37] formu-

lated by Chih-i (*fa-hua ch'an*) and doing circumambulation, he saw
the statue of P'u-hsien (Samantabhadra) holding a lotus flower in his
hand. Uncertain of its significance, he made out two divination lots.
One lot said: "Practice meditation and concentration all your life";
the other lot said: "Recite sutras, perform good acts, and glorify the
Pure Land." After much praying, he cast the lots, and the second
one came up seven consecutive times. From that time on, Yen-shou
devoted himself to Pure Land practice. In 961, he went to Yung-
ming monastery in Chekiang and led the dual cultivation of Ch'an
and Pure Land. It is said that he recited the Buddha's name a
hundred thousand times daily, and every night the sound of Buddha invocation reverberated from the mountain top. He told people
that, in Buddhism, mind was the underlying principle and that attainment of awakening (*wu*) was the goal. Using mind as a basis, he
tried to harmonize the doctrines of the T'ien-t'ai, Hua-yen, and Wei-
shih schools. Yen-shou remained in Yung-ming monastery for fifteen years and gathered seventeen hundred disciples around him.
Aside from practicing Buddha invocation and meditation, he also
stressed monastic discipline and performed Tantric rites such as
"feeding the hungry ghosts." He dedicated all the merit resulting
from these activities to the glorification of the Pure Land.

The seventh and eighth patriarchs of Pure Land, Sheng-ch'ang
and Tsung-tse, were noted for their successful organization of lay
associations to practice Buddha invocation. Sheng-ch'ang[38] was active during the Ch'un-hua era (990–994) of the early Sung. He lived
at Nan-shao-ch'ing yüan in Ch'ien-t'ang (in present day Chekiang)
and concentrated on the practice of Pure Land. Under his leadership, a Pure Land association called the Pure Behavior Society
(Ching-hsing she) was organized. It had eighty lay believers, among
them literati, members of the Hanlin Academy, and high government officials. Its membership also included a thousand monks. According to the stele inscription written by Sung Pai, a Hanlin
scholar, Sheng-ch'ang's society, though modeled after Hui-yüan's
Lotus Society, was much grander than the latter. The reason, as
Sung stated it, was because Hui-yüan lived during a chaotic period,
so his followers were mostly hermits or semi-retired people. Sheng-
ch'ang lived during a peaceful and prosperous age, and among his
followers were many famous and powerful persons.

Tsung-tse[39] was active around the Yüan-yu era (1086–1093) of the Sung. He made Ch'ang-lu monastery in Chen-chou (in present-day Kiangsu) his headquarters and proselytized in that area. In 1089 he organized the Lotus Convocation (Lien-hua sheng-hui) and advocated universal cultivation of *nien-fo* samadhi.[40] He stipulated that everyone should recite *A-mi-t'o-fo* every day as many times as possible. Under the date of each day, in order to keep track of the number of invocations, one should mark off each recitation with a cross.[41]

This brief review of the biographies of the eight Pure Land patriarchs suggests that, even though a lineage relationship as it would have been understood by the Ch'an school apparently did not exist, several points might have served to link these eight monks together. Chu-hung, who was concerned about the same points, can thus be regarded as an inheritor of the tradition connecting the eight patriarchs.

First of all, they all stressed the practice of *nien-fo*. As it is meant in the descriptions above, *nien-fo* can be understood to mean either Buddha contemplation or Buddha invocation. The ambiguity is related to the character for *nien*, which means to recite aloud, to think a thought, or in the technically Buddhist sense, to be mindful and to recollect, corresponding to the Sanskrit for *nien-fo, Buddhānusmṛti*.[42] Traditionally, there were four kinds of *nien-fo*. The fourfold categorization was first formulated by the Hua-yen master, Tsung-mi (779–841),[43] and Chu-hung gave his own interpretation in his *Fo-shuo A-mi-t'o ching shu-ch'ao* (Phrase-by-Phrase Commentary on the Smaller Sukhāvatīvyūha Sutra). The four kinds of *nien-fo* are enumerated in the following order: (1) *ch'eng-ming nien-fo,* or calling upon the Amitābha's name in the manner prescribed in the *A-mi-t'o ching;* (2) *kuan-hsiang nien-fo,* or concentrating one's attention on a statue of Amitābha made of earth, wood, bronze, or gold; (3) *kuan-hsiang nien-fo,* or contemplating the miraculous features of Amitābha with one's mind's eye in the manner described in the *Kuan-ching;* (4) *shih-hsiang nien-fo,* or contemplating Amitābha as no different from one's own self-nature, since both Amitābha and self-nature transcend birth and extinction *(sheng-mieh),* existence and emptiness *(yu-k'ung),* subject and object *(neng-so).* Indeed, since contemplation is free from the characteristics of speech *(yen-shuo hsiang),* name *(ming-tzu hsiang),* and mental cognition of external phenomena *(hsin-yüan hsiang),* it is therefore contemplation of the Buddha in accordance with reality.[44] According to the fourfold classification of *nien-fo*, Buddha invocation would correspond to the first kind of *nien-fo*, while Buddha contemplation could refer to any of the other three kinds. Thus, Hui-yüan, Ch'eng-yüan, and Fa-chao were primarily interested in Buddha contemplation, and Shan-tao,[45] Shao-k'ang, Sheng-ch'ang, and Tsung-tse were primarily interested in Buddha invocation. Yen-shou, consistent with his general effort to harmonize Buddhist schools, advocated both invocation and contemplation.[46] Chu-hung modeled himself after Yen-shou. Through a creative interpretation of the concept of "one mind," Chu-hung sought to establish the ultimate identity underlying the various forms of *nien-fo*.

The second point of congruence is that all eight patriarchs were interested in lay proselytizing. By accepting both monks and lay believers as members of the Lotus Society, Hui-yüan set an example for later Pure Land practitioners. Shan-tao and Shao-k'ang tried to turn Buddha invocation into a popular cult, while Sheng-ch'ang and Tsung-tse appealed to members of the social elite and organized associations along the lines of Hui-yüan's Lotus Society. As we will see in chapter IV, Chu-hung too devoted considerable effort to the development of lay Buddhism. He was interested in attracting both the literati-officials and the general populace. But there was a difference in the way Chu-hung presented Pure Land teachings to these diverse audiences. In general, he stressed the basic agreement between *nien-fo* and Ch'an meditation when he addressed himself to the elite, but used arguments and stories related to rewards and retribution to persuade ordinary men and women to call the Buddha's name.

Chu-hung was, however, reluctant to endorse the organization of lay associations. This was primarily due to his fear that they might be transformed into heretical societies such as the White Lotus sect. The White Lotus sect (Pai-lien tsung), founded by Tzu-yüan (1086–1166) in the Sung dynasty and revived by Yu-t'an P'u-tu (d. 1330) in the Yüan dynasty, was originally a popular movement based on Pure Land teachings.[47] It appealed primarily to the laity by emphasizing that one should not kill and stressing the performance of good deeds, filial piety, and respect for one's elders and teachers,[48] all of which, as we will see, were strongly advocated by Chu-hung as well. Indeed, Chu-hung demonstrated his approval of Tzu-yüan and P'u-tu by including the former in his *Wang-sheng chi* (Biographies of People Who Achieved Rebirth in the Pure Land)

and by crediting the latter with "the revival of Pure Land" (ching-t'u chung-hsing).[49] However, he never mentioned the White Lotus sect itself in any of his writings,[50] for it had become identified with heretical practices early on. The fact that members of both sexes could mix freely at meetings aroused considerable opposition from both Confucian officials and orthodox Buddhists. Tzu-yüan himself was exiled to Chiang-chou (present-day Chiu-chiang in Kiangsi) in 1131. Although he won pardon three years later, members of the White Lotus continued to be accused of "eating vegetables and serving the demon" (ch'ih-ts'ai shih-mo) and "gathering at night and dispersing at dawn" (yeh-chü hsiao-san). The White Lotus was officially banned during both the Southern Sung and the Yüan dynasties.[51] It was also branded unorthodox by the author of Shih-men cheng-t'ung (The Orthodox Tradition of Buddhism) seventy years after Tzu-yüan's death.[52] In order to avoid being associated with an outlawed sect, P'u-tu purposely dropped the word "white" from its name and called his school the Lotus School (Lien-tsung), claiming that both he and Tzu-yüan were merely continuing the orthodox Pure Land teaching handed down from Hui-yüan. Although this effort did not do much to clear the air, it did start a new tradition. Pure Land believers of the Ming period also avoided the word "white." Thus, the Lotus School became the standard designation for the Pure Land School.

The Joint Practice of Ch'an and Pure Land

Chu-hung frequently claimed that nien-fo was really no different from Ch'an meditation, for both could lead to the realization that one's self-nature and the Buddha were identical. In order to validate this view, he would cite examples of Ch'an monks of former times who also practiced nien-fo. A survey of his various writings[53] yields a roster of monks who carried out the so-called joint practice of Ch'an and Pure Land. Among them were Yung-ming Yen-shou (904–975), Yüan-chao Sung-pen (1020–1099), Chen-hsieh Ch'ing-liao, and Tz'u-shou Huai-shen of the early Southern Sung; three monks of the Yüan dynasty: Chung-feng Ming-pen (1262–1323) and his disciple T'ien-ju Wei-tse (d. 1354), and Tuan-yün Chih-ch'e (1309–1386); and five monks of the Ming dynasty: Ch'u-shih Fan-ch'i, K'ung-ku Ching-lung, Tu-feng Chi-shan (d. 1482), Ku-yin Ching-ch'in, and Hsiao-yen Te-pao (1512–1581), under whose direction Chu-hung himself studied Buddhism for a short time. Chu-hung cited these twelve Ch'an monks as models, even though he made it clear that a far greater number of monks actually practiced *nien-fo* along with other forms of Buddhist cultivation.

The joint practice of Ch'an and Pure Land was usually traced to Yen-shou, as is the case in Chu-hung's list above. Before Yen-shou's time, monks proclaiming allegiance to one school seldom approved of those who followed the other. In fact, Ch'an and Pure Land had been engaged in mutual criticism since the early T'ang. Among Pure Land believers, Hui-jih (679–748) and Fa-chao, although they never questioned the value of Ch'an practice itself, harshly criticized Ch'an monks as arrogant and undisciplined. Ch'an monks, on the other hand, tended to regard Pure Land devotion as simple-minded and suitable only for the ignorant.[54] It is possible that as a result of this mutual criticism some Ch'an masters came to encourage discipline and devotion. Pai-chang Huai-hai (749–814) was a celebrated example. He stressed monastic discipline and was credited with the writing of the first monastic code for Ch'an monks, the *Pure Rules of Pai-chang*.[55] The *Pure Rules* stipulate that the ritual performed during a monk's cremation ceremony must include the recitation of the Amitābha's name.[56] Chu-hung included Pai-chang along with the T'ien-t'ai master Chih-i and the Hua-yen master Ch'eng-kuan in his list of famous masters who practiced *nien-fo*.[57] To counter Ch'an criticism of Pure Land's simple-mindedness, the Pure Land people had long argued that *nien-fo* was really a form of Ch'an *kung-an*. Chu-lung recorded quite a few pertinent sayings on this point made by monks who advocated the joint practice of Ch'an and Pure Land, an aspect we will take up in detail later in this chapter.

Nien-fo as Buddha contemplation can lead to samadhi, a state in which the distinction between subject and object disappears. As the biographies of Hui-yüan and Fa-chao indicate, both men experienced *nien-fo* samadhi. To be specific, they were said to have seen Amitābha face to face. The attainment of this divine vision was always treated as the apex of the religious lives of these men, because the vision was understood by them as a guarantee that the beholder would be reborn in the Western Paradise. But it would appear that the vision had so much significance because it symbolized the mystic union between the meditator and the Amitābha—the object of his meditation. Because *nien-fo* had the power to procure

samadhi, both Chih-i and some of the Ch'an monks during the early
T'ang recommended it as an effective means for breaking through
the mind of delusion and reaching the state of nonduality.

Nien-fo samadhi appears in the Pan-chou san-mai ching [58] and
the Kuan-ching. Hui-yüan seems to have been especially influenced
by the former.[59] The Pan-chou san-mei ching defines nien-fo
samadhi as a form of mental concentration that enables the devotee
to behold all the Buddhas "as if they were presently standing before
his eyes" (hsien-tsai fo hsi tsai ch'ien-li san-mei). The sutra states that the
devotee should spend from one day and one night up to seven days
and nights contemplating the Buddha, at the end of which
Amitābha Buddha will appear to him in a dream, if not when he is
awake. When his mind is engaged in this contemplation, all the Buddha lands, Mt. Sumeru, and the hidden places as well will become
accessible to him. Without acquiring divine feet (shen-tsu), he can
travel to the Buddha land (Amitābha's land), sit at the feet of the
Buddha, and listen to his preaching. The devotee is especially enjoined to contemplate the thirty-two excellent marks of the Buddha's
body. This contemplation will enable him to achieve the "samadhi of
emptiness" (k'ung san-mei). Just as he dreams of eating delicious food
but wakes up feeling hungry, he comes to realize that everything is a
creation of the mind and has as much reality as his dreams. Contemplating the fact that the Buddha comes from nowhere and goes
nowhere, he realizes that he himself also comes from nowhere and
goes nowhere. By this contemplation, he reaches the awakening that
his mind is no different from the mind of the Buddha, and that neither can be seen or conceptualized. When there is thought, it comes
from the mind of delusion; but when there is no thought, it is Nirvana.[60]

The sutra goes on to say that four things will enable the devotee
to achieve this samadhi speedily. For a period of three months, he
should (1) be free from worldly thoughts, (2) not lie down, (3) walk
constantly without rest and never sit down except to eat and relieve
himself, and (4) not expect reward in the form of clothes or food
when preaching the sutra to others. The sutra assures the reader
that when these four conditions are fulfilled, he will be able to
achieve samadhi. No matter in which of the ten directions he faces,
he will see buddhas face to face.[61]

According to the Pan-chou san-mei ching, then, Buddha contemplation is a two-step process beginning with the visual or mental contemplation of the Buddha Amitābha and leading to the realization of the nonduality between the Buddha Amitābha (the object of contemplation), and the mind of the contemplator. The key factor in the transition to the second step lies in the experience of samadhi. The intense contemplation of the Amitābha, which can be accomplished either with a statue (equivalent to the second type of *nien-fo* in Tsung-mi's classification) or through mental visualization (equivalent to the third type of *nien-fo*), leads to the coalescence of the meditating subject and the object of meditation. Once samadhi is reached, the devotee awakens to the reality of emptiness whereby he sees everything nondualistically—without discrimination between subject and object.

The sutra does not mention Buddha invocation. Chih-i, however, using the method of *nien-fo* introduced in the *Pan-chou san-mei ching* as a basis, formulated the practice of the "constantly walking samadhi" *(ch'ang-hsing san-mei)*, one of the four types of meditation discussed in his *Mo-ho chih-kuan* (Great Concentration and Insight). Here Chih-i was employing *nien-fo* as both Buddha contemplation and Buddha invocation. In practicing this form of meditation, one sets a period of ninety days during which time he undergoes training in body, speech, and mind. He goes to a quiet isolated place, avoids contact with evil acquaintances, begs for food, and purifies both the place in which he carries out this meditation and his own body. He vows that until he achieves samadhi he will walk without ever resting. Then he constantly calls out the name of Amitābha—hence the name "constantly walking samadhi." At the same time, he also contemplates Amitābha. He can invoke the Buddha's name and contemplete him simultaneously, or first contemplate and then invoke the name, or first invoke the name and then contemplate. In any event, he is enjoined to practice both invocation and contemplation in succession *(ch'ang nien hsiang-chi)*. Each step, each sound, and each thought must center on Amitābha *(pu-pu sheng-sheng nien-nien, wei tsai Mi-t'o)*. Finally, contemplating the thirty-two marks of the Buddha's body, he experiences a realization on three levels. He first realizes that he can obtain Buddhahood through his own mind and body. Then he realizes that Buddhahood cannot be obtained through the mind or the body. He eventually realizes that one cannot obtain the Buddha's form through mind or the Buddha's mind through form. Enlightenment is achieved when one understands that there is originally not a thing.[62]

This kind of realization, achieved through Buddha contemplation, bears a striking similarity to the state of awakening reached in Ch'an meditation. In this case, one uses the contemplation of Amitābha as a means to reach the nondualistic state of having no mind and no thought. It is therefore not surprising to find that even before Yung-ming Yen-shou, some Ch'an monks were already using Buddha contemplation and Buddha invocation as methods of meditation. These Ch'an monks, practicing the "Ch'an of Buddha-contemplation" (nien-fo ch'an), were all disciples of the fifth patriarch and closely connected with Chih-hsien (607–702) of Szechuan.[63]

Chih-hsien had a disciple named Ch'u-chi who was the teacher of both Musang (Ch. Wu-hsiang, 684–762) and Ch'eng-yüan. Musang was a Korean monk. Since he bore the secular surname of Kim, he was also called Priest Kim. According to Tsung-mi, his teaching can be rendered with three terms: no recollection, no thought, and no forgetting. He instructed his students twice a year (first and twelfth months) on the method of Buddha invocation. First, one was to call upon the name of the Buddha in a loud voice (yin-sheng nien-fo). Then one would gradually lower one's voice until one became silent as one used up one's breath. The purpose of this invocation was to stop thought and to reach the state of no thought.[64]

Ch'eng-yüan, as we have seen, was Fa-chao's teacher. Although we have little information about Ch'eng-yüan's technique of Buddha contemplation, it is very likely that he influenced Fa-chao on this question. To some extent, Fa-chao's wu-hui nien-fo resembles Musang's yin-sheng nien-fo and the "constantly walking samadhi" of Chih-i. Wu-hui nien-fo refers to a method of sequentially invoking the Buddha's name in five consecutively altered voices. The tempo of invocation changes from slow to fast and the level of voice from low to high as one progresses from the first to the fifth assemblies (hui). Throughout the sequence, one concentrates on the three treasures (Buddha, Dharma, and Sangha) and keeps one's mind free of all extraneous thoughts. During the first assembly, one calls out na-mo A-mi-t'o-fo slowly and in an even voice (p'ing-sheng). During the second assembly, one still calls out the invocation slowly, but now in a slightly higher voice *(p'ing-shang-sheng)*. During the third assembly, one recites *na-mo A-mi-t'o-fo* in a way that is neither slow nor fast. The same invocation is called out at a much faster tempo during the fourth assembly. Finally, during the fifth assembly, one simply calls out the four sounds *A-mi-t'o-fo* at an extremely fast tempo.[65] While Musang's *yin-sheng nien-fo* starts in a loud voice and ends in silence, *wu-hui nien-fo* starts in a low voice and builds to a crescendo. Both use the sound of invocation as a device for achieving mental concentration.

Even though Musang and Fa-chao used *nien-fo* as a means for reaching samadhi, they did not advocate the joint practice of Ch'an and Pure Land. It was not until Yen-shou provided a conscious argument for the basic compatibility between *nien-fo* and Ch'an meditation that joint practice gradually became a self-conscious movement. Following Yen-shou's example, other Ch'an monks started to practice *nien-fo*. Hsüeh-tou Ch'ung-hsien (979–1052), T'ien-i I-huai (993–1064), Hui-lin Tsung-pen (1019–1099), and Tsung-tse and his teacher Ch'ang-lu Ying-fu were a few of the most famous *nien-fo* practitioners.[66] In his *Wan-shan t'ung-kuei chi* (Ten Thousand Virtues Return to the Same Source), Yen-shou listed ten arguments as proofs that Ch'an and Pure Land were complementary. Among those arguments, two were most frequently repeated: "universal and particular do not obstruct each other" *(li-shih wu-ai)* and "emptiness and existence complement each other" *(k'ung-yu hsiang-ch'eng).*[67] In contrast to the traditional Ch'an denigration of Pure Land, Yen-shou accorded it a position equal if not superior to Ch'an. His attitude is perhaps best illustrated by this famous "fourfold summary" of Ch'an and Pure Land *(ssu-liao chien):*

With Ch'an but no Pure Land, nine out of ten people will go astray. When death comes suddenly, they must accept it in an instant.

With Pure Land but no Ch'an, ten thousand out of ten thousand people will achieve rebirth. If one can see Amitābha face to face, why worry about not attaining enlightenment?

With both Ch'an and Pure Land, it is like a tiger who has grown horns. One will be a teacher for mankind in this life, and a Buddhist patriarch in the next.

With neither Ch'an nor Pure Land, it is like an iron bed with bronze posters. For endless kalpas one will find nothing to rely on.[68]

Nien-fo Kung-an

The joint practice of Ch'an and Pure Land rested on the assertion that the two paths were essentially the same because both led to the same goal: the stopping of wrong thoughts and the end of the cycle of samsara. But just how was this identity understood? How did Chu-hung see the relationship between the two?

Chu-hung compiled two works, the *Ch'an-kuan ts'e chin* (Progress in the Path of Ch'an) and the *Huang-Ming ming-seng chi-lüeh* (Selected Biographies of Famous Monks of the Ming Dynasty), which supply rich information on this subject. Since Chu-hung's own view of the joint practice reflects the influence of these monks, we present their opinions first and then discuss Chu-hung's ideas. He referred to these Ch'an monks: Chung-feng Ming-pen, T'ien-ju Wei-tse, and Tuan-yün Chih-ch'e of the Yüan, and Ch'u-shih Fan-ch'i, K'ung-ku Ching-lung, Tu-feng Chi-shan, T'ien-chi Ho-shan and Ku-yin Ching-ch'in of the Ming.

To these monks, the joint practice of Ch'an and Pure Land did not mean the simultaneous practice of Ch'an meditation and *nien-fo*. Instead, they regarded *nien-fo* as simply another form of meditation. Since the end result of *nien-fo* was to terminate discursive thought, it had the same effect as *kung-an* meditation in Ch'an. It is in this sense that practically all these people referred to the invocation of *A-mi-t'o-fo* as *nien-fo kung-an*. When one used *nien-fo* in this fashion, *nien-fo* was clearly no longer an expression of one's piety and faith, but became a means to arouse the "feeling of doubt" *(i-ch'ing)*, the critical mental tension that drove one to reach awakening. This kind of *nien-fo* was therefore also called *ts'an-chiu nien-fo*, the *nien-fo* of concentration and penetration. Chung-feng Ming-pen wrote 108 poems entitled "Longing for the Pure Land" *(Huai ching-t'u shih)*. Some of them express the identity between the Pure Land and Ch'an paths.

There is no need to talk about Pure Land aside from Ch'an,
One should know that there is no Ch'an outside of the Pure Land.
When one has solved these double *kung-an,*
A five-petaled lotus opens on the Bear Ear Mountain.[69]
Amitābha Buddha lives in the West, while the [First] Patriarch
    comes from the West.
To call on the Buddha and to do Ch'an meditation is of the same
    purport.

> Once the ball of doubt accumulated for aeons is broken wide
>   open,
> The flower of the heart blooms in the same fashion.[70]

T'ien-ju Wei-tse likewise regarded Ch'an and Pure Land as two
equally useful paths leading toward release from delusive thoughts:

The karmic root of transmigration lies with the one thought which chases
after sounds and forms and causes man's delusions. Therefore the Buddha,
because of his infinite compassion, taught you either to practice Ch'an or to
call on the Buddha's name. Either of these enables you to sweep away your
delusive thought and to recognize your original face so that you can finally
be a free man. . . . Some people think that Ch'an meditation and Pure
Land *nien-fo* are different. They do not know that there is no difference between realizing one's nature through Ch'an and awakening to the truth that
"self-nature is Amitābha, mere mind is Pure Land" through *nien-fo*. . . .
Treat the four sounds *A-mi-t'o-fo* as a *hua-t'ou* [critical phrase—the core of a
kung-an]. Work on it twenty-four hours a day. When you reach the state
where no thought arises, you are already a Buddha even though you have
not traversed any bodhisattva stages.[71]

Ch'u-shih Fan-ch'i defined the goal of both Ch'an and Pure
Land practice as an awakening to the identity between one's own
mind and the Buddha. The following is an excerpt from a letter he
wrote to one of his lay followers:

A person who practices *nien-fo* ought to know that the Buddha is none other
than the mind. If you do not understand what the mind is, then ponder
hard on this: Where does the mind that is contemplating the Buddha come
from? Furthermore, you must find out who the person is who is engaged in
this search. Once you gain an entry through this, you will know what the
Ch'an master Yüan-wu meant when he said: "What is it which is neither
mind, nor the Buddha, nor a thing?" What is meant by mind is not the phenomenal mind of delusion but the empty, bright, perfect, deep, and broad
mind which has no characteristics. What the Buddhas of the three ages of
past, present, and future have succeeded in realizing is none other than this
mind, and what sentient beings in the six realms of existence have failed to
realize is also this mind. Because the Buddhas have gained awakening
through realization, they possess *bodhi* [wisdom]. Because sentient beings are
confused through ignorance, they suffer from *kleśa* [defilement]. . . . If you
can firmly believe this, you will be no different from the Buddhas and patriarchs of former times who have achieved this realization.[72]

In a letter to another lay follower, Fan-ch'i discussed the relationship between thought *(nien)* and mind *(hsin):*

You must believe that your own mind is the Buddha. Thus you will know that *nien-fo* is the same as *nien-hsin,* "contemplation of the mind," and that *nien-hsin* is the same as *nien-fo.* When one thought is not forgotten in another thought, and one stirring of the mind is not interrupted by another stirring of the mind *(nien-nien pu-wang, hsin-hsin wu-chien),* all of a sudden your mental activities will come to a stop. Right away you will become separated from worldly thoughts and experience true emptiness. Only then will you know that there is neither thought nor mind and neither mind nor thought. . . . Therefore, it is said that one reaches no-thought through thought and realizes no-mind through no-thought.[73]

According to Fan-ch'i, this realization of no-mind can be accomplished by the constant repetition of the four syllables *A-mi-t'o-fo:*

You need not avoid daily noise and seek out a quiet place. Just sweep your breast clean of the ordinary knowledge and views you have accumulated every day, and fill it with the phrase *A-mi-t'o-fo.* Try to become identified with it *(t'i-chiu)* totally. Always generate the doubt, "Who after all is this person doing *nien-fo?" (Che-ke nien-fo-te pi-ching shih shui).* Dwell on this question constantly. You should not discriminate between existence and nonexistence. Neither should you purposely wait for awakening. The least bit of delusive thought will create obstacles. Empty your chest of everything. In walking, standing, sitting, or lying, in either solitude or company, leisure or engagement, always make your right thoughts succeed one another, your mind uninterrupted. After a long time, your effort will become pure and concentrated. There will naturally be quietude and ease, and then samadhi will appear. If you cannot achieve pure and single right-mindfulness and if torpor and distraction arise, do not drive them away consciously. Drop the *hua-t'ou [A-mi-t'o-fo],* turn the illuminating light of the mind inward, and find the source from which torpor and distraction come. As soon as they are caught by illumination, delusion and torpor will come to a stop immediately. When you persist in this way without sliding backward, one day all of a sudden the ball of doubt *(i-t'uan),* will be smashed to smithereens and your worries of endless kalpas will dissolve away like ice.[74]

As described here, the effect of "Who after all is this person doing *nien-fo?"* clearly resembles a *kung-an* or *hua-t'ou* of the Ch'an tradition, such as *wu* (nothingness). This explains why it was called *nien-fo kung-an.* Tu-feng Chi-shan elaborated on its functions to his followers in this way:

When you work on "Who is this person doing *nien-fo?*" concentrate your effort on this word "who." Deepen your sense of doubt. "Great doubt produces great awakening; little doubt produces little awakening." How true
this saying is! If there is uninterrupted concentration, that means your
doubt has become great. At that time, the *hua-t'ou* will naturally appear
before you. Following one another closely, your pure thoughts should be
continuous. . . . Hold on securely and do not let it break off. [The result is]
that not one thought arises. There is then only emptiness outside and nothingness within.[75]

Ku-yin Ching-ch'in summarized the power of *nien-fo* succinctly in a
poem entitled "Nien-fo ching-ts'e" (Instructions Urging One To Do
Nien-fo).

> This one phrase, *A-mi-t'o-fo,*
> Is indeed the foremost *kung-an* of the Ch'an school.
> No matter whether a person is a monk, a nun, a layman, or a
>   laywoman,
> One will experience results without fail when taking hold of it.
> In walking, standing, sitting, or lying,
> Do not break off the thought of *A-mi-t'o-fo.*
> If it is in every thought,
> Your thoughts will certainly become one great concentration.
> Realizing right away the true identity of the one who is doing *nien-*
>   *fo,*
> Amitābha and my true self stand side by side.
> One thus enters the samadhi of *nien-fo* and
> Experiences personally the inner court of the Western Paradise.[76]

When *nien-fo* is mentioned in these passages, they do not explicitly indicate whether the reference is to Buddha contemplation or invocation. But when it is used in the sense of *nien-fo kung-an,* it really
implies both. This comes through clearly in the interpretations of
both Tuan-yün Chih-ch'e and K'ung-ku Ching-lung. The first interpretation is Chih-ch'e's:

Call on the Buddha's name one, three, five, or seven times. Every time you
do so, ask yourself silently where this sound of invocation comes from. Also
ask yourself who is this person who is doing the Buddha invocation. If you
are seized by doubt, then just go ahead and doubt.[77]

The second is K'ung-ku Ching-lung's:

The path of *nien-fo* is indeed a shortcut in religious cultivation. . . . It does not matter whether you call the Buddha's name quickly or slowly, in a high voice or a low voice. Just relax your body and mind, dwell on the name quietly and without forgetting it for one instant. Do not change your course whether you are in quiet or noisy surroundings, whether you are busy or at leisure. When you suddenly meet with the right opportunity, you will hit upon the true meaning of this phrase. You will then know that the Pure Land of calm light is not different from this land and that the Amitābha Buddha is not separate from your own mind.[78]

A final statement representative of the views that have been mentioned is found in Te-ch'ing's definition of *nien-fo kung-an,* the use of which by his time was quite widespread:

The *kung-an* exercise of Buddha recitation uses the invocation of *A-mi-t'o-fo* as a *hua-t'ou.* At the very moment the name is uttered, it must be the focal point in respect to which all doubts and delusions are laid aside. At the same time you ask "Who is this person reciting Amitābha's name?" When you rely steadily on the *hua-t'ou,* all illusions and confused thoughts will be instantly broken down the way knotted threads are cut. When there is no longer any place for them to reappear, it is all like the shining sun in the sky. When illusion does not arise and when delusion disappears, the mind is all calm and transparent.[79]

Chu-hung's Ideas on Nien-fo

Chu-hung's view of *nien-fo* is set forth most methodically in his four-volume *Fo-shuo A-mi-t'o ching shu-ch'ao* (Phrase-by-Phrase Commentary on the Smaller Sukhāvatīvyūha Sutra). In general, Chu-hung's ideas were similar to those expressed by the monks we have discussed so far. However, he was even more emphatic in claiming that *nien-fo* was the best method to achieve both salvation and enlightenment for people living in the Age of the Degenerate Law. He was also more systematic in his formulation of a philosophy of *nien-fo.*

Chu-hung's *Commentary* states that the sole purpose of the Ta-thāgata's appearance in the world is to cause sentient beings to awaken to the knowledge of the Buddha. Now, since the *A-mi-t'o ching* assures us that we can reach the state of nonregression (*pu-t'ui*) by holding fast to the Buddha's name with one mind (*i-hsin ch'ih-ming*), this really means that ordinary people can become Buddhas through the realization of their own minds. As long as we have firm faith in the sutra, we can achieve sudden enlightenment with one instant of thought *(pu yüeh i-nien, tun cheng p'u-t'i)*. Isn't this, then, a great matter *(ta-shih)*?[80]

Chu-hung regarded the method of "Buddha-invocation with one mind" *(i-hsin nien-fo)*, which is found in this sutra, as the Buddha's greatest gift to man, for if a person can sincerely practice it, he is in fact training himself in the six perfections of a bodhisattva:

Now if a person practices *i-hsin nien-fo* [Buddha invocation with one mind], he will naturally stop clinging to external objects; this is the perfection of giving. If he practices it, he will naturally stop all evils; this is the perfection of discipline. If he practices it, his heart will naturally be soft and pliant; this is the perfection of patience. If he practices it, he will never retrogress; this is the perfection of vigor. If he practices it, no extraneous thoughts will arise; this is then the perfection of meditation. If he practices it, correct thoughts will appear distinctly; this is then the perfection of wisdom.[81]

Thus, when Buddha invocation is carried out with one mind, it can lead to Buddhahood. But, paradoxically, this one mind is best achieved through Buddha invocation, for according to Chu-hung, even though the mind is originally devoid of thought, sentient beings, because of their ignorance, have been accustomed to delusive thoughts since time immemorial. It is very difficult to cause people to stop their random thoughts. But when they recite the name of the Buddha, this one thought can crowd out the multitude of other thoughts. It is like "using one poison to counteract another poison, or using war to stop all wars." When delusive thoughts are thus stopped by the thought of *nien-fo,* it is nothing other than enlightenment.[82]

Chu-hung's concept of "one mind" is the crucial part of his theory of *nien-fo.* Although the term is originally to be found in the text of the *A-mi-t'o ching,* Chu-hung's interpretation of it is entirely his own. The sutra says that one will certainly be reborn in the Western Paradise, "if, when one hears *A-mi-t'o-fo,* one takes hold *(chih-ch'ih)* of the name for a time, from one day to seven days, with the unperturbed one mind *(i-hsin pu-luan)*." Commenting on this passage, Chu-hung states that the proper method of *nien-fo* is to "take hold of the name." When this "taking hold" is carried out to perfection, one reaches the "unperturbed one mind," which in Chu-hung's view is indeed the essence of the sutra.

According to Chu-hung, the compound term, *chih-ch'ih* (taking hold) really has two meanings. *Chih* means that when a person hears the name, he accepts it immediately and from then on resolutely refuses to be parted from it. *Ch'ih* also means to accept and keep the name, but it implies a further requirement: the constant remembrance of the name. Chu-hung felt that *ch'ih* contains both connotations, and a simpler definition is "to invoke the name with single-mindedness and never forget it" *(chuan-nien pu-wang)*.[83]

As for the ways by which one actually "takes hold of the name," Chu-hung lists three: the first is *ming-ch'ih*, or the invocation of the name in a clear voice; the second is *mo-ch'ih*, or the silent, secret contemplation of the name; and the third is *pan-ming pan-mo-ch'ih*, or the recitation of the name with slight movements of the lips and tongue without uttering a sound, which he compared to the "diamond recitation" of mantras by the Tantric Buddhists. When reciting the name, one may or may not count the number of recitations. This again is similar to mantra recitation of the Esoteric school.[84]

Chu-hung then distinguishes two kinds of "taking hold," which were on two levels corresponding to the two levels of "one mind," the latter being achieved through the former. Because of Chu-hung's high evaluation of Hua-yen philosophy, he uses Hua-yen terminology to name these two levels: the lower one is that of particularity *(shih)* and the higher one is that of universality *(li)*. *Shih-ch'ih* means to take hold of the name with uninterrupted recollection and mindfulness *(i-nien wu-chien)* and *li-ch'ih* means with uninterrupted experience and embodiment *(t'i-chiu wu-chien)*. The former results in *shih i-hsin*, the "one mind of particularity," and the latter results in *li i-hsin*, the "one mind of universality."

Chu-hung's own words serve to illustrate what he meant by "uninterrupted recollection and mindfulness," through which one takes hold of the name in the manner of particularity and achieves *shih i-hsin:*

When you hear the Buddha's name, you must always remember it and dwell upon it. Tracing each syllable [of *A-mi-t'o-fo*] distinctly, you think *(nien)* of the name in continuous and uninterrupted succession. Whether walking, standing, sitting, or lying, just have this one thought and let no second thought arise. You will then be undisturbed by greed, anger, the *kleśas,* or any other thought. This is to remain single-minded in leisure and quietude, to remain single-minded in various defilements. Whether you are praised or blamed, whether you win or lose, whether you are faced with good or with evil, you always remain single-minded.[85]

This single-mindedness is the one mind of particularity. According to Chu-hung, it can suppress delusion *(fu-wang),* but it cannot shatter delusion *(p'o-wang).* This is so because it is achieved by the power of faith. It pertains only to concentration but not to wisdom. Chu-hung next explains the "uninterrupted experience and embodiment" by which one takes hold of the name in the manner of universality and achieves *li i-hsin:*

When you hear the Buddha's name, you should not only remember and dwell upon it, but also turn inward to contemplate, investigate, and observe it, and try to find out its origin. When investigation and observation are carried to the utmost limit, it will suddenly achieve an accord with your original mind *(pen-hsin).*[86]

According to Chu-hung, *li i-hsin* consists of direct insight in two aspects: first, the insight that the recollector *(neng-nien)* and the recollected *(so-nien)* are not two different things, since they are only one mind; second, the insight that the one mind neither exists nor does not exist, nor both nor neither, since none of the four predicates applies to the one mind. The first insight implies "the identity between suchness *(ju)* and wisdom *(chih).*"

Outside the mind of the recollector there is no Buddha whom I recollect. This means that there is no suchness outside of wisdom. Outside the Buddha who is recollected there is no mind that recollects. This means that there is no wisdom outside of suchness. Since there is neither suchness nor wisdom, there is only one mind.[87]

The second insight implies that "calm *(chi)* and illumination *(chao)* are difficult to conceive."

If one says that they exist, then the objection is that the mind that recollects is in substance empty, while the Buddha who is recollected is absolutely unattainable. If one says that they do not exist, then the objection is that the mind which recollects is bright and unobscured, while the Buddha who is recollected is plain and obvious. If one says that they both exist and do not exist, then the objection is that he who has recollections and he who has none both disappear. If one says that they neither exist nor do not exist, then the objection is that he who has recollections and he who has none both exist. Since they are not existent, they are always illuminating. Since they are neither both nor neither, they are both noncalm, nonilluminating, and yet calm and illuminating. All avenues of speech and thought are cut off; there is no form to which one can give a name. Therefore, there is only one mind.[88]

Compared with *shih i-hsin, li i-hsin* is clearly of a higher level. Chu-hung says that it can destroy delusion, for it leads not only to concentration but also to wisdom. Using this two-level interpretation of Buddha invocation, that of the particular *(shih)* and that of the universal *(li)*, Chu-hung harmonizes the four traditional categories of *nien-fo*. For the one mind, realized in Buddha invocation, is not different from samadhi. Indeed, it is identical with the last and highest form of *nien-fo*, that of *shih-hsiang nien-fo*, for this one mind is absolute reality itself.

　　Chu-hung feels that people do not understand the true meaning of *nien-fo*. They regard it as appropriate only for those of dull intelligence, while only Ch'an meditation can lead them to enlightenment. He points out in the *Commentary* that the deeper form of *nien-fo* is in essence the same as Ch'an:

The *nien-fo* of "total experience and embodiment" has the same effect as working on *kung-an* or generating great doubts as taught by Ch'an masters of earlier times. That is why there is a saying that a person interested in Ch'an meditation should just concentrate on the four syllables *A-mi-t'o-fo*, and needs no other *hua-t'ou*.[89]

Similarly, Chu-hung feels that those Ch'an practitioners who denigrate Pure Land also fail to understand the true meaning of *nien-fo*:

Ch'an and Pure Land reach the same destination by different routes. Since the latter does not separate itself from the one mind, it is identical with the Buddha, identical with *dhyāna*. Therefore, he who clings to Ch'an and denigrates the Pure Land is denigrating his own original mind; he is denigrating the Buddha. He is denigrating his own Ch'an doctrine. How thoughtless![90]

　　The link between Ch'an meditation and *nien-fo* practice is then this one mind. Chu-hung states categorically that this one mind is exactly that at which Bodhidharma was "directly pointing" *(chih-*

chih). The difference between the two turns out to be no more than a difference in terminology:

When Bodhidharma talked about Ch'an, he was directly pointing at the luminous self-nature. The one mind of universality is exactly this luminous self-nature. Even though the two traditions use different terms, what they realize is the same mind. Well indeed did Chung-feng say this: "The *dhyāna* is the *dhyāna* of the Pure Land, and the Pure Land is the Pure Land of Ch'an." Some people might object by saying that Ch'an does not resort to the written word, whereas the Pure Land advocates the invocation of the name. But, they do not know that [in the Ch'an tradition] the Dharma is transmitted by the verse of four sentences and the imprinting of the mind is found in the four volumes of the scripture [the Laṅkāvatāra Sutra]. When these are compared with the four syllables of the name, they are indeed far more wordy. As a matter of fact, not to rely on the written word does not mean to annihilate the written word. An enlightened person knows that it really means one should refuse to adhere to the written word and yet, at the same time, not cling to this refusal.[91]

In claiming that Pure Land *nien-fo* was not different from Ch'an meditation and that *A-mi-t'o-fo* was the same as a Ch'an *kung-an,* Chu-hung obviously was within the tradition of the joint practice of Ch'an and Pure Land. But we must bear in mind that this did not mean the simultaneous pursuit of the two. For Chu-hung, it seemed to imply the following: (1) that *nien-fo* was not inferior to Ch'an; (2) that *nien-fo* could achieve the same goal as Ch'an—the realization of one's self-nature or original mind; (3) that *nien-fo* was more effective than Ch'an not only because of the efficacy of the name, but because of its suitability to contemporary needs. In a sense, Chu-hung incorporated Ch'an within the Pure Land path.

To recapitulate, we may say that Chu-hung, in his interpretation of *nien-fo,* combined the two trends in Pure Land discussed earlier in this chapter. He effected a synthesis between the tradition of *nien-fo san-mei* or samadhi of Buddha invocation, as represented by Hui-yüan, Ch'eng-yüan, and Fa-chao, and that of popular piety and evangelical salvationism as represented by the Buddha invocation of Shan-tao, Shao-k'ang, and Sheng-ch'ang. Even though we may hesitate to label Pure Land a separate school, in the last analysis the fact that Chu-hung was regarded as a Pure Land patriarch seems rather appropriate. Although Chu-hung was quite at home with doctrinal formulations, it was his influence as a leader of the lay Buddhist movement and his ability as a monastic reformer that distinguished him most among his contemporaries. In the next chapter, we turn to an examination of his role in the lay Buddhist movement during the late Ming dynasty.

CHAPTER FOUR

Chu-hung and the Late Ming Lay Buddhist Movement

THE DEVELOPMENT of lay Buddhism *(chü-shih fo-chiao)* and the combining of the three teachings *(san-chiao ho-i)* are two trends in the late Ming dynasty that stand out in the history of Chinese thought as a whole. The two trends do not, of course, first appear in the Ming. Their earliest manifestation can be traced as far back as the Eastern Chin dynasty (fourth century A.D.). The lively interest in Buddhism taken by the literati, as well as their attempt to combine Buddhism and Taoism, can be seen clearly in two works: the *Hung-ming chi* and the *Shih-shuo hsin-yü*. Nevertheless, even though Chu-hung's efforts were not unprecedented, they must be regarded as qualitatively different from earlier manifestations in their pervasiveness and thoroughness.

The rise of lay Buddhism in the Ming is sometimes attributed to the low moral caliber of the priesthood and the attractions of a career in officialdom through the civil service examination system.[1] Therefore, the theory is that the best minds went into official service, and only a few talented people became monks. The pious, unwilling to join a disreputable sangha, chose the practice of lay Buddhism as the only alternative. According to this theory, then, lay Buddhism arose in response to a decline in monastic Buddhism. Such an interpretation presupposes an inverse relationship between monastic and lay Buddhism. But this relationship is open to question, for in fact lay Buddhism has always been intimately linked with monastic Buddhism. Both in the T'ang and the Sung, when Buddhism was a

A longer version of this chapter appeared under the title "Chu-hung and Lay Buddhism in the Late Ming," by Kristin Yü Greenblatt, in Wm. Theodore de Bary, et al., *The Unfolding of Neo-Confucianism* (New York: Columbia University Press, 1975).

strong institutional religion, eminent monks attracted lay followers. The situation was similar in the Ming too, as lay Buddhists usually congregated around a few leading monks. The monk Chu-hung and his lay followers serve as a good example. If there had been no revival of monastic Buddhism in the late sixteenth and early seventeenth centuries, lay Buddhism would not have emerged. Lay Buddhism, then, reflected the new energy of monastic Buddhism in the late Ming. It did not emerge as a substitute for the latter.

To regard lay Buddhism primarily as an "alternative" to monastic Buddhism is also to accept another widely held view—namely, that since the T'ang Buddhism had declined continuously, and that it reached its nadir in the Ming.[2] The principal reasons usually advanced for this view are that after the T'ang no important sutras were translated, no new Buddhist sect was established, and no great master of originality and doctrinal brilliance appeared. The criteria that have been used so far to evaluate the growth or decline of Buddhism in China center on its institutional strength and philosophical creativity. But is this the only way to interpret the history of Buddhism in China?

Although this chapter deals primarily with the phenomena of the lay Buddhist movement and the combining of the three teachings in the late Ming, it also suggests a different criterion for evaluating post-T'ang Buddhism. It is not so much that Buddhism declined or degenerated as that the nature of Buddhist practice changed after the T'ang. One can say that post-T'ang Buddhism was different from Buddhism in earlier times, but one cannot say that it was necessarily worse. The main features characterizing this change were an increasing emphasis on self-enlightenment through a practical methodology and a growing openness toward Confucianism and Taoism. Eschewing doctrinal exclusiveness, post-T'ang Buddhism attempted to become fully integrated with Chinese society. It was during the Ming dynasty that this process of sinification was best exemplified in Buddhism.

When we probe for the circumstances leading to the rise of lay Buddhism during the late Ming, two stand out for special attention. The popularity of the school of Wang Yang-ming, especially its later offshoot, the left-wing Wang school (the T'ai-chou school), undoubtedly contributed in no small measure to the atmosphere of individualism and freedom in the sphere of religious as well as intellectual inquiry. The nonsectarian approach to spiritual realization advocated by the Wang school opened new ground for a rediscovery of Buddhism. It kindled a general appreciation of, and interest in, Buddhism.

Another important factor was the conscious effort made by monks like Chu-hung to propagate Buddhism among the educated literati-official classes—as well as among the common people—in a form that could be readily understood and easily appreciated. These monks also adopted a conciliatory attitude toward Confucianism and Taoism, although in truth some of them, like Chu-hung, did not really regard either as the equal of Buddhism. The important point to note here, however, is not so much that Chu-hung did not wholeheartedly welcome Confucianism and Taoism as equals; rather, it is that he did seek to accommodate Buddhism to the other two doctrines and to fit all three into a hierarchical pyramid, with Buddhism at the apex. Chu-hung's attitude toward the problem of the three teachings should be stressed, for without his posture of reconciliation it would have been impossible for him to have become the most influential figure in the formation of the lay Buddhist movement. This movement began in the late Ming, continued to flourish through the Ch'ing period, and is still active today in Chinese communities outside mainland China. The lay Buddhist movement and the combining of the three teachings laid a theoretical foundation for the absorption of Buddhism into the personal lives of members of the literati-official class. Conversely, the development of lay Buddhism within this same class was a concrete manifestation of syncretization and a tangible index of its success.

Two of Chu-hung's ideas exerted a great influence on his followers: first, compassion for sentient beings as manifested in the observance of nonkilling (pu-sha) and the release of life (fang-sheng); second, the promotion of popular morality through the system of merits and demerits outlined in his book, Tzu-chih lu (The Record of Self-knowledge, YCFH 15). As we shall see, Chu-hung was not the originator of these concepts, for both had long been accepted tenets not only in the Buddhist tradition, but also in Confucianism and Taoism. Nevertheless, his way of interpreting and presenting these ideas won him an immense following among both the educated elite and the common people.

Compassion for Life:
The Doctrinal Foundations of Lay Buddhism

The precepts of nonkilling and the release of life have firm doctrinal bases in Buddhism. They are, respectively, the first of the ten grave *(shih-chung)* precepts and the twentieth of the forty-eight light *(ssu-shih-pa ch'ing)* precepts. These two groups together form the entire set of bodhisattva precepts *(p'u-sa chieh)* promulgated in the second half of the chapter called "Ground of Mind" in the Sutra of Brahma's Net *(Fan-wang ching hsin-ti p'in)*. As the basic precepts of Mahāyāna Buddhism primarily addressed to lay believers, this set of fifty-eight precepts has always enjoyed great popularity as well as authority in China. There are numerous commentaries on this sutra; that by the T'ien-t'ai master Chih-i (538–597) is the most famous. Chu-hung composed a subcommentary on this work. It has a rather cumbersome title: *Fan-wang ching hsin-ti p'in p'u-sa chieh i-shu fa-yin* (The Elucidation of the Commentary on the Meaning of the Bodhisattva Precepts as Contained in the Chapter Entitled "The Ground of Mind" in the Sutra of Brahma's Net, *chüan* 5, *YCFH* 1–4). Since Chu-hung's understanding of, and attitude toward, the Buddhist Vinaya are both found in this work, it deserves our special attention. While *The Record of Self-knowledge* is a detailed prescription for a moral life, this subcommentary serves as a theoretical rationale permeated throughout with the spirit of Buddhist compassion.

The scriptural text of the precept of nonkilling reads:

The Buddha said: "It is incumbent on all sons of Buddha neither to kill by themselves *(tzu-sha)*, nor to cause others to kill *(chiao-jen sha)*, nor to offer others the means to kill *(fang-pien sha)*, nor to encourage others to kill *(tsan-t'an sha)*, nor to express joy when witnessing a killing *(chien-tso sui-hsi)*, nor to kill by uttering a spell *(chou-sha)*. These comprise the primary causes of killing *(sha-yin)*, the secondary causes of killing *(sha-yüan)*, all acts of killing *(sha-fa)*, and creating the karma of having killed *(sha-yeh)*.[3] As long as anything has life, you may not kill it intentionally. Therefore a bodhisattva must abide always in the mind of compassion *(tz'u-pei hsin)*, and the mind of filial obedience *(hsiao-shun hsin)*, and he must always save and protect all sentient beings by the use of expedient means."[4]

Regarding the last sentence, Chu-hung explains in his commentary that:

The two things [a bodhisattva] should have are compassion and filial obedience, and one thing he should do is offer salvation and protection. To kill is to act contrary to heaven and principle; therefore it is unfilial and disobedient. Moreover, since all sentient beings are [perhaps] our parents of many past generations, to hurt and harm them is to hurt and harm our own fathers and mothers. If one refrains from hurting them, one can avoid sin. But, unless one also saves and protects them, one cannot be called a bodhisattva. Therefore, while practicing nonkilling, we should also save sentient beings.[5]

Among the injunctions, nonkilling heads the list of ten grave precepts that a bodhisattva must observe. Its importance cannot be emphasized enough. However, for the advocates of compassion to animals through such acts as setting them free and keeping oneself on a vegetarian diet, the principal rationale is offered by another precept: the twentieth in the group of forty-eight light precepts. It is called "the prohibition against the nonpractice of releasing and saving [sentient beings]" *(pu-hsing fang-chiu chieh)*. It reads:

All sons of Buddha, because of their compassionate hearts, practice the release of sentient beings. All men are my fathers and all women are my mothers. All rebirths of mine without any exception, from one rebirth to another, I receive from them. Therefore all the beings in the six paths of existence are my parents. If I should kill and eat them, it is the same as killing my own parents. It is also the same as killing my own self. For earth and water are my former body, while fire and wind are my original substance. Thus one should always release sentient beings. Since to be reborn into one existence after another is the permanent and unalterable law, we should teach people to release sentient beings. When we see that domestic animals are about to be killed, we ought to save them by the use of expedient means and spare them the suffering. We ought always to preach the bodhisattva precepts and save sentient beings. On the day when our parents or brothers pass away, we should ask a Vinaya master to lecture on the doctrine and rules of the bodhisattva precepts so that, as the dead are aided by the merit [arising from this], they will be able to see the Buddhas and be reborn in the path of man or heaven. Those who do not do this commit a light offense.[6]

In his commentary on this passage, Chu-hung elaborates on this doctrine. Three main points are emphasized, and they are put in a question and answer format. The questions come from an imaginary interlocutor of decidedly Confucian persuasion. The first question is this: "Mo Tzu advocates impartial love and is regarded as a heretic.

Now, how can one say that all sentient beings are my father and mother?" Chu-hung answers:

Confucianism talks only of this life, but Buddhism also discusses our previous existences. Since a person is reborn in many lives, he must be reincarnated in all the various realms of existence. Then is it not natural that sentient beings in all six paths of existence may be my father and mother? When people look only at the traces that lie nearby but do not investigate their distant causes, they are naturally prone to fall into heresy.[7]

The second question is about the identity between the four elements (earth, water, wind, fire) and man's physical body. His interlocutor asks: "The four great elements are external things. How can they be related to our bodies?" The relationship, according to Chu-hung, is illusory. Man's true self is forever "empty" (śūnya), but out of ignorance he becomes attached to the phenomenal world and regards his temporal existence as real. Once this delusion takes hold, man is trapped in transmigration and remains inextricably entangled with the four elements that are merely symbols of the phenomena. Chu-hung's answer is this:

Sentient beings, suffering delusion, do not know their true selves, which are permanent and real. They regard outside things as their own selves and, seeking earth, water, fire, and wind, they take these as their own blood, flesh, body warmth, and breath. They are born when these four great elements are combined, and they die when the elements disperse and disintegrate. Except for death by transformation [death of beings such as arhats, who live in realms beyond transmigration], all other forms of transmigration [death in the three realms of desire, form, and formlessness] cannot survive in a body independent of this [the mortal] condition.[8]

Anticipating possible doubts on the part of the reader, Chu-hung poses two related problems regarding the correspondence between the physical universe and its human microcosm. He argues his case by analogies and inferences in a manner reminiscent of the fourth-century polemics between the Buddhists and their Confucian opponents, with particular reference to the controversy about the immortality or mortality of the soul. The foremost of these arguments, brilliantly presented by the anti-Buddhist Fan Chen (ca. 450–515) in his "Essay on the Extinction of the Soul" (Shen-mieh lun), took the view that the soul was mortal.[9]

The first question in Chu-hung's presentation is this: if all creatures are endowed with the same four elements, the natural consequence would be that we should be able to share each other's feelings and sensations. But how is it that when I hurt another being, I do not feel any pain? The answer is:

One's own body and the body of others are both the same and different. The difference is like the case when thousands of flowers grow on one tree, yet each has its own nature. So when one flower is plucked, the rest are not affected. Therefore, the food of one arhat could not satisfy the rest of the monks,[10] and a loving brother's voluntary cauterization could not lessen another brother's pain.[11] As for their being the same, we have such examples as this: when a mother bites her finger, the filial son feels it in his heart[12] or, when the statue of a rebellious subject is struck, his own head also falls off.[13] When somebody else eats a plum, one's own mouth often starts to water in anticipation of the sour taste. When we see another person stand on a cliff, we start to tremble ourselves. This is because all men share the same breath and blood. Therefore we can respond to each other.[14]

Chu-hung goes on to raise another question. If our physical bodies consist of the four elements, then how is it that we are mortally susceptible to their destruction? In other words, why does earth suffocate us, water drown us, fire burn us, and wind freeze us? Chu-hung answers this way:

There are two reasons for this. The first is the mutual antagonism of the elements, and the second is the self-cancellation of each element. In the former case, when earth accumulates, it blocks the wind; when the wind is strong, it disperses earth; when fire is fierce, it dries water, yet when there is much water, it extinguishes fire. In just the same way, the four elements outside our bodies are antagonistic toward the four elements inside our bodies. They check and hold each other in control. In the latter case [of self-cancellation of elements], just as the collapse of Mount T'ai would wipe out a mound of earth, or the waves of the ocean would absorb a spoonful of water, or a raging fire would eat up a flicker of fire, or a typhoon would draw in a light breeze, similarly, the external and internal four elements destroy each other because of the similarity of their essence.[15]

In the commentary, Chu-hung compares the Buddhist attitude toward one's parents with the Confucian and tries to prove the superiority of the former. Since the twentieth precept of the *Fan-wang ching* (the thirtieth of all the precepts, grave and light) places the salvation and release of sentient beings before religious services on the anniversary of one's parents' deaths, one may legitimately attack it for its slight against one's own parents. As Chu-hung had his questioner put it, there should be a natural order in expressing one's love and loyalty—one should start with one's immediate family, then extend to other people, and last include inanimate things. Now if, as the precept dictates, one put others before one's own family, would this not be acting contrary to nature? Chu-hung answers: "When you put your own before other people, then although you are concerned with others, you still make a distinction between yourself and others. This is ordinary compassion. But, when you put other creatures before your own family you are solely concerned with others and are no longer aware of yourself. This is compassion par excellence."[16] In other words, Confucian compassion is not as vigorous and thoroughgoing as Buddhist compassion.

On another occasion Chu-hung compared the Confucian moral precepts in general with those of Buddhism and arrived at a similar conclusion. He felt that, although they formally resembled each other, they were quite different in scope and intensity. Buddhist precepts, according to Chu-hung, were more demanding and far-reaching. They aimed at absolute perfection, whereas Confucian precepts aimed at goodness in moderation:

The precepts of Confucianism and Buddhism are similar, but as the first are limited and the other comprehensive in scope, they are quite different. Take the prohibition against killing, one of the five [basic] Buddhist precepts. In Buddhism, it means nonkilling in absolute terms. On the other hand, although Confucianism also teaches compassion, it says only that one should not kill cows, sheep, dogs, and pigs without good reason. It does not prohibit killing per se. Confucianism also advocates not fishing with a net or shooting at a nesting bird. Unlike Buddhism, however, it does not prohibit fishing and shooting under all circumstances. Therefore we know that Confucian precepts aim at the good of the secular society, while Buddhist precepts aim at the good in absolute transcendence. It is therefore not surprising that since ancient times individual Confucianists have accepted and observed Buddhist precepts.[17]

The influence of the precepts of nonkilling and the release of life on the practice of Chinese Buddhism has always been extensive. Although Chu-hung and his fellow monks emphasized abstention from killing and the release of living creatures, this was not the first time that these were advocated. A brief historical survey of attempts to institutionalize them may give us more perspective.[18]

Historical Precedents for the Advocacy of Nonkilling and Releasing Life

During the Sui dynasty it was legally stipulated in 583 that in the first, fifth, and ninth months of the year, as well as on the "six fast days" (eighth, fourteenth, fifteenth, twenty-fourth, twenty-ninth, and thirtieth days) of every month, no one should kill any living beings.[19] The choice of these particular dates was based on the rule set down in the Sutra of Brahma's Net.[20] It says that during these same three months and on these six days of every month a lay devotee should keep the eight precepts. Among them there are the prohibitions against killing and theft, and the rule of not eating after the noon meal. On the six fast days, the four Heavenly Kings would make an inspection of the world, observe the good and evil deeds of men, and make a record of these. Therefore, a person should be especially cautious on these days.

During the T'ang dynasty, a decree was issued in 619 forbidding the slaughter of animals as well as fishing and hunting during the first, fifth, and ninth months of every year.[21] This decree apparently met with varying degrees of success until the Hui-ch'ang persecution (845). As for the establishment of ponds for releasing life (fang-sheng ch'ih), the earliest reference dates back to the reign of Emperor Yüan of the Liang dynasty (552–555), when a pavilion was constructed for this purpose,[22] but we do not know the date of its construction or any details concerning its use. During the T'ang dynasty Emperor Su-tsung issued a decree in 759 setting up eighty-one ponds for releasing life.[23] The famous calligrapher Yen Chen-ch'ing (709–785)[24] wrote an inscription on a stone stele commemorating this event. According to the inscription, the area in which these ponds were established included parts of present-day Shansi, Hupei, Hunan, Szechuan, Yünnan, Kweichow, Kwangtung, Kwangsi, Kiangsi, and Chekiang: "Starting from Hsing-tao of Yangchow [Shensi], through the various districts of Shan-nan, Chien-nan, Ch'ien-chung, Ching-nan, Ling-nan, Kiangsi, Chekiang, and ending at the T'ai-p'ing Bridge over the Ch'in-huai River at Chiang-ning of Shen-chou [Nanking], every five li a pond for releasing life is set up by the river and near the city. All together there are eighty-one ponds."[25] Although we have access to government decrees and codifications giving some indication of the extent of official compliance, the evidence also suggests that popular practice was very limited. It is not until the Sung dynasty that we begin to see a pervasive popularization.

The gradual popularity of the practice of releasing life was due mainly to the successful evangelism of outstanding monks. Yungming Yen-shou (904–975),[26] the great synthesizer of all Buddhist sects, was a strong advocate of the amalgamation of Ch'an and Pure Land. When he was in charge of taxes for the king of Wu-yüeh before he became a monk, he used government money to buy fish and shrimps and set them free. Tz'u-yün Tsun-shih (963–1032),[27] a T'ien-t'ai monk who also advocated Pure Land practice, persuaded many fishermen to change their profession. It is said that when he was lecturing at the K'ai-yüan monastery, "People in the whole city stopped drinking wine, and butchers lost their business."[28] He was also instrumental in setting up new ponds for releasing life. In 1017 Emperor Chen-tsung issued a decree calling for the establishment of ponds along the rivers Huai and Che as well as in Hunan and Hupei, where fishing was also prohibited.[29] Tsun-shih sent a memorial to the throne in 1019 requesting that the emperor's birthday be celebrated by having the West Lake established as a pond for releasing life. From then on, every year on Buddha's birthday, the eighth day of the fourth month, "meetings for releasing life" (fang-sheng hui) were organized, and participation in the meetings became very fashionable. This custom apparently declined somewhat in later years, for Su Tung-p'o (1036–1101)[30] wrote a memorial in 1090 asking for its revival.[31]

Some Characteristics of Post-T'ang Buddhism

During the late T'ang and the Five Dynasties, after the monumental task of sutra translation, doctrinal elaboration, and sectarian systematization had been accomplished, the process of assimilation started in earnest. It had been, in a sense, impossible before the Sung. So the process flowered during the Sung, when Ch'an and Pure Land emerged as the dominant sects of Chinese Buddhism.

While different in approach—Ch'an being a form of self-realization effected through one's own efforts, and Pure Land emphasizing faith as expressed in the devotion and worship of the Amitābha Buddha—they both put practice ahead of doctrine. Religious salvation had to be sought through a religious life. This did not necessarily mean a monastic life, although the latter continued to be regarded as the preferred state for a person committed to Buddhism. Yet it certainly did entail a definite life style. The life of a Buddhist devotee was to embody both wisdom and compassion. When a Ch'an practitioner assiduously meditated on a *kung-an*, he was in fact gradually groping toward the realization of wisdom, which is the highest perfection in Mahāyāna Buddhism. Such wisdom could demolish the whole system of false and perverted thought constructions he had inherited as a human condition. In the same way, by performing such small acts of charity as setting free a captured fish or refusing to take meat on certain days, the Pure Land believer hoped to free himself from his innate desire, greed, and hatred.

The motivations for performing such acts were rooted not merely in ethical demands, but had deep religious and psychological roots. When a person killed another sentient being, he broke the hidden bonds among all forms of life. Violence alienated the violator not only from a sense of cosmic harmony but also, ultimately, from himself. For although the act of killing was an extreme assertion of the self, the self, which was so isolated and delimited, ironically ceased to have any real life or to have any real meaning.

Buddhist vegetarianism was significant when viewed in this context. For even though one did not kill the animal himself, every time one ate its meat, he denied the existence of any meaningful relationship between himself and other beings. By objectifying an animal as "food," one could become insensitive to its suffering and regard it as a mere thing. On the other hand, each time he released a creature from its impending death, each time he returned it to freedom, a person reaffirmed the original bond among all sentient beings. The act of releasing was a celebration of reunion, during which the selfish human will, which alienates, was momentarily obliterated. The person who released life in fact released himself from human selfishness.

The ordinary person who engaged in such acts might not consciously realize their significance. Nor can we assert that everyone could achieve this qualitative leap of transcendence by the quantitative performance of good deeds. Still, the rationale for this kind of piety is there. The fact that the two Sung monks mentioned earlier, who advocated nonkilling and the releasing of life, were regarded primarily as Pure Land believers comes as no surprise. What is particularly noteworthy is that general popular interest at that time affected even the teachings of the Ch'an masters whose concern was the attainment of enlightenment. The amalgamation of the Ch'an and Pure Land schools started during the Sung. The emphasis on practice, which both schools shared, provided a common ground for amalgamation. But as the years passed, popular Buddhism, which grew out of their common concern, came more and more to serve as a reinforcement for this syncretic trend.

During the Sung dynasty lay associations became increasingly popular in Buddhist circles. Such associations have been traced back to Hui-yüan's Lotus Society[32] and to the many organizations whose traces were found at Tun-huang. But as Suzuki Chūsei pointed out in his excellent study on Sung Buddhism,[33] these associations were quite different from their prototypes of the Northern and Southern dynasties, or the Sui and T'ang. In the first place, whereas the earlier associations were mainly organized for the purposes of erecting statues of the Buddha, building caves to store Buddhist treasures, copying and making sutras, reciting sutras, or organizing Buddhist feasts and religious festivals, the Sung associations were primarily "societies for reciting the Buddha's name" (nien-fo hui). During their periodic meetings members recited together the name of the Amitābha Buddha and transferred the merits thus accrued to their speedy rebirth in the Western Paradise. The members also engaged in philanthropic activities, but invocation of the Buddha (nien-fo) was the main purpose. In the second place, members of earlier associations tended to come from the upper classes, but membership during the Sung was much more diverse, and common people from ordinary walks of life tended to form the majority. Although they were called "societies," we do not find any formal organizational structure or institutional rules for these groups. They often consisted of indefinite numbers of people, and they met at unspecified times. In sharp contrast, the "societies for releasing life" (fang-sheng hui) of the late Ming and the Ch'ing were much better organized.

It was also during the Sung that tracts exhorting people to refrain from killing animals for food and to keep a vegetarian diet started to appear in great numbers. The ones I have read[34] are all quite short, and they appeal to ethical instead of religious considerations. The piece by Su Tung-p'o, probably the most prominent Sung lay devotee, is a representative example. Su stated that a meat eater invariably had to violate the five cardinal Confucian virtues: "To slaughter others in order to fatten oneself is inhuman; to tear it from its kith and kin in order to entertain one's own family is unjust; to offer its fleshy body to the gods is improper; to proclaim that what belongs to one as one's proper share must be beheaded is unwise; and to set bait and traps to ensnare it is to lack good faith."[35]

Chu-hung's Advocacy of Nonkilling and Releasing Life in the Ming

It was in this syncretic tradition that Chu-hung carried out his lay proselytism. His essays "On Refraining from Killing" and "On Releasing Sentient Beings" (Chieh-sha fang-sheng wen)[36] were reprinted and distributed widely. They were received with such enthusiasm and became so famous that the mother of the emperor sent a special emissary to seek further instruction from Chu-hung. As mentioned before, they also started the vogue among lay circles of organizing "societies for releasing life." These tried to raise funds to build ponds for releasing life and met together at definite intervals to set free captured birds, fish, and other domesticated animals (which they usually bought from fishermen or at the marketplace). In the twenty-eighth year of Wan-li (1600), as a result of his persuasion, Chu-hung's lay followers contributed money, redeemed two abandoned temples in the city of Jen-ho in Chekiang, where he was born, and established in each a pond for releasing life. These were the Shan-fang and Ch'ang-shou ponds.[37]

On the subject of organizing these societies, however, Chu-hung himself was curiously reticent, if not outright disapproving. The reason was, most probably, his fear of being connected with the notorious White Lotus Society and other secret societies which appeared periodically in history, and which various governments since the Sung had tried so hard to suppress.[38] Chu-hung warned his fol-

焦山放黿

6. Releasing a Tortoise at Chiao-shan Monastery (*Hung-hsüeh yin-yüan,*
chüan 2, p. 67a)

lowers that there were rascals in the society who used the name of the Buddha to do evil things.[39] They proclaimed the imminent coming of the future Buddha Maitreya and lured adherents with money, fame, material possessions, and women. The only way to disengage oneself from mistaken identification with these discredited groups was to try to practice cultivation by oneself. Societies should be organized with great discretion, and there should not be too many. In his own words:

Associations for the recitation of the Buddha's name *(nien-fo hui)* were started by Master Hui-yüan of Lu Shan, but among the organizers of societies today, can anyone be compared to Master Yüan? Can the members be the equals of the eighteen gentlemen of Lu Shan? Therefore, the societies should be few and not many. This is because people who are really interested in practicing the *nien-fo* of the Pure Land are as rare as dedicated monks sitting in the meditation hall. As for women joining an association together with men, this was something unheard of at Lu Shan. Women should practice *nien-fo* at home. Do not mix with men and cause society's criticism and suspicion. If you want to protect the true Law of the Buddha, this is most important. It is also better to have fewer societies for releasing life *(fang-sheng hui)* than many, inasmuch as people who are really interested in saving sentient beings are as rare as people in the recitation groups *(nien-fo hui)*. In my opinion, everyone should buy as many creatures as he can afford and release them whenever he sees them. At the end of a season or at the end of a year, everyone may go to one place, the number he has released can be tabulated, and his merit can be assigned. After this let everyone disperse quickly. Do not waste money to prepare offerings and do not waste time in socializing.[40]

The emphasis on flexibility and expediency was characteristic of Chu-hung's approach to problems of religious cultivation. Such organizations were not in themselves undesirable, but because of their tendency to become, among other abuses, formalistic, Chu-hung could not endorse them with complete enthusiasm. But on the subject of releasing life, he was consistently evangelical. In his essay "On Releasing Sentient Beings" *(Fang-sheng wen)*, he argues the case with many examples drawn from historical records, legends, contemporary reports, and personal experiences, to illustrate the efficacy of releasing life. More powerful than rational and doctrinal persuasion, these stories helped to convince not only his contemporaries but even later readers of the existence of a law which ensures that a good deed is always rewarded. Some stories may appear to be no more than superstitions, and one may marvel at the naïveté and gullibility of the people who believed them. Yet this realization does not prevent us from appreciating Chu-hung's skill in the presentation of his case and his ability to fathom the mysterious depths of human religiosity. By using a technique which stressed how the numinous worked in the miraculous, the magical, and the uncommon, he struck a responsive chord among the audiences of that time. The atmosphere of the Ming, as evidenced by the abundance of reported dreams, omens, and other inexplicable events in the *pi-chi* (notebook) literature of the day, was very hospitable to this approach.

Two anecdotes Chu-hung tells in this essay give us a good idea of the type of story he used. Both happened in his own day: one to himself, the other to someone in his native Hangchow.[41]

The first took place in the fourth year of Lung-ch'ing (1570). While Chu-hung was staying at a small temple during his wanderings after he had become a monk, he saw that someone had captured several centipedes and was fastening their heads and tails together with a bamboo bow. Chu-hung bought the centipedes and set them free. Only one was still alive and got away; the rest were dead. Later on, one night while he was sitting with a friend, he suddenly caught a glimpse of a centipede on the wall. After he had tried to drive it away and had failed, he said to the centipede, "Are you the one I set free before? Have you come here to thank me? If so, I shall preach the Dharma to you. Listen carefully and do not move." Then Chu-hung continued, "All sentient beings evolve from the mind. The ones with violent minds are transformed into tigers and wolves, and the ones with poisonous minds are transformed into snakes and scorpions. If you give up your poisonous heart, you can cast off this form." After he finished talking, the centipede slowly crept out the window without having to be driven away. The friend was greatly amazed.

The second anecdote took place in the ninth year of Wan-li (1581) in a household named Kan in Hu-lei near Hangchow. A neighbor was robbed, and Kan's daughter presented the neighbor's mother with ten eels when she went to commiserate. The eels were put away in a big jar and then forgotten. One night the mother dreamed that ten men dressed in yellow gowns and wearing pointed hats knelt before her and begged for their lives. Upon waking, she consulted a fortuneteller, who told her that some creatures were begging to be released from captivity. She searched all over the house and finally found the jar containing the eels. They had grown to enormous size in the meantime and numbered exactly ten. She was utterly astonished and set them free right away.

These and other stories were meant to prove that "of the persons who set creatures free, some receive honor and prestige, some receive added years of life, some are spared from disasters, some recover from mental illnesses, some achieve rebirth in heaven, and some attain enlightenment in the Way. There is clear evidence that as one releases life, he assuredly receives a reward."[42] Although rewards should not be the sole purpose in our performance of good deeds, Chu-hung told his readers, as a consequence of the good deed performed a reward will come, even though we may refuse it.

In fact, reward always served as an important argument in Chu-hung's advocacy of lay practice. In another article dealing with the same subject, in which he offered a complete list of all the reasons why a person should carry out the release of life, rewards again occupied a conspicuous position:

> As a man values his life,
> So do animals love theirs.
> Releasing life accords with the mind of heaven;
> Releasing life agrees with the teaching of the Buddha.
> Releasing life unties the snare of hatred;
> Releasing life purifies the taint of sin.
> Releasing life enables one to escape the three disasters [of fire, water, wind];
> Releasing life enables one to be free from the "nine kinds of untimely deaths *(chiu-heng)*."[43]
> Releasing life enables one to live long;
> Releasing life enables one to rise high in an official career;
> Releasing life enables one to have many children;
> Releasing life enables one to have a prosperous household.
> Releasing life dispels anxieties and worries;
> Releasing life reduces sickness and pain.
> Releasing life is the compassion of Kuan-yin [Avalokiteśvara];
> Releasing life is the deed of P'u-hsien [Samantabhadra].
> By releasing life one comes to realize the truth of no birth *(wu-sheng)*.
> By releasing life one ends transmigration.[44]

Here Chu-hung tells his readers that to release life is as much the will of heaven as a teaching of the Buddha. He attracts his readers with worldly honors and riches, promises them magical protection from disaster, and in the end holds out the loftiest ideals in Buddhism: "no birth" and the release from transmigration.

What are we to make of this mixture of religious, magical, moral, and materialistic rationales? Are we to presume that Chu-hung used material rewards only as a concession to popular superstition, while his true intention was to preach a higher Buddhism? Or should we argue that he could, in fact, do no better; that he was an ignorant monk peddling an adulterated version of Buddhism, that in order to make Buddhism palatable he had to exploit popular greed and superstition? I do not think that either was really the case.

It cannot be denied that Chu-hung consistently employed the theme of reward and punishment. But his credentials as an important Buddhist master were well acknowledged by his contemporaries. His knowledge and understanding of Buddhist philosophy, especially that of Hua-yen, were excellent. Following orthodox Chinese Buddhist tradition, he showed his ability as a scholastic commentator on sutras in his work *Fo-shuo A-mit-t'o ching shu-ch'ao,* a phrase-by-phrase commentary on the Smaller Sukhāvatīvyūha Sutra.[45] Yet, in advocating both nonkilling and releasing life, as well as in propagating the social ethics set forth in *The Record of Self-knowledge,* Chu-hung displayed remarkably little of his Buddhist learning; he relied much more on practical moral persuasion. This apparent contradiction can be resolved if we examine Chu-hung's purpose in encouraging lay Buddhism. When we do so, we discover that Chu-hung was not only aiming *for* something; he was also reacting *against* something.

The fact that Chu-hung proselytized in a nonintellectual, nonphilosophical manner was not an accident, but deliberate choice. He was in fact greatly distressed by what he considered to be the failure of Buddhism in his own time. This failure, as he saw it, was due mainly to the degeneration of Ch'an practice and the neglect of monastic discipline. Instead of working seriously on his enlightenment, the Ch'an devotee only discussed it cleverly and as an intellectual game. Ch'an was no longer a genuine living experience, but the mechanical mimicry of earlier *kung-an* and the fabrication of sophistries. Religious cultivation had come to signify learning by rote and the meaningless display of intellectual cleverness.

Neglect of monastic discipline was closely connected with the stultification of Ch'an. Ch'an masters in the T'ang and Sung frequently shocked their disciples by their unconventional behavior and by their refusal to admit the relevance of moral action to spiritual enlightenment. The truth discovered through enlightenment transcended human morality, and the person in a state of enlightenment might rightly regard all moral values as relative. This was not only a Ch'an position, for we can find it in the Wang Yang-ming school as well. The dictum "in the original substance of the mind there is no distinction between good and evil," as set forth in the famous colloquy at the T'ien-ch'uan Bridge, is also rooted in the genuine experience of enlightenment. Yet what is often easily forgotten is that this transcendence of human morality applies only to those who have already experienced enlightenment. To the person who is in the process of working toward enlightenment, monastic discipline is in fact indispensable.

Ch'an had lost vitality by Chu-hung's time. Yet people who had never gone through the transforming experience of enlightenment continued to denigrate morality as conventional, and looked down upon it. It was against this kind of irresponsible attitude that Chu-hung launched an attack. He saw a sense of moral seriousness as the most essential countermeasure. It could take the form of observance of Vinaya rules in the case of a monk, or of the practice of nonkilling, release of life, and social philanthropy in the case of a lay devotee. For Chu-hung the compelling question was how to save Buddhism from the deadening effect of routinization. Under the charismatic inspiration of strong Ch'an masters Buddhism had been able to retain its vitality even if it did not stress moral cultivation. But in the postcharismatic age of the Ming (which Chu-hung, along with other Buddhists, called the "degenerate age of the Law"), it would be dangerous for anyone to continue to neglect moral discipline. Indeed, moral discipline was the only effective means through which to bolster flagging energies and infuse vigor and direction into religious life.

In this context it is interesting to record Chu-hung's correspondence with Chou Ju-teng, a member of the T'ai-chou school. Chou was a disciple of Lo Chin-hsi, who introduced him to Buddhist writings.[46] It was Chou who once engaged in a debate with a fellow Confucian concerning the meaning of the famous "colloquy at the T'ien-ch'uan Bridge." He held to the interpretation then that the mind was neither good nor evil, and he wrote to Chu-hung about it saying: "If we realize the true self, then where is good and evil? It is like the moon as reflected in the river; how can one say whether it is clear or dirty?" To this question Chu-hung answered:

Even though the moon is pure, the reflection will become dull or bright depending on whether the water is clean or dirty. Although the mind is originally luminous, yet as one does good or evil deeds, their effects will make the mind soar high or sink to the ground. How can we say that the dirty water is good simply because the moon in its essence cannot be designated as clear or murky? How can we say that evil deeds do not matter simply because the mind in its essence cannot be designated as good or evil? If one is addicted to the biased view of emptiness, he will deviate from perfect understanding. Once you realize that both good and evil are nonexistent, it is all the better that you should stop evil and do good. If you insist on not stopping evil and not doing good, it shows that your understanding is not yet perfect.[47]

"To do good and to stop evil" (hsing-shan chih-e) was indeed the key to the entire Buddhist Vinaya. Chu-hung sought to use Pure Land faith and moral discipline to correct the penchant for "empty talk" current in his day.

Releasing life, then, was intended as a method of moral cultivation. One might wish that Chu-hung, in advocating the performance of good deeds, could have stressed the importance of nonattachment more, and the benefits of worldly rewards less. But he was as much a practical missionary as a Buddhist theologian. He knew the hopes and aspirations of his audience extremely well, and he used whatever arguments would be most effective in gaining wider acceptance.

Chu-hung's emphasis on concrete, practical methods of lay practice was adequately demonstrated in his essay "On Releasing Sentient Beings," especially at the end, where he offered concrete guidelines:

First, everyone is enjoined to buy animals whenever the opportunity presents itself. One should not begrudge the money spent, for money does not last, whereas the blessedness (fu) created by redeeming animals lasts forever. If a person does not have money, he accumulates blessedness so long as he has a compassionate heart and persuades others to buy animals and so long as he takes delight in such actions by others.

Second, it is the deed of releasing, not the size or quantity of the animals released, that counts most. The rich man who saves the lives of many animals and the poor man who saves only one insect are equally praiseworthy. What is most important is that it be done as often as possible—continuously. There are people who do not understand this principle. They buy a great number of creatures who are small in size in the hope of gaining more merit. This is no more than calculated greed; it is certainly not compassion for sentient beings.

Third, in releasing life, one is enjoined to try whenever possible to perform a religious ceremony at which sutras are read and the recitation of the Amitābha Buddha's name is carried out. For one should not only save the creature's physical body *(se-shen)*, but also its spiritual life *(hui-ming)*. However, if this cannot be conveniently arranged, one should be flexible. Where there is not time for sutra recitation, *nien-fo* alone is enough. If for the sake of the religious ceremony one keeps the animals overnight and allows some of them to perish, the consequences surely will negate the intention.[48]

Despite Chu-hung's hesitation about lay societies, he did organize one himself. The rules he drew up for it give us a good picture of its operations. Members of the society were to meet once a month (on the penultimate day of each month) at the Shang-fang Temple; hence its name, the Good Society of Shang-fang. At these meetings, members were to recite first one volume of the Vinaya sutras, accompanied by a monk who beat a wooden fish, then the name of Amitābha Buddha 500 or 1,000 times. They were each to contribute five *fen* (one *fen* being one-hundredth of an ounce) toward the preparation of fruit and vegetable offerings for the Buddha. Members were also urged to contribute money for the purpose of buying captured animals and setting them free, though the amount was not fixed. They were also to bring fish or birds to the temple and release them there. When members gathered together, no one was to be allowed to talk about worldly things; they were to discuss only unclear passages of scripture or essential points in cultivation. Discussions were to be short and to the point. Each member was to take a turn serving as chairman of the monthly meetings, and it was to be his responsibility to keep the account book for dues received and expenses paid. The chairman was to be the first to arrive and the last to leave.[49]

Some of Chu-hung's followers organized other societies along similar lines. T'ao Wang-ling,[50] who was a student of Chou Ju-teng and a close friend of Chiao Hung,[51] organized a society, together with some friends, in the southern part of K'uai-chi (in present-day Shao-hsing, Chekiang) during the summer of the twenty-ninth year of Wan-li (1601). The text of Chu-hung's essay "On Releasing Sentient Beings" appeared at the beginning of the society's register.[52] Another lay follower, Yü Ch'un-hsi,[53] organized a society named the Sheng-lien She (Luxuriant Lotus) which met on the West Lake. Except for minor details, the rules applied were identical to those described previously.

A companion piece to the essay "On the Release of Sentient Beings" was the essay "On Nonkilling" *(Chieh-sha wen)*. It comprised, in equal proportions, case histories and methodical directions for practice. Chu-hung believed that the killing and eating of animals was a habit formed gradually and by imitation. If someone ate human flesh, society would be rightly shocked, but if it had not been prohibited and had been consumed by ever-larger numbers of people, then after a few years cannibalism would have likewise become an accepted practice. That is why Chu-hung was convinced that the custom of killing animals for food had to, and could be, stopped. He listed seven occasions and situations when the killing of animals was most common, and in each instance he gave arguments to demonstrate its wrongness or irrationality.[54]

1. On your birthday you should not kill animals. Parents bear the burden of giving birth to you and bringing you up. On the day you are born, your parents have started the slow process of death. Therefore on this day you should do good deeds in order to help the souls of your parents achieve a speedy deliverance from suffering. If you indulge in killing, it will not only be disastrous for yourself, but it will also implicate your parents.

2. When you have a son, you should not kill animals. Since you know that all men are happy to have sons, is it hard to imagine that animals also love their young? If, to celebrate the birth of your son, you take the lives of their sons, can your conscience really be at ease? Furthermore, when your baby is born, you ought to accumulate merit for his sake. If on the contrary, you create bad karma by killing, this is stupidity beyond belief.

3. When you sacrifice to your ancestors, you should not kill animals. On the anniversaries of the dead, as well as during the spring and autumn visits

to ancestral graves, you ought to observe the precept of nonkilling in order to assist the dead by creating merit. Killing can only bring added bad karma upon the dead. For the body in the grave, even the choicest delicacies in the world will not be able to reawaken its sense of taste.

4. For the wedding ceremony, you should not kill animals. From the preliminary rite of asking names, to betrothal, and finally to the wedding, innumerable animals are killed for these ceremonies. But marriage is the beginning of the bringing forth of new life. It is contrary to reason to kill life at the beginning of life. Furthermore, the wedding day is an auspicious day. Therefore it is cruel to perform violent deeds on such a day.

5. In entertaining friends, you should not kill animals. Vegetables, fruits, and plain food are equally conducive to friendly conversation. There is no need for slaughtering animals and procuring extravagant dishes. When you realize that the meat you enjoy came from screaming animals, any person with a heart must feel sad.

6. In praying to avert disaster, you should not kill animals. When a person is sick he often kills animals to sacrifice to the spirits *(shen)*. But to kill another life in order to ask the spirits for the continuity of your own life is contrary to the principle of heaven. Moreover, spirits are upright and just, so how can they be bribed? Therefore not only are you unable to prolong your life, but you incur the evil karma of killing.

7. You should not kill animals as a livelihood. It is said that some people have to fish, hunt, or slaughter cows, sheep, pigs, and dogs for the sake of a livelihood. But people who are not engaged in such professions do not necessarily end up starving. To make a living by killing animals is condemned by the spirits, and no one who does this ever achieves prosperity. On the contrary, it will surely lead one to hell and make a person suffer retribution in the next life. Therefore it is imperative for such persons to seek another way of earning a livelihood.

At the end of the essay Chu-hung once again provided practical instructions[55] for the regular observance of the precept of nonkilling. If a person cannot stop killing on all seven occasions, he still should try his best to reduce the frequency of his violations. If he cannot give up meat, the least he should do is buy the meat from the market and not kill the animal himself. Thus, by nurturing the mind of compassion, one may hope to improve gradually the nature of one's karma.

There are, moreover, two further things one should do according to Chu-hung. First, one should pass this essay around among one's relatives, friends, and acquaintances. The more persons one converts to vegetarianism, the greater is one's own merit. Second, at the beginning of each year, one should paste up on the wall twelve pieces of paper with the name of the month written on each. When one does not kill anything for a whole month, one writes "no killing" on the piece of paper. If a person does not kill for one month, it is "inferior goodness"; for a whole year, it is "medium goodness"; for a whole lifetime, it is "superior goodness."

A Controversy between Chu-hung and Matteo Ricci

I have devoted considerable space to Chu-hung's ideas on non-killing and the release of life because I believe that these two concepts exerted the greatest impact on lay Buddhism not only during Chu-hung's time, but also in later generations—even to today. Compassion for animals, vegetarianism, and especially the practice of setting free captured animals often appear quaint and simple-minded to the modern reader. In fact, resistance to these precepts, based presumably on common sense and rationality, was voiced even during Chu-hung's lifetime. One attack emanated from Matteo Ricci (1552–1610), the Jesuit missionary who came to China in 1582; he was very successful and gained a considerable following among the Confucian gentry. Ricci's attack and Chu-hung's reply started a major controversy between Catholicism and Buddhism. The controversy, which is referred to as the Movement to Expose Heretical Teachings (p'i-hsieh yün-tung) among the Buddhists, was carried on energetically around Hangchow and Fukien, and lasted well into the early Ch'ing dynasty.[56]

Matteo Ricci's main thesis is neatly presented in his book T'ien-chu shih-i (The True Meaning of the Lord of Heaven),[57] which was written in 1603. In the fifth chapter, Ricci attacks the Buddhist doctrine of transmigration of souls. After listing five arguments against it, he arrives at his main point—namely, his proof that the Buddhist precepts of nonkilling and release of life are absurd:

Those who preach nonkilling fear that the cows and horses one kills might be the reincarnation of one's own parents and therefore they cannot bear the idea of killing them. But if they really think so, how can they bear the idea of forcing cows to till the land or drive the cart?—or of riding themselves on horses? For I think the crimes of killing one's parents and that of enslaving them with physical hardship are not different.[58]

He further argues that if one really believes in reincarnation, the logical conclusion would not merely be a prohibition on the killing of animals, but abolition of the use of animals for farming. More serious than that, the institution of marriage would have to be outlawed:

If we believe in the theory that a human being can be reborn as another human being, then we have to outlaw marriage and the employment of servants. For how can you know that the woman you are to marry is not the reincarnation of your own mother in your previous life? And how can you be sure that the servant whom you order around and on whom you heap abuse is not the latter-day manifestation of your brother, relative, sovereign, teacher, or friend? The canon governing human relationships will assuredly be wrecked by this.[59]

Citing the Christian concept of Creator-God, Matteo Ricci claims that everything in this world was created by God for the benefit of man.[60] Birds and animals were created to nourish the life of man. As long as men used natural resources within limits, killing was not necessarily an evil. In these beliefs Ricci was in complete agreement with the Confucian conservationists:

The universal law under Heaven is to prohibit the killing of man but not animals and birds. For animals, vegetables, and plants function in the same way as the economy. As long as we use them with restraint, it is all right. Therefore, Mencius taught the king that in fishing, men should not exhaust the pond, and in cutting down trees there should be a definite time for men to go to the mountains. But he did not say that men should not do such things.[61]

Chu-hung's defense consisted of three short essays entitled "On Heaven," (T'ien-shuo) which are found in his Chu-ch'uang san-pi (Final Jottings under a Bamboo Window).[62] The main portion of the argument runs thus:

The [Sutra of] Brahma's Net only strictly prohibits the taking of life. Since, from time immemorial, we have been bound to the wheel of transmigration and in each reincarnation we must have parents, then how can we be sure that they are not our parents of previous existences? But to say that they might be our parents is not the same as to say that they definitely are our parents. . . . Marriages between men and women, the use of carts and horses, as well as the employment of servants are all ordinary things in the world. They can never be compared with the cruelty of taking the lives of animals. That is why the sutra says only that one should not kill any sentient being, but does not say that one should not get married or employ domestic animals. The kind of sophistry [used by Matteo Ricci] is a clever play on words. How can it harm the clear teaching of the Great Truth?[63]

In the same year he finished this essay (1615), Chu-hung died. His lay disciple, Yü Ch'un-hsi, continued the defense of the Law. He exchanged letters with Matteo Ricci, taking the same position as had his master. Yü's letter and Matteo Ricci's reply are contained in a curious book entitled *Pien-hsüeh i-tu* (Remaining Letters Concerning the Elucidation of Learning),[64] which is attributed to Matteo Ricci and came out twenty years after Chu-hung's death. Besides the two letters, this work also contains a reply supposedly written by Matteo Ricci and directed against Chu-hung's essays called "On Heaven."[65] However, since Matteo Ricci died five years before the appearance of these essays, he could not have known about them, and it is clear that at least this part of the book is spuriously attributed to Ricci.[66]

This controversy is significant not only because it is of historical interest, but also because it illustrates an important doctrinal difference between Buddhism and other systems of morality. Buddhism requires that a man practice compassion not only in regard to his fellow man, but also in relation to all sentient beings. What the precepts of nonkilling and releasing life demand is precisely our extension to animals of the same feelings and sentiments we exhibit toward other human beings. This is different from the Confucian concept of *jen* (benevolence), which, though it requires kindness and sympathy toward animals because they share with us the same cosmic process of regeneration and decay, is concerned chiefly with human society.

In advocating Buddhist compassion, Chu-hung was in fact trying to effect a form of reevaluation that would reorient the people to a value system broader in scope than the traditionally family-centered social consciousness. In doing so, Chu-hung did not invalidate the Confucian moral schema. Filial piety, loyalty, and other Confucian virtues were accepted intact. (This explains Chu-hung's success in attracting Confucians.) But he did not merely superimpose Buddhist ethics on a Confucian structure. His method was to take a Confucian virtue, prove that Buddhism also valued it, interpret it according to the Buddhist understanding, give it back to society, and ask people to value it with this added dimension. Chu-hung's treatment of the concept of *hsiao* (filial piety) provides a good example. In the Sutra of Brahma's Net, before the Buddha gives the precepts, he says: "You are to act with filial piety toward your parents, to the monk who is your teacher, and to the Three Treasures. Filial piety is the law of ultimate truth. It is discipline *(śila).*" The original commentator on the sutra, Chih-i, did not comment on this passage, but Chu-hung built a major thesis out of it. He said:

If one is filial to his parents, he will naturally be pleasant in his voice and will not say crude and unreasonable things. This is the discipline for the mouth *(k'ou chieh).* He is forever solicitous and never disobeys: this is the discipline for the body *(shen chieh).* He is full of sincere love and his mind will not harbor disloyal thoughts: this is the discipline for the mind *(hsin chieh).* Filial piety has the power to stop evil, for one fears to disgrace one's parents: this is the discipline for proper conduct *(lü-i chieh).* It can also induce the performance of good, for one wishes to glorify one's parents: this is the discipline for good dharma *(shan-fa chieh).* Finally, filial piety also has the power to save others. Because of one's love for one's own parents, other people can often be moved to follow one's example. Thus, this is also the discipline for saving sentient beings *(she-sheng chieh).* To sum up, as long as one can be filial, his conduct will naturally be perfect. It is no wonder that the discipline is so interpreted. Aside from filial piety, is there any other discipline?[67]

Chu-hung went even further and subsumed the other five perfections *(pāramitā)* under filial piety:

In accordance with the mind of compassion, one does not indulge in stinginess; this is filial piety as charity. In accordance with the mind of submission, one does not indulge in anger; this is filial piety as patience. In accordance with the mind of perseverance, one does not indulge in laziness; this is filial piety as energy. In accordance with the mind of quietude, one does not indulge in absent-mindedness; this is filial piety as contemplation. And finally, in accordance with the mind of luminous knowledge, one does not indulge in delusion; this is then filial piety as wisdom.[68]

The Lay Devotees

Chu-hung had a wide lay following among the literati-officials of his generation. Two sources are particularly valuable in making a study of these lay devotees. The first is the *Chü-shih chuan* (Biographies of Buddhist Devotees),[69] compiled and edited by P'eng Shao-sheng, also named Chi-ch'ing, and Ch'ih-mu (d. 1796), who was the best-known lay Buddhist of the Ch'ing period. Of the three collections of biographies of lay Buddhists existing up to that time,[70] P'eng's was the most comprehensive. The biographies of twenty of Chu-hung's followers appear in this work. The other important source for our purposes is the collected correspondence between Chu-hung and some of his followers that forms the "I-kao" (Remaining Papers) section of the *Yün-ch'i fa-hui* (*YCFH* 30, 31). There are, in all, about two hundred replies written by Chu-hung, accompanied in most instances by the original letters addressed to him. The number of people actively engaged in this exchange of letters was about a hundred. Due to the nature of these sources, it appears that literati-officials predominated among Chu-hung's lay followers, because they were more likely to be included in P'eng's biography than common folk. It was also more likely that they corresponded more frequently with Chu-hung, although we do find letters from obscure people among the "I-kao." From the biographies of Chu-hung we know that he was much interested in the welfare of the common people in the neighboring villages. Some of the local townspeople and villagers undoubtedly also became his lay followers, but we do not know much about them because there are no sources.

The biographies and correspondence tell us a great deal about the backgrounds of lay followers, the forms of lay practice in which they engaged, the types of problems they encountered in their pursuits, and Chu-hung's approach to lay Buddhism in general. When we read these materials, several facts about the lay believers emerge immediately. Geographically, the majority came from Kiangsu and Chekiang, although there were also a few from Kiangsi, Fukien, Szechwan, Hukuang (Hunan and Hupei), and Shansi.[71] This fact is borne out by Sakai's observation on the geographical distribution of lay Buddhism.[72] Of the 107 lay Buddhists recorded in the *Chü-shih chuan*, Sakai found that 72 (67.3 percent) came from Kiangsu and Chekiang, while those from the inland provinces of Anhwei, Kiangsi, Szechwan, Hupei, and Hunan numbered only about 5 percent each. Another significant point about these 107 Ming lay Buddhists was their temporal distribution. Except for four of their number, they flourished during some 150 years spanning the end of the Ming and the beginning of the Ch'ing—the same time span during which Chu-hung and the three other prominent Ming Buddhist monks, Tzu-po Chen-k'o, Han-shan Te-ch'ing, and Ou-i Chih-hsü, were active. Thus we learn that the lay Buddhist movement of the

Ming was primarily a local phenomenon that sprang up during Chu-hung's lifetime and was centered around the lower Yangtze delta. This area had been the cradle of Buddhism since the epoch of the Five Dynasties (in the tenth century A.D.) and much, much earlier.

In terms of social status, the majority of the lay followers belonged to the so-called gentry class.[73] This, again, reflects more the bias of the samples than the actual constituency of Chu-hung's followers. From the biographies we learn that nine held *chin-shih* degrees, and two of these nine achieved such high position that they merited inclusion in the official history of the Ming dynasty, the *Ming shih* (Yen Min-ch'ing's biography appears in *chüan* 193, and that of T'ao Wang-ling in *chüan* 216). About a quarter of all the correspondents held official posts ranging from ranks 2A to 7B.[74] The most commonly held posts were those of prefect, magistrate, governor, judge, and compiler of the Hanlin Academy. They were thus middle-level officials, predominantly civil, but including military.

Among Chu-hung's followers (the literati-officials and the educated people who did not hold any office), a surprising proportion (about 60 percent) had religious names. These names were given to them by Chu-hung after they had taken the Three Refuges and received the first set of Buddhist precepts. In order of seniority, the names could have *kuang* (broad), *ta* (great), or *chih* (wisdom) as their first character. The interesting point is that the monks at Yün-ch'i Ssu were given their religious names in the same manner. In this way, Chu-hung made it clear that he regarded his lay disciples as the equals of the monks under his direction at Yün-ch'i. The monks and the "householders" (the original meaning of *chü-shih*) were indeed brethren in the faith.

The biographies give us glimpses, but never complete explanations, of the diverse motives prompting these lay devotees to embrace Buddhism. Some were drawn to it by their natures at an early age and in such an inexplicable manner that the Buddhists regarded it as *su-ken* (a propensity to Buddhism inherited from a previous existence). The most obvious examples were people who had suffered from long and incurable diseases. Personal suffering usually helped to draw people to religion, but we find that even a person who had led a so-called normal life could suddenly relinquish everything to take up the religious life. This was the case with Wang Meng-su.[75] After serving as a magistrate and waging a highly successful military campaign against local bandits, Wang suddenly became disgusted with everything, packed up his clothes, left his post, and started roaming the mountains. The refuge of Buddhism, then, was also sought after by men other than those with physical and psychological problems.

Several other aspects of the biographies catch our attention. First, there is the relationship between a man's religious beliefs on the one hand and his official behavior on the other. This is shown with equal clarity in the cases of Yen Min-ch'ing,[76] Ts'ai Huai-t'ing,[77] T'ao Wang-ling, Wang Meng-su, and Ting Chien-hung.[78] Compassion for the suffering of the common people and concern for the proper administration of justice were Confucian as well as Buddhist virtues. However, when Ts'ai Huai-t'ing prohibited the people under his jurisdiction from killing animals in their sacrifices and when Ting Chien-hung gave strings of beads to his prisoners and told them to recite the name of the Buddha, it was clearly a result of Chu-hung's influence. That these men carried out such measures in their capacities *as government officials* attests to the success of the integration of their inner faith and outward behavior.

Another aspect of the biographies is the close connection between family and friendship ties and the ways in which beliefs were shared and spread. This could take several forms. In the family it was usually the husband who became converted and the wife who followed his example (for example, the case of Wang Tao-an).[79] It could also be the older brother who introduced the faith to a younger brother (for example, in the cases of Yü Ch'un-hsi or Wang Jo-sheng);[80] or the relationship might be one between brothers-in-law (for example, Huang Yüan-fu[81] and Wen Tzu-yü).[82] The most common case, of course, was that of the father starting the practice at home and, by his influence, establishing the Buddhist belief as a family tradition (for example, the household of Yen Min-ch'ing). As for friendship ties, the teaching was usually introduced to, and discussed among, friends who either came from the same place or had some common background. This was the case with T'ao Wang-ling and Huang P'ing-ch'ing.[83] Both men attained the *chin-shih* degree in the same year. Each was closely related to a third friend, Chiao Hung, who also attained the degree in that year. It was with Chiao that T'ao discussed philosophy, and it was Chiao who introduced Huang to the works of Chu-hung (according to the accounts, during a dream of Huang's). Conversely, a shared belief could also be the basis for a new and lasting friendship. That of Wang Meng-su and Chu Pai-min[84] is a good example.

The organization of associations for releasing life was a natural extension of these family and friendship ties. They were in fact, often started by a few like-minded friends (for example, Yü Ch'un-hsi and T'ao Wang-ling) for the sake of mutual encouragement and consultation and were later enlarged to include others. Although they had a long historical development, as we have noted, these Pure Land societies could also have been enjoying popularity as the result of a current vogue in society at large. We are told that, in the late Ming, organizing societies was a national pastime.[85] "There were literary societies for essay writers and poetry societies for poets. For more than a hundred years [the reigns of Wan-li and T'ien-ch'i] in the provinces of Kiangsu, Chekiang, Fukien, Kwangtung, Kiangsi, Shantung, Hopei and everywhere we find this trend. . . . Not only did the educated want to establish associations, but even women took part in literary and drinking societies to show off their sophistication."[86]

A third aspect of these biographies is the fluidity of religious beliefs in Chu-hung's time. It was commonplace for a person trained in Pure Land practice to also engage in Ch'an meditation, Tantric exercises, and doctrinal discussion. More than this, we find that the boundary line between Buddhism and Taoism was, to say the least, rather blurred. Thus we read that several of Chu-hung's followers (for example, Chuang Fu-chen[87] and Chu Pai-min) were interested in the Taoist arts of longevity. Their interest in Taoism was often the path that led them to Buddhism. After they became Buddhist believers, they did not necessarily end their Taoist pursuits. Perhaps most interesting of all is their free and easy transition from the secular to the religious. They lived, in fact, the celibate lives of monks— shutting themselves into separate rooms (for example, Ko I-an);[88] refusing to take another wife after the first died (for example, Huang P'ing-ch'ing), living in a monastery (for example, Wang Tao-an), or traveling around like mendicant monks (for example, Wang Meng-su and Chu Pai-min). Some of them did, in fact, shave off their hair and become monks just before they died (for example, Huang Yüan-fu and Wen Tzu-yü). These tendencies also reflected Chu-hung's approach to religion—his aversion to sectarianism within Buddhist schools, his accommodation to other systems of thought, and his genuine desire to see monastic Buddhism become a secular as well as religious reality.

When we look into the contents of the correspondence, several themes recur with frequency. Perhaps foremost among them was that of religious cultivation. Chu-hung's followers wanted to know when and how to engage in religious cultivation. They were often confused by the multitude of methods available and they wanted Chu-hung to recommend the most effective ones. Chu-hung always recommended *nien-fo,* although he also discussed the Ch'an approach when someone specifically asked about it. The following excerpt, from a letter addressed to Hsü Ko-ju,[89] was typical of his advice concerning the efficacy of *nien-fo:*

To achieve an uninterrupted state of samadhi is not something a person leading a secular life can accomplish. Since it is difficult to achieve samadhi this way, it is best that you hold fast to the name of the Buddha. Whenever you have the time, after studying and managing household affairs, you ought to recite it silently. In doing so, you should be careful to articulate each word clearly and to dwell on each utterance with all your heart. If you can continue doing this for a long time without relapsing, your mind will naturally be tamed, and this state is none other than samadhi.[90]

To those who started out by following the Ch'an practice of meditating on *kung-an* and who held a strong belief in the wonders of *hua-t'ou* Chu-hung suggested that the very act of *nien-fo* could serve as a *hua-t'ou:*

For a long time, Ch'an masters have taught people to ponder over some *hua-t'ou,* whereby mental frustration could be aroused and, out of this, great enlightenment could emerge. They taught people to ponder the word *wu* [nothing] or the word "myriad dharmas." There are many things like these. I would say that the phrase "The myriad dharmas return to the One, and where does the One return to?" is extremely similar to this phrase: "Who is the one reciting the Buddha's name?" If you work hard at this "who," then the former puzzle will naturally become clear. That is why the ancient worthies said that if a Pure Land practitioner who called on Buddha's name desired to practice Ch'an meditation, he did not need any other *hua-t'ou.*[91]

Several followers wrote to Chu-hung complaining about one misfortune or another. In each case, while he offered his sympathy, he used the opportunity to turn their thoughts to salvation. The following are a few examples.

A devotee from Chiang-yin (in present-day Kiangsu), Feng Yün-chü, was in his late seventies and felt depressed. Chu-hung told him that the best time to practice *nien-fo* was in old age:

To live to one's seventies is a rare thing. In these twilight years of your life, you should open your mind and regard everything in the world as events in a play. Say to yourself that because I am reciting the Buddha's name, now I shall definitely be reborn in the West. When you are bothered by something, immediately turn to recitation and say to yourself, "I am a dweller in the world of the Amitābha Buddha. Why should I have the same attitude as ordinary men?" Thinking thus, you will be able to turn anger into happiness.[92]

To Wang Chung-ch'uan from Yü-hang, who had lost his son, Chu-hung wrote:

It must be ordered by fate that you should only have one son. This second one [who died] must have come into this world to seek payment for an old debt. So, after you brought him up, educated him, and set him up with a wife, he received whatever he came here for and then drifted away from you like a cloud. Since no feeling is left between a father and his dead son, you ought not to torture yourself with further remembrances. Instead, you should read Buddhist scriptures in order to break away from delusion. Do not live by yourself and harm your health with excessive sorrow.[93]

When another follower, a provincial graduate from T'ai-ts'ang named Wang Tzu-yu, became seriously ill, Chu-hung gave him this advice: "Illnesses usually are the result of much killing. Therefore to release life is especially important. Another thing you ought to know: the efficacy of inviting monks to perform the ritual of repentance is far inferior to that of repentance in one's own heart; so empty your mind, stop all distracting thoughts, and concentrate solely on the one name of Amitābha." [94]

A second much-discussed problem was that of whether a person educated in Confucianism and active in administrative affairs could conveniently pursue his Buddhist career. Chu-hung's answer was definitely in the affirmative. He did not see any conflict in a situation that was potentially full of conflicts, and his positive approach certainly encouraged many a doubtful soul and helped the growth of lay Buddhism. The following reply was directed to Wang Jo-sheng, a military commander:

In your letter you mentioned that you are burdened by worldly cares and therefore cannot rid yourself of secular impurities. But we cannot call the secular life a burden. The laws of this world—such as that a son should serve his parents with filial piety, a subject should serve his lord with loyalty, or any other principle governing human relationships—are not basically contrary to the Way. What one should do is follow the circumstances while holding to the principle. The only secret is to respond to the call of worldly duties with a free mind. Now the time for the examination is near. Please study hard. Should you succeed, you ought to make a vow on the day of success that you will never because of riches and power depart from what you have learned. If you can be a good minister in the tradition of the ancients, then this is saving the world. Make a vow that you will never lose your right mindfulness because of riches and power, that you will definitely realize the great reason why the Buddha came into the world. To do this is to leave the world. If you can do it, then literati will be able to serve as officials while engaged in meditation, and they will be able to enter the Way while still remaining in the sphere of the worldly.[95]

In a similar vein, but even more to the point, was Chu-hung's advice to another lay believer, one who was worried about not being able to fulfill a quota of performing "a thousand good deeds":

If you are pressed for time and cannot fulfill the number of a thousand good deeds, you ought to make this vow with a sincere heart: namely, that after you succeed in the examinations and become an official, you will try with redoubled effort to perform widely all kinds of good deeds. Never accept any request contrary to the principle of heaven; never do any unjust deed, never harm one innocent man, never hesitate at righting a wrong, and never refrain from performing beneficial acts required by duty because you feel a desire to protect your position. If you can do all this, then you will have performed not merely a thousand, but ten thousand, indeed a hundred million, good deeds.[96]

Here the Buddhist requirement to perform good deeds was skillfully identified with the Confucian ideal of an upright official.

Chu-hung's "skill in means" was shown in another instance, when he accommodated the rule of nonkilling to the exigencies of administrative life. One follower asked this question: "In carrying out one's official duty, it is sometimes unavoidable that one should have to pass death sentences. But this is forbidden to Buddhists. Now, as I want to take refuge in the Three Treasures, is it then necessary that I retire from office and come to the temple?"[97] The problem of reconciling one's duty with the demands of the religious prohibitions was indeed a perennial one for the believer's conscience. Chu-hung was well aware of the difficulty and, in fact, anticipated problems of this kind elsewhere. In his commentary on the first precept (nonkilling), the following passage appears:

Someone asks: "Monks specialize in works of compassion, but officials of the emperor are empowered to let [criminals] live or die. If a person commits a crime, and the official does not kill him, how can he serve the country?" My answer is, as stated in the *P'u-sa chieh-pen*:[98] "When a bodhisattva sees a thief or a robber who, because of his greed or profit, is about to kill many people or is about to harm a *śrāvaka* of great virtue, he ought to consider this carefully: If I should kill this evil man, I will fall into the Naraka Hell; but if I do not, he will create never-ending bad karma. I would rather enter hell myself than cause him to suffer the pain of unending punishment. This kind of killing does not constitute any violation, but on the contrary produces much merit." This is to say that one may kill as the occasion demands. So, if one kills a criminal, one does not violate any rule. The annihilation of the four ferocious tribes [Kung-kung, Huan-tou, San-miao, and K'ün] by King Yü, and the killing of the two rebels [Wu Keng and Kuang She] by the duke of Chou are examples of this kind. Moreover, if the official always cries after he passes a death sentence, and he carries out the execution only after thinking it over thrice, then he has manifested compassion over the killing, and even though he kills, he does not really kill. In this way, the Law is not abolished, and neither is kindness sacrificed. The affairs of the state and the mind of the Buddha do not obstruct each other.[99]

In his interpretation of the precepts, Chu-hung always adopted a flexible approach. He never demanded a literal faithfulness from his followers, nor did he adhere to the letter of the Law without regard to the actualities of secular life. To this particular follower, he therefore answered: "It is clearly recorded in the sutras that one may kill if an appropriate occasion demands it. As for people who attained enlightenment while they still served the state, you can also find many precedents since ancient times."[100]

Chu-hung never encouraged his lay disciples to enter the priesthood, especially if their parents were still alive or their children too young. The carrying out of the obligation of a filial son or a responsible father should come first. This brings us to a third theme running through the correspondence. The question was frequently asked: Is it true that no matter how diligently a lay believer engages in cultivation, he probably can never be compared with the monks? Chu-hung's answer was this: "If the lay believer can achieve enlightenment in the midst of the five passions, he is like a lotus flower in the midst of fire. When this kind of lotus receives water in the future, it can grow even taller. But for those that grow in the water [monks], they will probably wither away when they come into contact with fire." [101]

Chu-hung regarded monastic and lay Buddhism as mutually complementary, but nevertheless distinct, domains. He assigned equal value to each and made no one-sided judgments:

Those who have shaved off their hair ought to continue their early determination, while those who have not done so ought to realize the truth in the midst of worldly existence. Each can progress with single-minded diligence, and the purpose of either is to break down delusion and achieve enlightenment. As long as one can realize the nature of his own mind and obtain salvation, it is unnecessary to ask whether he has shaved his head or not. [102]

A Case History of a Confucian Monk

I will close this chapter with a story of a degreeholder (*chü-jen*) who eventually became a monk. Chu-hung's influence is clearly seen in each step this disciple took.

There are six letters from Chu-hung addressed to Feng Tai-ch'ü, a provincial graduate from Chiang-yin. At first we learn that Feng was contemplating going into retreat for a specific period of time. But Chu-hung said that, since Feng's father was not well, Feng should stay at home. Besides, contemplation did not necessarily have to be carried out in a definite place or for a definite period of time. As long as Feng could calm his mind, he could engage in cultivation even when taking care of his father. Otherwise to insist on seclusion for a set period of time would be a form of "obstruction." Feng apparently took the advice. In a subsequent letter, Chu-hung said, "Your father suffers from a slight discomfort. This is common with old people. You ought to amuse him all the time. This is most important." But Chu-hung did not want Feng to waver in his faith in the Pure Land: "In recent times, it has become fashionable to promote Ch'an meditation. I am both glad and worried because of this. There are also people who practice Ch'an but deprecate the Pure Land. I hope that you will be steadfast in your faith and not be weakened by such talk. Only then is there a possibility of success." [103]

Feng eventually became the monk Ch'ang-hsing. But it appears that he did not shave his head right away or go to a monastery for training. In one letter, Chu-hung advised him that he should receive the precepts for a monk (*pi-ch'iu chieh*) in front of a statue of the Buddha. This was a contingency measure, as the normal procedure was to receive the precepts at a monastery with an ordination platform (*chieh-t'ai*). But in the late Ming, all ordination platforms were made inoperative by imperial decree.

If the circumstances do not allow for the regular procedure, one may prostrate oneself in front of the Buddha and receive [the precepts] by oneself. If you should doubt this procedure because in the scriptures there is only the text saying that one can receive the bodhisattva precepts by oneself, but not those for a monk, I now tell you this: if under normal circumstances, when the ordination platform is in operation, a person does not go there to receive the precepts on purpose, but performs the rite himself, he is indeed in error. But now, since the law of the land prohibits the operation of the ordination platform, one should indeed perform the rite in front of the Buddha by oneself. You need not have any doubts about this.[104]

Feng's unorthodox behavior (remaining in the household after announcing his determination to leave the world) caused some gossip. Chu-hung defended Feng and offered two reasons: First, Feng's son was only twelve years old, and this was a critical time for the lad's education; second, Feng's daughter was still unmarried. In regard to the latter, Chu-hung had this advice for Feng: "I hope that you will marry off your daughter soon; you and your son are welcome to come to my temple. Your son can then return home every two or three months to visit his mother, and eventually he may take care of the household by himself. Thus you will be able to manage your worldly affairs without causing unnecessary gossip."[105] Feng eventually went to the Yün-ch'i monastery and became one of Chu-hung's most trusted disciples.

CHAPTER FIVE

~~~~~~

Syncretism in Action:
Morality Books and
The Record of Self-knowledge

Morality Books: Some General Characteristics

CHU-HUNG WAS a syncretist. Syncretism is often taken to mean the blending or mixing of different elements. One writer defines it: "Syncretism is used to denote any mixture of two or more religions, as for instance in Hellenistic syncretism, where elements from several religions are merged and influence each other mutually. It might also be used to refer to cases when elements from one religion are accepted into another without basically changing the character of the receiving religion (because of the relatively small quantity of adopted elements)."[1] This definition, as the writer himself readily admits, is really too broad to be very useful. In fact, our difficulty in giving syncretism a clear and unambiguous definition reflects the lack of theoretical refinement and sophistication in this area of research. Even though syncretism has taken place among religions since antiquity, both in the West and the East, the syncretic process as a distinctive religious phenomenon has until recently not received much scholarly treatment.[2] Perhaps as a result of this, the term has usually taken on a rather pejorative connotation[3] and come to denote an indiscriminate mixture of disparate or even contradictory ideas.

I would like to suggest that syncretism, on the contrary, can be regarded as a creative enterprise. As traditions interact, ideas in one tradition become developed as a result of the stimulation supplied by compatible ideas from other traditions. This is neither artificial grafting from other sources nor cooption or capitulation to them.[4] Chu-hung, for example, never ceased to be a Buddhist, yet he welcomed and incorporated ideals and practices from Confucianism and Taoism, and in doing so, helped to bring about the Buddhist adaptation to Ming society. One example of his creative use of syncretism was his compilation of the *Tzu-chih lu* (The Record of Self-knowledge). *The Record of Self-knowledge* belongs to the genre of Confucian-Buddho-Taoist popular books and pamphlets usually designated as "morality books." These works were written for the purpose of inculcating moral values in their readers. Simply stated, their goal was "to propagate good and to stop evil." In order to convince readers of the necessity to do good and refrain from evil, the authors appealed to the prevailing belief in rewards and retribution that served as the theoretical basis for the morality books. Originally, these books contained either ethical aphorisms of a general nature or lists of specific moral acts that should be performed and immoral acts that should be avoided. In time, however, a voluminous collection of "case histories" was added to the original morality books to illustrate the infallible working of the law of rewards and retribution. Thus, when someone performed a certain good act, he received a suitable reward; when another man committed a certain bad deed, he met an appropriate retribution. The cases, which often read like short stories, concretized general moral injunctions and no doubt encouraged popular appreciation and acceptance of the ethical standards they expounded.

The earliest work belonging to this genre is *T'ai-shang kan-ying p'ien* (The Treatise of the Exalted One on Response and Retribution), which dates from the latter part of the Northern Sung dynasty, was first published in the Southern Sung, and apparently was in circulation after the beginning of the eleventh century.[5] But it was not until the late Ming and early Ch'ing period, around the seventeenth century, that morality books were actively compiled and distributed. During the Ming dynasty, Kao P'an-lung, the leader of the Tung-lin faction showed his approval of the *Treatise* by writing a preface to a new edition of that work, by practicing the moral precepts contained in it, and by forming with his friends a Society of Common Goodness (T'ung-shan hui).[6] The famous Ming writer T'u Lung and several other late Ming figures also wrote prefaces to various morality books.[7] *The Treatise of the Exalted One* was officially endorsed by the Emperors Shun-chih and Yung-cheng of the Ch'ing dynasty, and two great Confucian scholars, Hui Tung (1697–1758) and Yü Yüeh (1821–1906), wrote commentaries on it.[8] Hui Tung wrote his commentary in order to fulfill a vow he made during his mother's illness. He prayed for her early recovery and promised to write a commentary on *The Treatise of the Exalted One.* That Hui Tung, a Confucian scholar noted for his historical and exegetical research, should have made such a vow affords striking evidence for the remarkable influence of the *Treatise.*[9]

For scholars interested in the formation and transformation of Chinese popular moral values, a study of morality books should be of considerable value. By comparing and analyzing different types of morality books composed in different periods, one can say something about the salient values and concepts underlying all these works. One may also trace the process of change by noting the displacement of old values by new ones as well as the gradual shift of emphasis from the original reliance on supernatural sanction to moral internalization and religious consciousness. Yet their significance is not always immediately appreciated. These morality books were printed in huge quantities and distributed widely. Despite the fact that individual scholars wrote commentaries or prefaces for them, morality books as a genre were never looked upon as literary or philosophical works. As a result, except for *The Treatise of the Exalted One* and *The Ledger of Merits and Demerits,* they were not included in any canonical collection, whether Confucian, Taoist, or Buddhist. This might be one of the reasons why few scholars have given them the kind of attention that a text of the "great tradition" would receive.[10] However, morality books are a useful source in helping us to locate the kind of values spokesmen for the "great tradition" were most desirous to inculcate in late traditional China.[11]

Because of their popular and syncretic nature, some scholars saw the morality books as the moral and theological justification of what Wing-tsit Chan called the "religion of the masses."[12] Although it was true that morality books were intended primarily for the moral education of the common people, their readership was not restricted to the masses. They were read by people at all levels of society. As Tadao Sakai put it, "By calling them 'popular' I mean that these books served not only the lower levels of society, but all types and classes of people irrespective of social status, economic position, and religious affiliation. In fact, so basic was their appeal to the common denominator in ethical thought that they were read and used even by scholars identified with Ch'eng-Chu school."[13] Morality books then, were written by people who were well versed in the basic tenets of Confucianism, Buddhism, and Taoism. They were people who, though educated in these literary traditions, were also aware of popular aspirations and beliefs. The morality books were read by both gentry and common people eager to mold their destinies and willing to accept more than one teaching as their guide in order to achieve this goal.

Morality Books and
the Trend of Syncretism

The writings of any number of Ming literati testify to their interest in a syncretic trend. Li Chih, the iconoclast, provides the following testimony:

Those who claim that the sages of the three teachings differ are indeed deluded. Now examine these three pithy phrases which the three teachings use [to describe the state of perfection or enlightenment] and tell me if they are the same or different. For the Taoists, it is "all of a sudden I see it" *(li-ti i-sheng);* for the Buddhist, it is "your original face before you were born" *(pen-lai mien-mu);* and for the Confucians, it is "equilibrium before the arousal of emotions" *(wei-fa chih chung).* The person who is sincerely concerned with his nature and life *(wei-chi hsing-ming)* will know in his heart that the answer is positive. This is because the sages of all three teachings regard nature and life as the essence of their teachings.[14]

His friend Chiao Hung, a great classical scholar and historiographer, shared this feeling. He said:

The teaching of Confucius and Mencius is a teaching that exhausts the mysteries of human nature and life. But because their language is simple and their meaning vague, the teaching is not completely elucidated. What is elucidated in the various Buddhist scriptures is none other than this principle. If they can explicate this principle and become a guide to my nature and life, then Buddhist sutras are no other than commentaries to Confucius and Mencius. Why should we reject them?[15]

Such statements tell us that the combining of three teachings in one was favored by some leading literati, but they do not tell us much more. If we want to know how this doctrine was concretely understood and actually practiced, morality books are more useful.

Li Chih wrote a work called *Yin-kuo lu* (The Record of Causes and Effects) to illustrate the workings of Buddhist karma. Following the general conventions for morality books, he cited case histories to prove the law of karma. His work is divided into three sections: the first deals with the experiences of good people, the second with those of evil people, and the third with the lives of people who practiced the Chinese Buddhist precept of releasing animals. The first section contains stories in which reward or punishment was visited upon domestic slaves, government runners, prison wardens, monks, women, rich merchants, doctors, officials, and other persons from different social strata.[16] In a morality book of this kind, the actual fusion of the three teachings is represented much more graphically than it might be in a philosophical context. For even though the Buddhist karma is given predominant emphasis, the workings of karma are also illustrated by Taoist and Confucian deeds and thoughts.

To give another example, in *The Record of Self-knowledge* we find that each action, whether good or bad, is given a certain number of points. A practitioner's purpose is to increase good points, or merits, and to decrease bad points or demerits. Among those actions earning one good point are the following: (1) for each day one serves one's parents with filial piety and one's sovereign with loyalty, count one good point; (2) for every 100 cash[17] of unjust profit one refuses to take, count one good point; (3) for the refusal to eat the meat of an animal that one sees being slaughtered, count one good point; (4) for each monk one feeds in offering food to a monastery, count one good point; (5) for passing to others one book of life-preserving recipes or five medical prescriptions capable of effecting a cure, count one good point; (6) for picking up and burning every piece of paper with 100 characters written on it, count one good point.[18] The first two embody the Confucian virtues of filial piety, loyalty, and righteousness. The third and fourth underline the Buddhist virtues of nonkilling and almsgiving, the fifth refers to typical Taoist concerns, for the art of curing disease and prolonging life is traditionally regarded as a specialty of Taoists, while the sixth, the reverence for written characters, is a Chinese value which is not restricted to any one tradition. By assigning equal merit to all of them, the book not only propagates the combination of three teachings in one, but impartially endorses various tenets of the three teachings and recommends them for general observance.

From the printing of the earliest prototype to their general pro-
liferation in the late Ch'ing, the morality books underwent continuous transformation both in content and in emphasis. This process
naturally reflected changes in society as a whole, for an author or
compiler could never completely transcend his social milieu. At the
same time, by incorporating new values and giving new interpretations to old concepts and practices, morality books also contributed
to value changes in society. The processes were intimately linked, as
an examination of two morality books will illustrate. *The Treatise of
the Exalted One on Response and Retribution* and Chu-hung's *Record of
Self-knowledge* have been chosen for comparison both because they
are separated by some six hundred years and represent, respectively,
the earliest and the most developed types of morality books, and
because they are very different in character and embody exactly the
changes of content and emphasis in which we are interested.[19]

The Treatise of the Exalted One:
An Early Prototype

The Treatise of the Exalted One is a rather brief essay that consists
of some 1,200 characters.[20] It begins with a saying attributed to the
Exalted One (T'ai-shang), a title given to the deified Lao Tzu: "The
Exalted One says: 'Curses and blessing do not come through doors,
but man himself invites their arrival. The reward of good and evil is
like the shadow accompanying a body, and so it is apparent that
heaven and earth are possessed of crime-recording spirits.' "[21]

Everyone is supposed to have an allotted life span, but because
of transgressions, the span may be reduced. This is the underlying
principle of the *Treatise*. Four deities are connected with the job of
recording a man's transgressions and reducing his life span. The
relationships of the deities are confusing, and the *Treatise* does not
attempt to place them in a systematic hierarchy but simply preserves
popular beliefs dating as far back as the Chou dynasty. First of all
there is the Crime-recording Spirit *(Ssu-kuo chih shen)*,[22] who later in
the *Treatise* is also called the Director of Fates *(Ssu-ming)*. Then there
are the three stars of the North Dipper *(San-t'ai pei-tou shen-chün)*.[23]
Next come the Three Corpses *(San-shih shen)* who reside in man's
body and report to heaven on the *keng-shen* day (the fifty-eighth day
in the sexagenary system).[24] Finally, there is the God of the Stove

(Tsao-chün) [25] who, at the end of every month, also makes a report on man's sins. Punishments are meted out according to the gravity of offenses. In the case of a serious offense, one *chi* (a unit of 300 days), and in the case of a light offense, one *suan* (a unit of three days) are taken away from the transgressor's total life span. When one's life span is reduced, he is liable to suffer poverty and become unlucky. People will avoid him and curses will follow him. When the allotted number of years is exhausted by the deduction, the transgressor dies. If there are still offenses left unexpiated, then the curse will be transferred to his descendants.[26] For the grave sins of robbing others' property or killing other men, punishment comes in a more dramatic form. The *Treatise* says:

All those who wrongly seize others' property may have to compensate for it, with wives or children or other family members, the expiation to be proportionate up to a punishment by death. If the guilt is not expiated by death, they will suffer by various evils, by water, by fire, by theft or by robbery, by loss of property, by disease and disputation, and by ill repute, to compensate for any unlawful violation of justice. Further, those who unlawfully kill men will in turn have their weapons and arms turned against them, and they will kill each other.[27]

The *Treatise* contains sixteen categories of good deeds and ninety-four types of bad deeds.[28] If a person avoids committing these bad deeds, he can achieve longevity. On the other hand, if he can perform three hundred good deeds, he can expect to become an earthly immortal *(ti-hsien)*; and if he performs 1,300 good deeds, a heavenly immortal *(t'ien-hsien)*.[29]

The belief in various deities who control the length of man's life span and the methods for achieving immortality are, of course, authentic Taoist concerns. In dealing with these concepts, the *Treatise* merely repeats passages found in the inner chapters of the *Pao-p'u-tzu*, written in A.D. 317 by the Taoist eclectic Ko Hung as "a kind of encyclopaedia on the art of becoming a *hsien* [an immortal]."[30] In the concluding paragraph, however, the *Treatise* introduces some non-Taoist ideas. It contains a quotation from the Dhammapada *(Fa-chü ching)*: "Those who have hitherto done evil deeds should henceforth mend and repent. If evil be no longer practiced and good deeds done, and if in this way a man continues and continues, he will surely obtain happiness and felicity. He will indeed, so to speak, transform curses into blessings."[31] This is followed by a tripartite distinction in ethical behavior: man's speech, thought, and action.

Blessed is the man who speaks what is good *(yü-shan)*, who thinks what is good *(shih-shan)*, and who practices what is good *(hsing-shan)*. If but each single day he would persevere in these three ways of goodness, within three years Heaven will surely shower blessings on him. Unfortunate is the man who speaks what is evil *(yü-e)*, who thinks what is evil *(shih-e)*, and who practices what is evil *(hsing-e)*. If but each single day he would persevere in these three ways of evil-doing, within three years Heaven would surely shower curses on him.[32]

Except for this passage, the *Treatise* is entirely free from Buddhist influence. This is possibly because at the time of writing of the *Pao-p'u-tzu,* which the *Treatise* follows in principle, Buddhism had not yet been sufficiently rooted in the popular consciousness. But by the ninth or tenth centuries, when the *Treatise* might have been first composed, Buddhism had become so much a part of the Chinese tradition that the author could not ignore it completely. He therefore concluded his essay by quoting from the popular Dhammapada and formulated another theory of rewards and punishments based on the Buddhist tripartite distinction of speech, thought, and action. But since he made no effort to coordinate this statement with the earlier Taoist method of achieving immortality, there is in fact little relationship between the two. What interested the author were the doctrines concerning the prolongation of life and the acquisition of blessings. When he found them, he simply included them in the essay without bothering to form any kind of synthesis. Whether the three hundred good deeds required for becoming an earthly immortal were to be understood to mean simply "good actions," or good speech and good thought as well, and how, if good speech and good thought were included, points were to be tabulated, the author does not say. This blithe indifference to detail and total neglect of specificity could conceivably have been a source of annoyance for at least some pious practitioners of the *Treatise.* The lack of specificity was also one of the most important differences between the *Treatise* and *The Ledger of Merits and Demerits,* for the latter puts exclusive stress on the practical and ritualistic aspects of moral behavior.

Before we begin to analyze the content of the *Treatise,* it may be interesting to consider the beliefs it propounded in regard to man's fixed life span and supernatural sanctions on man's moral behavior. As has been mentioned earlier, the *Treatise* followed the fourth-century *Pao-p'u-tzu* on these points. But these ideas were already quite prevalent long before the appearance of the *Pao-p'u-tzu*. The *T'ai-p'ing ching*, the Taoist scripture of the Han dynasty, says: "No matter whether it be a great offense or a small one, Heaven knows about them all. There is a book in which both good and evil are recorded. This is checked by the day, the month, and the year. Days or years are deducted from a man's life." [33] Thus, moral perfection and the confession of sins were early accepted as basic tenets of religious Taoism. Pursuit of moral perfection and confession of sins were designed to influence divine judgment and to attain physical immortality.

These beliefs were so strong that Buddhists who could not find similar views in Buddhist scriptures sometimes forged sutras to provide doctrines to rival those of the Taoists. [34] In the *Ssu-t'ien-wang ching* (the Sutra of the Four Heavenly Kings) the following passage appears:

Each of the four Heavenly Kings takes charge of one direction. . . . They survey the whole world and investigate the good and bad thoughts, speech, and actions of kings, officials, subjects, dragons, ghosts, insects, and crawling creatures. After noting them down, they report to Indra. If a person cultivates virtue and perseveres without relaxation, Indra will issue an order to the Director of Fates and increase a person's life span. [35]

It is also stated that the four Heavenly Kings personally came down to the world on the eighth, fifteenth, and thirtieth of every month and sent down messengers on the fourteenth, twenty-third, and twenty-ninth to make their investigatory rounds. These were called the six fast days *(liu-chai-jih)*, when Buddhists observed the eight precepts, not eating for a day, listening to religious lectures, and giving alms or doing other meritorious deeds such as releasing life. [36] Professor T'ang Yung-t'ung has offered conclusive proof that this passage was a forgery produced by Chinese monks with strong Taoist inclinations. [37] Incidentally, the triad of speech, thought, and action featured in this sutra might well have been the inspiration for the Buddhist ending of the *Treatise* mentioned earlier.

The predominance of Confucian and, to a lesser extent, Taoist values shows through clearly when we analyze the content of the

Treatise. It has less to say about good deeds; they are listed in the essay at a one-to-ten ratio to bad deeds. The good deeds exalted here are conventional virtues that would be endorsed by all ethical thinkers the world over; they are not uniquely Chinese. Fourteen of the sixteen injunctions are as follows:

Do not proceed on an evil path.
Do not sin in secret.
Accumulate virtue, increase merit.
With a compassionate heart, turn toward all creatures.
Be faithful, filial, friendly, and brotherly.
First rectify yourself and then convert others.
Take pity on orphans, assist widows, respect the old, be kind to children.
Be grieved at the misfortune of others and rejoice at their good luck.
Assist those in need, and rescue those in danger.
Regard your neighbor's gain as your own gain, your neighbor's loss as your own loss.
Do not call attention to the faults of others, nor boast of your own excellence.
Renounce much, accept little.
Show endurance in humiliation and bear no grudge.
Extend your help without seeking reward.
Give to others and do not regret or begrudge your liberality.

Most of the injunctions consist of four or six characters. Their brevity and symmetry could have greatly facilitated their oral transmission and memorization. Several injunctions are "four-character phrases,"[38] the use of which is still current today. The section on evil deeds is more interesting for our purposes because of its specificity and scope. Evil deeds can be classified into several categories, although in the essay they occur in a rather random fashion, and the author gives no indication that he is aware of their divergent characteristics.

The first category deals with breaches of social ethics. Although most social relationships are touched upon, failure to fulfill family or clan-centered moral obligations receives more emphasis. Some of the censured actions include: "Stealthily to despise superiors and parents; to disregard and rebel against elders; malevolently to attack and slander kith and kin; to be ill-humored and angry towards one's teachers and instructors; to resist and provoke one's father and elder brothers; to make light of an ancestor's spirit." Within this category there are a few evil deeds specifically related to wrong behavior on the part of husbands and wives. The *Treatise* condemns the actions of husbands who are unfaithful, unkind to wives and children, or who listen to the gossip of wives and concubines so that they disobey parents; and the conduct of wives who are disrespectful to their husbands, act improperly toward parents-in-law, or are jealous of other women.

The second category includes evil deeds against people in general when it comes to relations that go beyond the five cardinal relationships. The more serious ones are these:

Molesting orphans and wronging widows; appropriating the accomplishments of one's neighbors, concealing their good qualities and exposing their secrets; assisting others in doing wrong. When seeing the success and prosperity of others, wishing failure on them; when seeing the wealth of others, wishing that they would go bankrupt; when seeing beauty, cherishing thoughts of seduction; and engaging in lawsuits.

A third category includes evil deeds committed by specific classes of people. Officials, merchants, and farmers are especially selected for attention. Thus, officials are enjoined "not to: reward the unjust, punish the innocent, kill those who surrender, take bribes, disregard public duties for private gain, be unfair in giving out awards or in meting out punishments, demote the upright and expel the virtuous." Merchants are cautioned not to use two measures or scales in dealing with customers, or to adulterate genuine with inferior articles, and not to engage in usury. Farmers are likewise warned against destroying other people's crops and fields and against misdirecting the course of water, or setting others' houses on fire.

The last category of evil deeds bears on religious taboos. The origin of some of them can be dated back to Chou times,[39] and they shed much light on popular religion and beliefs. We may further subdivide this category into two subcategories: those of Taoist origin and those of Confucian origin. Among the former are instructions such as "not to spit at falling stars or point at the many-colored rainbow," "not to point at the three luminaries irreverently," and "not to use vile language while facing the north." Among the latter are instructions such as "not to shoot the flying bird" or "chase the running animal," "not to expose a hibernating animal" or "surprise nestlings," "not to close up entrance holes," "upset nests," "injure the pregnant," or "break the egg"; "not to execute criminals during the eight seasonal days"—the equinoxes, the solstices, and the first day of each season: such execution was called *pa-chieh hsing-hsing*—"not to hunt with fire in the spring months," and "not to kill snakes and tortoises without cause." Some scholars[40] have taken certain items in this category as evidence of Buddhist influence. In fact, these are not so much manifestations of Buddhist compassion for sentient beings as examples of the Confucian extension of humaneness—a point well established by Hui Tung, the Ch'ing commentator of the *Treatise*, who documented his view by tracing these prohibitions to the *Record of Rites.*[41]

Some Differences between the *Treatise* and *The Record of Self-knowledge*

This final category of religious injunctions, with a few exceptions such as those extolling kindness to animals, is entirely absent from *The Record of Self-knowledge*. This is the most conspicuous, though not necessarily the most important, difference between the two works. The other main differences include the following: (1) The *Treatise* usually lists its good and evil deeds in a general way and does not follow any clear criteria. It is primarily concerned with ethical ideals. The *Record* not only classifies merits and demerits into several categories (filial piety and loyalty versus unfiliality and disloyalty; kindness versus unkindness; piety versus impiety, and so on), but also assigns a specific number of merits and demerits to each act. In other words, the *Record* not only tells its reader what particular things related to his different spheres of life he should or should not do, but also tells him the relative importance of each act by measuring it against some standard. The emphasis here is on the implementation of ethical ideals.

(2) The *Treatise* appeals to supernatural sanction either by threatening the reader with reduction of his allotted life span or by tempting him with the promise of physical immortality. Both ultimately come from some superhuman agencies. The *Record,* on the other hand, presupposes the existence of an impersonal law of karma. Following the inner logic of the law of karma, man himself has power over his own destiny. It is true that a person's moral performance still affects his fate, but the authority of deities is no longer

invoked. In fact, the law of karma makes the deities superfluous. In the preface to *The Record of Self-knowledge*, Chu-hung claims that if a person has a wish to make, he should simply make a vow to perform five hundred, a thousand, three thousand, five thousand, and ten thousand meritorious deeds, instead of praying to gods or sacrificing to heaven. As soon as the promised number of meritorious deeds is accomplished, the wish will immediately come true.[42] This implies a conviction that as long as a man keeps his part of the agreement by fulfilling his vow, his fate cannot but change for the better. The process is automatic—one might even say mechanical.

(3) Compared with the *Treatise*, the *Record* places a greater premium on moral internalization and ethical intention. For instance, for an official to save one person from the death penalty theoretically earns him the maximum one hundred merits. However, if he does so because he has taken bribes from the accused, there is no merit. In another case, to remain chaste when faced with sexual temptation earns fifty merits, but no merit is earned if one does nothing only because the circumstances prevent it.

This awareness of the distinction between overt behavior and covert motivation is not limited to the *Record* but is a common feature of morality books since the late Ming. A case history originally used as an illustration of the teachings of the *Ledger of Merits and Demerits* is found in a Ch'ing edition of the *Ledger,* and it brings forth with compelling simplicity the striking advancement in spiritual awareness.

The story purports to be a true case history of one Mr. Yü Tu of Kiangsi who lived in the Chia-ching era (1522–1566) of the Ming dynasty.[43] Mr. Yü was a very talented and learned man, having passed the local examination at the age of eighteen. He made his living by teaching pupils and, together with his classmates, organized a religious society called the Wen-ch'ang Society (Society for the Worship of the God Wen-ch'ang, the god of learning) which promoted such things as releasing life, cherishing written characters (not putting paper with characters written on it to improper use, picking up such papers lying in the street and burning them reverently, and so on), observing precepts of nonkilling, chastity, and telling the truth. He engaged in these good deeds for many years, yet he was visited with constant misfortune. He took and failed the provincial examination seven times. He had five sons, but four of them died in infancy and the third one, who was both clever and good-looking, suddenly disappeared when he was eight years old. Of the four daughters born to him, only one lived. His wife became blind because of constant weeping. He was, in the meantime, reduced to utter poverty. He could not understand why he had to suffer all these misfortunes. Therefore, the last day of every year he wrote supplications to heaven and prayed to the God of the Stove asking for help.

In his forty-seventh year, while he was sitting with his blind wife and only daughter on New Year's Eve, feeling overwhelmed with self-pity, the God of the Stove came to visit him in the form of a Taoist priest. The priest accused Mr. Yü of harboring evil thoughts and of performing good deeds only in name. He also informed Mr. Yü that his supplications, which were full of bitter complaints, might have angered heaven even more. Mr. Yü, of course, felt very hurt and protested that he and his friends had observed moral precepts for years. How could he be accused of doing all those good deeds only for the sake of a reputation? The answer given by the God of the Stove is the highlight of this story and expresses the heart of this new awareness:

I will examine your conduct according to the rules of your society one by one. You advocated the cherishing of written characters. But when you saw your pupils or friends use old notebooks to paste windows or to wrap things, you never uttered one word to reprimand them. Of what use was it to pick up one or two pieces of paper from the streets and burn them at home? Every month you followed others in buying some living creatures and setting them free. But if the others did not do it, you also let it pass. In fact, you did not really feel compassion in your heart. Besides, shrimps and crabs were also cooked in your own kitchen. Can we say that they are not living creatures? As for speaking the truth, because you are quick-witted and people are attracted by your eloquence, even though sometimes you knew that what you said was unkind, you could not stop yourself. As a result, you have angered spirits and gods. Finally, it is true that there is no evidence for your unchastity, but whenever you saw a beautiful woman, you always gazed at her with much interest. It was only because of the lack of opportunity that you have remained chaste. The Director of Fates has examined you every day, but he cannot find one single bit of evidence of goodness in you. What he sees are thoughts of greed, licentiousness, jealousy, impatience, and arrogance, as well as all kinds of evil intentions.[44]

After hearing this lecture, Yü repented and promised to work hard to reform himself. On New Year's Day, he changed his name to

Ching-i (pure intention) and, kneeling before the image of Kuan Yü, the God of War and Righteousness, vowed to have only pure thoughts and engage only in good deeds from then on. Yü attained great happiness in the end. He succeeded in passing the provincial examination in the fourth year of Wan-li (1576) when he was fifty-one years old. The next year he qualified in the national examination and became a *chin-shih*. Soon afterward, by chance, he found his long-lost third son. His wife regained her eyesight after her son licked her eyes. Yü resigned his official post and devoted the rest of his life to doing good deeds and teaching his countrymen. He had seven grandsons and lived to the age of eighty-eight years.

The story of Yü Tu is interesting because of the distinction it makes between inner thought and outer action and the recognition of the discrepancy between cognitive avowal and behavioral manifestation. The story makes it clear that one's intentions as well as acts really count. This story is also interesting in its vision of the good life. Academic success, public recognition, numerous male progeny, and a ripe old age—these are the qualities of the blessed in the Chinese popular view of life.

It would be natural to ask what happened between the composition of the *Treatise* and that of the *Record* to bring about this remarkable emphasis on moral internalization. The most obvious factor would be the rise and development of Neo-Confucianism. With it, classical Confucian concepts such as sincerity of will *(ch'eng-i)*, rectification of mind *(cheng-hsin)*, being cautious when alone *(shen-tu)*, and reverence *(ching)* all received profound reinterpretation. At the same time, new doctrines about "mind," "nature," and "innate good knowledge" were being constantly expounded and discussed by all Neo-Confucians. Their uniform emphasis on spiritual enlightenment [45] was certain to produce far-reaching changes in popular consciousness. I use the general term "popular" here advisedly, because I do not believe that gentry-literati were the only group thus affected. Starting with the Ming dynasty, social mobility, large-scale printing, and the increased availability of education all helped to blur class distinctions and facilitate the interchange of ideas between the cultured elite and the uncultured masses. The new conviction that a man was the master of his own fate could also be reinforced by the credo of the Wang Yang-ming school that everyone could become a sage. Both ideas expressed the exhilaration and exaltation of self-confidence. Both opened the door to a new world.

An equally important factor was the rise and development of lay Buddhism since the Sung. The Buddhist belief that all sentient beings possess the Buddha-nature, the Ch'an emphasis on the attainment of enlightenment here and now, the Pure Land hope of universal rebirth in the Western Paradise through invocation of the name of the Amitābha Buddha and through the practice of compassion all implied a basic optimism. Furthermore, the emphasis on self-realization is a common link between Neo-Confucianism and Buddhism. Even without going into detail as to the areas of Buddhist influence on Neo-Confucianism, it is obvious that between the Buddhist belief in universal Buddhahood and the Confucian belief in universal sagehood, there is a fundamental agreement in spirit.

However, although the Neo-Confucian movement had undoubtedly played a major role in deepening the religious consciousness of the Chinese people, this was not readily acknowledged by the compilers of morality books. In the later books, when an author or a compiler justified his approval of this kind of literature, he invariably either used a statement from the *Book of Changes* (for example, "In a household which accumulates evil, there must be excessive disaster") or drew heavily from Buddhist sources. For some curious reason Neo-Confucianism was comparatively underrepresented in these statements.

In the preface to his *Record of Self-knowledge,* Chu-hung discusses the possible attitudes toward the *Record* that would be expressed by different sorts of people. He says:

When an inferior man *(hsia-shih)* gets hold of it, he will laugh at it with glee. He will not even read the work, much less record his actions. When a man of medium quality *(chung-shih)* gets hold of it, he certainly will record his actions diligently. When a superior man *(shang-shih)* gets hold of it, it makes no difference whether he records his actions or not, as long as he refrains from doing any evil but persists in practicing good. This is because he does good for its own sake, not because he hopes to gain blessings. Similarly, he avoids evil not because he fears punishment. The truth is that when a person stops evil and cultivates good all day, there is neither the characteristic *(hsiang)* of good and evil outside him, nor a mind which can stop and cultivate anything inside him. For both blessing and punishment are empty in nature.[46]

Two points are worthy of note here. First, Chu-hung maintains that a system of moral cultivation, like *The Ledger of Merits and Demerits* and his own *Record,* is useful only for the middle range of humanity; neither the very wise nor the very depraved need it.⁴⁷ Second, Chu-hung makes creative use of the Buddhist idea of "skill in means" *(upāya, fang-pien)* and appropriates it as the rationale for the *Record*. A particular teaching is expounded more because of its effectiveness for a particular group of people than because of its intrinsic truth. Chu-hung uses the Buddhist theory of "double truth" to spiritualize an essentially mechanistic system. On the level of mundane truth, a person is told to carry out certain good deeds and avoid doing certain bad things. He is further told that the former brings reward and the latter, retribution. But, on the level of ultimate truth not only are blessing and punishment nonexistent, but neither a doer nor a deed can be predicated. Other writers besides Chu-hung also used this postulate of the "double truth" to harmonize the utilitarian and spiritual sides of moral cultivation.

In a similar vein, the use of the Buddhist concepts of "skill in means" and "double truth" to interpret the law of moral causality from a Confucian viewpoint is apparent in the following passage, drawn from an enlarged nineteenth-century edition of *The Ledger of Merits and Demerits:*

The sage exemplifies the way of serving gods in his service to man. Since loyal ministers, filial sons, virtuous men, and chaste women move heaven and earth, they are protected by spirits and gods. This is not something a person who flatters spirits and gods can ever hope for. Therefore, if one can sincerely respect heaven, it is all right not to talk about spirits or gods. If one can sincerely serve men, it is all right for him not to talk about serving spirits and gods. This is the true teaching *(shih-chiao)*. Although the theory of cause and effect as it is worked out in the three generations *(yin-kuo san-shih)* touches on the supernatural, its intention is to frighten people, make them examine themselves, and thereby activate their minds to respect heaven. Therefore, even though it talks about spirits and gods, its true purpose is to make people do good and avoid evil. This is to perfect his way of serving men, and it is therefore the provisional teaching *(ch'üan-chiao)*. The sage establishes his teaching according to the appropriateness of time. He establishes the teaching in order to save the world. [Whether it is the ultimate teaching or the temporary teaching, his intention is always the same.]⁴⁸

The argument used here, just like that used by Chu-hung in the previous paragraph, is persuasive enough. Superior men did not need any theory of reward and punishment, for they practiced morality for its own sake. Whether it is the hope of Nirvana for a Buddhist or the ideal of sagehood for a Confucian, the intense yearning for the transcendent serves as the fuel for moral life. In this case, morality is a natural by-product of spiritual awakening. However, since there was never an abundance of superior men in any time and any society, morality had to be made imperative to ordinary (Chu-hung's "middling") people by appealing to their belief in reward and punishment. Abstract ideals of charity and righteousness were thus made more readily appreciable. Moral perfection and spiritual felicity are distant and abstract concepts, but they could be made concrete and appealing if one were told that daily advances in small good deeds can accumulate and result in future blessedness. There is the same tacit assumption at work here that we saw in connection with the practice of releasing life: quantitative yet methodical performance of good deeds can eventually lead to a qualitative transformation in the spiritual and moral outlook of the performer. Therefore, even though the belief in reward and punishment was only a conventional teaching and did not represent the ultimate truth, Chu-hung appreciated its value, took the system of merits and demerits very seriously, and based the *Record of Self-knowledge* on it.

The Record of Self-knowledge

The *Record* is a revised and expanded version of an earlier morality book entitled *T'ai-wei Hsien-chün kung-kuo-ko* (Ledger of Merits and Demerits According to the Immortal T'ai-wei), which is contained in the Tao-tsang or the canonical collection of Taoist scriptures.[49] According to the preface to the *Ledger,* which is dated the eleventh year of Ta-ting (1171) during the Jurchen Chin dynasty, the content of the work was imparted by the Immortal T'ai-wei to a Taoist priest by the name of Yu-hsüan-tzu of the Wu-yu (Devoid of Care) Pavilion, Hui-chen (Meeting Truth) Hall of Hsi-shan (Western Hills). The *Ledger,* therefore, had a mythical origin. Although we do not know the actual date or any concrete events in the life of the privileged "transmitter" of this divine document, his identity, fortunately, is less obscure. It has been suggested by both Sakai and Yoshioka that Yu-hsüan-tzu may have belonged to a Taoist sect called the Ching-ming Chung-hsiao Tao (The Pure and Bright Way of Loyalty and Filial Piety). The sect, as the name indicates, stressed loyalty and filial piety.[50] Its founder was Hsü Chen-chün, who lived in the third century A.D. Despite its ancient lineage, the sect became active only after the fall of the Northern Sung. From then on, through the Southern Sung, the Jurchen Chin, the Yüan, the Ming, and the Ch'ing dynasties, the sect continued to exist in North China, and was especially active along the middle and lower reaches of the Yellow River, where it exerted considerable influence on the common people.[51] According to this hypothesis, Yu-hsüan-tzu was a member of this sect. As shown by the content of the *Ledger,* he shared the same concern for moral perfection stressed by the sect.

More significantly, it has also been suggested that the *Ledger* may have been influenced by or even copied from similar handbooks used by members of the sect. These handbooks have unfortunately been lost, but from the scriptures and rules of the sect, we know the names of two of them. *Ling-pao ching-ming-yüan hsing-ch'ien-shih* (Rule Book for Neophytes in the Pure and Bright Hall of Spiritual Treasure) stipulates that every sect member must have a copy of the *Kung-kuo-pu* (Notebook of Merits and Demerits).[52] In another sacred scripture of the sect, the *T'ai-shang ling-pao ching-ming fei-t'ien tu-jen ching* (The Exalted Scripture of Pure and Bright Spiritual Treasure that Saves People and Enables Them to Fly to Heaven), sect members are advised to keep a so-called *Daily Record (Jih-lu).* The date of the first *Rule Book* is uncertain, but the composition of the latter scripture has been dated in the first year of Shao-hsing (1131), about forty years prior to the date for the publication of the *Ledger.*[53] The amazing similarity between the titles of the *Ledger* and the *Notebook (Kung-kuo-ko* and *Kung-kuo-pu,* respectively) must be more than coincidental. Given also the possible proximity in time, it is indeed tempting to suppose that the *Ledger* was derived from the *Notebook* or vice versa. Although the precise format of the *Notebook of Merits and Demerits* and the *Daily Record* is unknown, these works, like the *Ledger,* emphasized the importance of reflection on one's behavior and the keeping of a record of good and bad acts.

Chu-hung wrote the *Record of Self-knowledge* in the thirty-second year of Wan-li (1604), when he was already seventy years of age.[54] By that time, he had long been an influential Buddhist leader. His temple, the Yün-ch'i Ssu, was looked upon as the model of Pure Land meditation and strict Vinaya observance. His lay disciples included high-ranking officials and famous literary figures, as well as obscure common people from within the locality of the temple. We may therefore assume that his decision to write the *Record* was not a frivolous act, but one designed to serve some meaningful function in his general plan of revitalizing Buddhism. Chu-hung tells us that he first came across the *Ledger of Merits and Demerits* when he was still a young man, long before he became a monk. When he read it, he was so overjoyed that he had it reprinted and distributed to people free of charge.[55] Now, in the twilight of his life, he took out the work he had so valued in his youth and, using it as a model, wrote one of a similar nature. That Chu-hung should have discovered the *Ledger* when he was a young man and become so interested in it is not particularly strange, for the *Ledger* had spread beyond the original confines of the sect and become quite influential among the general population by the time of the late Ming. Yüan Liao-fan (1533–1606), in an essay written for his son entitled "Li-ming p'ien" (Establishing One's Destiny), wrote how he had been a confirmed fatalist until he was given the *Ledger* by a Ch'an monk, Yün-ku, in the third year of Lung-ch'ing (1569), and how his life was completely changed when he faithfully practiced the rules set forth in the *Ledger*.[56] Many people must have had similar experiences.

If the *Ledger* served so well, why did Chu-hung write *The Record of Self-knowledge*, a larger and a better work of the same kind? Chu-hung never made his reasons clear. It is more than likely that he advocated the system of merits and demerits as one more effort in his overall plan to promote lay Buddhism. Precisely because of the concise and practical nature of this system, Chu-hung decided to make it his own, adding to it many new items, subtracting and changing old ones. By the time Chu-hung finished his revisions, a work that was originally mainly Taoist and Confucian in orientation had been turned into a document of Buddhist and Confucian concerns. It could and did now serve to further the cause of lay Buddhism.

Before analyzing the contents of the *Record* and comparing it with the *Ledger*, it will be useful to examine how the system of merits and demerits was actually practiced, and in this connection to venture a few hypotheses concerning its origins and the reasons for its popularity.

Early in *The Ledger of Merits and Demerits* we find this passage addressed to a would-be practitioner:

As for the way of practice, one should always have a pen, an inkwell and a notebook ready by the head of the bed in the bedroom. First one should write down the month, then write down the day of the month. Under each day, make two columns for merits *(kung)* and demerits *(kuo)*. Just before one retires for the night, one should write down the good and bad things one has done during the day. Consult the *Ledger* for the points for each deed. If one has done good acts, record them in the merit column. If one has done bad things, record them in the demerit column. One should not just write down good acts and conceal bad ones. At the end of each month count the total of merits and demerits. Compare the two. Either subtract the number of demerits from the number of merits or use the number of merits to cancel out the number of demerits. After subtraction or cancellation, the number of merits or demerits remaining will be clear.[57]

In the preface to *The Record of Self-knowledge,* Chu-hung gives us a similar picture of how the system works:

The Immortal (Hsien-chün) says that all men ought to have a notebook by their beds. When they go to sleep, they should write down both the merits and the demerits they have achieved during the day. Accumulating the days to a month, and then accumulating the months to a year, they can either cancel demerits by merits or vice versa. By looking at the number of merits or demerits they will know themselves their blessing or punishment.[58]

We now know why the title of the first work is *Kung-kuo-ko* (The Ledger of Merits and Demerits). As Sakai correctly suggests, *ko* has the meaning of standard and regulation.[59] The book was intended to serve as a guide to ethical living. One might consult it to find out what good deeds one should do and what bad actions one should avoid. But *ko* also means a frame, a limit, a pattern, or ruled lines for writing. As the passages quoted above make clear, the practitioner of this system of merits and demerits is urged to keep an account of his daily behavior. In this sense, *ko* has been appropriately translated as "ledger." The most striking feature of the *Ledger* is its quantification of morality. Each act, be it moral or immoral, is assigned a certain number of points. By keeping a daily tally of merits and demerits, and by taking monthly and yearly inventories, one was always able to determine how his account stood. In this way, he could measure the distance between his present status and future blessing or disaster.

In theory and practice this system of merits and demerits bears strong resemblance to the ritual complex of merit-making in contemporary societies where Theravāda Buddhism is practiced. In Sri Lanka and Burma, for example, both monks and Buddhist laymen firmly believe in the necessity of increasing merit (Pali, *pin;* Burmese, *ku-thou*) through good actions and reducing demerit (Pali, *pav;* Burmese, *aku-thou*) by avoidance of bad actions.[60] The balance of one's merits and demerits determines the state of one's next rebirth. In the understanding of the common man, karma is "the net balance, the algebraic sum, of one's merit and demerit."[61] One accumulates merit or demerit, and once acquired, it brings automatic consequences. This ideology of merit-making is clearly shared by the compilers of morality books. Merit is similar to money. Spiro tells us that the Burmese do careful merit bookkeeping in order to "calculate the current state of their merit bank."[62]

Yüan Liao-fan, a fervent practitioner of the *Ledger*'s prescriptions, left behind a vivid description of his conversion and the subsequent fulfillment of his most ardent wishes as a result of moral practice. His testimony is extremely valuable because it tells us, first, how one could not only affect his future life but also manipulate his fortune in the present life by accumulating merit, and second, how the system actually worked. Yüan was originally a fatalist. He believed what a fortuneteller had predicted and thus was quite resigned to the prediction that he would not get his *chin-shih* degree, that he would not have a son, and that he would die in his fifty-third year.[63] However, after he met the monk Yün-ku, who gave him the *Ledger* in 1569, he decided to give this new approach a try.

The first wish Yüan made was to be successful in the provincial examination. He promised to do three thousand good deeds in order to fulfill this wish. The next year (1570) he passed the examination with the highest score. But it took him ten years to accumulate the three thousand deeds he had pledged to perform. Yüan explained why it took him such a long time.

My motivation, in carrying out righteousness, was not completely pure, and when I examined my behavior there were many mistakes. Sometimes when I saw a chance to do good, I did not do it wholeheartedly. Other times, after I saved a person, I would have second thoughts. Sometimes, I worked hard to do good, yet I would say something wrong. Other times, although I behaved well when sober, I would let my restraint go when I became intoxicated. As a result, my demerits often outweighed my merits, and I would pass the days in vain.[64]

After he had accumulated three thousand good deeds, his next wish was to have a son, and for this he also promised three thousand

good deeds. In 1581 a son was indeed born to him. This time, however, the quota was fulfilled in a shorter time. Only four years
elapsed between the time he made the pledge and the time it was
fulfilled. His essay records that he told his son that both he and his
wife performed good deeds together. "As soon as I did one good
thing, I would record it with a brush. Your mother did not know
how to write, so whenever she did one [good] thing she would make
a red circle with a goose quill on the calendar. She would either give
food to the poor or buy fish and shrimp to set them free. Sometimes
she would have more than ten circles on a single day."[65] When he
had accumulated three thousand good deeds for the second time, he
promised to perform another ten thousand good deeds in order to
satisfy his last wish, which was to pass the *chin-shih* examination. This
he succeeded in achieving in 1586, and he was appointed magistrate
of Pao-ch'ih. When he wrote his essay describing these experiences,
he was sixty-eight years old, long past the year for which his death
had been predicted.

In reading Yüan's essay, one is struck by the automatic consequence of doing good deeds. In order to obtain a certain goal, one
had to perform a number of meritorious deeds. Having entered into
such a pledge, one was assured of the achievement of his goals. It
was up to the party in question to keep his side of the bargain by fulfilling the quota pledged. It seems that the only reason Yüan decided to do good was to obtain some reward. In such a system it is
possible to practice morality for personal benefit rather than for its
own sake. Despite Yüan's rationalization, it was not wrong to do
good for ulterior and utilitarian purposes.

It should come as no surprise to find that this kind of utilitarian
consideration appalled the purist sensibilities of at least one contemporary literatus.[66] Even to advocates of this system, the pitfalls of its
literal interpretation were obvious. In a legalistic and calculative religious system like this one, it was quite conceivable that one might
find piety and immorality intermixed in the motivations of its practitioners. Such a possibility was clearly foreseen by the compiler of the
nineteenth-century edition of the *Ledger* which was mentioned earlier, for in the preface we read:

Generally speaking, law only gives important guidelines. Now the *Ledger*
regulates that merit and demerit can cancel each other out. This is true in
principle, but if one holds the literal meaning to the letter and ignores the

spirit, one will be mistaken. The *Ledger* regulates that to kill a person counts three hundred demerits, to save ten very tiny creatures counts one merit, and to spend one hundred cash [for good purposes] also counts one merit. Suppose there is a rich man who has murdered a man. But since he has also saved a great many tiny creatures and contributed a great amount of money, would his demerit then be canceled out? In my opinion, this problem is indeed a delicate one.[67]

This author resolves the dilemma by stressing the necessity for repentance, thus reaffirming the importance of intention. But the question still remains: how did such a quantitative and classificatory approach to morality come into vogue in the first place?

Beyond Karma: Other Ideological Sources of the Morality Book

The sources for this kind of morality, first represented in the *Treatise of the Exalted One*, most probably resulted from the following three spheres of influence: the governmental censorate, Pure Land pietism, and the penal code. Sakai Tadao, in his *Chūgoku zensho no kenkyū* (Studies of Chinese Morality Books), mentions the first two briefly.[68] The influence of the penal code, however, may prove to be most significant.

Effective rule of the empire had been a serious issue ever since China's unification under the Ch'in dynasty. The ideology of the vast bureaucracy that was established in the Han to administer the empire absorbed both Confucian and Legalist assumptions. The practice of periodic review of officials' performances and the application of reward or punishment in accordance with their achievements certainly emphasized the central role of personal merit and demerit. Later, with the introduction and popularization of Buddhism, this same idea was reinforced and legitimized by the theory of karma. The rationale for this breucratic control, however, came from Legalism. Specifically, it derived from Han Fei Tzu's stress on the correspondence between actuality and name and his famous slogan of the "two handles"—reward and punishment.[69] What interests us here, however, is the idea of accountability as a factor in individual behavior. Accountability is central not only to Legalist concepts of control but also to the system of merits and demerits. The difference between the two is that whereas the former holds subjects accountable to their rulers, the latter holds the practitioner accountable to a supernatural ruler of destiny or the immutable law of karma. But both systems make reward and punishment the essential means for enforcing the accountability.

From the Han dynasty on, special officials were entrusted with the supervision and review of subordinates' performances. Thus, in the *Hsü Han-shu*, we find that a grand commandant *(t'ai-wei)* was in charge of military officials, a chancellor *(ssu-t'u)* was in charge of civil officials, and a minister of works *(ssu-k'ung)* was in charge of construction and waterworks officials. At the end of the year each of the three reported to the court on these officials' grades, and reward or punishment would then be meted out.[70] According to Sakai, this practice was continued in subsequent dynasties, and during the T'ang a regulation concerning the examination of achievements defined four kinds of good performance and seventeen kinds of superior performance *(ssu-shan shih-ch'i tsui)*.[71] Earlier, during the Han, the practice of permitting an official to use his merits to cancel out his demerits was also established.[72] Besides these particular examples, one might refer to the censorial system of China as a whole as evidence of the concern for self-examination and institutional control. Officials throughout the country were constantly kept under surveillance by the Censorate, which dispatched censors on provincial inspection tours.[73]

Some of the methods bureaucrats devised to classify the populace might also have had some influence on popular morality. One example is that of the "nine-grade classification" of candidates for office as applied by inspectors known as the "impartial and just" *(chiu-p'in chung-cheng)*. This system was reportedly instituted by Ch'en Ch'ün of the Northern Wei dynasty.[74] Each prefecture had a "small impartial and just" *(hsiao chung-cheng)*, who would examine the people in the district and classify candidates for office into nine classes, three classes of superior *(shang)*, middle *(chung)*, and inferior *(hsia)*. Each class was then further subdivided into three: the superior-superior *(shang-shang)*, the superior-middle *(shang-chung)*, and superior-inferior *(shang-hsia)*, and so on, to a total of nine classes. The results were reported to the "great impartial and just" *(ta chung-cheng)* at the county level who, after having checked the facts, reported to the chancellor. After a final review, candidates were recommended to the master of documents *(shang-shu)*, who made the final decision on their employment. In actual practice this system of election by merit was seldom impartial or just. Since the electors themselves came from a "superior class," they usually recommended only those of similar background. As a result, "the superior class has no poor families, neither does the inferior class have aristocrats."[75] This system helped to create and perpetuate class distinctions for several hundred years until it was abolished at the beginning of the Sui.

The second probable source for quantitative morality derives from a totally different sphere, that of Pure Land pietism. In the *Kuan wu-liang-shou ching* (the Amitāyurdhyāna Sutra), one of the three most important scriptures of the Pure Land school, people who are destined to be reborn into the Western Paradise are classified into nine classes. Since the sutra was translated during the Yüan-chia era (424–453) of the Liu-Sung dynasty,[76] and thus came later than the time of Ch'en Ch'ün, it is unlikely that it had any influence on the nine-grade classification of candidates described above. Nevertheless, both were based on a classificatory approach toward election, whether bureaucratic or spiritual. According to the sutra, depending upon the believer's spiritual maturity and religious cultivation, he may be classified into any one of nine gradations. The nine are classified as superior *(shang-p'in)*, middle *(chung-p'in)*, and inferior *(hsia-p'in)*. Each of these is then subdivided into three classes. Thus, within the superior grade there are the following possibilities: rebirth in the highest form of the superior grade *(shang-p'in shang-sheng)*, in the middle form of the superior grade *(shang-p'in chung-sheng)*, and in the lowest form of the superior grade *(shang-p'in hsia-sheng)*. The same procedures apply to the middle and inferior grades.

The spiritual reward one receives at rebirth in the Western Paradise differs in degree according to the particular grade to which one is assigned. For example, beings who will be born in the highest form of the superior grade must be those who, first of all, wish to be born there, and second, have the "true and sincere thought" *(chen-ch'eng hsin)*, the "deep-believing thought" *(shen hsin)*, and the desire to be born in the Pure Land by "bringing one's stock of merit to maturity" *(hui-hsiang fa-yüan hsin)*. Generally, three kinds of people are included in this category:

First, those who are possessed of a compassionate mind, who do no injury to any beings, and who accomplish all virtuous actions according to the Buddha's precepts; second, those who study and recite the sutras of the Ma-hāyāna doctrine, as for instance, Vaipulya sutras *(fang-teng);* third, those who practice the sixfold remembrance [i.e., of the Three Treasures, the precepts, the charity of the Buddhas, bodhisattvas, and the world of de-vas].[77]

He who belongs to this group is a religious virtuoso, a member of the spiritual elite. His reception in the Pure Land is suitably grandi-ose. Among other marvels to be witnessed are these: "He will see the Buddha's form and body [Amitābha's] with every sign of perfection complete, and also the perfect forms and signs of all the bodhisatt-vas; he will also see brilliant rays and jewel forests and hear the bodhisattvas propounding the excellent Law."[78] By contrast, beings who are born in the lowest form of the inferior grade can expect to receive completely different treatment. They are the great sinners who have committed many crimes. But, just before they die, should they meet good friends who teach them to recite the Amitābha's name and should they succeed in reciting it ten times without inter-ruption, they can be reborn in the Western Paradise on the strength of this merit alone. However, they will have to wait for twelve great kalpas *(ta-chieh)* inside lotus flowers before the flowers will unfold, thus enabling them to see the Buddha and bodhisattvas and to listen to their teachings.[79] If the first case describes the religious virtuoso, the second describes the religious amateur, the spiritual proletariat. There are seven other categories between these two extremes.

In stressing the importance of reciting the Buddha's name, Pure Land pietism sometimes lent itself to a quantitative approach toward spiritual cultivation. The number of times a believer recited the Buddha's name was often taken as a better indicator of faith than the quality of his inner life. One very famous example of this kind of quantitative piety was set by the monk Tao-ch'o (562–645), who ad-vised people to use beans to count the number of times they recited the Amitābha's name. Every time one recited *na-mo A-mi-t'o-fo* (hom-age to Amitābha), he was to put one bean aside. It is said that there were individuals who eventually accumulated several million pecks of beans. Tao-ch'o proselytized in the Shansi area, particularly in the districts of Hsin-yang, T'ai-yüan, and Wen-shui. He even taught children from the age of seven on to recite the Buddha's name. Moreover, he divided his followers into three classes according to the number of beans they accumulated to mark their recitations.

Thus, a most vigilant person *(shang-ching-chin che)* would accumulate eighty to ninety piculs of beans; a person of middling vigilance *(chung-ching-chin che)* would get fifty piculs, while a barely vigilant person *(hsia-ching-chin che)* would only get twenty piculs.[80]

These same attitudes and practices persisted well into the Ming period. Chu-hung had ambivalent feelings toward them. In one instance he disapproved of such practices. But, as is evident from the following passage, we cannot be sure whether he disapproved because of their intrinsic nature—the mechanical emphasis on quantity—or simply because of the clumsiness of the procedures involved:

There are some monks who ask donors for beans. Each time they recite the Buddha's name, they put one bean aside. In the beginning there may be only one person who does this. But soon many people imitate him. They are called "masters of Buddha beans" *(tou-erh-fo shih-fu)*. But the Buddha instituted the rosary in order to teach people to recite the Buddha's name.[81] Why do they not follow the Buddha's practice and save their energy instead of doing such a strenuous thing? Moreover, when one finishes with the one hundred and eight beads of the rosary, one can start all over again. In this way one can recite a hundred, a thousand, ten thousand, a million, all the way to an infinite number of times but still not exhaust it [the rosary].[82]

In the passage that follows, Chu-hung once again expresses his disapproval of mechanical piety. He undertook an experiment and concluded that mere quantitative recitation was not only impractical, but also detrimental to spiritual growth:

It is reported that master Yung-ming (904–975) recited Amitābha's name a hundred thousand times during one day and one night. I once tried to do it. From the first hour of one day until the first hour of the next day, in twenty-four hours, I recited the name exactly a hundred thousand times. But I recited only the four characters [*a-mi-t'o-fo*, Amitābha]. Had I recited the six characters [*na-mo-a-mi-t'o-fo*, homage to Amitābha], I would not have been able to reach this number. I never stopped reciting it while eating, drinking, or going to the toilet. I also did not sleep or speak. Otherwise, I also would have been unable to reach this number. Even so, I was as hurried as a traveler desperate to reach his destination and did not have the leisure to concentrate carefully on what I was reciting. Otherwise I also would not have been able to reach this number. From this we can understand that "a hundred thousand" probably meant constant and perpetual recitation. It does not necessarily mean the actual figure of one hundred thousand.[83]

The relationship between religious belief and penal law in traditional China has generally been regarded as a close one.[84] But attention is usually focused on the effect of religious beliefs on the formulation of the penal codes, not the reverse. The influence of religious
belief on the law is especially conspicuous with regard to bans on executions and other legal activities on days of religious significance.
This practice can be traced to very early origins: "There is abundant
evidence that by the Han dynasty the restriction of executions and
serious legal proceedings to autumn and winter was not only an idea
but an accepted practice. . . . In addition to this general ban on
spring and summer executions, it seems probable that in Han times,
as later, the summer solstice and especially the winter solstice were
specifically included in a similar ban."[85] Such prohibitions were designed to prevent human interference with cosmic change. In the
T'ang Code, periods regarded as taboo for executions were greatly
increased. "Many of the new taboos are inspired by the then extremely powerful influence of Buddhism with its opposition to the
taking of life."[86] When all the taboo days were subtracted, less than
two months a year in which executions were permitted were es-
timated to remain.[87] The taboos of the T'ang Code were said to have
been retained virtually unchanged in subsequent codes through
those of the Ming dynasty.[88] The violation of such taboos was punishable by law. We are told, for instance, that, according to the T'ang
Code, any official who failed to observe the regulation that no execution was to take place between the period of the "beginning of
spring" and the "autumn equinox" was subject to a year's imprison-
ment. According to the Ming Code, that same official would be subject to eighty strokes.[89]

Another example of the influence of religious beliefs on the law
is evident in the way some judges passed verdicts. Ch'ü T'ung-tsu
notes a few instances where the judge's concern for gaining personal
merit overrode his obligation to justice:

After the introduction of Buddhism into China, the idea of not killing and
secret reward had more influence on the Chinese than before. Believing that
"not to kill" would count as a secret merit, and that killing the innocent was
sinful and subject to retribution, many officials avoided killing and sought to
be merciful. Kao Yün [390–487], an official of Northern Wei, thought that
he would live to be a hundred years old because he had accumulated many
secret merits for having saved the lives of many persons. [Wei-shu, 48.] Some

officials went so far as to consider not killing a secret merit, and for this reason tried to save the lives of persons who deserved death.

Chu Hsi remarked that most of the Legalists in his time were deluded by ideas of sin, blessedness, and retribution and liked to reduce the punishment of others in order to seek blessedness and reward for themselves. In cases of crimes deserving the death penalty, they always tried to find some excuse for the criminals and to present their cases to the emperor in the hope that the punishment would be reduced. Thus those who deserved beheading were banished; those who deserved banishment were imprisoned; and those who were to be beaten received fewer strokes or none at all [*Chu Wen-kung cheng-hsün*].

Both Yüan Pin (eighteenth century) and Fang Ta-chih (nineteenth century) complained that many officials who believed in secret merit sought to protect those who were guilty of rape from death, although this was a punishment accorded by the law.[90]

Religious scruples clearly played a role in the administration of justice. However, it is equally important to note that the legal codes also reinforced religious beliefs and influenced popular morality. Although this aspect of the relationship between religious behavior and law has seldom been examined, even a cursory study of the morality books attests to its importance. Here, we shall examine three specific areas in which the legal codes could have had a direct influence on morality books, including Chu-hung's *Record of Self-knowledge*.

First, the emphasis on the deterrent function of the criminal law could explain why both the *Treatise* and the *Record* devoted so much more space to the category of evil or bad deeds. The compilers of these books shared a conviction similar to that held by the Legalists who believed "that dire threats would forestall all wrongdoing."[91] Admittedly, the legal codes, at least in theory, supported threats with their actual enforcement, while morality books had no such power. Through psychological encouragement and deterrence, however, the morality books, like religion in general, helped to popularize and support the secular moral values embodied in the legal codes. When one examines the contents of the morality books and the specific moral behavior encouraged or condemned by their compilers, the influence of the penal code is even more evident. For in both the *Treatise* and the *Record,* except for a small proportion concerning religious values (religious taboos in the *Treatise* and sections on deeds beneficial or harmful to the Three Jewels in the *Record*), the majority of deeds included reflect secular values.

This interest in social ethics and the general lack of specifically religious values illustrates what C. K. Yang has termed the "diffused" nature of Chinese religion.[92] Diffused religion—that is, syncretic religion—lent its support to secular moral rules by giving them supernatural sanction, by making them "sacred and awe-inspiring." It also "helped to remedy the fallibility of ethical values in their actual operation."[93] Thus, stealing money (demerit 173), and despoiling graves (demerit 100), both crimes punishable by law, were also condemned by the *Record*. Even if the wrongdoer were lucky enough to escape legal punishment, he could not escape a bad conscience. What is perhaps more important is that the victim of crime had the benefit of the same knowledge as the criminal. He might be unable to seek legal redress for the wrongs committed against him, but he could seek comfort in the thought that the culprit would not escape supernatural judgment (in the case of the *Treatise*) or the justice guaranteed by the law of karma (in the case of the *Record*). Any injustice or imperfection in the legal system was thus made bearable.

Second, the orderly arrangement of graduated punishments in the legal code could have served as a model for the morality books' assignment of merits and demerits. Some students of Chinese law have termed this arrangement "the Chinese penal ladder," for from the lightest punishment of ten blows with a light bamboo rod, the various punishments progress, step by step, all the way to "death by slicing." "We may interpret this system as a complex device for measuring morality with quantitative exactitude or again as constituting a graduated continuum whereby any offense, ranging from the most trivial to the most serious, may be requited with the utmost precision."[94] These two characteristics—the attempt to measure morality with quantitative exactitude and to form a self-sufficient schema by which each good or bad deed, no matter how serious or how trivial, could be appropriately evaluated—apply equally to the *Record of Self-knowledge*. The maximum number of points for merits or demerits is one hundred, while the minimum is one. Between these extremes, two, five, ten, twenty, thirty, forty, fifty, and eighty points mark the gradations. For instance, a very serious offense such as successfully plotting for someone's death sentence (demerit 41) or intentionally murdering a person (demerit 56) results in the maximum one hundred demerits, but a trivial offense such as keeping birds in a cage or binding animals with string for one day (demerit 80) results in one demerit. The range of points for behavior between one and one hundred, just like that between the five grades of punishment, is considerable. However, except in the most obvious instances, no strict logic governing the assignment of points is immediately discernible for actions in the middle range between the two extremes.

Third, the minute differentiation between offenses in the legal codes could have inspired a similar treatment of moral behavior in the *Record of Self-knowledge*. We are told that "the codes always endeavor to foresee all possible variations of any given offense and to provide specific penalties for each."[95] This may account for the abundant and at times tedious enumeration of acts done for slightly different purposes, to slightly varied recipients, with slightly altered consequences, under slightly changed circumstances. To cite a few of the many possible examples in the *Record,* we find the following provisions under the category of good deeds:

In an official proposing a benevolent policy, when it benefits one person, it counts as one merit. [merit 9]
When it benefits a region, it counts as ten merits. [merit 10]
When it benefits the whole country, it counts as fifty merits. [merit 11]
When it benefits the country in later generations, it counts as one hundred merits. [merit 12]

While the examples just cited differentiate acts according to their consequences, the following do so according to the recipients of the action:

When one saves domestic animals capable of repaying kindness, for each animal thus saved count twenty merits. [merit 42]
For each domestic animal saved that has no power to return human kindness, count ten merits. [merit 43]
For each small animal saved, count one merit. For ten very small creatures saved, count one merit. [merit 44]

In the Ch'ing Code, which was modeled on the Ming Code, homicide is classified into over twenty varieties. These detailed differentiations derive from one or another of three major principles according to which differentiation takes place: (1) the motivation for the homicide (premeditated, intentional but unpremeditated, homicide in an affray, by mischance or accident, in roughhousing, or by inducing the victim to commit suicide); (2) the status, social or familial, of the killer vis-à-vis his victim; (3) the means or the situation through which or under which the homicide is committed (homicide caused by poison, by improper administration of medicine, by introducing harmful objects into the nostrils, ears, or other orifices of the victim's body, and so on).[96]

The same three principles apparently governed the differentiations found in the *Record*. The emphasis on the motivation of the doer and on his interiorization of morality was the most striking difference between the *Treatise* and later books such as the *Ledger* and the *Record*. The last two made a clear distinction between intentional and unintentional acts and provided different treatment for each. For example, to sentence one person by mistake to the death penalty counts eighty demerits, but to do so intentionally counts one hundred demerits (demerits 30–37). Again, the principle of differentiating acts according to the status of the wrongdoer vis-à-vis the victim is well illustrated in the following cases:

An official of high position who obstructs his subordinate's future advancement earns thirty demerits. [demerit 106]
To lock up a maid or a concubine counts as one demerit. [demerit 109]
A judge may clearly know that the defendant is innocent, yet either because of outside pressure or because the verdict has been given in a lower court or by a previous judge, he does not clear the person of guilt. Count eighty demerits if the death sentence results from this. Military exile or penal servitude counts thirty demerits. Heavy bambooing counts eight demerits. Light bambooing counts four demerits. If the judge receives a bribe and passes the death sentence, it is one hundred demerits. The number of demerits is counted the same as above in regard to other sentences. [demerits 49–53]

Finally, the principle of differentiating acts according to the means by which or situation under which they are committed is paralleled by the provision in the *Record* that any act committed as a result of bribery or the absence of an alternative does not count as a merit. Thus, if one cancels someone's debt only because the court refuses to deal with the complaint, no merit is earned (merit 71). In a more specific example, when one cooks a living creature in a strange way and makes it suffer excruciating pain, he gets twenty demerits (demerit 74). The variation in the severity of the penalty is apparent when one reads that to kill a small animal intentionally counts only one demerit (demerit 60). Although harming a creature is bad, if one does so in the course of doing some good work such as repairing bridges, paving roads, or building temples, no demerit will accrue (demerit 78). In this way, a certain flexibility and a great deal of common sense are built into an otherwise mechanical system.

Unique Features of the *Record of Self-knowledge*

The real innovativeness of the *Record* can be appreciated only after comparing its contents with those of its predecessor, the *Ledger*. Chu-hung added a great many new entries to those found in the latter work.[97] These fall into one of three categories: (1) loyalty and filial piety and their opposites, (2) Buddhist practice, and (3) social ethics.

As we have noted earlier, the *Ledger* might have been written by a Taoist priest belonging to the Ching-ming Chung-hsiao Tao (The Pure and Bright Way of Loyalty and Filial Piety). But, although loyalty and filial piety are mentioned sporadically in the *Ledger,* they constitute a full section (1–18 in both categories) in the *Record.* Their importance for Chu-hung is undeniable, and this accords well with his general stress on Confucian values in other parts of the *Record.* Most of the new entries under social ethics are equally Confucian in orientation. In the *Record,* the interest in social ethics is not very different from the *Treatise,* and like the *Treatise,* the *Record* singles out a few classes of people for special attention. Aside from rules of good and bad behavior that apply to all, there are specific warnings directed at officials, gentry, merchants, and farmers. Officials are given detailed guidelines of a legal and administrative nature. They are not to take bribes or to be subject to social pressure. Most important of all, they are not to be unnecessarily harsh when passing sentences. Householders of the gentry class are told not to encroach on other people's property or force them to sell land. They are enjoined to be generous with money and to construct bridges and repair roads for the public weal; to take care of the poor and the helpless; not to ill-treat servants, but to try to redeem them and return them to their families; not to use coercion to make the poor repay their debts. Since cases of official corruption, legal injustice, and gentry oppression of the common people abounded in the latter part of the Ming, Chu-hung had good reason to pay so much attention to these particular problems.

The prominent place given to Buddhist practices sharply distinguishes the *Record* from both the *Treatise* and the *Ledger*. It also tells us much about Chu-hung's attitude toward Taoism. Both the *Treatise* and the *Ledger* are a mixture of Confucian and Taoist values, but the *Record* is definitely a mixture of Confucian and Buddhist values. The sections called "deeds beneficial to the Three Jewels" are Chu-hung's additions. These deal with specifically Buddhist practices. But even in other sections of the *Record*, there is frequent reference to lay Buddhist values, such as vegetarianism, nonkilling, and the release of living creatures. These innovations consitute the most significant aspects of the *Record*. Through such provisions as these, Buddhist values were for the first time formally incorporated into the general content of popular morality books. Thus the *Record* also served to reinforce the tenets of lay Buddhism discussed in chapter IV.

Chu-hung's attitude toward Taoism, however, was highly critical if not downright hostile. For instance, he stipulated that to refuse to accept instructions about the Taoist technique of making cinnabar counted thirty merits (merit 200). Similarly, Chu-hung also discouraged the use of counterfeit silver, which was produced by this process. He assigned thirty merits to a person who refused to use a piece of this kind of silver worth one hundred cash (merit 201).[98] According to Chu-hung, this technique of making counterfeit silver was specifically a Taoist specialty.

Although it is true that he also encouraged the distribution of books on hygiene, the preservation of life, and medical prescriptions (merit 194, 195)—practices originally advocated and developed by religious Taoists—these were activities also considered meritorious by Confucians and Buddhists. By the Ming dynasty they were completely integrated into the popular consciousness. Picking up papers with characters on them from the street and burning them at home (merit 197) was another practice belonging to this category. It is instructive to note that the only entries in the *Ledger* Chu-hung either eliminated or changed considerably had to do with Taoist practices. The two sections entitled "doctrinal texts" (*chiao-tien men*) and "worship and cultivation" (*fen-hsiu men*) in the *Ledger* were replaced by the section entitled "On the Three Jewels" in the *Record*. In the new section, Chu-hung did not include entries concerning the transmission of Taoist charms, spells, and registers (fa-lu).[99] He recommended the Tantric Buddhist ritual of "bestowing food" (shih-shih, merit 118) and the "ritual to divert disaster" (pao-jang tao-ch'ang, merit 121) to replace the Taoist rites of burning incense and cultivating virtue and the Taoist sacrificial services (chang-chiao).[100]

Chu-hung's attitude toward the three teachings is revealed by the *Record* in another interesting fashion. He assigns twice the number of merit points when an act benefits Buddhism as he does when the same act benefits Taoism or Confucianism. For instance, in making Buddhist images each one hundred cash spent counts one merit, but in making images of deities of other religions, each two hundred cash spent counts only one merit (merit 90, 91). Similarly, every one hundred cash spent in building Buddhist temples counts one merit, but every two hundred cash spent in building other kinds of temples counts only one merit (merit 96, 99). Whereas writing one volume of commentaries on Mahāyāna sutras, shastras, and vinayas counts fifty merits, writing one volume of ethical texts counts only one merit (merit 106, 107). This is another indication of Chu-hung's reconciliatory, yet hierarchical attitude toward Confucianism. Confucian values are accepted, but they are subordinate to Buddhist values.[101]

In the final analysis, the quantification of morality exhibited by the *Record* may not escape criticism. Its practice could easily lead to a purely utilitarian and mechanical approach to morality. But one should not lose sight of the social and historical background to such a system. Concretized injunctions of the kind illustrated here did and may still serve the purpose of making general moral concepts such as justice, integrity, and kindness pertinent to everyday behavior. Social mobility created new opportunities for the lower classes, but it also induced a sense of uncertainty and anxiety. A poor farmer's son who had recently entered the official classes through successful passage of the examinations needed practical guidance to be able to carry out in the concrete and workaday world the weighty moral values of the classics. Such guidance was offered in numerous sources, and morality books were one of them. The versatility of the morality books is remarkable. To every hopeful aspirant to success, they served as guides to what he should and should not do in order to achieve his goals. To the perplexed and the anxious, they served as guides by which the individual, in whatever new setting he might find himself, could determine what constituted appropriate moral behavior. The peculiar contribution of *The Record of Self-knowledge* is that it introduced Buddhist values into the general moral schema of the traditional morality books.

CHAPTER SIX

~~~~~~

The Condition of the Monastic
Order in the Late Ming

IF WE TURN from lay to monastic Buddhism in Chu-hung's time, the overall picture is indeed depressing. It is true that as a result of the trend of combining three teachings in one, contemporary Confucian literati showed remarkable tolerance as well as appreciation of Buddhist philosophy and meditational discipline. It is also true that Buddhist practices such as fasts, vegetarianism, release of animals, and recitation of the Buddha's name had become so pervasive that one is almost tempted to view them as ubiquitous manifestations of popular morality. Yet it would be wrong to conclude that society held the monastic order in high regard. On the contrary, the reputation of monks in general was very low. The high esteem enjoyed by Ta-kuan, Chu-hung, and Te-ch'ing was always accompanied by the impression that they were exceptions to the rule. It is no wonder that Chu-hung, a religious leader with a profound sense of responsibility, should feel despair and shame.

In Chu-hung's writings one of the most persistent themes is the decline of discipline among his fellow monks. These passages, together with what we find in novels and notes written around the same period, furnish a most vivid and damaging picture of the sangha.

Causes of the Decline of
the Monastic Order

The decline of the sangha was tied to the inexorable logic of Buddhist eschatology. Both Theravāda and Mahāyāna Buddhism believe in the cyclical destruction and regeneration of innumerable world cycles[1] and in the decline and eventual disappearance of Buddhism itself sometime after the Buddha's Parinirvana. Both also agree that Buddhism will be revived again with the coming of the Future Buddha (Maitreya for Mahāyāna Buddhists and Metteyya for Theravāda Buddhists.) The second belief played a central role in religious reforms and popular millenarian movements in China and Japan. Differing somewhat from the Theravāda apocalyptic tradition,[2] Chinese Buddhists believed that the world would undergo three stages of varying duration from the Buddha's death or Parinirvana to the final disappearance of Buddhism in the world. These are the Age of True Law *(cheng-fa)*, when people would study the scriptures, practice disciplines, and realize the Dharma; the Age of Counterfeit Law *(hsiang-fa)*, when people would adhere to the externals (scriptures and disciplines) of the religion but become incapable of realizing the Dharma for themselves; and last, the Age of the Degenerate Law *(mo-fa)*, when people would lose respect for Buddhism and neither practice nor study the teaching, and the Dharma would eventually disappear as a result of public indifference and internal atrophy.

The idea of the three periods is found in various Mahāyāna sutras, such as the Lotus Sutra and the *Ta-pei ching* (Mahākaruṇā-puṇḍarīka Sutra), and there are four different ways of computing the three periods.[3] Generally speaking, the prevalent view is that the True Law lasts five hundred years after the Buddha's Parinirvana, the Counterfeit Law continues for another thousand years, and after that the Age of Degenerate Law takes over and lasts for ten thousand years. Even though the age of *mo-fa* was computed to begin some fifteen hundred years after the Buddha's death in 480 B.C., many in the Northern and Southern Dynasties already spoke of its arrival. This is because Buddhists in the sixth century generally accepted the date 949 B.C. for the Buddha's death, so that fifteen hundred years after that would have been A.D 550. The most famous example of the prevalence as well as the power of this belief was probably the ill-fated San-chieh chiao (Sect of the Three Stages), founded by Hsin-hsing (540–594).[4] Yet throughout the succeeding centuries this idea continued to exert its influence. For Chu-hung, as well as other contemporary Buddhists, *mo-fa* was an existential reality. This was why, according to him, Buddhism at the end of the Ming was in such a disreputable state. Specifically, it was believed that in this age of *mo-fa* one could not find any eminent monk on a par with those of earlier dynasties. Thus, Chu-hung says:

From the Hung-wu period [1368–1398] until now, very few great masters have appeared in this dynasty. We need not mention those masters of the T'ang and the Sung dynasties. Even masters Chung-feng[5] and T'ien-ju[6] of the Yüan dynasty probably would only find in Ch'u-shih Chi[7] of our dynasty their lone companion. If one tries to compare the present with the time before the T'ang, it is even more impossible. Is not this because the more recent the time, the more deluded the people become?[8]

In view of the fact that Chu-hung compiled *Huang-Ming ming-seng chi-lüeh* (Brief Record of Famous Monks in the Ming Dynasty, *YCFH* 17), in which he recorded biographies and selected saying of eighteen Ming monks, one ought to take with caution the remarks he made belittling his immediate predecessors. Moreover, in another important work, *Ch'an-kuan ts'e-chin* (Progress in the Path of Ch'an, *YCFH* 14), in which he collected those teachings on Ch'an cultivation that he considered most helpful, Chu-hung also saw fit to include the instructions of five Ming monks. Nevertheless, despite his respect for individual monks in the Ming, Chu-hung did take a rather dim view of the majority of his fellow monks. He also found it difficult to uphold the claim that monks were always more religious than laymen. As he said, "In this Age of the Degenerate Law, it is rather common for monks who have left the world to have less faith *(hsin-hsin)* than the laymen who stay in the world. It is also not unusual for laymen to have less faith than laywomen. No wonder that of the many people who aspire to become Buddhas, so few accomplish their goal."[9]

Chu-hung's low evaluation of the monastic order was confirmed by other contemporary opinions. Novels and *pi-chi* (notes, short essays) are useful sources and provide an impression of monks probably shared by society at large. *Chin-p'ing-mei* (The Golden Lotus),[10] a novel written during the Wan-li period, provides two seemingly contradictory impressions of Buddhism. On the one hand, Buddhist beliefs and practices are treated as deep-rooted and pervasive social realities. Buddhist rites are always performed after a person's death (chapters 8, 62). Almsgiving to individual monks, contributions toward repairing a local monastery, and donations for printing and distributing scriptures are gladly undertaken by the principal characters in the novel (chapters 57, 88). One of the most frequent pastimes among Hsi-men Ch'ing's wives is listening to the preaching of sutras and the retelling of Buddhist stories (*fo-ch'ü*) by nuns who are invited to the women's quarters for this purpose (chapters 39, 51, 59, 74). The popularity of nuns with the women is probably equal to the popularity of singing girls with the men. The representative of the faithful in the *Chin-p'ing-mei* is Hsi-men Ch'ing's first wife, Wu Yüeh-niang. Through her the author expounds the Buddhist concepts of karma, transmigration, and release. He deals with these most explicitly in the final chapter (chapter 100), when Lady Wu is made to see everything in the light of karmic retribution and agrees to let her only son become a monk.

On the other hand, the novel depicts individual monks and nuns in a very unflattering light. The author is most unrelenting in accusing them of two cardinal sins: greed and unchastity. "Let me tell you, readers, that in this world there are three kinds of people who will open their eyes only at the sight of silver: [Buddhist] monks, Taoist priests, and singing girls. They despise the poor and flatter the rich. For the sake of money they will employ lies, tricks, and everything they can think of." [11] And it is against monks' supposed immorality that the author of *Chin-p'ing-mei* directs most of his satirical darts.

Superficially these two attitudes are contradictory and puzzling, yet they are typical of institutionalized religious life in East and West. In Europe dissatisfaction with the Church and the clergy caused the laity to find its spiritual leaders among dissenters and heretics. There was a continuous tradition of religious movements led by various messiahs, renegade monks, mystics, and prophets from the time of the early Crusades until the Reformation. [12] These movements were inspired by the millennial eschatology of Christianity and in turn helped to strengthen its tradition. In China the belief in the Age of the Degenerate Law and the coming of Maitreya Buddha led to the organization of secret religious societies. From the Sung dynasty, and possibly earlier, most peasant rebellions derived their ideologies from these secret societies, especially the White Lotus and Maitreya sects. [13] Political and religious interests were intermingled, and these societies were both persecuted by the government and condemned by orthodox Buddhists. In this respect they shared a certain similarity with the millennial movements of medieval Europe.

For the majority of people the dissatisfaction with monastic Buddhism facilitated two phenomena: the rise of lay Buddhism and the absorption or cooption of some Buddhist ideas by the Confucian tradition. In the case of lay Buddhism there was also considerable accommodation to Confucian tenets.[14] But the individual lay Buddhist at the very least had to take refuge in the Three Jewels and be committed to keeping the five basic precepts. Therefore his primary allegiance was still to Buddhism, although he was expected and even encouraged to find ways to meet the demands of a Confucian society. In the latter case, when Confucianism coopts Buddhist ideas, a person can hold certain views and practice certain rites which are Buddhist in origin, but he may not acknowledge his ideological allegiance to Buddhism at all.

The *Chin-p'ing-mei* may again serve as an example. With the possible exception of Lady Wu, we cannot find any person in the book who can be called a professed lay Buddhist. Pan Chin-lien and Hsi-men Ch'ing certainly are not, yet they ask monks to perform funeral services, "soul masses" *(shui-lu)*,[15] and memorial services for family members. Another character, Li P'ing-erh, also has no deep interest in Buddhism, but when her infant son becomes seriously ill, she donates money for the purpose of printing sutra (chapter 58). The printing of sutras and the distribution of them free are meritorious acts much advocated by Buddhism. But in this case the acts are performed for the explicit purpose of effecting a fast recovery for Li P'ing-erh's son and are carried out in the spirit of propitiation, so that they do not indicate the doer's desire to propagate Buddhist teaching or her intention to thereby enlighten unbelievers.

Inviting Buddhist priests to officiate at funeral services, as Pan Chin-lien and Hsi-men Ch'ing did, is a good example of appropriation. Funeral rites, together with mourning and sacrifice to the departed, form the core of the Chinese family religion, often called "the cult of ancestor worship." The rationale and practice of this family religion had been in existence in China long before the introduction of Buddhism, and the rules governing these rites were codified in the *Li-chi* (Record of Rites). After Buddhism came to

China, the doctrines of karma and transmigration were incorporated into the traditional belief in the immortality of the soul. The doctrine of transmigration in particular merged with the Chinese idea of the ghost, which is associated with the *p'o* part of a person's soul (the coarse part of the soul formed by the yin in contrast to the *hun* or subtle part of the soul formed by the yang). From this fusion there arose the belief in purgatory and the necessity of performing religious rites that could help the wandering, suffering ghost to achieve early salvation. The irony is, of course, that doctrinal Buddhism did not accept a theory of the existence of the soul. Thus, the incorporation of Buddhist soul masses into the traditional funeral rites served to strengthen the Confucian value of family cohesion but did violence to the integrity of Buddhist doctrine. This is why many Buddhist masters, including Chu-hung, discouraged their disciples from engaging in funeral ceremonies.

If monks and nuns were already as immoral and contemptible as depicted in some contemporary sources, what were the reasons for the further decline of the monastic order? The process of monastic decay had started long before the Ming dynasty. It is customary, when discussing the history of Chinese Buddhism, to regard the T'ang as the zenith and to describe the period from the Sung dynasty onward as one of gradual decline. Since Buddhism puts equal emphasis on the Three Jewels—the Buddha, the Dharma, and the Sangha—the decline must necessarily refer to the stultification of doctrine and the demoralization of the priesthood.

Although commentaries and treatises were continuously produced, no monk after the T'ang created a philosophical synthesis to compare with those of Chih-i, Fa-tsang, or Tsung-mi. Of far greater significance, however, was the gradual decline of the monastic order. Traditionally, the monastic order had always relied on imperial patronage and popular contributions for its sustenance and prosperity. The most important single factor which assured this support was the demand that the monks maintain a certain standard of pure conduct. Indeed, this was the most powerful justification for lay support of an otherwise "parasitic" group, for the assembly of monks could theoretically transfer merit accrued from a life devoted to meditation and morality to their lay patrons for the sake of the latter's salvation. It is also interesting to note that it was the monks' failure to keep discipline that always evoked the ire of the public, while their lack of doctrinal originality or intellectual brilliance was apparently a matter worthy of little comment.

Two broad categories of causes may be adduced to explain the decline of the monastic order. First, there were external causes, those related to governmental intervention in the form of: (1) limitations on the number of monasteries and temples, (2) political manipulation of ordination certificates, and (3) establishment of monk-officials for bureaucratic control. Second, there was the internal disintegration of the monastic ideal, which in turn, resulted from three factors: (1) the degeneration of Ch'an practice, (2) the neglect of the discipline, and (3) secularization. This internal disintegration seems to have had a more lasting impact on the quality of monks and accounts for their loss of public esteem. It was also the internal disintegration that Chu-hung discussed in much greater detail. It is conceivable that he refrained from criticism of governmental policies out of fear, but more likely he felt that the crucial factors underlying the decline lay within the sangha itself.

Limits on the Number of Monasteries

All the major policies concerning Buddhist as well as Taoist orders were laid down during the reign of T'ai-tsu. There were both political and economic motives for instituting such laws, and in this respect the Ming attempt to impose religious control was no different from similar attempts made by earlier dynasties. But, aside from these practical reasons, there appears in T'ai-tsu's edicts a note of genuine dismay over the deplorable condition of the monasteries and an indication of his desire to reform the Buddhist establishment. Typical is this edict issued in 1391 stating the emperor's views on Buddhism:

Since Buddhism was introduced into China during the Han dynasty, one thousand three hundred and thirty years have passed. Therefore, it is not something which has existed only in one dynasty. The reason it has not perished lies in its doctrine of nonkilling and reverence for life. Its original tradition lies precisely in hard discipline and absolute quietude. But at present under heaven monks for the most part mingle with the common people. Furthermore, there are many who are even inferior to the common people. Although the teaching is the same as before, the monks' conduct has degenerated. It is therefore necessary to purify the practice and to classify Buddhism into sects.[16]

Unlike other emperors, T'ai-tsu could claim a personal knowledge of the life of a Buddhist monk. As a younger son in a poor family, he became a novice at the age of seventeen[17] in a small, and probably typical, rural temple. There he lived the life of a mendicant monk for several years.[18] The temple, Huang-chüeh Ssu, was under the direction of abbot Kao-pin, who was not only married but had children.[19] There is good reason to believe that this kind of temple, under the direction of abbots like Kao-pin, was by no means an exception to the rule. Indeed, to become a monk in the chaotic years marking the end of the Yüan usually involved motivations other than religious ones. This point is made succinctly by Wu Han, the historian of the Ming dynasty, in the following passage:

At that time it was regarded as a means of livelihood to leave the world and become a monk. Some people, it is true, did so because they thought that by becoming monks they could become buddhas. But they definitely constituted the minority. More often it was for the following reasons: they entered the monastic life either because of a guilty conscience as a result of their having done evil deeds, or to escape from the penal laws of the government, for the temple was a sanctuary beyond the reach of the secular law. More often people became monks because their families were too poor to raise their children. But once one became a monk, he could get food everywhere. He could live forever on the donations of pious men and women.[20]

T'ai-tsu's firsthand knowledge of monastic life clearly played a part in prompting him to institute new measures and reinforce old statutes in an effort to regulate Buddhism. It will be useful first to review these measures and statutes and then to determine to what extent they were in fact implemented.[21]

Limitations on the number of monasteries were imposed early in 1373. In the *Ming shih-lu* (The Veritable Record of the Ming), under the twelfth month of the sixth year of Hung-wu, it is recorded:

Right now the Emperor feels that in recent years people have believed excessively in Buddhism and Taoism. As a result, monks and priests have increased day by day. They eat without labor and there is nothing more wasteful to the national economy than this. Therefore, it has been decreed that in each prefecture (*fu*), district (*chou*), and county (*hsien*), only one large

Buddhist monastery and Taoist temple will be allowed to exist. All monks and priests are to be housed in one place, and persons with good discipline will be chosen to lead them.[22]

The purpose of this regulation was twofold: to assemble all the monks in each county into one temple to facilitate their control, and to prohibit the building of new temples, or the rebuilding of old ones destroyed in the course of war, so as to conserve human and material resources. But according to Ryūchi Kiyoshi,[23] this regulation was neither nationally applied nor enforced for more than a few years in the areas where it was applied. Geographically, the decree was carried out only in the six prefectures near the capital: Ying-tien, T'ai-p'ing, Chen-chiang, Ning-kuo, Hui-chou, and Kuang-te. Economic factors accounted for its enforcement in these areas; for, as Ryūchi points out, it was around the same time that T'ai-tsu also excused these prefectures from payment of grain taxes for four years.[24] The six prefectures had contributed heavily in grain and money to the military campaigns in the early years of T'ai-tsu's career. As a gesture of appreciation, taxes were reduced, and regulations to limit the number of temples were enforced in order to relieve the people of both the tax burden and the financial burden of supporting the temples in the area. But even within these limited areas the order was not observed for very long. Ryūchi, spot-checking the section on monasteries and temples recorded in the prefectural history of T'ai-p'ing, discovered that the same monasteries that were abolished in 1373 had been rebuilt as early as the next year.[25]

The proclamation issued in the twenty-fourth year of Hung-wu (1391) gives further proof of the ineffectiveness of the earlier decree. After lamenting the current state of the sangha it stated again that, because of devastating wars, monks had lost discipline. It suggested that henceforth officials in each prefecture, district, and county were to inspect monks under their jurisdiction, find out which monks had left their temples to live among the common people, gather all the monks together, house them in a "public monastery" (ts'ung-lin; literally, "forest"), and enforce monastic discipline.[26] This was to be institutionalized in a decree. Under the seventh month of that year the Shih-lu says, "It is decreed that when any Buddhist or Taoist builds a temple, nunnery, or monastery, if it does not come under the old quota (chiu-e), it must be destroyed." Since "old quota" (one temple per county) was reiterated, it is clear that the implementation of the 1373 decree had been less than satisfactory. That this was indeed so is confirmed by an entry in *Ta Ming hui-tien* (The Complete Institutes of the Great Ming): "In the twenty-fourth year of Hung-wu (1391) the government issued this order: in each prefecture, district, and county only one large Buddhist monastery and Taoist temple will be allowed to remain. All monks or priests must live in them."[27] The intention of this decree was similar to that of 1373: to concentrate monks or Taoist priests in one place for easy supervision.

The one large monastery that was allowed to remain was the so-called public monastery or *ts'ung-lin* (sometimes called *shih-fang ts'ung-lin*, "forest of ten directions"). This term has been traditionally contrasted with "private temple" *(chia-i yüan)*. The difference lies principally in the method for choosing the abbot. In the public monastery, the abbotship was determined by public recommendation. According to the *Ch'ih-hsiu Pai-chang ch'ing-kuei* (Pure Rules of Pai-chang, Compiled under the Imperial Order of the Yüan), "When the abbotship is vacant, the authorities must be notified, and one must wait for the order of appointment from the authorities."[28] Furthermore, the opinions of resident monks as well as lay patrons of the monastery were to be considered. Their recommendations had as much weight in the appointment of the new abbot as did orders from higher authorities. In contrast to this practice, the succession of abbots in the hereditary temple was purely a private affair; since it was owned by one particular monk, the temple was private property. When this monk died, the position of abbot passed on to one of his tonsured disciples. It has been suggested that the name *chia-i* probably originated because of the rules of succession to the abbotship: tonsured disciple A (or *chia*) preceded tonsured disciple B (or *i*).[29] T'ai-tsu's edicts abolishing monasteries were aimed mainly at the private temples.

T'ai-tsu classified the public monasteries into three types. This was what he meant when he said in his 1391 edict that Buddhism must be "classified into sects." During the Sung and Yüan dynasties there were three types of monasteries specializing in meditation *(ch'an)*, doctrine *(chiao)*, and discipline *(lü)*, respectively. This classification had always been followed in the local gazetteers.[30] T'ai-tsu dropped the classification referring to temples specializing in discipline and replaced it with a classification for those specializing in religious rituals. The change was formally announced by the Ministry of Rites in 1382.³¹ The revised classification now read *ch'an*, or meditation, *chiang*, or doctrine, and *chiao*, or practical instruction. The exact meaning of these terms becomes clear when we read the following explanation:

He who practices *ch'an* does not rely on words, but must seek to see his nature. He who practices *chiang* must understand the meanings of the various sutras, and he who practices *chiao* should know how to perform the Buddhist method of teaching the common people by means of benefiting and helping them. He extinguishes all the evil karma of the living and wipes away all past wrongs of the dead.³²

From this passage it is clear that the *chiang* spoken of here is the same as the *chiao* of former times; it referred to the temples that stressed doctrinal study. Though the term itself was retained, it was now the last category of temples; the ones that stressed *chiao*, ritual performance, were a new category. Sometimes these temples were also called *yü-chia* or yoga.³³ They specialized in the performance of Tantric rituals, conveniently summed up in the term *ching-ch'an*, namely chanting sutras *(sung-ching)* and reciting penances *(pai-ch'an);* funeral services and plenary masses *(shui-lu fa-hui),* as well as rites for seeking long life, early recovery from disease, and so on also fall under this general rubric. Because monks living in this type of temple went out to lay devotees' homes to perform ceremonies, they were called "monks responding to calls" *(ying-fu seng).*³⁴ The effect of T'ai-tsu's reclassification of Buddhist temples proved to be far-reaching in the long run and therefore more significant than his other control measures. Since monasteries stressing discipline were now replaced by those specializing in religious ritual, discipline was gradually neglected and a steady commercialization of monks took place. These two changes might very well have been under way before T'ai-tsu took action, but we can be sure that his measures intensified the process.

In the edict of 1391 the amount of compensation for monks performing rituals was also specified. Each monk who participated in a service was to be paid five hundred in cash *(wen)* per day, but the three chief monks, who had the task of striking hand gongs *(chu-ch'ing),* writing supplications *(hsieh-shu),* and calling Buddhas, bodhisattvas, and spirits to the service *(chao-ch'ing)*, were to be paid one thousand *wen* per person per day, respectively.[35] Whether this rule was in fact followed is difficult to know, but as time went on, income for performing services did indeed become a major source of the monks' livelihood. More than five hundred years after this edict, in 1934, a prominent Buddhist monk, Fa-fang (1904–1951), commented sadly on the prominence of ritualism in Chinese monasteries:

In every temple of China, although the plaque on the main gate says it is such-and-such Meditation Hall, inside the Meditation Hall one realizes that it has been changed into the Hall for Chanting Sutras and Reciting Penances *(ching-ch'an t'ang)* or the Inner Altar of the Soul Rite *(shui-lu nei-t'an)*. As for the monks living there, even though they call themselves Ch'an monks, they are simply monks specializing in chanting sutras and reciting penances *(ching-ch'an shih)*.[36]

At the same time that the new classification of monasteries was announced, the colors of robes for monks belonging to each school were also regulated. Under the twelfth month of Hung-wu, fifteenth year (1383), we read in the *Shih-lu* that "the Ch'an monk wears an ordinary brown robe, green stole, and a jade-colored cassock. The *chiang* monk [one specializing in doctrine] wears an ordinary jade-colored robe, deep red stole, and a light red cassock. The *chiao* monk [one specializing in rituals] wears an ordinary black robe, black stole, and a light red cassock."[37]

According to Ryūchi Kiyoshi's study of the monasteries of the early Ming, among the three kinds of temples, those specializing in rituals constituted the majority, as shown in local gazetters.[38] Ryūchi regarded this development as a direct result of the favorable treatment the *chiao* temples received at the hands of imperial authorities. This partiality toward *chiao* monks was strikingly evident in an edict issued in 1394:

As for the monks belonging to the two schools of *ch'an* and *chiang*, aside from traveling abroad in order to seek instruction *(yu-fang wen-tao)*, they ought to stay inside their own temples and truthfully practice their own teachings. They may not do anything else. They may not live separately, nor may they enter into cities or marketplaces. But in the case of the *yü-chia* monks, if they have old patrons and donors who ask them to perform Buddhist services, they may do so according to the set rituals. In doing so, they

teach the people to be filial sons who remember to repay the kindness of
their ancestors. They also teach people to think of their own future. In this
way the purpose of compassion is well served. People ask the monks to perform the services out of their own wishes, but not because monks beg to do
it for food and clothing. Therefore any person, be he official or common citizen, who dares to insult the monks is to be punished by the law.[39]

   This edict shows most clearly the intention behind T'ai-tsu's
reclassification of Buddhist schools. Doctrinal study and meditation,
the dual paths leading to wisdom, were always emphasized by Buddhists. But T'ai-tsu put all kinds of restrictions on the freedom of
movement of monks belonging to these schools. He accorded the
monks specializing in rituals (especially funerals for the dead) particular favor. Although there is no concrete evidence to indicate that
T'ai-tsu was so motivated, he might have argued that these monks
were to be given more freedom precisely because they were less
"Buddhist" in their commitments and training and therefore could
pose no threat to the dominant Confucian orthodoxy. In fact, their
expertise in ritual matters concerning the dead made them ideal
functionaries in Chinese family religion. What they offered could
easily be incorporated into Confucian familism: filial piety was reinforced but never challenged by Buddhist rituals for the dead. Indeed, the music, the chanting, and the paraphernalia of ritual instruments added color and solemnity to funeral or memorial
services.
   The other schools presented an entirely different problem. If
the common people were to come into close contact with monks
from these schools and discuss Buddhist doctrines or practice meditation, it was conceivable that given sufficient time they might become, if not converted, at least sympathetic to the Buddhist way of
life. Although we cannot confirm that such an argument did in fact
underlie T'ai-tsu's prohibition, he did on different occasions insist
upon the strict separation of monks from the common people. He
even raised the specter of legal prosecution to prevent inter-
mingling. Interestingly, the reason T'ai-tsu gave for such a policy was
that it protected the purity of Buddhism. A few rulings on this subject are cited below:

Monks who ought to shun the public [i.e., *ch'an* and *chiang* monks.] are not
allowed to go into cities or villages. If they use begging *(hua-yüan)* as an ex-

cuse and thereby harm Buddhism by provoking unnecessary public insults, they should be seized and handed over to the local authorities. They will then be punished for the crime of corrupting the Buddhist tradition (pai-huai tsu-feng).[40]

If an abbot or any other monk dares to communicate with officials and thereby becomes good friends, he ought to be punished severely.[41]

If the head of the family, whether he be a civil official, military man, or a common citizen, encourages his wife or daughter to offer incense at a Buddhist or Taoist temple, he is to be whipped with light bamboo forty times. When there is no husband, then the penalty is meted out to the woman herself. The abbot and gatekeeper of the said temple who fail to prevent her from entering the temple are punished with the same severity.[42]

Henceforth, when a junior scholar (hsiu-ts'ai) or people from other walks of life enter temples without sufficient reason and eat monks' food, they are to be punished by law.[43]

This form of prohibition has a long history. In the Ch'üan T'ang wen (Complete Collection of T'ang Writings) we find edicts of a similar nature issued during Hsüan-tsung's reign.[44] The reason was probably political, for monasteries could and did serve as meeting places for outlaws and rebels. Since the White Lotus and Maitreya societies had participated in the civil war at the end of the Yüan, it is possible that T'ai-tsu looked upon friendships between monks and the common people with great suspicion and that he might for this reason have tried to constrain them through legal sanctions.

T'ai-tsu's justification for this particular prohibition, however, was anything but political. He blamed the low moral caliber of the monks for the public's lack of respect. In prohibiting free communication between the monks and the public, T'ai-tsu again claimed that he was protecting the sangha's reputation by making monks "scarce." This argument was ingeniously presented in the edict issued in 1394:

There are some men of superior caliber (kao-ming chih-jen) who come to temples in order to carry on discussions with monks and propagate Buddhism. But, unfortunately, most monks are of inferior quality. As soon as some people show friendliness to them, the monks immediately start thinking about asking for donations. For this reason, people shun their company. Now if monks obey my orders, they will not bother the common people, whether the monks live in mountain retreats or regular monasteries, or travel about to seek instruction. Since they do not go into cities or villages frequently, it will be difficult for officials as well as common people to seek them out for the purpose of listening to sutras. If this is the case, good people will respect the monks. They will go where the monks are and make requests of them with burning incense and folded hands. Now is this not excellent? After this is practiced for a long time, Buddhism will certainly prosper.[45]

Limits on the Construction of Monasteries

The prohibitions against building new monasteries were repeated in succeeding reigns. For example, the same prohibition was issued in 1402, 1417, 1441, and 1445.[46] To what degree these edicts met with compliance is difficult to establish, but there is no reason to believe that they had better success than those issued during T'ai-tsu's reign. The policy of limiting the number of Buddhist monasteries was, in fact, little more than a statement of purpose. When one examines the situation in the late Ming, one finds that it was not even maintained as public policy. Chu-hung had no difficulty in rebuilding the Yün-ch'i monastery, which was located on the site of an old temple dating back to the Northern Sung and which, presumably, was not included in the ban. But other monks, notably Te-ch'ing, built many new temples without any interference from the authorities. A precedent for disregarding this prohibition was, in fact, set by several emperors themselves. Emperor Ying-tsung (during the year immediately following that in which he reissued the prohibition against rebuilding any monastery that had fallen into decay), started a large-scale rebuilding project. The Ta-pao-en Ssu and the Ta-hsing-lung Ssu of Nanking were rebuilt in 1447 and 1449, respectively. The eunuch Wang Chen played a major role in these projects. Since the emperor was young and very close to Wang, he was amenable to the latter's suggestions. This coalition, incidentally, served as a forerunner of the alliances between monks and eunuchs, and it has been suggested that, by the time of Hsien-tsung's reign (1465–1487), it had become usual for monks and eunuchs to work hand in hand.[47] Concerning the reconstruction of Ta-hsing-lung Ssu, the *Shih-lu* reports:

The eunuch Wang Chen said that the monastery was old and dilapidated, so the emperor ordered ten thousand soldiers and civilians to rebuild it. The building materials cost several tens of thousands. After it was finished, its beauty and grandeur outshone the several hundred monasteries both inside and outside the capital. . . . It was called "the number-one public monastery of the nation." The emperor personally attended the services performed by monks.[48]

Labor and expenses multiplied several times when, a few years later, Emperor Ching built the Ta-lung-fu Ssu. It is recorded that by the time the monastery was completed some nine months later, in 1453, tens of thousands of soldiers had been employed, and several hundred thousand taels of silver had been spent. When one recalls that this event took place during a national crisis and that only a few years earlier Emperor Ying-tsung had been captured by enemy forces during the debacle of the battle of Tu-mu, the lavishness of the project assumes added significance. The ban on monastery building above and beyond the established quota, to which successive emperors paid lip-service, turned out to be entirely ineffective.

During Chu-hung's lifetime, imperially sponsored building projects were carried on an unprecedented scale. First, Empress Dowager Tz'u-sheng, who was a great patroness of Buddhism, donated money from her own coffers to start the building of Tz'u-shou Ssu in 1576. Because the empress showed special interest in it, members of the imperial and other aristocratic families contributed generously to the project. The monastery took two years to complete and was reputed to have "cost a great deal of money."[49] The very next year Emperor Shen-tsung himself initiated the building of yet another monastery in Peking. This was the Wan-shou Ssu, which was said to have been even more splendid in construction than the Tz'u-shou Ssu.

We have examined the legal prohibitions against the building of new monasteries and looked at examples illustrating how this ban was at times ignored by the court itself. The apparent inconsistency suggests that the emperor's like or dislike of Buddhism usually had a more important impact on the condition of Buddhism than the political, legal, or institutional measures applied by the central government. When we examine the religious preferences of the various Ming emperors, the picture that emerges is again one of marked inconsistency and repeated change.[50]

The Yung-lo emperor, Ch'eng-tsu (r. 1403–1424), regarded the Lamaist monk Ha-li-ma (De-bshin-gśegs-pa) as his teacher, and

called himself the Son of the Buddha of the Western Heaven
(Hsi-t'ien fo-tzu). Imperial patronage of Buddhism continued until
Hsien-tsung's reign, when Taoism suddenly gained the upper hand.
Hsien-tsung showered favors on the Taoist priests Li Tzu-sheng and
Teng Ch'ang-en. The next emperor, Hsiao-tsung (r. 1488–1505),
reversed the trend by ignoring the Taoists. Buddhism once again
was heavily patronized by the court. Hsiao-tsung's successor, Wu-
tsung (r. 1506–1521), showed even more enthusiasm for Buddhism.
He studied chanting and singing with lamas and participated in
Buddhist services held inside the court. Like the Yung-lo emperor,
Wu-tsung also gave himself a religious title: The Great and Auspicious Dharma-King *(Ta-ch'ing fa-wang).* With the ascension of Shih-
tsung (r. 1522–1566), however, Taoism once again took precedence.
The emperor had absolutely no interest in Buddhism, but was an
ardent practitioner of Taoist *chai-chiao* rites. At the beginning of his
reign he adopted a proposal submitted by Chao Huang, a vice-
minister of the Ministry of Works, to scrape gold surfaces off
Buddhist statues cast during his predecessor's reign to yield 1,300
ounces of gold for the imperial coffers. During his later years he
gave his trust to the Taoist priest T'ao Chung-wen, and at T'ao's
instigation he had 2,000 catties of Buddhist relics burned. Buddhism
suffered a severe blow and reached its lowest point during the entire
Ming period. But this was not the end of the story for Buddhism,
for with the reign of the new emperor, Shen-tsung (r. 1573–1619), a
final reversal took place. It coincided almost exactly with the career
of Chu-hung.

It has already been noted that it was during the Wan-li period
that temple building approached its most lavish scale. It was also at
this time that the printing of Buddhist scriptures was undertaken in
earnest. The Tripitaka was printed and distributed to temples all
over the empire. There was also a revival of the curious practice of
ordaining young monks to serve as substitutes for the emperor,
heirs-apparent, and princes. Concerning this custom, there seemed
to exist two opinions. According to Shen Te-fu, the author of *Wan-li
yeh-huo pien* (Literary Gatherings of a Rustic Scholar of the Wan-li
Era), this was a custom inherited from the Yüan dynasty. In one
place, Shen states:

When a new emperor first ascends the throne, he immediately has a person
ordained as a monk. This is called "to leave the household life as a substi-

tute" *(tai-t'i ch'u-chia)*. The monk receives the same kind of superior treatment in food and lodging as a duke or lord. It is said that before the monk is finally chosen, he must be the one having the best fate as decided by fortunetellers.[51]

In still another passage, Shen appears to offer a different opinion. "When the emperor, the heir-apparent, and the various princes of the present reign are born, they all have young boys ordained as monks and have them serve as substitutes."[52] From this statement, it appears that the custom was practiced only during Shen-tsung's reign. Wu Han offers a second and more plausible version. In his essay about the novel *Chin-p'ing-mei* and its social background, he writes: "Substitute monks *(t'i-shen-seng)* existed for all the emperors of the Ming. The only difference during the Wan-li period was that the prestige and status of the substitute monk reached an unprecedented height."[53]

It is hard to believe that only twenty-odd years separated the period when Buddhism reached this height from the time of the burning of relics and the destruction of statues. But the contrast in treatment, though more dramatic here than in other periods, was not unique in the history of Buddhism in China. Buddhism's fortunes were always intimately tied to the personal whims and changing interests of the emperor.

Government Control of Ordination Certificates

One of the most striking differences between the Chinese sangha and its Indian counterpart was that the former had to submit to a far greater degree of government control. One concrete example of the monk's formal submission to secular authority was the institution of ordination certificates *(tu-tieh)*. In China if someone wanted to become a monk or nun, he or she had to obtain an ordination certificate issued by the Bureau of National Sacrifices of the Ministry of Rites. Only then could one shave off one's hair and formally enter a monastery. By limiting the number of certificates issued, the government could control the population of monks and nuns. Since the sangha had always enjoyed exemption from taxes and corvée labor, the state was not eager to increase its financial burdens by extending this privilege. In every dynasty the government tried to impose varying restrictions on those who sought certificates.

But on certain occasions when, either because of famine or military need, it was sorely pressed for money, the imperial house also turned to the certificates as a lucrative source of revenue. From the standpoint of the individual monk, the certificate served the same function as an identification card. He was recognized as a monk only by his possession of this particular document. Yet possession of the certificate was usually a mixed blessing, for although it assured monks of free lodging and food at any monastery, as well as lifelong exemption from taxes and corvée labor, it also limited the autonomy to which, according to the Buddhist Vinaya, monks were entitled.

Government control of the ordination certificates was first instituted during the T'ang dynasty, but regulations concerning ordination requirements and quotas varied in subsequent dynasties. Before the government decided in 747 to inaugurate a system of official ordination, private ordination (ssu-tu) was the prevailing practice.[54] After the decree of 747, private ordination was ostensibly prohibited and those who engaged in it were subject to one hundred strokes of heavy bamboo.[55] To qualify for the government's ordination certificate, a citizen (pai-i) had to be able to recite five hundred pages of Buddhist sutras.[56] This requirement was further elaborated in 955 in a decree that remained effective through the Sung. According to this decree of the Latter Chou period,[57] a person who wished to leave household life had to obtain permission from his parents and grandparents. If he was an orphan, then the permission of uncles and older brothers sufficed. Men had to be over fifteen years old. They had to be able to recite one hundred pages by heart or read five hundred pages of scripture. Women who wanted to become nuns had to be over thirteen and able to recite seventy pages of scripture by heart or able to read three hundred pages of scripture. Only after local magistrates had tested the applicant's proficiency was the request processed. Anyone caught receiving private ordination was not only forced to return to lay life, but the monk officiating at the ceremony was subject to three years penal servitude, followed by laicization. Quotas establishing the number of new monks allowed to receive ordination in each department (chou) were decided during the Sung on the basis of the number of monks already in residence. For every one hundred monks already resident in a department, the law permitted one new monk to receive ordination. For every seventy after the first hundred, one more was allowed to receive ordination.[58]

Like most bureaucratic regulations, those aimed at monastic control were not always enforced. As early as the T'ang, ordination through imperial favor *(en-tu)* and by the purchase of ordination certificates *(chin-na)* was practiced.[59] In 758, during Su-tsung's reign, people were allowed to buy the certificate for one hundred strings of cash *(pai-min)*. It is said that after the An Lu-shan rebellion, more than ten thousand Buddhist and Taoist monks purchased their certificates.[60] Although the practice of selling certificates *(mai-tieh)* started during the T'ang dynasty, it did not become national policy until the reign of Shen-tsung during the Sung. From 1067 on, the sale of ordination certificates was carried out regularly to produce badly needed revenues.[61]

The contradictory policy of restricting ordination on paper but selling certificates in actuality continued during the Ming. But the Ming rulers brought that contradiction to a new height of absurdity. On the one hand, they tightened quotas on the number of monks. On the other, they indulged in the sale of certificates on a much greater scale. Early in T'ai-tsu's reign, in the fifth year of Hung-wu (1372), the emperor issued the following edict:

Buddhist and Taoist monks are to be given ordination certificates. Right now there are under heaven more than 57,200 [Buddhist] monks and nuns, [and] Taoist priests and priestesses. They should all be given ordination certificates so that imposters can be found out. In former dynasties, ordination certificates were sold to aid the national treasury. This was called the money to avoid corvée *(mien-ting ch'ien)*. From now on we decree its abolition and we shall have this codified into law.[62]

As this edict made clear, T'ai-tsu intended to abolish the notorious custom of selling certificates and imposing religious taxes, which had been practiced in both the Sung and the Yüan dynasties. As was the case in the decision to limit the number of monasteries, the primary purpose of this edict was to enable the state to achieve firmer control over the monastic community, both quantitatively and qualitatively. In 1373 the government ruled that a person seeking ordination had to take an examination and prove his proficiency in Buddhist sutras. This was reaffirmed in 1395, when it was stated that all Buddhist and Taoist monks had to go to the capital to take the examination and that those who failed would then be laicized.[63]

Meanwhile, in 1391, in order to restrict the religious community further, the Ministry of Rites was instructed to put Buddhism and

Taoism into better order *(ch'ing-li shih-tao)*. From then on, ordination was to be performed only once every three years, and the number of Buddhist and Taoist monks was not to exceed forty per prefecture, thirty per department, and twenty per district. In order to leave household life, men had to be over forty and women over fifty.[64] In 1392, in order to test the genuineness of monks, the Central Buddhist Registration *(Seng-lu ssu)* was asked to prepare a register *(seng-chi ts'e)* listing monks residing in monasteries both inside and outside the capital. The register contained each monk's name, year of ordination, and certificate number. Once completed, it was distributed to all the monasteries in China. Whenever a monk arrived at a monastery and asked to stay, his name was checked against the register. If he was not registered, he was exposed as an imposter and sent to the capital to receive severe punishment. All those who accepted his claim were subject to the same punishment.[65]

Although the government took painstaking precautions to ensure the quality and quantity of monks, private ordination was never successfully stamped out. In 1407, about 1,800 people, said to be children of military and civilian households *(chün-ming tzu-ti)* in Chih-li and Chekiang (perhaps draft dodgers), had been secretly ordained as monks. When they came to the capital to ask for certificates, they were apprehended. The emperor ordered the Department of Military Affairs to change their status to that of soldiers and to exile them to Liao-tung and Kansu.[66] Undoubtedly this was not the only time a private ordination had taken place. The incident in question left a historical trace only because it was discovered by the authorities. Many more probably were not.

It is, however, safe to argue that before the mid-fifteenth century the government never condoned private ordination. On the contrary, it consistently reinforced T'ai-tsu's policies. Ch'eng-tsu in 1418 issued an edict reaffirming the previous quotas and adding a few new requirements. Except for provisions lowering age limits, the new requirements were no different from those applied during the Sung dynasty:

Henceforth those who desire to become monks may not exceed forty per prefecture, thirty per department, and twenty per district. One must be over fourteen but under twenty. He must have his parents' permission. After having reported to the magistrate and been recommended by his neighbors, he may go to a monastery to study under a teacher. After five years, when he is well versed in the scriptures, he may go to the Bureau of Buddhist Affairs for examination. If he is proved to be proficient in the scriptures, only then is he given an ordination certificate. If he cannot pass the examination, then he is returned to lay life. If his parents are unwilling, if there is no other son or grandson to serve the parents or grandparents, a person is not allowed to leave household life. If anyone is over thirty or forty years of age, has previously been a monk but later returned to lay life, is an escaped convict, or has been tattooed for committing some crime, he will not be allowed to leave household life.[67]

As we have seen, T'ai-tsu set the age limit for people who wanted to become monks and nuns at over forty and fifty, respectively. Ch'eng-tsu changed this restriction to read above fourteen and below twenty for monks (age limits for nuns were not given). We are not told whether this regulation superseded or complemented T'ai-tsu's. But despite Ch'eng-tsu's efforts, private ordination continued to be a vexing problem. In 1435 another imperial edict was issued prohibiting monks from shaving off their hair secretly *(ssu-tzu tsan-t'i)*.[68] This edict referred to private ordination. According to the procedure of the Chinese sangha, the first step on the path to becoming a monk was to obtain parental and official permission, to find a monastery, and to be received as a postulant *(t'ung-hsing)*. After a few years' study, during which one kept one's hair, one had to become familiar with the Buddhist scriptures. The next step was to apply for an ordination certificate. By demonstrating that he possessed the required knowledge, one signaled his readiness to take the third step and have his hair shaved off. This procedure was disrupted by anyone who simply shaved off his hair and assumed the appearance of a monk without further ado. As the practice of private ordination increased, it became more difficult to prevent undesirable elements from entering the monastic community. In 1436, investigating censors of the thirteen circuits memorialized the throne with this observation:

Within the monasteries and temples of the capital, there are criminals, artisans, and others desiring to escape from military service, who secretly shaved off their hair to become Buddhist and Taoist monks. There are also women who, because of family disputes, have left their parents or husbands and blatantly become nuns. Moreover, they do not observe monastic rules but give public lectures in temples at festivals or on the first and the last days of the month. Several thousand men and women are often attracted to attend. They gather at dusk and disperse at dawn. Since they corrupt public morals, we beg you to order the Censorate to prohibit this.[69]

In two very important respects, the Ching-t'ai era (1450–1456) marked a crucial turning point. Before this time, the government issued ordination certificates free of charge and generally observed the quotas set down in previous edicts. After this time, neither was true. As we mentioned earlier, from the beginning of the Ming, ordination was held once every three years, and a definite quota was set for each prefecture, department, and district. Since there were 147 prefectures, 277 departments, and 1,145 districts, the total number of monks permitted to receive ordination should have been 37,090. However, in the second year of Ching-t'ai (1451), the emperor suspended the rule restricting ordination to once every three years. At the same time, the eunuch T'ai-hsing, acting on an order from the empress, had more than 50,000 Buddhist and Taoist monks ordained. This was only the beginning; during Hsien-tsung's reign, there was a further escalation. In 1477, 100,000 monks were ordained; in 1487, it was 200,000.[70]

The first government sale of ordination certificates also occurred during the Ching-t'ai era. Within a short span of four years, the government repeated such sales three times (in 1451, 1453, and 1454). The immediate cause for the first sale was relief for a famine in Szechuan. The left vice-minister of the Ministry of Justice, Lo Chi, memorialized the throne saying that if a person could contribute five piculs of rice and transport it to Kuei-chou, he should be able to receive an ordination certificate. His suggestion was apparently accepted. The next two sales were also occasioned by economic need.[71] When this policy was first carried out, it was regarded as an emergency measure. Once undertaken, however, it offered a convenient precedent. In subsequent years, whenever there was a famine, the government repeatedly resorted to the sale of certificates. But at this early stage, there was still some semblance of governmental control. Theoretically at least, the government knew the name of the person to whom it sold the certificate, for the practice was called "ordination certificate with name" (*chi-ming tu-tieh*). Starting with Hsientsung's reign, however, the situation got increasingly out of control. In 1484, 10,000 blank certificates (*k'ung-ming tu-tieh*) were given to the grand coordinator and the censor-in-chief of Shansi and Shensi. In exchange for one certificate a person had to contribute ten piculs of grain to areas suffering from famine. In the following month of the same year 60,000 certificates were sold for twelve ounces of silver apiece in the thirteen provincial administrative offices. The number of Buddhist and Taoist monks ordained reached 370,000, prompting one official to remark that "at present monks are about half our population."[72] In this instance, the government did not even bother to record the buyer's name.

As Ryūchi Kiyoshi has carefully documented, government control of monastic life underwent a steady decline from Hsien-tsung's time onward. Not only did the government drop any pretention of demanding proof of an applicant's suitability, but it also indulged in indiscriminate sale of certificates. As the years passed, the price went up and the procedure was made simpler. During Wu-tsung's reign, the price for a certificate was quoted in silver instead of rice (eight to ten ounces of silver bought a certificate at this time). The substitution of silver for rice continued in subsequent reigns. Although the next emperor, Shih-tsung, was hostile to Buddhism, he was not at all averse to the sale of certificates. In 1540, a few years after Chu-hung was born, a new regulation went into effect. Now if a person desired to become a monk but did not live in the capital, he could deposit ten ounces of silver at the provincial administrative office. He did not even have to go to the capital.[73]

This procedure was further clarified in a 1555 edict that contained the following provisions: A person who wanted to become a monk was to pay the necessary amount of money to the district, departmental, or prefectural offices. At the end of the year these offices were to compose a register to be sent, together with receipts, to the Ministry of Revenue, which would then issue certificates (hao chih) made out to the purchasers. With such certificates, they or others could go to the Ministry of Rites to have them formally filed as ordination certificates.[74] According to this, it appears that the purchaser did not have to go to the capital himself, but could get his certificate by proxy. This impression is confirmed by a 1573 ruling which said that the Ministry of Rites could print blank ordination certificates (k'ung-t'ou tu-tieh) and distribute them to different places for sale. If anyone chose to come to the capital, he could do so and pay five ounces of silver to the Ministry of Revenue to get a certificate. After that, he could go to the Ministry of Rites to apply for a formal ordination certificate.[75]

This last ruling remained in effect until the end of the dynasty. When the sale of certificates was institutionalized in this way, anyone who could pay the price had no difficulty in becoming a monk. All the qualifications and quota limitations, which the two earlier emperors had set out so elaborately, were set aside. It was up to the abbots of individual monasteries to keep up whatever standards there were. As we will see in chapter VIII, Chu-hung set down specific requirements for people who sought to stay at the Yün-ch'i monastery as postulants or who wished to receive ordination and the precepts. In most cases, the requirements he set were similar to the earlier government regulations; in other cases, they were even stricter. When the government gave up its attempt to control the quality and quantity of monks, the monastic community had to assume responsibility for self-examination and self-criticism. In a curious fashion, autonomy was finally restored to the sangha.

Monk-Officials

The institution of the monk-official *(seng-kuan)* had a long history. Traditionally, Yao Hsing of the Later Ch'in dynasty (384–417) was credited with its establishment. Ch'i-sung (d. 1072), the Sung Buddhist master, traced the evolution of monk-officials as follows:

The practice of appointing *seng-cheng* [monk regulators] was not an old one. It started with the Later Ch'in. The next four dynasties, Sung [420–478], Ch'i [479–501], Liang [502–556], and Ch'en [557–587], all followed the practice of the Later Ch'in. The Western Wei [535–554], the Eastern Wei [534–549], the Northern Ch'i [550–577], and the Northern Chou [557–581] abolished the Ch'in system but substituted *seng-t'ung* [monk governors]. The Sui dynasty [581–617] followed this practice, but the T'ang [618–906] replaced it with the establishment of *seng-lu* [directors of the Buddhist registry]. The present dynasty [Sung] followed this system. In the two capitals there are *seng-lu* and in the various prefectures, *seng-cheng*.[76]

In another place, Ch'i-sung expressed his dissatisfaction and questioned the rationale for monk-officials. He also remarked that this was an innovation started some five hundred years after the introduction of Buddhism into China, giving a date somewhat later than the one usually given.[77]

> The control of monks did not exist in ancient times, but was due to the wish of the tyrant Chou [Emperor Wu of the Northern Chou, who reigned 561–577]. Monks avoid the secular world and live apart from the four classes of people [scholars, peasants, artisans, and merchants]. To control monks by bureaucratic means is to treat them as ordinary subjects. In the time of our Sage [Shakyamuni?] monastic laws were used to rule monks, and secular laws were used to rule ordinary people. Each was ruled by different laws, and to control monks with secular laws was something unheard of.[78]

This feeling of resentment toward the institution of monk-officials was typical among Buddhist monks after the T'ang, for the T'ang dynasty was a turning point in its development. Before the T'ang, the degree of bureaucratization was comparatively low, and a certain amount of autonomy was enjoyed by the Buddhist sangha. Except for grave crimes such as murder, monks were subject only to the judgment of monk-officials, who used monastic laws, not state statutes, in passing sentences. We find that in the Northern Ch'i dynasty, there was a monk-official with the title *tuan-shih 'sha-men* (the monk who deliberates cases), whose job was to judge erring monks.[79] Starting with the T'ang dynasty, monk-officials had only nominal juridical authority. Except for minor infractions of monastic rules, in which case the abbot of the monastery had the right to mete out punishment, monks who committed crimes against civilians were liable to civil prosecution. The monastic order no longer enjoyed its former special privilege of extraterritoriality vis-à-vis the central authority.[80]

The T'ang dynasty was decisive for the institutionalization of monk-officials in other aspects as well. It was during the T'ang that the number, title, and duties of monk-officials of both the central and the local levels were first formalized. In the beginning, Yao Hsing named only four monk-officials. The highest post was the *seng-cheng*, who was supposed to supervise the entire sangha. He held a post equivalent to a *shih-chung* (attendant to the emperor) and occupied the third degree in the civil service hierarchy. He was assisted by the *yüeh-chung* (the one who pleases the sangha), whose function was like a general manager of Buddhist affairs. He had a grade lower than that of the *seng-cheng*. Under these two, there were two *seng-lu* (monk recorders), whose job was to keep a record of affairs relating to the sangha as well as to take note of translation projects and other important events. All four positions were filled by monks. They received government salaries and were given carriages and servants by the state.[81] There were no monk-officials on the local level.

During the Wei dynasty officers of individual monasteries were first created. They were the so-called three principals: *san-kang*, which comprised the *shang-tso*, "superior"; the *ssu-chu*, "rector"; and the *wei-no*, "precentor." These offices, whose exact titles sometimes varied, have continued to exist until the present day.[82] Generally speaking, the superior, who was the highest of the triad, was to be a monk of seniority noted for his learning and virtue. He was the head of the monastery. The rector took care of the daily affairs related to the monastery as a whole, while the precentor was responsible for matters related only to the monks.

Throughout the early years of the T'ang dynasty the three principals were the only monk-officials; the government did not create any other positions.[83] During the early T'ang monks and nuns had been put under the jurisdiction of the Bureau of Ceremonies for Foreigners *(Hung-lu-ssu)*, but the Empress Wu in 694 changed this and put them under the control of the Bureau of Sacrifices *(Tz'u-pu)*. This signaled a change of attitude toward the monastic community, for whereas before monks and nuns were seen as foreigners, now they were regarded as no different from other Chinese subjects. However, this did not stabilize the status of Buddhists in China once and for all. In later periods, they were again shifted back and forth between the two offices.[84] The decision reflected the emperor's general attitude toward Buddhism. Even as late as the Sung, shifts and changes still occurred.[85]

During the reign of T'ai-tsung (763–779), special monk-officials were created. They were called "commissioners of good works" *(kung-te shih)* and were in charge of the entire Buddhist community. All things having to do with ordination requirements, such as permission to enter monastic life, examination of the proficiency of an applicant, granting of the ordination certificate, and so on, were theoretically under their jurisdiction. They stood between the Bureau of Sacrifices and the sangha. In 779, after Tai-tsung's death, the office was divided into three positions—a commissioner of good works for the left part of Ch'ang-an, one for the right part of Ch'ang-an, and one for the eastern capital of Lo-yang.[86] These positions, however, were not always filled by monks. We are told by the Sung monk Tsan-ning (d. 996), who wrote the *Ta Sung seng-shih lüeh* (Brief History of the Sangha in the Sung Dynasty), that frequently eunuchs or military commanders who had made special contributions to the state were given these positions as an imperial favor.[87] This practice differed sharply from earlier times, when monks were the sole appointees to the office of monk-official.

Around the beginning of the ninth century two more central monk-officials were created. These were the directors of Buddhist registration for the left and right parts of Ch'ang-an *(tso-yu-chieh seng-lu)*. The positions were filled by monks, who were also said to be in charge of the entire monastic community in their area.[88] They were under the nominal supervision of the commissioners of good works, who usually held only honorary titles but did not carry real authority or have real functions. The directors of the Buddhist registration had the actual duty of overseeing the Buddhist community.[89]

The Japanese pilgrim Ennin (793–864), who visited China from 838 to 847, made an entry in his diary in 839 describing the hierarchy of monk-officials as he knew it at that time:

As a rule in China there are three categories [of Buddhist officers]: ecclesiarchs [the directors of Buddhist registration] sacrists, and monastery supervisors *[chien-ssu]*. Ecclesiarchs control the monasteries of the whole land and regulate Buddhism. Sacrists control only the area of jurisdiction of a single government-general, and monastery supervisors are limited to a single monastery. Aside from these there are also monastic officers *(san-kang)* and the monastery stewards *(k'u-ssu)*.[90]

According to Ennin, by the mid-T'ang there were monk-officials on the central and the local levels. This system was also followed in the Sung dynasty.[91] However, the division between central and local Buddhist offices was more theoretical than actual, for the duties and functions of monk-officials of the two levels coincided to a large degree. It was often difficult to tell the exact relationship between them. For example, although the directors of Buddhist registration were supposed to nominate the local directors, in actual practice, as

Ennin indicated in one anecdote, it was a civil official (the minister of state) who made the nomination.[92] By the Sung dynasty, the central directors had only nominal control over the sangha. In fact, they had a say only in affairs relating to the monasteries within the capital.[93]

Monk-Officials during the Ming

One of the very first administrative measures undertaken by T'ai-tsu of the Ming dynasty on assuming the throne was to install officials to control the religious communities. In the first month of the first year of Hung-wu (1368), he set up the Shan-shih-yüan (Buddhist Worthies Department) at the T'ien-chieh Ssu in Nanking to take charge of all affairs relating to the Buddhist sangha. He also set up the Hsüan-chiao-yüan (Taoist Department) to supervise the Taoist community.[94] We know the titles of the four officers of the Buddhist Worthies Department, and a monk named Hui-t'an, abbot of the T'ien-chieh Ssu, headed the list.[95] Although the details of their jobs were unclear, their main duties were to appoint and dismiss abbots of famous public monasteries as well as to punish monks who had committed crimes. But this first attempt to institute monk-officials in the Ming was short-lived. It seems that when Hui-t'an retired in the following year, the system again collapsed. It is unclear when the Buddhist Worthies Department was abolished,[96] nor is it known when the Central Buddhist Registration (*Seng-lu-ssu*) was set up to take its place. Nevertheless, by 1383 it was already in existence, for an entry concerning the officers of the Registration together with the definition of their duties is found in the *Shih-lu* under this year.[97]

According to the 1383 regulation, the Central Buddhist Registration had jurisdiction over monks living in the capital and those living in other localities. There were eight monk-officials in the capital: left and right *shan-shih* (worthies), whose rank was sixth grade; left and right *ch'an-chiao* (instructors) whose rank was the sub-sixth grade; left and right *chiang-ching* (lecturers on sutras), whose rank was the eighth grade; and finally left and right *chüeh-i* (enlighteners), whose rank was the sub-eighth grade. On the local level, at first there was to be a Prefectural Buddhist Registration (*Seng-kang-ssu*) in each prefecture manned by one supervisor (*tu-kang*) and one deputy supervisor (*fu-tu-kang*), a Subprefectural Buddhist Registration *(Seng-cheng-ssu)* in each subprefecture manned by one regulator *(seng-cheng)*, and a County Buddhist Registration *(Seng-hui-ssu)* in each county manned by one coordinator *(seng-hui)*. The supervisor was assigned a sub-ninth grade, while from the deputy supervisor downward the officers were unclassified *(wei ju-liu)*. But some of the local officers existed in name only. Only the Prefectural Buddhist Registration was ordered to be set up in the latter part of 1383; the subprefectural and county registrations were deemed unnecessary and were never established.[98]

The officers of the Central Buddhist Registration not only received administrative ranks, but from 1342 on they also received stipends. Although a worthy received a monthly stipend of ten *tan* of grain, those for an instructor, lecturer, and enlightener were eight, six and a half, and six *tan,* respectively. On the local level, a supervisor received five *tan,* but there was no stipend for monk-officials from deputy supervisor downward.[99]

The duties of the monk-officials in the capital were carefully defined. The left worthy was responsible for supervising meditation, study of *kung-an,* and general religious practices. The Right Worthy oversaw the work of the seven other officers in the registration and presided over the examination of monks seeking ordination certificates. The two instructors assisted in the supervision of meditation. The two lecturers took care of donors and explained Buddhist teachings to them. The duty of the two enlighteners was to govern monks according to monastic discipline and punish a wrongdoer whose crime was strictly intramural (a quarrel with another monk). When a monk committed a civil or criminal offense against society at large, he had to be handed over to the regular civil authorities, for this was beyond the jurisdiction of the monk-official. The duties of the local monk-officials were not as clearly defined as those of the higher ones.

When the capital was in Nanking, the Central Buddhist Registration was situated within the T'ien-chieh Ssu, which was the primary public monastery in the city. Monk-officials were usually officers of this monastery. For instance, the left worthy was the superior *(shou-tso)*, the lecturer could be the guest prefect *(chih-k'o)*, and the enlightener the treasurer *(chien-ssu)*. Although the monk-officials appeared to hold independent positions, in fact the monastic officers of T'ien-chieh Ssu held these positions concurrently. After the capi-

tal was moved to Peking, the registration was again located in a great
monastery, most probably the Ching-shou Ssu.[100] The same arrangement held true for the Prefectural Registration; it was also usually
located in the largest or the most famous monastery in a prefecture.

The efficiency of the monk-officials in the Ming was highly
questionable. As with T'ai-tsu's other measures directed at Buddhism, the design was more impressive than its implementation.
Monk-officials were intended as intermediaries between the government and the sangha. They were supposed to rule the monks as del-
egates from the government, and they were thus accountable to the
government. Another attempt on T'ai-tsu's part to achieve accountability may be seen in the curious and short-lived institution of the
chen-chi-tao-jen (the man of the Way who takes care of the land with
buildings on it).[101] The Ministry of Rites was ordered to make a
proclamation that in every large monastery in the country there
should be a *chen-chi-tao-jen* who took care of the *chen-chi-pu* (record
of land with buildings on it), paid land taxes for the monastery, and
served generally as its representative. He was the only monk permitted to have any dealings with the government. If there were any
questions or difficulties, the monks of the monastery were to address
themselves to him; no one was allowed to bypass him and go to the
local authorities directly.[102] But this policy was soon discontinued,
because someone who acted as the *chen-chi-tao-jen* had abused his
power and maltreated his fellow monks.[103]

Like the *chen-chi-tao-jen,* the institution of monk-official was primarily designed to facilitate bureaucratic control. Monks were seg-
regated from the population at large and especially barred from
any contact with government officials. If this system functioned ideally, the monk-officials would serve as administrators governing the
total monastic population. The government could keep a watchful
eye on all monks simply by holding the monk-officials responsible.
At the same time, government officials with orthodox Confucian
views could be protected from the possible undesirable influence of
frequent exposure to monks in general.

Although the office of monk-official had a much longer life
than that of the *chen-chi-tao-jen,* its record was by no means more
successful. Whatever functions monk-officials may have performed
in the early Ming, they stopped having any real effect after Ying-
tsung's time in the mid-fifteenth century. As the sale of ordination

certificates gained momentum, the sale of this office also became a profitable business. According to the *Shih-lu,* the going price for an office in 1482 was 120 ounces of silver or 100 *tan* of grain. The number of monk-officials also increased rapidly. During the Ch'eng-hua reign (1465–1487), the rate of increase was phenomenal. In 1486 there were ninety-eight monk-officials instead of the original eight stipulated for the Central Buddhist Registration. The number rose to 120 in the next reign and finally reached 182 in the early Chia-ching (1522–1566).[104] The government from time to time tried to reduce their numbers, but it was not until the Wan-li reign (1573–1619) that they were finally reduced to four (one left enlightener and three right enlighteners).

As the number of monk-officials increased, the nature of their offices also changed considerably. Instead of having real administrative power over monasteries and monks, the title of a monk-official gradually came to denote only some dubious honor. In fact, an abbot of a famous monastery was often far more powerful and prestigious. Examples of this change may be found in the following two cases. During the early Ming, in 1388, monk Hung-tao, who was the left worthy at the time, was entrusted with the power to choose the new abbot if the abbotship should become vacant in a great monastery in the capital, such as the Ling-ku, T'ien-chieh, Neng-jen, or Chi-ming Ssu. The qualifications for the abbotship were strict observance of monastic discipline and a good knowledge of Buddhist scripture. The left worthy had the power to examine candidates from all over the country. If he did not find a suitable person, he could leave the post vacant.[105]

This was no longer the case by the late Ming.

According to Shen Te-fu's (1578–1642) description of some abbots in Nanking during the Wan-li reign, as given in his *Wan-li yeh-hu-pien* (Literary Gatherings of a Rustic Scholar of the Wan-li Era), the situation had altered markedly. It is true that abbots still had to be examined by the Ministry of Rites, although no longer by the left worthy. But Shen was most impressed by the power, the glory, and the worldly sophistication of the abbots, and any hint that monk-officials were important is absent from his account. It is also interesting to note that the Buddhist elite now paid more attention to literary accomplishments than to religious cultivation. They were consciously modeling themselves on the Confucian literati. According to Shen:

Monks in the two capitals [Peking and Nanking] are under the supervision of the Ministry of Rites. Whenever an abbotship becomes vacant, the director of the Ministry of Rites examines the monks in these areas. The one who comes out on top fills the vacant post. Formerly I visited the three big monasteries in Nanking and found the abbots very elegant. This is probably because the three monasteries of Ling-ku, T'ien-chieh, and Pao-en were the largest in the area, and the monks living there number several thousand. The abbot of Ling-ku Ssu was barely twenty. His appearance was very handsome and delicate. The examination papers he showed me were no different from those of a Confucian scholar, being composed in "eight-legged" style. There were also elegant poems and novel verses. The titles of these compositions usually were taken from the Diamond and the Sūraṅgama sutras. The monk who passed the examination also called the director of the Ministry of Rites his teacher *(tso-shih)* and addressed his fellow monks who took the examination with him as "classmates" *(pi-yin)*. This is all very amusing.[106]

CHAPTER SEVEN

≈≈

Internal Causes of
Monastic Decline in the
Ming Dynasty

IN THE previous chapter, we discussed some factors that historians of institutional Buddhism have suggested contributed to the decline of the sangha. Yet one must accept their explanations with great caution. For one thing, most government measures did not originate in the Ming, but were reiterations of earlier policies. If government control were the sole cause, evidence of monastic decline should have emerged long before the Ming, and the notoriety of the sangha should have elicited about the same amount of concern in the Sung as in the Ming. But, although complaints about the sangha were heard in the Sung, they were neither so frequent nor so vociferous as during the Ming. Indeed, the Sung period has been looked upon as the mature age of the Ch'an school, and many Confucian scholars were impressed by the lofty behavior of Ch'an monks. Also, except for the sale of ordination certificates, which definitely did continue to adulterate the composition of the sangha, attempts to limit the number of monasteries and to control monks with monk-officials failed to accomplish the purposes for which they were designed. Even in the case of the sale of certificates, had the monastic order itself been stronger, it should have been capable of either transforming bad elements into acceptable monks or of expelling undesirables. If the monastic order had both well-established standards of discipline and the power to enforce them, corruption induced by factors external to the sangha itself might not have been so devastating.

As Chu-hung and other monks saw so accurately, the source of decay came as much from within as from without. This inner decay, which was far more difficult to combat, was helped along by the influx of unqualified and uncommitted monks. In order to reverse this trend, Chu-hung prescribed internal reform. Rather than demand that the government stop the sale of certificates or raise the requirements for ordination, he demanded that the monastic community reexamine itself. Chu-hung gave eloquent testimony to the spiritual and moral stagnation of his fellow monks during the late Ming. Roughly speaking, we may divide his criticisms into three categories: abuses of Ch'an practice, neglect of discipline, and secularization.

Abuses of Ch'an Practice

Ever since the Ch'an school had become predominant during the Northern Sung, Buddhism had been virtually synonymous with Ch'an Buddhism. It was the monk proficient in Ch'an meditation and successful in gaining enlightenment who was the object of universal admiration. Scriptural understanding and devotional acts, though encouraged by some monks and pursued by others, could not match the mastery of Ch'an meditation in the estimation of the general public as well as the monks themselves. By Chu-hung's time, it was no longer a question of whether one should engage in scriptural study or Pure Land devotionalism instead of Ch'an. For Chu-hung, the question was how to combine Pure Land devotion, scriptural study, and monastic discipline *with* Ch'an meditation. Never for one moment did he belittle or discourage Ch'an practice. Chu-hung's innovation lay in the fact that he saw compatibility between Buddha invocation and traditional Ch'an meditation.

Despite its popularity, the Ch'an school of the Ming was quite different from that of the T'ang and the Sung. Since the Ch'an experience was, and still is, basically nonintellectual, nothing was more fatal to its spiritual efficacy than taking an intellectual approach to it. Ch'an experiences could not be verbalized. The utterances of a monk after achieving enlightenment were an immediate and spontaneous expression of his spiritual awakening. They were not literary compositions that required the intermediation of deliberate thought. Unfortunately, as time went on, the sayings of Ch'an masters were gradually collected, memorized, and what is worse, imitated. There were *kung-an* "public cases," published in collected works, the more famous being the *Pi-yen lu* (Record of the Blue Cliff) and the *Wu-men kuan* (The Gateless Gate).[1] By Chu-hung's time, people interested in Ch'an were doing things diametrically opposed to the original spirit of Ch'an, and he was understandably horrified by them:

The decline of Ch'an Buddhism is the fault of people who talk about it in order to make clear its principles. How can I say that they corrupted it? I say that because the sutra, Vinaya, and shastra all have a conceptual aspect *(yu i-lu)*. Unless we talk about it, it cannot be made clear. But Ch'an does not have any theory. The more one talks about it, the more obscure it becomes. The best way is to let a person meditate and achieve [the truth] by himself.[2]

More seriously at fault than those engaging in pedantic discussions of Ch'an were people who liked to show off their spiritual attainments by making up clever phrases:

The ancient worthies used to instruct beginners by saying that as long as you could present an appropriate "turning phrase" *(chuan-yü)*,[3] it would be unnecessary for anyone to fathom your concentration, wisdom, eloquence, or magical powers. Now a beginner, upon hearing this, starts to learn to compose clever phrases day and night. This is really a mistake. The phrase must naturally flow from genuine enlightenment. If a person seeks it from the scripture or recorded dialogues of former sages, and imitates them with clever ingenuity, it is no more than scratching an itch from outside one's boots.[4]

As Chu-hung makes clear in the following passage, quite a number of people were expert in creating new "public cases." Since there was no genuine enlightenment behind it, they were merely charlatans sporting counterfeit testimonials:

Nowadays, there are people who do not have any enlightenment in their hearts, but because they are quick-witted and clever with words, they sneak a look at various recorded dialogues and imitate some of the phrases. They only value the absurdity and strangeness of the phrasing. As long as the phrases can delight and startle the ordinary people, they are satisfied. For instance, you have such creations as these: "The third watch occurs at high noon, the sun rises at midnight." "Waves rage on top of the mountains, dust gathers at the bottom of the sea." "Beat him [the Buddha] to death with a club and feed him to a dog." "Is the patriarch here? Call him over to wash my feet." They open their mouths to say all kinds of nonsense. People who do not know better praise them with one voice and frequently imitate them. To talk about wisdom foolishly and vainly is indeed a great sin.[5]

The fad of composing clever, enigmatic phrases that passed as "public cases" naturally served to discredit the serious pursuit of Ch'an practice. The real victim, however, was the monk who engaged in such vain tasks himself. For without a genuine and often tortuous process of cultivation, no one could ever achieve lasting enlightenment. As much as Chu-hung was annoyed by the nonsense these monks produced, he was even more horrified by the facile and reckless attitude they took toward religious cultivation as such. They made a caricature of the Ch'an enterprise. What in fact they were saying was that there was nothing to enlightenment. One needed only to be clever, to glance occasionally at some recorded saying of former Ch'an monks, and one would easily arrive at the desired goal. This was untrue, and as Chu-hung tirelessly attempted to demonstrate, Ch'an was a painfully long and difficult path to take. There was no shortcut to real enlightenment. One had to seek teachers, work ceaselessly on meditation, and—most important—be consumed by commitment so great that no amount of physical hardship would become an obstacle to progress.

But monks of his own time fell short of this ancient ideal in many ways. First of all, they would not exert themselves to seek out teachers:

When the ancients had the slightest doubt in their minds, they would not cheat themselves, but had to find out the answer from a teacher. Thus they did not regard going a long distance as a tiresome task. But nowadays people are otherwise. If it is for seeking out a teacher and asking about the truth, they knit their brows even if they have to cover only the distance of a frog's leap. But if it is for fame and profit, they can easily start a journey of ten thousand *li*.[6]

Second, many monks had the mistaken notion that physical hardship was not only undesirable but also unnecessary. They made an artificial distinction between themselves as the elite and other monks who engaged in physical labor. As an elite, they wanted to be waited on hand and foot. Like the Confucian literati, most of them disdained menial tasks that required physical exertion:

[Speaking of people in former times] while they managed various affairs, they were not deterred from study. While they worked in the kitchen, they also went into the master's room to discuss the Way *(ts'an-tao)*. They say, "I am only interested in cultivating the Way *(pan-tao-che)*, unlike those other monks who manage mundane affairs *(hsing-wu-che)*." How different they are from the ancients![7]

Young people nowadays won't touch water with their ten fingers, and nothing deserves their concern. After holding begging bowls, they complain about sore arms. When they have to carry a broom, they say that their backs hurt. If someone advises them to work hard on their cultivation in the early morning or at night, they say: "My health is poor and I am often sick." If you ask them further, they say: "The stupid use their bodies, but the wise use their minds. The stupid cultivate blessedness, but the wise cultivate wisdom." If this were true, then both Kāśyapa and the Sixth Patriarch were stupid men, for the former engaged in austerities *(t'ou-t'o)*, and the latter worked as a rice-pounder.[8]

Due to their arrogance and indolence, few of Chu-hung's contemporaries practiced the time-honored Ch'an customs of visiting teachers everywhere *(ts'an-fang)* and touring on foot *(hsing-chiao)*. A Ch'an monk, when first embarked on his career, was usually advised to visit various masters in the country until he found one who could help him. In his search for the ideal teacher, he toured the country on foot, stayed at different monasteries, and in the process gained physical stamina and spiritual maturity. Although the Ch'an school did not emphasize scriptural learning, the importance of a teacher was recognized from the beginning. A teacher might not impart any theoretical knowledge about Ch'an Buddhism, but he did give practical guidance on meditation and steer his students on an appropriate course. He plotted programs of cultivation, watched over the student's progress, and authenticated the final breakthrough.

Moreover, the relationship between the teacher and student was a subtle one. Temperamental and psychological compatibility between the two was essential if the student was to benefit from the teacher. As numerous anecdotes in the *Ching-te ch'uan-teng lu* (The Transmission of the Lamp) and other Ch'an works testify, finding the right teacher was often the first step in the process leading to enlightenment. In the first interview, one might well be subjected to intolerable humiliation, to jeering and taunting from one's teacher. This was usually a ploy for testing a student's temperament, determination, and endurance before the latter would be accepted. If a student discovered that after some time under one teacher he was still getting nowhere, either his teacher would recommend another master or he himself asked leave to seek out another teacher. Thus the search for a right teacher was a two-way process and a crucial first step in Ch'an training.

Chu-hung repeatedly warned his fellow monks that they should never rest before they reached the state of enlightenment. The best way was to follow the traditional method of traveling widely to test and temper themselves. We are told what monks in former times were like: "Before their understanding reached clarity, they sought out teachers regardless of the distance. No sooner had they left one monastery than they entered another. They traveled far and wide, and never had the time to rest. Only after they attained enlightenment did they choose a site near the water or under the trees to nurture the embryo of sagehood *(sheng-t'ai)*. [9] Compared to this earlier model, how did his contemporaries fare? Chu-hung looked around him and saw very different practices indeed:

As soon as they join the monastic order they can live in a nicely established monastery. They can have everything they desire. Just like sons of a millionnaire, they have no knowledge of the sufferings of the common people. Even though they might be more intelligent than ordinary people, since they do not engage in study tours but arrogantly take pride in themselves behind closed doors, they retain their basic ignorance. [10]

On the other hand, one could go to the other extreme. Chu-hung said he knew some monks who, though shunning the luxury and comfort of monastery living, ended up in an equally deplorable state when they failed to seek instruction. Chu-hung cited the example of a monk named Hsing-k'ung from the Ssu-chou temple in Kiangsu. Probably imitating the famous example of Master Kao-feng of the Yüan, This monk shut himself up in a hut on Mt. Kao-feng and sat in confinement *(pi-kuan)*. Since he did not have enough spiritual maturity, he went crazy and eventually died. The reason, according to Chu-hung, was that he had faith but did not possess wisdom:

When a person has just left a burning house [the househouse life], he should not go into retreat right away. If he does so, he cannot know his mistakes, nor can he dispel his doubts. He may want to climb higher, but in truth he will fall lower. . . . I have seen quite a few beginners in Buddhist cultivation who built huts in some remote mountains and lived there alone. They regarded themselves as lofty and refined. Although they may not all go mad in the end, I am sure that they all lose much benefit. [11]

Kung-ku Lung, an early Ming monk, had already deplored the practice of sealed confinement and regarded it as a corruption of the Ch'an tradition:

During the T'ang and Sung dynasties, there was no such thing as sealed confinement. It was only in the Yüan dynasty that people constructed confinement houses *(kuan-fang)* and sat there waiting for enlightenment. Nowadays people imitate this custom. But if you are genuinely interested in awakening, you should not sit in a confinement house, where food and robes are prepared for you, and pass your days at ease. Moreover, sometimes companions and lay patrons drop by for a visit. You then gossip for half a day in the confinement house. Is this the way of true cultivation? Master Kao-feng sat in the "cave of death" *(ssu-kuan)*, but he did it after awakening in order to nurture the Way. Unlike people of today, the ancients treasured every moment of time. Wasting not even the time to cut their fingernails, they sought enlightenment regardless of the cost to life and limb.[12]

Neglect of Discipline

Although Chu-hung considered it vital to study under a good teacher, he thought it extremely difficult to find many monks who could qualify as teachers. Therefore, along with his advice on undertaking study tours, he also impressed upon his fellow monks the necessity of choosing the right teacher:

When a monk lives in the age of the True Law, he should never make discriminations in regard to people. But when a monk lives in this age of the Degenerate Law, he should fear nothing more than failing to make discriminations in regard to people. The reason is that in this last age of the Law, good and bad elements mingle together. If one does not make a right judgment but chooses the wrong person, if one regards him who is heterodox as orthodox, if one becomes friendly with him whom he ought to avoid and avoids him whom he ought to be friendly with, one will surely become the same as one's teacher. Furthermore, in future lives he will always be a companion to Māra. Is it then not apparent that one has to be watchful in seeking out a teacher?[13]

The cause for such concern had to do with the general lack of discipline among the monastic community. Even though what was under immediate discussion here was the Ch'an method of reaching enlightenment, for Chu-hung, as for all orthodox Buddhists, the search was not an isolated endeavor but an integral part of the total

Buddhist training. This training traditionally consisted of the three interrelated areas of discipline *(chieh)*, concentration *(ting)*, and wisdom *(hui)*. Chu-hung witnessed both the corruption of Ch'an practice and the neglect of monastic discipline. Although Chu-hung decried the fall of both with equal vehemence, he in fact devoted much more energy to reviving the spirit of discipline than to restoring the Ch'an tradition. He rightly felt that the emphasis on discipline was especially important, for this was the foundation of a monk's career. Concentration and wisdom must rest on the foundation of good discipline.

In order to highlight the significance of moral discipline, Chu-hung wrote *Tzu-men ch'ung-hsing lu* (Record of the Exalted Conduct of Buddhist Monks, *YCFH* 15), and intended it to be read and emulated by his fellow monks. In the preface, Chu-hung made clear the fundamental importance of discipline for a Buddhist:

A monk asked me, "What did the Buddhist order serve?" I answered that it served the Way *(shih-tao)*. When he asked what the basis of serving the Way was, I said that it was moral conduct *(te-hsing)*. The monk laughed at me saying: "You are indeed very obstinate. The smart enter the Way through wisdom and the stupid by cultivating blessedness. Therefore it will be sufficient if monks just seek after wisdom." To this I answered in the following manner: "The ancients said that moral conduct was the basis for a man. They also said that those who could go far were first recognized for their capacity. How can the wonderful Way of Supreme Enlightenment be realized by someone who does not have the correct capacity? Lion's milk must be stored in a bottle made of precious stones, for if we put it in any other container, the container will burst. If we put a tripod of enormous weight in a leaf-like boat, what can we expect but that it will capsize and sink right away? Nowadays, monks who have some ability engage in studying historical documents and writing commentaries like Confucian students. If they are more gifted, then they repeat bits and pieces of earlier masters' sayings. It is like following the echo or chasing after the shadow. No wonder that people in the know laugh at this. The utterances of these monks sound grander than those of the patriarchs, but their conduct is inferior to that of ordinary people. This is the extreme degeneracy of the last age of the Law."[14]

The decline of monastic discipline had many causes. When the government began to sell ordination certificates to anyone who could afford the price, whatever institutional control there was on moral and intellectual standards disappeared. This no doubt contributed to the general indifference to discipline. But a more important cause probably was the increasing commercialization of funeral services and sutra chanting. Since the Sung, Buddhist monasteries had been divided into the *ch'an*, the *chiang* (scriptural study), and the *lü* (discipline). T'ai-tsu, as I mentioned earlier, replaced the Lü division with the *chiao* (or *yü-chia*). This act officially relegated discipline to limbo. Chu-hung lamented that in his day all monasteries had turned into lecture halls, and none specialized in Ch'an and discipline.[15] Although this might be an exaggeration, the fact remained that most monks were interested only in performing funeral services or giving lectures on sutras.[16] This, however, was only one manifestation of the overall secularization of the monastic order in the late Ming.

The Worldliness of the Monks

As monks paid less attention to Vinaya and the true spirit of Ch'an practice, they became more open to unorthodox pursuits and material comforts. Worldliness indicated a lack of spirituality. In turn, it served to prevent the reemergence of religious fervor. Thus it is not surprising that Chu-hung devoted much space in his writings to the exposure of the various worldly foibles of the monks of his day. He insisted that monks should return to the strict observance of Vinaya rules, sutra studies, Ch'an, and Pure Land cultivation. He also insisted that they must give up non-Buddhist interests and pursuits.

On this latter point, he showed a remarkable departure from the conciliatory attitude toward Confucianism he adopted in winning lay believers: He demanded strict adherence to Buddhist orthodoxy from his fellow monks. This is an example of the complex nature of the problem of syncretism. In studying syncretism, one has to identify the syncretist's degree of involvement with each constituent ideology. The statement that everyone in the late Ming was a syncretist really does not help much; one must try to approximate the points along the continuum between complete rejection and complete acceptance that best describe the subject's affiliation. At the same time, one also has to identify the particular circumstances as well as the reason for which a person advocates this syncretism. Thus, when Chu-hung showed open-mindedness toward Confucianism and to a lesser extent toward Taoism before his lay fol-

燭影風飄香霧雲飄
貪看嬌娥燭燼香消
之璜

7. A Buddhist Service (*Ming-tai pan-hua hsüan ch'u-chi*, vol. II, p. 226–27)

lowers, he knew this would help his cause. Ming China was a Confucian society, and any outright rejection of Confucian values would only cause official censure and public alienation. As eagerly as Chu-hung wanted to convert people to Buddhism, he was aware that the task could not be accomplished overnight. The people must be shown that there was no basic incompatibility between the tenets of Confucianism and Buddhism. In the case of lay Buddhism, the main problem was how to integrate Buddhism into a Confucian society.

He faced a different situation, however, in his attempt to reform monastic Buddhism. His task here was to extricate the monks from secular concerns and instill in them a sense of dedication to Buddhism. Monks were to serve as models for lay Buddhists—even though, in his anger and exasperation, Chu-hung often regarded monks as inferior to the latter in spirituality. Love of Confucian learning was naturally different from material indulgence, yet in the final analysis it also distracted a monk from his proper goal.

When we see these quite contrary attitudes toward non-Buddhist preoccupations, it is easy to say that Chu-hung was simply inconsistent and hypocritical. But a study of his intentions in both cases is of critical importance. In encouraging the lay movement, he wanted to incorporate and integrate Buddhism into the larger society. But in reviving monastic Buddhism, he had first to isolate the community from the distractions of the secular world. He stressed the importance of Buddhism's entering into and merging with the larger society in the first case, that of withdrawing and separating from it in the second one. His intentions in both cases were the same: to rejuvenate Buddhism. The difference in approaches was only a tactical one. One might say that it was another example of Chu-hung's "skill in means."

The secularization of the monastic order manifested itself in three general aspects: the monks' pursuit of non-Buddhist interests and avocations, their greed for donations, and their love of material comforts.

Chu-hung noted with great dismay that monks of his day liked to dabble in calligraphy, poetry, and the art of letter writing, the three genteel pursuits of the literati.[17] He felt that this amateur interest could only hinder their progress in Buddhist understanding, which should be their true profession. Yet this does not mean that Chu-hung felt Confucian learning was worthless; on the contrary, he valued it highly. However, he thought that the Confucian classics were good for Confucians and should be studied primarily by them, just as Buddhist scriptures should be the primary concern of Buddhists. He approved the single-minded dedication of Confucian scholars who would study only Confucian classics. For him, whether one was a Confucian or a Buddhist, one's principal task was to become firmly grounded in one's own tradition. Only when this was accomplished could one approach the other tradition from a standpoint of strength:

The learning of a Confucian is based on the Six Classics, the *Analects,* and *Mencius.* He does not study *Lao Tzu, Chuang Tzu,* or Buddhist scriptures. Each profession has its specialty. As this is the correct principle, we do not blame him. The same holds true for monks. But monks nowadays do not study Buddhist scriptures. On the contrary, they study Confucian works. Not only do they study Confucian works, but they also study *Lao Tzu* and *Chuang Tzu.* Those who are slightly more quick-witted write commentaries. Furthermore, they learn to write poems and essays; they practice calligraphy and letter writing. All these are signs of the decay of the monastic order.[18]

Although some monks did not hesitate to imitate Confucian literati in their pursuit of literary and artistic virtuosity, in Chu-hung's view they failed to learn the single-minded dedication of the Confucian student. This manifested itself in the careless attitude the monks took toward the study of Buddhist scriptures:

The sutras and shastras are numerous, and it is very difficult to be proficient in them all. That is why the ancients usually specialized in one work, such as the Lotus or the Avataṁsaka Sutra. People nowadays, however, lecture on all the sutras and discourse on all the shastras. Does this mean that they are more intelligent than the ancients? [Of course they are not.] Therefore, you have people who do not study under anybody but, relying on their own opinion, advocate new-fangled theories. You also have people who wantonly criticize former worthies with their new ideas. Or else they rework ever so slightly some passages [in the scriptures] but in fact have nothing new to say.[19]

What offended Chu-hung here was again the lack of discipline. He contrasted the lighthearted attitude of these monks with the seriousness of Confucian scholars and showed the former to great disadvantage:

Among the stories about ancient scholars was one about how a scholar did not even look at the garden for three years; there was another about a person who shut his doors and would not step over the threshold; then there was a third about a person who, after receiving a letter from home, as soon as he read the words "Everyone is well" would throw it in the water without reading the rest. They did these [things] in order to become single-minded in their study. Yet monks whose concern should be the study of the other-worldly Dharma often let profane affairs confuse their minds. When we read these stories, we should feel deep shame and thereby learn a lesson.[20]

The rejection of the traditional emphasis on scriptural specialization, the disrespect toward established views, and the boldness of unorthodox opinions all reflected the prevailing spirit of individualism. This independence from the past could theoretically lead to innovation and inject new life. Yet in Chu-hung's view it worked to the disadvantage of Buddhism, for the lack of intellectual conscientiousness, like the disregard of monastic discipline and the true spirit of Ch'an training, would lead inevitably to laxity and dilettantism.

Not only did Chu-hung feel that monks of his day failed to devote themselves to the study of Buddhist scriptures or to observe Vinaya rules, but he also thought that their amateur approach had destroyed the very effectiveness of Buddhist rituals. As we saw in the previous chapter, during the Ming dynasty monks specializing in Tantric rituals were grouped under the *yü-chia* sect. They were presumably not required to have deep scriptural learning or expertise in Ch'an cultivation. Yet the performance of these rituals presupposed great sincerity and concentration on the part of the performer, a quality which, in Chu-hung's estimation, was in short supply among his contemporaries. In order to impress on his readers the dire effects of an ill-performed ritual, Chu-hung did not hesitate to tell stories of monks who had allegedly suffered painful retribution as a result of their neglect. In the following passage, Chu-hung first talked about the proper way to perform the ritual of feeding the hungry ghosts, and then described the terrible consequences of performing it incorrectly, as apparently happened quite frequently in his day:

The ritual of feeding the burning mouths (*yen-k'ou shih-shih*) was first instituted by Ananda and was included in the teachings of the Yogācāra school. The Yoga teaching came to be propagated by the two masters Vajrabodhi (d. 741) and Amoghavajra (d. 774) of the T'ang dynasty. It could command gods and spirits and move mountains and oceans, its majestic power being beyond human imagination. After it was transmitted for a few generations, there was no one capable of inheriting it. The ritual of feeding the hungry ghosts was the only one preserved. [In performing this ritual], one makes signs with hands *(chieh-in)*, recites spells orally *(sung-chou)*, and enters into a trance *(tso-kuan)*. Because the three acts must coordinate with each other, it is called yoga [i.e., a yoke]. This is indeed not at all easy to do. Nowadays few people are proficient in employing *mudrās* and *dhāraṇīs*, not to mention the ability to enter into a trance. Since this is the case, they cannot achieve coordination. Once coordination is lost, then not only will they not be able to help sentient beings, they will also end up harming themselves.

Not long ago a monk living on this mountain became seriously ill. One evening when food was laid out for the hungry ghosts, he said to the monk who was tending him: "Just now some ghosts wanted to drag me out to get food. I refused, but they came back soon afterward and said to me that the master who was performing the ritual was insincere and therefore they did not get any food. After they go back, they will definitely avenge themselves. So saying, they grabbed my arms and forced me to go with them. Some ghosts took out robes and chains and said that they would drag the officiating priest to the ground. I was greatly frightened and cried out for help. Only then did they depart." This same monk died a few days later. Alas, even before he died, he had become friends with ghosts. If he had not cried out, the monk performing the ritual probably would have been endangered. This was not an isolated case. I have heard of one monk who because of insincerity was dragged by ghosts to a river and almost drowned. I have heard of another monk who had lost the key of his trunk and thought of the key while performing the ritual. As a result, the ghosts could not eat the rice because it was covered with iron pieces. I have heard of a third monk who had put out his blanket to air and before he took it indoors it rained. While he was performing the ritual, he thought about the blanket. As a result, the ghosts could not eat any of the rice because it was all covered with animal fur. Each of these monks received retribution in their lifetime. Once there was a man who visited the nether world and saw several hundred monks in a dark room. They were emaciated and dried out and appeared to be in extreme pain. When he asked about their identity, he was told that they were all monks who had officiated at the ritual of feeding hungry ghosts incorrectly in their previous existences. Thus you must believe me when I say that it is indeed not at all easy to perform such a ritual.[21]

Among the various forms that secularization took, the penchant for Confucian embellishment was certainly the least serious. Next on the list of Chu-hung's indictments were the Taoist practices in which some monks engaged. His attitude toward Taoism, as we saw in chapter V, was consistently critical. He said disapprovingly that "among the monastic community, some monks acted as geomancers, some as mediums, some as pharmacists, some as healers of female diseases, while there were also some who practiced the art of making elixirs and cinnabar."[22] He had the utmost disdain for some Taoist beliefs which he regarded as especially superstitious. One was the practice of communicating with spirits by the use of a planchette. He gave the following advice to one of his lay disciples, warning him of its bad effects: "Spirits called forth by divination are seldom real. They pretend to be such and such a spirit, but in truth they are not. If one engages in this practice, one's spirit (*shen*) and vital breath (*ch'i*) will be harmed. In the triple world, only the Buddha is the great teacher. Recite the Buddha's name with one mind, and then all demons will cease of their own accord."[23] Spirit and vital breath were two favorite and central concepts in religious Taoism. It is ironic, perhaps, that even in attacking Taoism, Chu-hung could not avoid using its terminology.

Another target for Chu-hung's attack was the popular belief in alchemy:

Everybody knows that alchemy is nothing but a sham. One might ask why there are still so many people who become deceived by its claims. The ancient sage [Confucius] said: "The wise are not perplexed." Therefore those who are deceived by the practitioners of alchemy are people deficient in wisdom. However, one can forgive the ordinary people [who believe in alchemy], but what amazes me is that within the sangha there are also monks who are deceived by it. This is truly regrettable. Ordinary people of the world regard money as their life. Thinking that cinnabar could be transmuted into gold, even emperors could not help being deceived by the talk of Taoists. That is why it is not strange that lay people should believe in it. But have monks forgotten the words of the Buddha? The Buddha says that there are 84,000 rays of light issuing from the white curl between his eyebrows (*pai-hao*). When even one ray of light is bestowed universally on the disciples in the age of the Degenerate Law, it will not become exhausted. Then what need is there for them to engage in alchemy?

I know of an old monk in Soochow who wanted to build a temple. He used to recite the seven volumes of the Lotus Sutra and call on Buddha's name ten thousand times in the hope of helping the success of a project in alchemy. Even though he had been cheated repeatedly, he still did not repent. . . . He eventually ended up in utter failure. His desire to build a temple for the Buddha is, of course, a good one. Yet a temple will cost no less than ten to twenty thousand ounces of gold. It is indeed naïve to believe that he could do so with the success of alchemical transmutation. On the other hand, if he had sought for the Way with the same dedication as he sought for the cinnabar, if he had served the good friends of the world with the money he spent in serving the alchemists, . . . if he had transferred the merits accrued from reciting the seven volumes of the Lotus Sutra and calling ten thousand times the Buddha's name to the rebirth in the Western Paradise, he would have succeeded in building his temple even if he had not erected one beam.[24]

Indeed, the old monk in this anecdote typified the misguided piety that Chu-hung regarded as prevalent at the time. Monks wanted to promote Buddhism by engaging in temple building and other projects, yet they did not realize that these were peripheral when compared with what should be their proper concern—the search for wisdom. Chu-hung contrasted good works, which he called "the cultivation of blessedness" *(hsiu-fu)* with religious enlightenment, which he called "the cultivation of wisdom" *(hsiu-hui)*. In an interesting passage, he made clear where his own sympathies lay and showed himself once again to be unconventional and yet strangely conservative:

There is a verse written by the ancient worthies that says: "If one cultivates wisdom but not blessedness, he will become an arhat who enjoys little offering; if one cultivates blessedness but not wisdom, he is like an elephant wearing a necklace made of precious stones." Now there are people who are deeply impressed by the first sentence. They are busy all day long trying to get donations. They tell people that they want to make images of the Buddha, or build temples, or feed the monks. Now although these are accepted acts of a good Buddhist, we must be careful about two things: namely, first of all we must know distinctly what is the cause and what is the effect; second, we must deal with the affair of our own salvation before we do anything else. You may accuse me by saying that if people really do what I advocate, then who will repair the Buddha's image when it becomes damaged, who will rebuild the temple when it crumbles, and who will save the monks when they fall by the wayside because of hunger? If everybody is concerned only about his own salvation, then the Three Jewels would undoubtedly become neglected.

My answer to this is that what you have said is not true. We should fear only the neglect of the Three Jewels inside ourselves *(i-t'i san-pao)*. As for the Three Jewels of the world *(shih-chien san-pao)*, ever since Buddhism was introduced into China, there has never been a time when the casting of images, the building of temples, and the feeding of monks was not carried out. You can see this is still being done everywhere. What need is there for you to worry yourself about these things excessively? I am alone in feeling sorry for the monks who are engaged in these projects. We do not have to talk about those monks who are ignorant of cause and effect, who do not

fear punishment and retribution but cheat the sangha and deceive the faithful laity.

Even in the case of honest monks, because they do not know the Vinaya
rules, they think it is all right as long as they do not embezzle public funds.
Consequently, they use the money intended for one thing to do something
else. . . . They do not know that if they use the money set aside for buying
food to buy bricks for the construction of a temple hall, they will receive
only punishment for their pains. . . . In this case, not only have they
created no merit, but they have done positive harm. Master Chung-feng
once told the assembly: "Having the one mind is the root, and the myriad
good acts must occupy a secondary place." This is exactly what I mean when
I say that one must first devote oneself to the affair of one's own salvation.
After one has done so, only then should he concern himself with the cultivation of blessedness. All monks must keep firmly in mind this true advice.[25]

The tendency to lay more stress on blessedness than wisdom led
to other abuses. In order to repair or build temples, to cast images
and to print sutras, it was necessary to ask for lay donations. Among
the monks who went around asking for money, there were no doubt
some who sincerely wanted to do good deeds, but there were also
many more who were using the donations for selfish aggran-
dizement. Regarding the former, Chu-hung's feeling, as is made
clear in the passage cited above, was that these monks were
misguided in their efforts. In the case of those who asked alms out
of greed, his judgment was much harsher. In the following passage,
he reported a dialogue between himself and a Taoist priest who
ridiculed the monks' greed for donations. This Taoist priest also
claimed that far more Buddhist monks than Taoist priests engaged
in this endeavor. Chu-hung, whose aversion to Taoist practices and
animosity toward Taoism in general are by now familiar to us, could
only agree, for the charges were undeniably true:

A Taoist priest said to me, "We keep our hair under a cap, but you monks
shave off your hair. A man who has shaved off his hair ought to isolate himself from the secular world. Why is it that among those who roam the streets
for lay donations, one seldom sees a Taoist priest, but always encounters
Buddhist monks? Some monks carry pledge books in their hands and look
like those infernal judges in front of the City God. Some beat their wooden
fish, while others sing loudly and talk about the law of karma in the manner
of blind storytellers. Some carry images of bodhisattvas on their shoulders
and, accompanied by drums and gongs, ask people for donations. Some
drag iron chains that weigh several tens of catties behind them like prisoners. Some beat their bodies with rocks as if they were wronged and are

full of hatred. Finally, there are monks who wear formal clothes and carry incense sticks going from door to door and doing obeisance all the way. They are like census takers. Aren't they a blemish to your religion?" I could make no answer.[26]

As a matter of fact, the Taoist priest's caricature of the money-crazed monks appear rather mild when it is compared with Chu-hung's own description. In the following passage, Chu-hung described some favorite austerities that monks practiced in order to attract the attention, sympathy, and, most important, the money of the gullible passers-by:

Recently there have been Buddhist and Taoist priests who build brick walls around themselves. The space is so small that it can contain only one person. They stand inside as a sword inside its sheath or a clam inside its shell. Some put nails on the four sides and make the space into a box bed. There are some who cut off one hand and wrap the stump in a piece of cloth which is covered with dirt and tar. They show this mutilated hand to passers-by. There are some who dig a pit into the ground. They then bury their heads in it and stick both feet upward. Some people either beat their backs with large bricks until they turn green and swollen, or they go barefoot in winter. Some only drink water but never touch any grain. Some stand on the balustrade of a bridge and read sutras, and thus amaze everyone walking by. There are also some people who walk around dragging iron chains weighing more than a hundred catties. Strange deeds like these cannot be exhaustively enumerated. If we want to know the reason, they use these methods to attract people's attention and beg for alms. They fool the world and deceive the people. Whether it is out of greed or stupidity, they deserve our pity. All enlightened people should advise such persons to give up this kind of evil practice and to concentrate on practicing the right Way. If this advice is taken, it will be a great good fortune for Buddhism.[27]

The most conspicuous sign of a monk's worldliness was his interest in material luxury and personal comfort. Chu-hung saw the danger of succumbing to these temptations and felt it to be most damaging to a spiritual progress. In a letter to a fellow monk, he had this advice:

As long as one seeks perfection in food, clothing, and housing, one cannot be perfect in regard to the Buddhist Law. You should be able to get by with the hall you have already built; the rest of the rooms can wait for the future. In former times, they often built rooms gradually, one after another. For if you want to finish the whole temple all at once, you will have much difficulty and this will obstruct your work in the Way.[28]

The disdain for physical labor, which was usually thought to be peculiar to the Confucian literati, was also shared by monks in this period. Despite the high value put on work in the Ch'an tradition (which was epitomized by Master Pai-chang's dictum, "If one does not work one day, he should not eat for one day"), monks of Chu-hung's time seldom practiced this virtue. Instead, they bought and kept servants: "Nowadays, monks cherish their disciples as if they were sons of rich families. They do not let their disciples work but spend money to buy servants who cook food, carry firewood, and hold umbrellas and traveling staffs for them."[29]

Chu-hung was well aware that the surrender to materialism was not entirely due to a monk's ingrained greed and weak character. Recalling his own initial hesitation to head the Yün-ch'i monastery, he often repeated the warnings against a monk's becoming too interested in the power and prestige of being a religious leader. For fame always led to corruption. He felt that a monk had to renounce the world twice: once when he first entered the sangha, and again when he had to renounce the temptation of personal fame:

When a man first becomes a monk, no matter whether he has a great or a slight commitment, inevitably he is full of good intentions. Yet after a long time, as a result of circumstances, he becomes influenced by the desire for fame and profit. So he seeks to build temples and add new rooms to the temples already built; he wants nice clothes and buys land; he keeps servants and disciples; he hoards money. In order to get all these, he works hard at different projects and behaves in no way different from the men of the world. . . . I once knew of a monk who had practiced austerity deep in a mountain. As soon as he left the mountain, he was surrounded by several dozens of the faithful who wanted to serve and take care of him. In this way, whatever he had achieved in his life was now completely lost. . . . To "leave the household" the first time is easy, but to "leave the household" the second time is difficult. I tremble at this thought morning and night.[30]

Elsewhere Chu-hung told a similar story of how a serious-minded monk became corrupted by well-meaning admirers. This monk, of whom Chu-hung claimed to have personal knowledge, lived in a hut deep in the mountains for over ten years. During that time he worked hard at religious cultivation. Then, because his admirers respected him, they built a temple and invited him to live there. Consequently the monk began to indulge himself in material comforts and retrogressed spiritually beyond hope.[31]

Since indiscriminate lay support sometimes created this undesirable effect, Chu-hung, who devoted so much effort to winning lay support, found himself in the curious position of discouraging certain types of lay patronage. There is an interesting passage in which he laid down guidelines for the lay patron who wanted to promote Buddhism. The message, which was formulated in various ways throughout his writings, is that the religious community must reform itself first. Otherwise, outside protection would not only fail to revive Buddhism, but would hasten its downfall:

Everyone knows that the duty of protecting Buddhism lies with kings and ministers, but few know that monks who receive such protection must be extremely careful. There are three kinds of lay patronage: first, the building or restoring of temples; second, the propagation of the great teaching; and third, the help and protection extended to the sangha. However, in the case of restoring a temple, one must be sure that it was indeed originally a Buddhist temple. If it was once a Buddhist temple but later was taken over and occupied by someone forcibly, then it is justified that we should return it to the Buddhists. . . . But if some monk makes a powerful personage believe in gaining merit by turning an old temple over to the Buddhists without making sure it was originally a Buddhist temple, he is not thinking of the Buddha's equal regard for all sentient beings. This results only in demerits, not merits. In the case of propagating the teaching, if a monk's writing really conforms to the intention of the Buddha and the principle of the scriptures, it is justified to praise it and spread it abroad. But if his theory is biased and heretical, it should not be praised. When a monk asks famous persons to write a preface or a postscript for his writing, he is not aware of the danger that he might mislead people of later generations. This too will result not in merits, but in demerits. Finally, in the case of protecting the sangha, if the monk has indeed achieved genuine enlightenment and possesses great knowledge, he should of course be respected. Moreover, if a monk observes discipline and sincerely practices the religious life, people should of course believe in and draw near to him. But if the monk is a vulgar fake, then respect and devotion is naturally out of the question. When a monk ingratiates himself with the rich and powerful, he hopes to take advantage of their patronage. This is like using silk and brocade to cover up a festering sore. It can only help the poison grow worse, and lead to demerits. Even though kings and ministers are willing to protect Buddhism, monks often harm it. How sad![32]

CHAPTER EIGHT

~~~~~~

Chu-hung's Monastic Reform:
The Yün-ch'i Monastery

AS THE previous chapter makes clear, Chu-hung felt that the main cause for the decline of Buddhism was the neglect of monastic discipline. Therefore, throughout his long career he tirelessly stressed the importance of strict adherence to Vinaya rules. A concrete example of his achievement in monastic reform was the success of the Yün-ch'i monastery. From the founding of the monastery until his death at the age of eighty-one, Chu-hung worked continuously to make Yün-ch'i a model of religious cultivation and Vinaya observance. The fame of Yün-ch'i attested to Chu-hung's gift as an administrator. Undoubtedly, his personal charisma as an inspiring leader contributed to the ready cooperation provided by the monks at Yün-ch'i. But it was primarily his ability to put theory into practice, his astute sense of the essential, and his fine eye for administrative detail that enabled him to create order and discipline at Yün-ch'i.

When Chu-hung set out to build Yün-ch'i as a model of "pure living," he was faced with a serious problem. Despite various governmental measures aimed at control, the monastic order was by and large left to regulate itself because the measures were ineffectual. There were, in fact, no uniform and effective regulations governing the recruitment, training, and supervision of monks. It was up to the individual abbot to make sure that sincere applicants were brought in and that a good standard of behavior was maintained. When we examine the content of the *Yün-ch'i kung-chu kuei-yüeh* (Rules and Agreements for Communal Living at Yün-ch'i, *YCFH* 32), we cannot but be impressed by Chu-hung's penetrating and comprehensive insights into the problems of running a monastery. Starting with the requirements for an applicant who desired to join Yün-ch'i, Chu-hung laid down clear and concise rules concerning every aspect of monastic life. In the following pages we will examine in some detail areas of special interest, such as the formal requirements for joining the monastery (*ch'u-chia*) and for receiving the tonsure (*t'i-tu*) and the precepts (*shou-chieh*), as well as the general principles governing life at Yün-ch'i and the structure of its religious and liturgical life.

It has been traditionally asserted that the first Ch'an monk to have drawn up rules and regulations for monastic life was Pai-chang Huai-hai of the T'ang dynasty. He was supposed to have set down "monastic statutes for the arrangement of buildings, the order of the monastic administration, special ascetic practices during the course of the year, as well as penalties for causing disturbances and transgressing the rules." [1] However, recent scholarship has cast doubt on this tradition. There is no evidence that Pai-chang in fact wrote a monastic code. In the writings of his contemporaries and disciples, neither the term "Pure Rules of Pai-chang" nor the fact that he had compiled a code is mentioned. If Pai-chang had compiled a code, this silence is remarkable. The extant version of the *Pai-chang ch'ing-kuei* (Pure Rules of Pai-chang) was compiled by imperial order during the Yüan dynasty. It was a synthesis of various monastic codes compiled in the Sung, the earliest being the "Ch'an-men kuei-shih" (Rules of the Ch'an Order, 1004). [2] Chu-hung followed the tradition that Pai-chang set down the first Ch'an code, but he was dissatisfied with the Yüan version of the *Pure Rules* and cast doubt on its authenticity:

The *Pure Rules* is a work expounded by later writers, but is not that written by Pai-chang. . . . It is undoubtedly true that Pai-chang was the first one who established the system of "public monasteries" and made rules to govern the monastic community. But the complexity of the *Pure Rules* and the triviality of its fine points only make a person befuddled and bewildered. Since he will have to spend all his time trying to study the intricate details, how can he devote his energy to pursuing the Way? That is why I believe that the *Pure Rules* as we know it now is a product of latter-day busybodies, and does not represent Pai-chang's original intention. [3]

The purpose of drawing up a code was to regulate monastic life so that monks could pursue meditation and study in an orderly fashion. But if the code were to become too complex and legalistic, it

五雲山
壁觀峯
金液泉
聖義泉
青龍泉
華藏堂
演法堂
藏經堂
靜室
禪堂
西堂
雲棲
天池寺
迴耀峯
大師塔院
孝義庵塔
普同塔
放生所
三聚亭
天竺路
七佛寺
余氏宅

8. Panoramic View of Yün-ch'i Monastery (*YCFH* 33, p. 2a–b)

would interfere with rather than help the work of spiritual cultivation, which should be the primary task for all Buddhist monks. Chu-hung therefore did not use the *Pure Rules of Pai-chang* but worked out his own code for Yün-ch'i because he felt the former was too cumbersome and detailed for practical use. As its formal name, Ch'an Monastery of Yün-ch'i (Yün-ch'i Ch'an Ssu) indicates, Chu-hung considered Yün-ch'i to be within the Ch'an tradition, but Pure Land devotionalism and Ch'an meditation were combined in the work of the monks at Yün-ch'i.

The Requirements for Entering Yün-ch'i

The first step a layman had to take in joining the monastic order was to become a postulant *(t'ung-hsing)*. While serving as a postulant, he did not have to shave off his hair, but he did have to observe the five precepts: not to kill, not to steal, not to engage in sexual activities, not to lie, and not to drink wine. For this reason, postulants were referred to as the "five-precepts class" *(wu-chieh pan)* at Yün-ch'i.

A person desiring to join Yün-ch'i had to meet the following four requirements.[4]

1. The postulant must be personally accompanied by his parents. If his parents are dead, then his next closest kin ought to accompany him.
2. He must satisfy the following eight conditions: (1) He is not a disobedient and unfilial son; (2) he is not an escaped convict; (3) he is not forced to enter by external circumstances and poverty; (4) he is not interested in an easy and desultory life; (5) he has not done evil deeds; (6) he is not a member of a prosperous and famous family *(ta-chia)*; (7) he does not have any unpaid debts; (8) he does not have any unfinished family business.
3. He should know the rudiments of sutra chanting. He should be familiar with sutras such as the Heart Sutra and the Smaller Sukhāvatīvyūha Sutra, which are used in morning and evening devotions.
4. He must be fairly proficient in reading and writing. Even though he does not have to be well read, he should have some background in reading. He does not have to be a calligrapher, but he should be able to write characters with ease.

The emphasis on parental approval and the applicant's moral character are two points that immediately strike the reader. In this regard, Chu-hung followed similar requirements found during the

Sung. Their purpose was to protect Buddhism from the charges of disrupting family cohesion and harboring criminal elements. Especially interesting among Chu-hung's requirements are those which stipulate that the postulant must not be a member of a prosperous and famous family and that he must not have any unfinished family business. As far as I know, these two conditions are not found elsewhere. Did this conscious avoidance of gentry families and government officials reflect Chu-hung's attitude toward officialdom, an attitude instilled in him by his father and one that remained with him throughout life? One can only speculate.

Once a person became a postulant, he lived in the monastery but was not yet counted as a full-fledged member of the community. He was not, for example, qualified to enroll in the Great Hall to engage in meditation work, nor was he qualified to hold responsible monastic offices. Neither was he exempted from paying taxes and serving as a corvée laborer. The next step was to become a novice (*sha-mi*). This step was highlighted by the ceremony of tonsure, which signified a final and radical break with the secular world and was therefore treated with appropriate solemnity. At this ceremony, he also received the ten precepts and advanced to the "ten-precepts class." The ten precepts consisted of the five previously described plus five more: not to use perfume or a decorated headdress; not to sing and dance or attend the same; not to sleep on big beds; not to eat at improper times; and not to handle gold, silver, or precious jewels. A commentary on the ten precepts together with some twenty-four rules regulating a novice's deportment were included in Chu-hung's *Sha-mi-lü-i yao-lüeh* (Essential Rules and Ceremonies for a Novice, *YCFH* 13). A novice was expected to observe the ten precepts and become thoroughly familiar with the contents of this work. If he failed to convince the examiner of his knowledge of the book, he would not be allowed to receive the complete precepts for a monk (*chü-chieh*).

The requirements for receiving the tonsure at Yün-ch'i were as follows: [5]

1. Before tonsure is given, the postulant must be reexamined to see if he qualified in the four areas as stated in the requirements for joining the sangha. After this, he must satisfy the examiner that he knows the sutras for the morning and evening devotional services [6] and that he has committed no offenses against the sangha.

2. The tonsure is performed only once at the end of a year in this monastery. But if someone comes here to seek tonsure and leaves soon afterward, this can be done at any time during the year. In the latter case, the person has to be examined in great detail as well. Tonsure is given to no one lightly.

3. If a woman seeks the tonsure, she must be accompanied by her parents, parents-in-law, husband, son, or grandson. Otherwise, she must be strictly refused.

The decisive step in joining the sangha was formally to shave off one's hair. Henceforth, as a novice, one was counted as a full member of the monastic order and could enjoy the privileges of tax and corvée exemption. It was for this reason that the central government, since the T'ang dynasty, had sought to control the number of novices and monks by reserving the right to issue ordination certificates. Theoretically, during the Ming a postulant had to secure an ordination certificate before he could ask to have his hair shaved off. The fact that ordination certificates were not even mentioned in the requirements cited above indicates that this practice was no longer followed in Chu-hung's time. Private ordination was now the rule of the day.

Most members of the sangha in China remained novices, while a monk, or bhikshu (*pi-ch'iu*), had an exalted status.[7] At Yün-ch'i, however, novices were encouraged to advance to the bhikshu stage, to take the full ordination for a bhikshu by receiving the complete set of 250 precepts. After that they were encouraged to advance even further by receiving the fifty-eight precepts for a bodhisattva. He who desired to receive the full ordination had to be equipped with the *Ssu-fen-chieh pen* (Extracts from the Four-Division Vinaya) and the *Essential Rules and Ceremonies for a Novice*. He should, presumably, already be familiar with both. For those who wanted to receive the bodhisattva ordination, familiarity with one section of an additional scripture, the bodhisattva precepts from the chapter called "Ground of Mind" in the Sutra of Brahma's Net (*Fan-wang ching (hsing-ti p'in)* was also required.[8]

When one became a novice at Yün-ch'i, he was subject to periodic examinations on his knowledge of the Vinaya rules as well as other Buddhist scriptures. The occasion for this examination was provided by the semi-monthly recitation of the *prātimokṣa (pan-yüeh sung-chieh shih)*, for the test was carried out the day before this cere-mony took place. (Details concerning the test will be supplied in the section dealing with the administration of the Vinaya Hall.)

The point that must be stressed once again is Chu-hung's orga-nizational skill. No rule was ever made without the support of other measures that could serve to reinforce its implementation. The method of inculcating novices with a knowledge of the scriptures was similarly designed. First of all, only a selected list of sutras and other religious texts was stipulated as required reading. They were given in the following order: the complete texts of certain sutras, and mantras for morning and evening devotional services.[9] The sutras included the Sutra in Forty-two Chapters, the *Fo-i-chiao ching*, the Admonitions of Master Kuei-shan,[10] the *Essential Rules and Ceremonies for a Novice*, the *Extracts from the Four-Division Vinaya*, the bodhisattva precepts in the chapter called "Ground of Mind" in the Sutra of Brahma's Net, the *Kuan-wu-liang-shou ching*, the Larger Sukhāvatīvyūha Sutra, the Awakening of Faith, the Diamond Sutra, the Sutra of Perfect Enlightenment, the Vimalakīrti Sutra, the Śūraṅgama Sutra, the Laṅkāvatāra Sutra, the Lotus Sutra, and the Avataṁsaka Sutra.[11] Second, no one was permitted to change the prescribed order. One had to master one sutra before he was per-mitted to take up the next, following the sequence just given. Viola-tion of this rule resulted in a fine of one cash.[12]

The Ritual of the Semi-monthly *Prātimokṣa* Recitation

The technical term for this ritual is *poṣadha (pu-sa)*. The recital of the *prātimokṣa* (the 250 precepts for a bhikshu) forms the central part of this ritual. The ritual originated in India and was at least as old as the Vinaya Piṭaka.[13] Twice monthly, on the days of the full moon and half moon, monks gathered together to listen to the reci-tation of the *prātimokṣa*. Any monk who committed an offense while the rules were being read aloud had to confess in front of the as-sembly. He would then receive either absolution or punishment, depending on the nature and severity of the offense. According to Chu-hung, this ritual had utmost significance for the maintenance of a highly disciplined monastic life. Although there is some indication that the ritual had long ago been performed in China, it had apparently fallen into disuse. In the *Record of the Exalted Acts of Bud-dhist Monks,* Chu-hung included the story of Seng-yün, a Northern Ch'i monk, to highlight the importance of this ritual:

Seng-yün of the Northern Ch'i dynasty [550–589] lived in Pao-ming Ssu, and he was famous for his ability to lecture. On the fifteenth day of the fourth month during the ceremony of reciting the *prātimokṣa,* he told the as-sembly: "Everyone can recite the precepts, and it is unnecessary to listen to them so often. Why don't we simply have one monk explain the meaning to young novices for their understanding?" No one dared to object to him, and from then on the practice of reciting commandments was abolished. On the fifteenth day of the seventh month, when the monks assembled, Yün was missing. They went out to search for him everywhere and finally found him in an old tomb. His body was covered with blood. When asked, he said that a ferocious being with a huge knife had scolded him, saying: "Who did you think you were that you dared to abolish the ritual of reciting precepts and substitute for it having a monk lecture on their meaning?" After that the being stabbed him with the knife, and the pain was unendurable. The peo-ple took Yün back to the monastery. He repented sincerely and for the next ten years observed the ritual of semi-monthly recitation of the *prātimokṣa* faithfully. On the day he died, a strange fragrance filled the room, and he died joyfully. The people all respected him for his ability to acknowledge his mistake and correct it during his lifetime.[14]

After relating this dramatic anecdote, Chu-hung concluded with the following observation:

In the present age, it is fashionable to study sutras and shastras, but dis-cipline is treated with neglect. For over two thousand years, the practice of semi-monthly recitation of the *prātimokṣa* has not been continued. Though I am not talented, I have revived this practice in my mountain monastery. Some people have reservations about this, but in the story of Seng-yün, reward and retribution is as clear as day and night. I hope readers will pon-der this well.[15]

According to Chu-hung, before he revived the semi-monthly *prāti-mokṣa* recitation at Yün-ch'i, the ritual had not been performed for over two thousand years. This was obviously an exaggeration, since 'he had already told us, in the story of Seng-yün, that it was still being observed during the Northern Ch'i, which was about a thou-sand years before Chu-hung's time. Be that as it may, Chu-hung did restore a long-neglected ritual to its rightful place.

Since there was no established format for the performance of the ritual, Chu-hung had to write his own text. What he wrote, which was called *Pan-yüeh sung-chieh i-shih* (Rite of Semi-monthly Recitation of the Precepts, YCFH 13), deserves a brief description. The text starts with the five and ten precepts. Those who have received these two classes of precepts are called upon to listen. After the precepts are read aloud one by one, the text concludes with this statement: "Members of this assembly, if anyone has broken the basic precepts [*ken-pen chieh*, the four unpardonable sins: unchastity, theft, killing another man or encouraging a person to kill himself, and falsely claiming to understand truth], he is expelled from the monastery. If anyone has committed minor mistakes *(hsiao kuo)*, he should come forward to confess."[16] This statement is followed by a section on the full precepts which is more elaborate in the liturgy. It begins with a hymn to the Shakyamuni Buddha and the Extracts from the Four-Division Vinaya. Then the reciter asks if all the monks in the monastery have assembled and if they are now of one mind *(ho-ho)*. When he has been answered in the affirmative, he makes sure that the audience consists entirely of fully ordained monks, and all those who are not are asked to leave. A short speech by the reciter then follows:

Reverend sirs, I would now like to recite the *prātimokṣa*. As you are all gathered here, you ought to listen attentively and consider it well. If anyone has committed an offense, he should make a confession. If no one has done so, then remain silent. From your silence, I know that you are pure. If anyone should want to ask, you should answer him truthfully. Now if anyone among you upon being asked three times remembers his sin but does not reveal it, he commits the sin of lying. The Buddha has said that lying obstructs the Way. Therefore, that monk who knows he has sinned ought to confess if he desires to be pure. Confession will bring ease and comfort.[17]

This passage incidentally, agrees almost verbatim with a passage from the Mahā-Vagga.[18]

Once the speech has been completed, the reciter proceeds to read the 250 precepts. He reads the full texts of the four unpardonable sins *(pārājika)* one by one and says, "Now I have recited the four *pārājikas*. Any monk who has broken any one of these is not permitted to live with the other monks in the same place." He then repeats three times: "Are you all pure with regard to these?" If there is silence, he says: "Since you have proven your innocence by re-

maining silent, then take and cherish these precepts as before."
After the four *pārājika* the text simply names the thirteen *saṅghā
vaśeṣas*, the two *aniyatas*, the thirty *naiḥsargikāyattikas*, the ninety
prāyaścittikas, the four *pratideśanīyas*, the one hundred *śikṣākaraṇīyas*,
and the seven kinds of regulation for ending disputes, without de-
tailing each individual precept. After each group has been called
out, the assembly is once again questioned three times. The final section deals with the bodhisattva precepts. The format is similar to that
given for the full precepts but for the fact that it begins by invoking
the Vairocana Buddha, who is the Buddha of the Sutra of Brahma's
Net. Of the fifty-eight precepts, the first five are read in full; only
the titles of the others are read.

Judging from the rules of the Yün-ch'i monastery, this ritual
was apparently practiced in good faith. It also appears that not only
resident monks at Yün-ch'i but also monks from elsewhere attended
the ceremony. The latter would come to Yün-ch'i for this express
purpose. Unfortunately, we have no way of knowing whether this
custom was continued after Chu-hung's death, or whether it was imitated by other monasteries.

General Principles Governing Life at Yün-ch'i

The principles behind Chu-hung's code for Yün-ch'i are forcefully and succinctly set forth in two short documents translated
below: Agreement with the Sangha *(Seng-yüeh)* and Ten Things for the
Cultivation of the Self *(Hsiu-sheng shih-shih)*. In their insistence on the
strict observance of discipline, these have the power of a credo.
There is no doubt that discipline must have been the beginning and
the end of monastic life at Yün-ch'i. By and large, these rules were
designed to curb the trend toward irreligiosity and worldliness, some
characteristic manifestations of which were pointed out in the last
chapter. They also shed light on Chu-hung's understanding of
Buddhist discipline. Chu-hung clearly did not advocate a slavish adherence to the letter of the *Vinaya Piṭaka*. Rather, he adapted the
Vinaya to the needs of his own times. Because Buddhism was in
serious competition with Taoism throughout the Ming, Chu-hung
was a harsh critic of the latter. He prohibited his followers from
learning or practicing Taoism. On the other hand, as we have noted,

he tended to be conciliatory toward Confucianism. It is interesting to note that he used the Confucian expression, "cultivation of the self" *(hsiu-shen)*, for the title of the second document. Indeed, some of the virtues he elaborated in this document are as much Confucian as they are Buddhist.

Agreement with the Sangha [19]

What is the goal you seek in renouncing the world and entering the mountain? It is for the sake of cultivation that you leave the society of men far behind. If it is not for this purpose, what is the good of coming here? Now I wish to make an agreement with the assembly. Those who abide by this can live here together, but those who will not are asked to leave.

1. Reverence for the discipline: The following people are asked to leave the temple: those who break any one of the four basic precepts for a monk; those who without a valid excuse do not join the assembly of monks in reciting the *prātimokṣa;* those who are unfilial to parents; those who cheat and oppress their teachers and elders; those who willfully disobey governmental prohibitions; those who habitually consort with women; those who though they received the precepts years ago do not know the distinctions between rules nor the appropriate way of performing each rule *(chieh-hsiang);* those who go near heretical teachers.

2. Poverty and contentment with the Way: The following people are to be expelled from the monastery: those who are unwilling to eat simple and plain food; those who wear colorful and fine clothes; those who go out of their way to give Buddhist services; those who fight over money given by a donor; those who engage in farming, or raising silkworms and livestock; those who gather together men and women to set up vegetarian feasts for worldly purposes.

3. Holding to the root: The following people are to be expelled from the monastery: those who without reason often go out to the outside world or return to their secular homes; those who study rhymed poetry, music, and other miscellaneous arts for social purposes; those who study such heretical learning as astrology, geomancy, healing water with spells read over it *(fu-shui)*, and the Taoist alchemy *(lu-huo);* those who study heretical practices such as holding the breath *(pi-ch'i)*, unnatural feats of meditational sitting *(tso-kung)*, and the five divisions and six volumes *(wu-pu liu-tse);* [20] those who like to start unbeneficial enterprises.

4. Justice and uprightness: The following people are to be expelled from the monastery: those who use force to get lay contributions; those who take financial advantage of lay believers for personal gain; those who use things belonging to transient monks without their permission; those who destroy utensils and articles but fail to compensate; those who eat food behind others' backs and by themselves; those who appropriate an article that does not belong to anyone without telling the others; those who pocket money

illegally and secretly; those who evade hard work stealthily and without excuse.

5. Gentleness and endurance of insults: The following people are to be expelled from the monastery: those who curse and beat others with their fists; those who oppress people by force; those who insult elder monks who have much learning.

6. Deportment: The following people are to be expelled from the monastery: those who joke and laugh without restraint; those who pollute sutras and images; those who purposely wear clothes and caps different from the others; those who argue in a loud voice and will not stop even after having been warned three times.

7. Diligence of cultivation: The following people are to be expelled from the monastery: those who repeatedly fail to attend sutra recitation and worship services without excuse; those who are in charge of temple affairs but do not perform their duty; those who hate to be warned in meditation but persist in indolence; those who continue to fail in the examinations on understanding of the scriptures; those who do not believe in the teachings of Pure Land.

8. Dealing with the assembly with a straight mind: The following people are to be expelled from the monastery: those who incite others to quarrel; those who establish cliques and parties; those who employ cunning and dishonest means; those who ridicule the pure rules and the pure assembly; those who make friends secretly with bad people.

9. Circumspection and contentment with one's status: The following people are to be expelled from the monastery: those who boldly create disturbances; those who falsely expound sutras and shastras; those who wantonly imitate the expedient acts and utterances of famous Ch'an masters in former ages; those who have no knowledge but write books to fool people; those who accept persons unlike ordinary men (fei-jen) into the assembly; those who build up their own disciples and following; those who keep young children and male novices without permission; those who have a weak understanding themselves but like to be others' teachers; those who encourage another's disciple to disobey his original teacher; those who go to government offices without permission and without serious reasons; those who wantonly criticize and judge the right and wrong or the good and bad of current political affairs; those who condemn sages and good men of former ages with a light heart; those who give away permanent property [of the monastery]; those who encroach on other people's property; those who have their own kitchens apart from the group.

10. Obedience to the rules: The following people are to be expelled from the monastery: those who do not do a thing when ordered and do not stop [doing it] when prohibited; those who though they commit errors do not accept the punishment; those who live in the temple but do not enter their names in the monks' register; those who hinder the law and do not allow a functionary to carry out his duty; those who, though functionaries, change what is already established; those who do things as they please

without informing anyone; those who purposely socialize with someone who has committed mistakes and been expelled from the monastery.

Ten Things for the Cultivation of the Self [21]

Before one studies Buddhism, one first studies the cultivation of the self. Now the ten matters are listed below to which everyone should pay strict attention.

1. Do not cheat: This means to steal permanent objects belonging to the temple, to get things out of a donor by ruse, to use money intended for the making of images of the Buddha, the printing of scriptures, preparing vegetarian feasts for monks, building temples, casting bells, repairing bridges and paving roads . . . to do any of these things for one's own purposes; to deceive people, officials, heaven, and the gods—all such murky dealings are called "to have a cheating heart."

2. Do not be greedy for money: Even though one does not cheat and steal as mentioned above, yet if one likes to accumulate wealth, is stingy in giving money away, buys land to receive rent interest, or gives loans for interest, he will be regarded as greedy.

3. Do not be crafty: If one keeps back and does not say what ought to be said, if one sits to one side and does not remonstrate against a mistake that ought to be remonstrated against, or if one appears to be stupid and slow-witted yet harbors contempt inside, these are all called "being crafty."

4. Do not use designs: If one is dissatisfied with his natural lot but uses designs to get a living place, to attract a following among disciples, to perform confessional services, to seek donations, to become a master of the Dharma or a teacher of the discipline, even to the point of befriending evil men, of going into government offices to plot for one's own benefit with the aid of partisan help, and of carrying out plans contrary to principle, . . . such a man is then regarded as using designs.

5. Do not create disaster: To slight and laugh at others, to scold and slander others, to envy others' ability and broadcast others' shortcomings, to keep articles others have lost, to take others' property, to delight in lawsuits and be unwilling to concede to others; all these will create disaster.

6. Do not be extravagant: To build spacious rooms, to eat rich food, to wear beautiful clothes, to buy a lot of property, to use refined utensils, to waste grain, to engage in excursions as one pleases, to keep slaves and servants, to be generous to undeserving acquaintances; to do all these without shame is called "being extravagant."

7. Do not go near women: If one enters into friendship with young nuns, adopts a woman from the outside world as a godmother, goes frequently to relatives' homes to visit relatives and dependents, or even if one lives with his mother who is not yet seventy, oblivious of ridicule and suspicion; all these are regarded as being near women.

8. Do not busy oneself with outside affairs: To hurry to rich families and visit noble households in order to beg for poems and essays or a hori-

zontal plaque with an inscription; to run around all day long either to avail oneself of their power and prestige or to extort money forcibly, but not to think about quiet preservation—this is to busy oneself with outside affairs.

9. Do not be lazy: If one repeatedly makes mistakes in morning and evening worship; if one does not follow the others in performing duties and labor; he is regarded as lazy.

10. Do not lose time: Life rests with one breath and time does not wait for men. Before one realizes the Great Matter [of Birth and Death], even one second is precious. If one passes time with apathy, this is wasting time. The nine matters above should be observed closely, while this final point should be taken as a goal to be striven for.

Role Models

Chu-hung stated in the rules for the Dharma Hall that all monks had to familiarize themselves with the *Record of the Exalted Acts of the Buddhist Monks*. They were, moreover, to be examined on it from time to time. This work, like his *Wang-sheng chi* (Record of Rebirth in the Western Paradise, *YCFH* 16), was compiled to supply role models for emulation. Brief biographies of some one hundred and thirty-two monks were provided in which unusual and exemplary acts were singled out. In order to give more emphasis to such acts, Chu-hung often appended remarks to the end of one biography or a group of biographies.

The work itself is divided into ten sections, each of which concerns one type of ideal behavior. In the order of their appearance, they are: pure and unadorned conduct *(ch'ing-su chih hsing)*, strict and upright conduct *(yen-cheng chih hsing)*, acts of respect for the teacher *(tsun-shih chih hsing)*, acts of filial piety *(hsiao-ch'in chih hsing)*, loyalty to the sovereign *(chung-chün chih hsing)*, compassionate acts toward living creatures *(tz'u-wu chih hsing)*, noble and lofty behavior *(kao-shang chih hsing)*, persevering and serious conduct *(ch'ih-chung chih hsing)*, acts of austerity *(chien-k'u chih hsing)*, and acts calling forth supernatural response *(kan-ying chih hsing)*. Chu-hung explained in his preface, which is given below, why he regarded these ten kinds of behavior as ideal models, and why he arranged them in this particular order:

Since to be a monk is to depart from worldly impurities, pure and unadorned conduct heads this collection. But purity unaccompanied by strictness is the purity of a wild man, for the teaching of all the Buddhas insists on the discipline of body, speech, and mind. Therefore, the next category is strict and upright conduct. This strictness and uprightness is inculcated by the instructions of one's teacher, for the teacher is a model for men. Therefore, respect for the teacher forms the third category. Since we can receive instruction from our teachers only after our parents give us birth, to leave out parents is to forget our origins. Within the Buddhist discipline too, although there are ten thousand rules, filial piety is regarded as their basis. Therefore, to be filial to parents is the next category. Filial piety and loyalty to the sovereign come from the same principle. To know the existence of only one's parents but not that of one's sovereign is selfishness. That one can enjoy the luxury of living in the forest and by the mountain stream is because of the grace of one's emperor. Since nothing is greater than the grace of the emperor, loyalty to the sovereign constitutes the next category. However, if one is loyal to one's superior but is unkind to those under oneself, one will be deficient in the way of salvation. Therefore, kindness to living creatures is discussed next. Kindness is close in nature to love and affection. Since affection gives rise to attachment, which is an obstacle to one's leaving the world, I put lofty conduct next. Loftiness does not mean that one should keep oneself aloof and forsake sentient beings. Since we hope that by accumulating virtue we can radiate the brightness outward, the next category is about deliberate and serious conduct. Yet since to sit there solemnly all day long without doing anything is undesirable, we complement it with hardship and suffering. If labor does not bring results, then people will stop when they encounter difficulties. Since the law of cause and effect is really true, we conclude the entire collection with the category of conduct which brings response. When one cultivates these ten kinds of conduct, his virtue will be complete, and he can be a utensil worthy of containing the true Law. Only when the earth is fertile do we plant good seeds. Only when the heart is pure can it receive the inpouring of true words. It is only then that we can possibly hope to achieve enlightenment. Otherwise one is merely a lowly person who, not having even fulfilled the way of humanity, can never hope to know the way of the Buddha. Even if he is endowed with sharp understanding, cleverness will only serve to create more obstacles. With so many obstacles, what use can he make of his intelligence?[22]

In the following pages, one or two biographies from each category are presented to give some idea of the kinds of behavior Chu-hung hoped to inculcate in the monks at Yün-ch'i. Since the biographies are clearly written and make their point eloquently, further analysis may not be necessary. Two points, however, stand out. First of all, among the ten categories of ideal behavior, at least three—respect for the teacher, filial piety, and loyalty to the sovereign—are also basic Confucian virtues. Indeed, one may legitimately argue that the story of Fu-shang represents the Confucian value of integrity as much as the Buddhist value of purity. The glorification of these traditional Chinese virtues derives from Chu-hung's general attitude toward syncretism. We see it at work in his organization of the lay movement, and it forms the motivation behind the compilation of this present work as well. Chu-hung wanted to show the basic compatibility of the Buddhist and the Confucian moral ideals.

The second point deserving notice is that the entire collection, like the fifteen examples included here, consists predominantly of biographies of pre-Sung monks. This agrees with Chu-hung's low opinion of his contemporaries and recent predecessors. As we have seen on different occasions, Chu-hung firmly believed that he was living in the last epoch of the Law. Yet instead of feeling regret and manifesting nostalgia for the lost golden age, he hoped to recapture the best of the past by studying and incorporating it into the present. Chu-hung was both practical and realistic, but he was not a pessimist.

Selections from the *Record of the Exalted Acts of the Buddhist Monks*

I. Pure and Unadorned Behavior
Refusal to Organize Vegetarian Feasts
Seng-min of the Liu-Sung Dynasty [420–479] left household life at the age of seven. He was foremost in the country in his understanding of Buddhist doctrine, and the people called him Dharma Master Min. He never tired of building temples, printing sutras, casting images, releasing captured creatures, and giving alms. Someone said to him: "The merits you have created are indeed numerous, but perhaps the blessing is still incomplete, as we have never heard of your organizing a great vegetarian feast." Min answered: "Vegetarian feasts are seldom ideally done. Furthermore, to do it one must use rice, vegetables, salt, vinegar, boiling water, and burning charcoal, and consequently a lot of tiny creatures are harmed, if not by water and fire, then by being trampled underfoot. This is why I do not perform the service. If one has to ask favors from the imperial family, high officials, or some prestigious people for help, it will be even more difficult to achieve satisfactory results. Therefore it is better not to do it."

[*Chu-hung's praise*]:
Nowadays when people perform any act to obtain blessings, they must always organize a vegetarian feast, and call this "perfection." Some monks even start to plan for it after they have spent half the intended time living in sealed confinement. They plan for the vegetarian feast day and night in their closed rooms and can no longer have right thought. How sad! What Master Min said above can serve as a valid instruction for ten thousand generations. [*YCFH* 15, 8a–8b]

Disregarding the Money Left Behind

Fu-shang of the Sui Dynasty [581–618] lived in Ching-te Ssu in Yi-chou [in present-day Szechuan]. He used to put up a large bamboo hat by the roadside and sit under it reading sutras. When people walked by him, he would not ask for alms; and if someone gave him something, he would not thank him. Since the street was in a quiet neighborhood, he never got much. A man said to him: "In the northwest section of the city there are many people and I am sure that you will get a lot of contributions. Why do you stay here?" Fu answered: "As long as I get one or two copper coins, it will be sufficient to keep me alive. I have no use for lots of money." Chao Chung-shu, the governor of Ling-chou [in present-day Szechuan], was a notoriously harsh official. He neither respected nor trusted anyone. When he heard of this, he wanted to test Fu. One day he rode by Fu and purposely dropped a string of cash on the ground. Fu read his sutra as usual and did not even glance at the money. After Chao went some distance, he had his followers pick up the money. When this happened, Fu still did not pay any attention. Finally, Chao asked him: "You sit here all day and only get a coin or so. Now you see a whole string of cash lying on the ground. Why don't you stop the man who takes it away?" Fu answered: "Since it does not belong to me, how dare I claim it to be mine?" Upon hearing this, Chao got off the horse and paid Fu his respects. [*YCFH* 15, 9b–10a]

[*Chu-hung's concluding remark*]:
In Chinese "bhikshu" is rendered *ch'i-shih*, that is, a mendicant who lives in purity. To seek a lot, to have a lot, or to busy oneself with a lot all contradict the title. Starting with Master Min, the acts of all these masters have not been forgotten to this day even though a thousand years have elapsed. Whoever hears of them and fails to rise up is not worthy of being called a bhikshu. [13a–13b]

II. Strict and Upright Conduct

Refusal to Look at Women

Tao-lin of the T'ang Dynasty was a native of Ho-yang, T'ung-chou [in present-day Shansi]. When he was thirty-five years old, he became a monk and went to live as a hermit on a remote cliff on Mt. T'ai-pai. He was empowered by an imperial decree to live in the Ta-hsing-huo Ssu, but he soon left quietly for the north side of Mt. Liang. He was diligent and thrifty all his life. Since he regarded women as the source of transmigrations and impurity, he never went near them. He did not preach to them, receive food from them, nor allow them to enter his room. Just before he died, a woman came to inquire about his illness. When he found out about it, he had someone stop her far away, so that he did not have to look at her.

[*Chu-hung's comment*]:
The Vinaya allows preaching to women provided the monk does not show his teeth; nor should he say much. That this master should refuse to preach at all may seem to be overly strict. However, in this demoralized last age of the Law, we do not have to worry about not preaching to women, but should

worry about being contaminated by desire through preaching to women. We who have come after this old master ought to imitate him. [15a–15b]

Closing the Door in His Son's Face
Ts'ung-chien of the T'ang dynasty was a native of Nan-yang [in present-day Honan]. He became a monk in middle age, and soon understood the deep principle completely. During the Hui-ch'ang persecutions [845], he took refuge by living in the villa of the Huang-fu household. When the religion was reestablished at the beginning of Ta-chung [847–860], he returned to his old abode in Lo-yang. His son came to see him from Kuang-ling [in present-day Kiangsu] and met Chien at the door of the temple. His son did not recognize him and asked him where Master Ts'ung-chien was. Chien pointed to the east. After his son left, he closed the door and did not go out. Such was his resolve to cut off his family attachments. [16b]

[*Chu-hung's concluding remarks*]:
Some people may say that since a monk must pay attention to the six kinds of monastic harmony[23] and also practice the perfection of patience, strictness should not apply. Yet what I mean by strictness is not of harshness (*yen-li*) but that of sternness or seriousness (*yen-cheng*). If one controls one's mind with seriousness, then his mind will become correct. If he holds the Law with seriousness, the Law will also be established. This is the exact opposite of gaining notoriety by strange behavior or showing off one's power with a vicious temper. Monks should be careful in making the distinction between the two. [18a–18b]

III. Respect for the Teacher
Blaming Oneself for the Failure of a Disciple
Fa-yü of the Chin Dynasty served Tao-an [312–385] as his teacher. Later on he stayed at Ch'ang-sha Ssu in Chiang-lin [in present-day Hupei] and lectured on various sutras. More than four hundred monks studied under him. One day one of the monks drank wine. Fa-yü punished him, but did not drive him out of the monastery. When Tao-an heard about this, he sent Fa-yü a bamboo tube that contained a thorn stick. As soon as Fa-yü opened the sealed tube and saw the stick, he said: "This must be about the monk who drank. My neglect of instruction has caused my teacher who is far away to worry and send me this." He then beat the drum and assembled all the monks. When this was done, he put the bamboo tube in front, burned incense, lay on the ground, and asked the precentor (*wei-no*) to beat him three times with the stick. He reproached himself with tears in his eyes. Both monks and laymen in the neighborhood were greatly moved, and the people who were thus encouraged to strive for progress became more numerous. [19a]

[*Chu-hung's comment*]:
Suppose nowadays a person does what Master An did. I would not be surprised if the receiver smashed the bamboo tube, broke the stick, and more-

over cursed while doing so. Such a good teacher and disciple have been hard to find over the past thousand years. [19b]

Reproaching Oneself for Having Left the Teacher

Ch'ing-chiang of the T'ang dynasty understood the transitory nature of existence when he was still a child. He later studied under the Vinaya master T'an-i. Whether reciting sutras or expounding doctrines, he understood their meaning completely as soon as he laid his eyes on them. All the people who knew him said: "This is the hope of the Buddhist order." Once, after he had a slight disagreement with the teacher, he left. He wandered to different places and attended many lectures. Finally, he reproached himself, saying: "I have walked over half the country but seldom is anyone as good as my own teacher." So he went back to his teacher. When the monks were all assembled, he came forward and declared: "I would like to present myself once more as your disciple. Pray accept me." In reply, Master T'an-i gave him a vigorous scolding. Chiang cried and said in repentance: "I was ignorant before, but realized my mistake later on. Please show compassion to me and bestow joy." After repeated pleading, Master Tan-i finally took pity on him and, as before, treated him as his disciple. When Tan-i died, Chiang went to study with the National Master Chung, who secretly passed on to him the essentials of the doctrine. [20b]

[*Chu-hung's concluding remarks*]:
In former times, a disciple's faith in the master was even stronger after the latter's death. But, nowadays even during his teacher's lifetime a disciple shifts his loyalty. Why is this so? We feel that this is because when he first became a monk, he did not originally desire to rely on a true teacher who could resolve his doubts about life and death. He went to a teacher only as a result of coincidence. That is why he can shift his loyalty when he sees profit, when he is persuaded by evil friends, or when he is angry because his teacher has reprimanded him. . . . It is truly sad. [23a]

IV. Acts of Filial Piety
Saving One's Mother by Praying at the Tower

Tzu-lin of the T'ang dynasty was formerly surnamed Fan. His mother, whose surname was Wang, did not believe in Buddhism. He escaped to the Eastern Capital and received the tonsure from the Vinaya master Ch'ing-hsiu of the Kuang-shou Ssu. Then one day he suddenly missed his parents and went back to see them. But by this time his father was blind, and his mother had died three years before. So he went to the temple of the God of the Eastern Peak (Mt. T'ai), sat on the mat he brought with him, and chanted the Lotus Sutra. He vowed that he would see the God of Mt. T'ai and ask him the place of his mother's rebirth. That night he was summoned by the god, who told him his mother was imprisoned in hell and was at present suffering all kinds of torture. Lin cried bitterly and begged for his mother's absolution. The god of Mt. T'ai said to him that in order to save his mother, he should go to pray at the stupa of King Ashoka on Mt. Mo [east of Chin *hsien* in present-day Chekiang]. Lin immediately went to the stupa and, crying bitterly, prostrated himself forty-thousand times in front of the stupa. Then suddenly he heard someone call him. When he looked up, he saw his mother in the sky thanking him. She said that she was enabled by his help to be reborn in Trāyastriṅśā Heaven [*Tao-li-t'ien*, the heaven of the thirty-three devas, the second of the desire heavens, the heaven of Indra.] After she said this, she disappeared. [25a–25b]

[*Chu-hung's concluding remarks*]:
People in the world used to accuse monks of not recognizing their fathers, but it is abundantly clear from historical records that monks were more filial than ordinary people. If today there are still people who regard monks as snakes and scorpions, this is surely the fault of monks. Three sins committed by monks should be hated most grievously: first, to enjoy offerings from ten directions but fail to think of one's parents; second, to sit in the boat and cart oneself and make one's parents carry the reins or drag the chains as servants; third, to respect someone else as a parent after one has cut off ties with one's own. It is hoped that the public will not blame monks in general on account of the renegades who commit these three sins. [27b]

V. Loyalty to the Sovereign
Preaching the Dharma to Enlighten the Sovereign
Seng-ch'ou of the Northern Ch'i dynasty was a native of Chang-li [in present-day Jehol]. When he was twenty-eight years old he followed master Shih of Chü-lu [in present-day Hopei] and became a monk. Emperor Wen-hsüan [550–559] of the Northern Ch'i called him to court, but he refused to go. When the emperor came to visit him, he welcomed the emperor inside and preached the Dharma. He said that the three worlds [of desire, form, and formlessness] were all illusory, and the kingdom was the same. After he talked of the transitory nature of all worldly things, he expounded the method of fourfold mindfulness *(Ssu-nien-ch'u-fa)*.[24] When the emperor listened to this, he was so shaken that he perspired profusely. Consequently, the emperor took the bodhisattva precepts, forswore meat and wine, released his falcons and sparrow-hawks, did away with fishing and hunting, forbade slaughtering, and ordered his subjects to keep the fast during the six days of the month and the three months of the year. [30b]

[*Chu-hung's concluding remarks*]:
In the previous section, I recorded acts of loyalty. Does loyalty contradict loftiness? I do not think so. For everything depends on what one holds to be true. When one's virtue fills the mountain cave and one's fame reaches the imperial court, it is certainly one's true obligation to save one's emperor as well as the people. Yet it is a shame for us monks if we seek only glory by demeaning ourselves when the Great Way is not established. For monks have to respect themselves for the sake of the Way. If there be monks who enjoy the search for Truth but forget about power and positions, emperors

and officials will be amazed and moved. This is loyalty. For loyalty does not come into being only after one serves the emperor face to face. [45a]

VI. Compassion for Creatures
Cutting Off One Ear to Save a Pheasant
Chih-shun of the Sui dynasty [589–618] was a native of Chao-chou [in present-day Hopei]. He went north to Mt. Ting [in Shantung] and stayed in a little temple there. One day a pheasant who was being chased by a hunter ran into his room. The hunter was adamant, despite Shun's pleading. Shun cut off his own ear and gave it to the hunter, who was shocked into enlightenment, laid down his arrow, and released his falcon. After this people in several villages gave up hunting as their profession. Whenever Shun saw anyone suffering from poverty, he would cry copiously and give him whatever food and clothing he had. [34b–35a]

Attending Filthy Diseases without Complaint
Tao-chi of the T'ang dynasty was a native of Shu [Szechuan] and lived in Fu-kan Ssu in I-chou [in present-day Szechuan]. He was compassionate by nature. There was a man who suffered from dysentery, and the smell from the rotten flesh he excreted was so strong that everyone near him had to cover their noses. Yet Chi took care of the patient with single-minded attention. He would eat from the same bowl which the sick man used, and he often washed and mended the latter's clothes. When people asked him why, he said: "Purity is what the mind loves and filth what the mind hates. I take this as an exercise to unify my mind." [36b]

VII. Lofty Behavior
Refusing To Obey Imperial Summonses
Lan-jung of the T'ang dynasty lived on Mt. Niu-shou in Chin-ling [near present-day Nanking and Chiang-ning] as a hermit. The emperor heard about his fame and sent a messenger to fetch him. When the messenger arrived, Jung was sitting on the ground and, with mucus dropping from his nostrils [it was very cold], eating sweet potatoes he had cooked in cow dung. The messenger said: "The emperor has sent for you. Please get up." Jung looked at him intently but did not stir. Then the messenger smiled and said: "You have mucus on your cheeks." Jung said, "I haven't got time to wipe away the mucus for a worldly man." When the emperor learned of this, he was amazed and he properly glorified Jung by bestowing gifts upon him. [41a–41b]

Putting the Recommendation Letter Away
Ch'an master Hsüeh-tou Hsien of the Sung dynasty attained enlightenment under Master Chih-men Tso and planned to go to the Chekiang area. Mr. Tseng, a Hanlin scholar, said: "Lin-yin Ssu is one of the excellent places in the world, and I know Ch'an master Shan there very well. Take the letter I write recommending you." Hsien came to Lin-yin and stayed there incon-

spicuously for three years. Then suddenly Mr. Tseng was sent to the area on official business. When he came to Lin-yin to look for Hsien, nobody had ever heard of him. At that time there were more than a thousand monks in the monastery. He had his followers look in the dormitory, and there they found Hsien. Tseng asked about the recommendation letter he had written, and Hsien took it out from his sleeve. It was sealed as before. He said: "You are very kind to me. But I am just a mendicant monk who desires nothing from the world. How dare I hope to gain notoriety by using your recommendation letter!" Mr. Tseng laughed heartily, and Master Shan was amazed. [43b]

[Chu-hung's comment]:
Nowadays monks treasure letters from great officials like precious jade. They hope to sell themselves day and night. Is it possible that no one has heard of Hsüeh-tou's behavior?

VIII. Persevering and Retiring Acts
        Mingling with Woodcutters and Cattle Herders
P'u-yüan of the T'ang dynasty was a native of Hsin-cheng, Cheng-chou [in present-day Honan]. He first studied under the Ch'an master Ta-hui of Mt. Ta-wei, and achieved enlightenment under the great master Ma-tsu of Chiang-hsi. After this, he hid his brilliance and acted as if he had lost his power of speech. In the tenth year of Chen-yüan [794], he came to Mt. Nan-ch'üan in Ch'ih-yang [in present-day Anhwei]. Wearing a bamboo hat, he tended cows with the local herdsmen. He went into the forests and worked as a woodcutter. He sometimes also worked in the rice fields. For thirty years he did not leave Mt. Nan-ch'üan. In the middle of the Yung-ho era [827–835], the governor of Ch'ih-yang as well as other prominent officials asked him to preach the Dharma. His teaching attracted a universal following, and he was called the Ancient Buddha of Nan-ch'üan. [46b]

IX. Hardship and Suffering
        He Will Not Drive Away Fleas and Lice
T'an-yün of the T'ang dynasty was a native of Kao-yang [in present-day Hopei] and stayed in Mu-kua Ssu on Mt. Wu-t'ai. He wanted to be alone and lived by himself in a cave made of bricks. His clothes became rags after many years, and they were covered with fleas and lice. He let them suck his blood, using the suffering as a means to subdue his mind. During the summer retreats, fleas became even more numerous in the place he stayed. Since he would not drive them away, his body was covered with dried blood like a blanket. He felt that to feed the fleas with his blood was a proper way to expiate his past transgressions, and he had no hesitation. He practiced charity in this fashion for more than forty years.

[Chu-hung's comment]:
Although somebody may think that to let fleas and lice feed on his body is similar to the self-mortification practied by heretics, yet in truth there is a

difference. For if one desires to gain truth by mortification, it is indeed a heretical view. But what he was doing here was expiating his past transgressions by benefiting other creatures. This should not be regarded in the same way as the practices of the heretics. [52a]

X. Acts That Call Forth Supernatural Response
Sutra Chanting Prolongs the Life Span
Chih-tsang of the Liang dynasty [502–557] was a native of Wu [present-day Kiangsu] and lived at K'ai-shan Ssu on Ch'ung-shan. One day he met a fortuneteller who said to him: "You are unsurpassed in intelligence, but unfortunately you have not long to live. Your life span is only thirty-one years." At the time Chih-tsang was twenty-nine. After this conversation, he stopped giving lectures. He took out the Diamond Sutra from the library and chanted it with utmost sincerity. He confessed his sins and worshipped the Buddha day and night. When the time predicted for his death arrived, he suddenly heard a voice from the sky declaring: "Your life span should end now. But because of the merit of chanting the Wisdom Scripture, it is doubled." Later he met the fortuneteller again and the latter was amazed to see him still alive. Chih-tsang told him what had happened, and he then understood the unthinkable power of the scripture. [58b]

[*Chu-hung's comment*]:
In recording the exalted deeds of the ancients, I conclude the record with the chapter on supernatural response. There may be someone who will laugh at me and say, "There is no way that can be cultivated or realized. Since there is no way to cultivate it, there is no one to receive a reward, and since there is no way to realize it, there is no one to receive punishment. When you talk about reward and punishment, doesn't this indicate a mind that calculates merit and schemes for profit?" I would answer him: "The drum is beaten by a drumstick and responds with sound. The water is touched by the moon and responds with reflection. Where is the calculating and scheming here? There is a reason why a loyal official can make a withered bamboo sprout with his vows and a filial son can dissolve ice with his tears. If there were no reward and punishment through stimulation and response, then the law of cause and effect would become invalid. Talking about emptiness in such manner can only get one into trouble. We must be careful." [61b]

Religious Life at Yün-ch'i
The arrangement of buildings and daily schedules at Yün-ch'i reflected Chu-hung's ideal of a monastic community. There were two main halls where the principal activities were carried out. In the Great Hall (*Ta-t'ang*), monks worked on Pure Land meditation. Behind it, in the Vinaya Hall (*Lü-t'ang*), they studied precepts, performed the *prātimokṣa* ceremony, and perfected their understanding

of the Vinaya. The same hall was also used as the Dharma Hall *(Fa-t'ang)*, in which monks chanted sutras, listened to lectures, and mastered Buddhist doctrine. In this way doctrine, meditation, and discipline, the three branches of Buddhist cultivation, were given equal emphasis. However, the Great Hall was Yün-ch'i's nerve center, just as Pure Land meditation was the primary task of every monk living there. The schedule of the Great Hall determined the rhythm of the entire monastery.

Chu-hung fixed the number of monks admitted to live in the Great Hall at forty-eight. Before they were admitted, they had to prove that they had been ordained as novices for at least five years, that they observed discipline, understood Pure Land teaching, and had a general idea of the teachings of other schools. These forty-eight were chosen from among those residing at Yün-ch'i. In addition, twenty-four vacancies were reserved for visiting monks, who were housed in the Western Hall *(Hsi-t'ang)*. They too had to satisfy the four conditions for admission mentioned earlier, and two additional requirements were demanded of them. They had to have a subtle grasp of doctrine, and they had to manifest a sincere desire for cultivation.[25] The visiting monks followed the same schedule as that for monks at the Great Hall, although they carried on the work of silent contemplation in their own Western Hall. Only for the morning devotional services did they join the monks in the Great Hall.

The actual size of the community at Yün-ch'i was much larger than the forty-eight noted above, for it included functionaries, postulants, and persons not enrolled in the Great Hall. But since the Great Hall was the place where the principal work at Yün-ch'i was carried out, it was a symbol for the entire monastery. Chu-hung realized that some Ch'an monasteries of the T'ang could accommodate several hundred monks in their meditation halls. By comparison, Yün-ch'i had facilities for only forty-eight. But the limitation was consciously imposed by Chu-hung, who felt that quality was more important than quantity, and that the only way to ensure a standard of quality in his own time was to keep the enrollment small:

When masters in former times established monasteries to take in monks, they often gathered around themselves three hundred or five hundred followers. The fifth patriarch, Hung-jen, had seven hundred. Master Hsüeh-feng [I-tsun, 822–909] had over a thousand, and Master Ching-shan [Tao-ch'in, 713–792] had seventeen hundred disciples. I was very anxious at first and regretted very much that I was born too late to take part in these assemblies of dragons and elephants. Now that I am getting old and realize that the differences between the True, Counterfeit, and Degenerate Law were indeed real ones. In the present age, it is hard to find even one sincere seeker of the Way among large multitudes of people. . . . What use is it if one has numerous followers but few of them ever achieve true understanding? In my monastery, the meditation hall can accommodate only forty-eight persons. This accounts for one-tenth the number of former masters' disciples. Yet I still feel this is too many and want to further reduce the number. This is not because I am not interested in universal salvation. It is rather because the epoch of the Degenerate Law makes this necessary.[26]

Monks enrolled in the Great Hall followed a fixed daily schedule of silent Buddha recollection (chih-ching), devotional chanting (li-sung), and meditation (ju-kuan). As Chu-hung made clear in his rules on the Great Hall (rule 5), the orthodox method of religious cultivation being pursued here was nien-fo san-mei. Earlier (chapter III) we discussed Chu-hung's view on nien-fo. In these rules for the Great Hall, he put his theories into practice. In the course of a day's work, monks enrolled in the Great Hall had to practice all four kinds of nien-fo. Chih-ching refers to silent nien-fo; while one recites the Buddha's name silently, one also tries to achieve mental concentration by dwelling on the image (either actual or mental) of Amitābha. Ju-kuan, on the other hand, denotes a higher form of contemplation and concentration. The purpose is to actualize nien-fo san-mei, to achieve the coalescence between the meditator and the object of meditation, or identity between Amitābha and oneself. Throughout the four periods, the invocation of the Buddha's name is also carried out.

The essential rules of the Great Hall, the Vinaya Hall, and the Dharma Hall follow. They give us a fairly clear picture of religious life at Yün-ch'i. Titles of monastic personnel appear, along with frequent mention of punishment for any failure to observe the rules. For details of personnel and their functions, and the regulations regarding punishment, see Appendixes II and III.

Rules of the Great Hall[27]
1. The daily schedule is as follows: There are four periods (ssu-shih)[28] of silent Buddha recollection,[29] three periods of devotional chanting, and one period of meditation.

a. After the fifth watch [about 6 A.M.], it is the first period. When the incense for silent Buddha recollection is finished, recite the Śūraṅgama Mantra *(Leng-yen chou)*, the chapter on superior rebirth as the superior [of nine] grades [of the Amitāyurdhyāna Sutra], then call out the Buddha's name aloud a thousand times. Recite the shorter version of the "Essay on the Pure Land" *(Hsiao ching-t'u wen)*.[30] Transfer the merit *(hui-hsiang)*.[31]

b. After daybreak, it is the second period. This lasts until the incense for silent Buddha recollection is finished. Then comes the noon meal. After the noon meal, recite the forty-eight vows, and call out Buddha's name a thousand times. Transfer the merit as before.

c. After midday, it is the third period. It lasts until the incense for silent Buddha recollection is finished. After that, at the evening service, read the Smaller Sukhāvatīvyūha Sutra and the *Confessional (Ch'an-hui wen)*.[32] Put out an offering for sentient beings *(ch'u-sheng)*.[33] Then call out the Buddha's name a thousand times, recite the longer version of the "Essay on the Pure Land,"[34] and transfer the merit.

d. After dark, it is the fourth period. It lasts until the incense for silent Buddha recollection is finished. After that, call out the Buddha's name a hundred times. Retire to your sleeping place, and enter into meditation. Sleep peacefully.

Thus silent Buddha recollection, devotional exercise, and meditation form a day's pure work *(ching-yeh)*. They are neither too complicated nor too simple and can be continued without interruption. In the summer months, the devotions in the third period may be changed to before noon.

2. One is admitted into the hall only after he has the following four qualifications: (a) he has finished five summer retreats; (b) he observes discipline strictly; (c) he understands the teaching of the Pure Land; (d) he has a general concept of the teachings of other schools.

3. The meditation patrol *(hsün-hsiang)* in the hall uses a small flag. The flag is to be two inches long and the handle one foot two inches. If someone has dozed off, tap his knees with the flag handle, but do not hit him carelessly. When a person has sat for a long time, flash the flag in front of his eyes. If he is not asleep, he has to call out the Buddha's name once. When a person does not wake up after being warned three times, wake him up by beating on the patrol board. He who refuses to leave his seat is fined twenty *wen*. If he does not reform after several times, he is expelled from the hall.

4. Four semesters *(ssu-ch'i)* are instituted according to the four seasons. In winter and summer, the semesters last three months; in autumn and spring they are shorter and last about two months and ten days. When the semester is over, monks from outside are dismissed, and they can come and ask to be enrolled when a new semester starts. For the monks of this monastery, there is a fixed rule for their rotation. When a se-

mester is over, neither those who do not want to leave the hall nor those who want to enter the hall by force are allowed.

5. There may be someone in the assembly who, though enrolled in the Hall of Pure Deeds, does not practice the samadhi of Buddha recollection, but practices other methods. If such is the case, we do not dare retain him and thereby obstruct his progress, for this hall practices only *nien-fo*. He may come again if later on he should make a fervent decision to do the same.

6. Everyone in the hall should have studied and possess the three sutras of the Pure Land school [the Larger Sukhāvatīvyūha Sutra, the Amitāyurdhyāna Sutra, and the Smaller Sukhāvatīvyūha Sutra.] He should also have studied and own the following: the Commentary to the Smaller Sukhāvatīvyūha Sutra, the Commentary to the *Kuan-wu-liang-shou ching*, the ancient version of the Larger Sukhāvatīvyūha Sutra, the Forty-eight Vows, the Vow to be Reborn in the West (*Hsi-fang yüan-wen*)³⁵ (both of the latter have been newly reprinted), and the rosary. There are altogether six items. None who lacks one of them is allowed to enter the hall. No one is allowed to borrow any item from another person.

7. The forty-eight vows included in the old version of the Larger Sukhāvatīvyūha are to be read aloud during the third period. Each time only sixteen vows are recited, and it takes three days to complete the cycle. But in summer, when the weather is too hot, the recitation may be omitted.

8. The Buddha instituted the practice of sitting in meditation in winter and summer and of doing austerities in spring and autumn when begging is carried out. But even in the time of the Sage, if one had no elder teacher for guidance, one was apt to be troubled by Māra. Now it will be more so as we are in the last epoch of the Law. So for the sake of expediency, begging ought to be replaced by doing chores. Begging is practiced only when necessary.

9. When old acquaintances meet in the hall, they should not enter into conversation. They may converse in the sacristy (*hsiang-teng liao*), but even there, they should not talk long. Those who talk a long time are fined ten *wen*, and those who linger too long, thirty *wen*.

10. If one has to go out of the hall on business, he has to ask for a plaque [on which "leave to go out" is written] from the rector (*shou-tso*). If he leaves without the plaque, he is fined 20 *wen*. Outside the hall, anyone below the prior (*chih-yüan*) may report him.

11. When one leaves the monastery grounds with permission, if he exceeds a day in spring, summer, and fall, he is fined 10 *wen*. He is counted as absent when he exceeds three days. During the winter semester, he is counted absent as soon as he asks for permission. When a leave is granted, the time limit varies according to the distance he is going.

12. People enrolled in the hall are excused from these tasks: carrying rice and firewood, lecturing on scriptures, taking care of the sick, doing rou-

tine duties, and so on. But they have to work as instructors (*ching-ts'e*) and patrol just like everybody else.

13. Whenever one has doubts, he must ask. One should not conceal them.

Rules of the Vinaya Hall[36]

1. Each person should have the Vinaya Sutra, whose commandments he has received, the *Rules and Ceremonials for a Novice*, the *Extracts From the Four-Division Vinaya*, and the *Further Elucidation of the Commentary on the Bodhisattva Precepts*. When any one of the above is missing, he is fined 30 *wen*. Each person should have his own robes and bowls. When one is missing, he is also fined 30 *wen*.

2. One day before the recitation of the *prātimokṣa*, novices who are recently tonsured are examined on the *Rules and Ceremonials for a Novice*. Those who have imperfect understanding of its meaning are fined five *wen*. Those who have imperfect memory in reciting it by heart are fined 10 *wen*. Those who fail to memorize anything are demoted to the five-precepts group. The format for examining those who have received the precepts for a bhikshu and a bodhisattva is similar to this.

3. Those who have received the ten precepts should study Vinaya for five years. During this time, they are not allowed to go out to attend lectures, but they may study sutras inside the monastery. They take turns in setting grains of rice in the courtyard for [hungry] ghosts, attending semesters in the Great Hall, serving as acolytes, and taking care of the sick when there is no one else to do so. If a person falls short in observing precepts, on the day of *prātimokṣa* recitation the leader says loudly: "So-and-so who has received the ten precepts does not study or learn; therefore he is now demoted to the five-precepts group." After three months, when he has accumulated fifty good points,[37] he is restored to his original group.

4. Those who have received the bhikshu precepts may take turns leading prayer, teaching required sutras, chanting the five, ten, and bhikshu precepts, and delivering admonitions. Anyone who falls short in observing the precepts is demoted to the ten-precepts group on the day of *prātimokṣa* recitation in the manner described before. After three months, when he has accumulated seventy good points, he may be restored to his original group.

5. Those who have received the bodhisattva precepts may take turns chanting the bodhisattva precepts, lecturing on Buddhist teaching, teaching Mahāyāna scriptures, performing almsgiving [of goods and doctrine], delivering admonitions, serving as priors, and receiving robes from the laity. Anyone who falls short in observing the precepts is demoted to the bhikshu group on the day of *prātimokṣa* recitation, in the manner described before. After three months, when he has accumulated ninety good points, he can be restored to his original group.

6. When one fails to attend the *prātimokṣa* recitation and does not express his intention beforehand, he is fined 10 *wen*.

7. At the semi-monthly Vinaya recitation, when a person reports that someone has violated the ten monastic agreements or has committed some

other serious offense, the reciter should acknowledge his report right away. If the one who is so named is innocent, he should step out of the assembly and say: "I want to defend myself." The proctor (*yüen-ch'ung*) should answer: "You may do so tomorrow." The person should then step down. If he creates further disturbance, he is fined 50 *wen*.

8. People who come to the monastery to attend the *prātimokṣa* ceremony should arrive on that day. If they come from far away, then they may come a day before. They should return when the ceremony is over. Those who come too early or leave too late do not really come for the purpose of attending the ritual.

9. To cheat officials and conceal from the rest of the monks such things as not paying taxes, hiding grain, or using dishonest scales are all considered theft. One is either given first-degree punishment or expelled from the monastery.

10. If one falsely claims to have his master's order and cheats the brothers in the monastery or any other people, he is fined 500 *wen*. If the matter is serious, he is expelled after paying the fine.

11. If one accepts women as lay disciples before he is sixty years old, he is fined 500 *wen* [roughly $50 in today's currency] and after that expelled from the monastery.

Rules of the Dharma Hall[38]

1. In the hall, make sets of the Avataṁsaka Sutra available in spring, summer, and autumn. Choose people who know how to chant and put their names on a board. Each day they take turns chanting one *chüan*. After the whole sutra is finished, begin again. During the three months of winter, no chanting is practiced.

2. In studying the sutras, one ought to follow the order stipulated, but not disregard the order. If one does, for each sutra of great length he is fined 100 *wen*, and for each sutra of short length, 50 *wen*. The money is used to buy scriptures and to give to monks from other monasteries.

3. Everyone should memorize by heart the *Fo-i-chiao ching*, the *Instructions of Kuei-shan*, and the *Record of the Exalted Acts of Buddhist Monks*, and conscientiously act in accordance with the teachings embodied in these works. Every fifteen days, several persons are selected at random and examined on these.

4. Lecturers take turns lecturing on the Pure Land sutras, first the Smaller Sukhāvatīvyūha Sutra and next the *Kuan-wu-liang-shou ching*. After these, they lecture on the Lotus Sutra, the Sūraṅgama Sutra, and the others. When they finish the cycle, they start again.

5. People who study doctrine are divided into two groups: those of dull intelligence should read the text, and those of sharp intelligence should study its meaning. Those of the latter group should be further differentiated into two groups: one group practices according to the teaching, and the other group gives lectures to make clear the doctrine. Those who are chosen to be lecturers on the sutras must be persons endowed with sharp in-

tuition and persons who act with strict discipline. They must be chosen with great care and become a select group, lest they bring shame to Buddhism.

6. He who secretly studies the ritual of "bestowing food on hungry ghosts" without telling his superior or who merely studies the text is fined 500 *wen*.

7. The printing office must keep a careful account of the wooden blocks used for printing sutras. If no person of sincere faith can be found to take care of them, then choose several persons who will take turns in taking charge.

8. The person who proofreads sutras is given special food by the business office. When he discovers one mistake, he is given five good points; but if others point out a mistake, he is deprived of five good points.

9. Sutras which are kept in the monastery permanently: twenty-four sets of the Avataṁsaka Sutra, forty-eight sets of the Lotus Sutra and the *Confessional of Emperor Wu of Liang*. The extra copies are kept in the Pavilion of Many Buddhas *(To-fo-ko)* and given away. Those that are given to the monastery to be kept permanently do not come under this limitation.

CHAPTER NINE

Conclusion

THE FOCUS of this study has been the career of Yün-ch'i Chu-hung, and his ideas on *nien-fo,* lay Buddhism, and monastic reform. In tracing his career, I have also touched on the general condition of Ming Buddhism. This concluding chapter will recapitulate the main findings reached and offer some observations and evaluations concerning Chu-hung and Ming Buddhism.

One of the conspicuous features of Buddhism in the Ming dynasty was its syncretic nature. Although Ch'an Buddhism, in the form of its two subschools, Lin-chi and Ts'ao-tung, was nominally the dominant school of Buddhism, the impression one gets from Chu-hung and other Buddhist monks is that a pure Ch'an tradition of meditation and manual work had ceased to exist. Although the lineages of the schools were carefully maintained and monks continued to receive training in how to sit and work with *kung-an,* their affiliation with Ch'an usually amounted to mere lip-service. It seldom meant that they were engaged in the exclusive pursuit of training in Ch'an meditation. It was far more likely that although they affirmed their allegiance to the glorious memory of the Ch'an tradition, they were also concurrently engaged in Pure Land devotionalism, study of the Buddhist scriptures, performance of religious rites and rituals, and other secular and non-Buddhist interests and vocations. Since a person's sectarian identity no longer denoted actual expertise or genuine commitment, monks such as Chen-k'o, Chu-hung, and Te-ch'ing could view their exclusion from the Ch'an lineage as a matter of little consequence.

When we examine the thought and careers of these three prominent monks of the late Ming, we find that all advocated some kind of syncretism both within Buddhist schools and between Buddhism and Confucianism. We also discover that although all three received

Ch'an training and even practiced Ch'an meditation, they were listed in the "lineage unknown" section of contemporary and later biographical works of Ch'an monks. It is tempting to suggest that they advocated syncretism because they represented the minority point of view, because they were outcasts from the established families of Lin-chi and Ts'ao-tung, the assumption being that all the time there was a Ch'an tradition of strictness and purity which rejected any admixture of alien elements. But such an interpretation would hardly accord with the true situation. In fact, monks throughout the Ming period (and especially in the later years of the Ming) already practiced different types of syncretic mixes of Buddhism. Chu-hung and other Buddhist leaders were not offering syncretism as an alternative to a monolithic orthodoxy. On the contrary, they were interested in imposing a sense of order on and establishing some criterion of values for what must have appeared to them as a state of chaos. Since most people were practicing one type of syncretism or another, they felt it desirable to seek out the best possible mixture.

This tendency toward sectarian syncretism was, of course, not unique to Ming Buddhism. Both T'ien-t'ai and Hua-yen, in their comprehensive, architectonic approach toward the entire corpus of Buddhist teaching, as evidenced by their "classification of Buddhist doctrines" (p'an-chiao), were in their own way syncretic systems of thought. They also provided theoretical rationales for the sectarian syncretism of later periods. To give a few examples, both Yen-shou and Te-ch'ing used the T'ien-t'ai concept of "one mind" (i-hsin) or "true suchness" (chen-ju, bhūtatathatā) to justify the simultaneous adoption of different paths for reaching enlightenment. Chu-hung, on the other hand, turned to the Hua-yen philosophy of dharmadhātu to establish his claim that nien-fo was no different from Ch'an meditation. Specifically, he held that one could view the act of reciting the Buddha's name on two levels, or in two realms: that of li or universality, and that of shih or particularity.

But to acknowledge the inherent comprehensiveness of T'ien-t'ai and Hua-yen is not to equate these systems of thought with the general looseness and fluidity that characterized the outlook of most Ming monks. Indeed, the difference could not be more striking. While the former was a syncretism born of strength, the latter was born of weakness. Chih-i, Fa-tsang, and others like them could accept other approaches in Buddhism as valid because they could find

an appropriate place for such approaches in their systems, and sub-
sume all views and practices under a comprehensive vision of Truth.
A monk in the early Ming period pursued various paths because he
did not have a central vision that could serve as an integrating and
unifying force in his life. One might say that what Chu-hung tried to
do was change a prevailing sense of weakness into a sense of
strength. He sought to establish a center and to impart a vision, and
he tried to do this through his theory and practice of *nien-fo*.

Before we take up a critical review of Chu-hung's efforts as a
leader of the lay Buddhist movement and of monastic reform, it may
be helpful to review briefly the condition of the Buddhist order in
the Ming. We have little information about the overall composition
of the Buddhist order in any dynasty, and therefore it would be dangerous to make sweeping comparisons between the sangha in the
Ming with, let us say, the sangha during the T'ang and Sung. It is,
however, still possible to agree with Chu-hung and other witnesses
that the sangha had suffered a considerable loss of prestige, and that
it seemed to have declined intellectually, religiously, and morally
from the standards of former days. What led to this decline? Chu-
hung frequently explained it by referring to *mo-fa*, or the Age of the
Decay of the Law. But in moments of critical reflection he suggested
that the neglect of Vinaya rules and the lifeless formalism of Ch'an
training were most responsible for the secularization and degeneration of the order.

The review in chapter VI of some of the major government regulations enacted during the Ming concerning the control of the
Buddhist order shows that most laws and statutes were seldom enforced and hardly effective, with the sole exception of those which
divided Buddhist monasteries into three categories: *ch'an* (meditation), *chiang* (scripture study), and *chiao* (religious services). Even
though the tripartite division of monasteries was already to be found
in the Sung, T'ai-tsu made a significant change when he substituted
for the former category of *lü* (discipline) that of *chiao* or *yü-chia*.
Henceforth, the *lü* monasteries, which theoretically made ordination
and the study and observance of Vinaya their exclusive concerns,
were no longer recognized by the state. Moreover, T'ai-tsu tried to
encourage the growth of *chiao* at the expense of the other two
categories. Although monks specializing in religious rituals were
given privileged treatment, laws were created to restrict those special-

izing in meditation and doctrinal study from free association with the general population. It matters little whether T'ai-tsu's laws created the conditions for the secularization and commercialism of the monastic community or merely exacerbated an existing condition; their effect was to contribute to the decline of the order. When a monk made skill in performing religious rituals (mostly funeral rites, "soul masses," and other related rituals concerning the dead) his primary function, he was merely an instrument of potential customers. Such a monk indeed no longer deserved the title of "bhikshu."

Living in the inauspicious age of *mo-fa*, what was Chu-hung's answer to the need for revitalizing Buddhism? His concern was essentially twofold: on the one hand, he was interested in securing the survival of the monastic order and guarding it against the inroads of mercantilism and formalism; on the other hand, he wanted to help Buddhist values and ideas penetrate the larger society through the spread of the lay Buddhist movement. The motivating and integrating force behind both was his comprehensive understanding of *nien-fo*.

Chu-hung is usually regarded as the proponent, if not the originator, of the joint cultivation of Ch'an and Pure Land Buddhism. This is generally taken to mean the simultaneous pursuit of Ch'an meditation and Pure Land devotionalism. However, I believe that Chu-hung intended to make *nien-fo* central for himself and his followers. In supplying *nien-fo* with a new theoretical framework, Chu-hung attempted to make it so comprehensive that it would contain Ch'an meditation within itself. As chapter III has shown, quite a few monks before Chu-hung advocated the use of *A-mi-t'o-fo* as a *kung-an*. It thus may appear that Chu-hung was simply reiterating a well-worn theme, but a careful analysis of his views on the subject suggests otherwise. Although there is much similarity between his *i-hsin nien-fo* (recitation and rembrance of Buddha's name with one mind) and the *nien-fo kung-an* of earlier monks, there is, in fact, a major difference. When earlier Buddhists used *A-mi-t'o-fo* as a *kung-an*, they incorporated *nien-fo* within the overall framework of Ch'an meditation. They argued that the intense concentration on *A-mi-t'o-fo* could lead to enlightenment. Since it had the same usefulness as other Ch'an *kung-an*, it ought to be accepted as one of them. Chu-hung, however, argued that as long as one focused on *nien-fo,* other *kung-an* and Ch'an practices would be unnecessary, because *nien-fo* already contained the Ch'an path and was a more suitable form of religious cultivation during the age of *mo-fa.*

Chu-hung also showed himself to be an innovator in his success with the lay Buddhist movement. Although its essential components were drawn from Pure Land Buddhism, the lay Buddhist movement was syncretic in nature. It emphasized recitation of the Buddha's name, nonkilling, and compassion both for one's fellow human beings and for animals, and concretized this compassionate attitude in acts of social philanthropy and the release of animals from captivity and slaughterhouses. Although there were historical precedents for all of these, the late Ming movement was more than a revival of earlier movements. One of the principal reasons for this was Chu-hung's success in affecting lay practice as well as reorganizing the monastic order. Not only did he accord the lay devotee the same attention as the monk, but he gave him detailed, practical, and programmatic directions for his religious practice. Chu-hung's choice of nonkilling and the release of life as central themes in lay proselytization was another reason. Since the Confucian tradition did not put particular emphasis on reverence for the life of animals, lay Buddhist practice could serve to complement and even deepen the religious consciousness of lay devotees. It definitely facilitated the eventual syncretizing of Confucian and Buddhist values in their lives.

A more striking feature of Chu-hung's approach to the lay Buddhist movement was his emphasis on moral action and his relative neglect of theological speculation. Instead of viewing the human condition as transient, illusory, and painful, Chu-hung regarded it as the best opportunity to realize the Truth. In his eyes, therefore, one should cherish and use this life to achieve enlightenment and not look at the human condition with horror and disgust. Instead of viewing human relationships and social obligations as obstacles to one's salvation, Chu-hung regarded them as among the appropriate means to salvation. One did not have to reject the world or escape from society in order to find release; one could find it in the midst of secular activities. To be a filial son and a loyal subject did not bar one from enlightenment. On the contrary, if one failed to be a filial son and a loyal subject, one also failed to be a true Buddhist. The Ch'an saying that carrying water and chopping wood are in the Way was now brought to its logical conclusion.

The lay Buddhist movement at the end of the Ming was more activist than contemplative, more moralistic than theological, more world-affirming than world-rejecting. All these signify a considerable transformation, if not a complete about-face, from the traditional Buddhist teaching. Complex social, political, economic, and historical factors were involved in this eventual "Confucianization" of Buddhism. Because Confucianists had consistently attacked Buddhists for their alleged suppression of natural feelings and disregard for social and familial obligations, the Buddhists had to come to terms with the realities of a Confucian state in order to survive. It was also undoubtedly true that unless Buddhism had broken away from monastic isolation, doctrinal rigidity, and scholastic obscurity, it would have had a poor chance of reaching the general populace. Chu-hung, in some measure, did exactly this with his innovations in lay Buddhism. Precisely because the lay movement did not demand a radical break from the social system in which it existed, it not only survived but continued to flourish throughout the Ch'ing and to some extent into the present time. During this period, those who were responsible for the two major attempts at revitalization, Chou Meng-yen (1655–1739) and P'eng Shao-sheng (1739–1796) in the K'ang-hsi and Ch'ien-lung eras, and Yang Wen-hui (1837–1911) in the late Ch'ing and early Republican periods, all claimed Chu-hung as their source of inspiration. In Chu-hung's work lay the movement's strength. The lay movement, then, was neither ephemeral nor sporadic. On the contrary, it became a permanent and pervasive phenomenon.

It would be an oversimplification, however, to attribute the changes in Buddhism to its accommodation to Confucianism, for in truth Confucianism (and Taoism) had also been greatly affected by Buddhism. This brings us back to the problem of syncretism in Chinese thought. Syncretism usually has negative connotations. It frequently suggests or implies an indiscriminate mixture of disparate elements, accompanied by vulgarization of doctrine, weakening of commitment, and corruption of practice. It is perhaps for this reason that purists tend to condemn the syncretic practices of post-T'ang Buddhism as impure and degenerate. Yet I feel that the late

Ming case offers a positive example of syncretism. The lay movement proved to be durable and workable, important criteria for the evaluation of any religious movement. Similarly, the combining of the three teachings generated an openness and a receptivity in spiritual, moral, and intellectual spheres of life. What is more significant, it made the separation of the three spheres unnecessary. It was in this fusion, I believe, that late Ming thought gave new expression to an underlying tendency of Chinese thought.

Finally, I will discuss briefly Chu-hung's achievement as a monastic reformer and his possible influence over the sangha of later generations. When compared with the preceding remarks on his contribution to the lay Buddhist movement, the assessment that follows will appear to be less enthusiastic and more ambivalent. The reasons are twofold: first, despite the existence of copious rules and regulations at the Yün-ch'i Ssu, we have no way of ascertaining whether they were indeed implemented. We have only the laudatory testimony of his followers and associates to go by, which quite possibly contains hagiographic exaggeration. Furthermore, if these rules were implemented at Yün-ch'i during Chu-hung's residence there, we still have no way of knowing *how* they were implemented. Were all the rules in his code carried out to the letter? Were some of them implemented and others abrogated or ignored? Or were only a few rules (such as the semi-monthly recitation of *prātimokṣa* and the schedules of the Meditation Hall) faithfully observed because of their importance or because of the ease of detection if they were neglected? Likewise, were more rules in fact overlooked because of their comparative triviality and the difficulty of supervision (such as the system of counting good points and the apparatus for imposing fines)? Again, we are in the dark. If we know little of actual conditions at Yün-ch'i during Chu-hung's lifetime, we can claim to know even less of prevailing practices at other monasteries both in the late Ming and afterward. Since we have only written documents but no first-hand testimony, the difficulty presented by this kind of problem seems insurmountable. There are no living witnesses to cross-examine; neither are there contemporary sources for corroboration, so far as I know. We are forced to deal with only the ideal picture suggested by the written word.

Another reason for ambivalence toward Chu-hung's monastic reforms has to do with their very nature. It was doubtless true that the sangha of the late Ming was, by and large, in a sorry state. The monks probably were, just as he claimed, worldly, ill-disciplined, poorly informed in Buddhist doctrine, and not adept at or interested in religious cultivation. It is also undoubtedly true that Chu-hung managed to instill a new sense of commitment and dedication in his followers at Yün-ch'i. But was the revival seriously affected by his insistence on discipline? Although we have no conclusive evidence to the contrary, my conjecture is that Chu-hung's personal charisma probably contributed just as much to his success at Yün-ch'i. The leadership of strong masters has always been one of the deciding factors behind the rise or fall of a school, a sect, or a monastery in Chinese Buddhism. By laying special emphasis on discipline and the organizational aspects of monastic life, Chu-hung had hoped to create a kind of institutionalized charisma. He intended to invest the body of monastic codes with a new authority parallel, if not superior, to that of personal leadership.

Keenly aware of the critical challenges the sangha faced in his time, Chu-hung's primary goal was to seek a way of survival for monastic Buddhism. He succeeded in winning the case for discipline; the Chinese monastic community, even in the twentieth century, is famed for its meticulous observance of rules such as chastity and vegetarianism. For this reason, one may credit Chu-hung with the achievement of preserving Buddhism. One may argue that Chu-hung helped to make the monastic order institutionally viable and thereby provided an environment for the rise of future Buddhist leaders.

Yet one can also see his influence on the monastic order in another light. By overemphasizing strict observance of rules and regulations, Chu-hung had a tendency to lapse into legalism. One reads that if a dish steward at Yün-ch'i broke a dish out of anger, he had to repay tenfold, and if he refused to pay, he was expelled from the monastery. When one recalls that expulsion from the monastery was the most severe penalty for a monk, and that it was reserved for the monk who committed the four unpardonable sins, one is left to wonder at the judiciousness and practicality of such a ruling. This tendency to evaluate qualitatively different acts in terms of quantitative equivalents already appears in his adoption of the merits and demerits system in *The Record of Self-knowledge*. As I pointed out in chapter V, a legalistic and mechanical treatment of morality leads to moral petrification. Reward and punishment may serve as incentives and deterrents, but they cannot be substituted for the life-spring of moral action—conscience. In a similar way, discipline must be closely interwoven with meditation and wisdom. When the latter two are absent, discipline easily degenerates into sterile conservatism.

Chu-hung showed that he was fully aware of the complexity of the question. He tried, both in his writing and in his work at Yün-ch'i, to strive for a balanced development of discipline, meditation, and doctrinal study. He criticized the rules of Pai-chang because they were too detailed and hard to implement. Yet his own rules could be criticized as having some of the same shortcomings.

Having said this, however, I do not intend to end the book on a negative note. Buddhism indeed experienced a renewal in the late Ming and received new life energy. It penetrated deeply into the fabric of Ming society. Buddhist ideas and values were accepted widely by the general population and formed integral parts of their mental universe. As a result, monastic Buddhism also maintained its institutional viability throughout the Ch'ing and down to the twentieth century. Without Chu-hung and the other Buddhist leaders of late Ming, the renewal of Buddhism might not have happened.

APPENDIX ONE

~~~~~~

A Translation of
The Record of Self-knowledge
(Tzu-chih Lu)

CATEGORY OF GOOD DEEDS (SHAN-MEN)
Loyal and Filial Deeds
(chung-hsiao lei)

1. Serve parents with the utmost respect and loving attention; one day, one merit.

2. Observe their instructions righteously and do not disobey them; each instance counts as one merit.

3. When parents pass away, help their deliverance by performing Buddhist rites; each hundred cash spent counts as one merit.[1]

4. Preach the worldly goodness *(shih-chien shan-tao)* to one's parents; each time this is done, count ten merits.

5. Preach the supramundane goodness *(ch'u-shih-chien shan-tao)* to one's parents; each time this is done, count twenty merits.

6. Serve a stepmother with the utmost respect and loving attention; each day counts as two merits.

7. The same goes for serving one's grandparents.

8. Serve the emperor with the utmost loyalty; each day counts as one merit.

9. If you are an official, propose a benevolent policy; when it benefits one person, it counts as one merit.

10. When it benefits a region, it counts as ten merits.

11. When it benefits the whole country, it counts as fifty merits.

12. When it benefits the country in later generations, it counts as one hundred merits.

13. Observe the laws and the institutions of the present dynasty without violation; each instance counts as one merit.

14. Be honest and undeceiving in managing affairs; each instance counts as one merit.

15. Treat teachers and elders with respect; each day counts as one merit.

16. Follow the teacher's good advice; each instance in which the advice is heeded counts as one merit.

17. Respect elder brothers and love younger brothers; each time one does so counts as one merit.

18. Love and respect stepbrothers; each time one does so counts as two merits.

Altruistic and Compassionate Deeds
(jen-tz'u lei)

19. To save one person afflicted with serious illness counts as ten merits.

20. To give a person a dose of medicine counts as one merit.

21. For each sick person one meets in the street and carries back to one's home by carriage for rest and treatment, count twenty merits.

22. No merit is earned if one accepts a bribe. (It is a bribe if one accepts the sick person's money.)

23. To save one person from the death penalty counts as one hundred merits.

24. To pardon one person sentenced to the death penalty counts as eighty merits.

25. To reduce one person's sentence from the death penalty counts as forty merits.

26. No merit is earned for a deed done under bribery or out of personal sentiment.

27. To save one person from military exile (chün-hsing) [2] or penal servitude (t'u-hsing) [3] counts as forty merits.

28. To pardon one person from military exile or penal servitude counts as thirty merits.

29. To reduce one person's term of military exile or penal servitude counts as fifteen merits.

30. To save one person from heavy bambooing (chang-hsing) [4] counts as fifteen merits.

31. To pardon one person from heavy bambooing counts as ten merits.

32. To reduce one person's sentence of heavy bambooing counts as five merits.

33. To save one person from light bambooing *(ch'ih-hsing)* [5] counts as five merits.

34. To pardon one person from light bambooing counts as four merits.

35. To reduce [6] one person's sentence of light bambooing counts as three merits.

36. No merit is earned if the above is done under bribery or out of biased and unfair judgment.

37. The same merit scheme applies to a household head when he pardons or reduces the punishment of his men and women servants.

38. To save an infant from being drowned and bring it up oneself counts as fifty merits.

39. To persuade others not to drown an infant counts for thirty merits.

40. To adopt a deserted infant counts for twenty-five merits.

41. To refrain from killing a soldier who has surrendered or a person coerced into surrendering counts for fifty merits.

42. When one saves domestic animals capable of repaying human kindness *(yu-li pao-jen)*, for each animal thus saved count twenty merits.

43. For each domestic animal saved that has no power to return human kindness *(wu-li pao-jen)*, count ten merits.

44. For each small animal saved, count one merit. For ten very small creatures saved, count one merit.

45. If one saves only small creatures but not large ones because small creatures are easy to add up into merits, or if for the same reason one saves only large animals regardless of their cost, neither is meritorious. [7]

46. For the saving of each animal that harms others, [8] count one merit.

47. In preparing for sacrificial ceremonies or banquets, it is customary to kill animals. If one does not kill but buys already cooked dishes, every hundred cash thus spent yields one merit.

48. When one's hereditary profession is taking care of silkworms, if one refuses to look after them, he earns five merits. [9]

49. Talking to fishermen, hunters, and butchers in order to make them change their professions counts as three merits.

50. To succeed in making one of them change his profession counts as fifty merits.

51. When one is an official, officially to prohibit slaughtering for one day counts as ten merits.

52. When domestic dogs, domesticated water buffalo, or draft horses die, bury them. For each large animal buried, count ten merits.

53. For each small animal buried, count five merits.

54. If one further helps animals through religious services for speedy deliverance, each animal counts five merits.

55. In helping widows, widowers, orphans, the childless, the blind, the bedridden, and the poor, for each hundred cash spent, count one merit.

56. If small amounts of money are spent at different times for charity, when they accumulate to one hundred cash, count one merit.

57. If rice, wheat, cloth, and money are given out, they should be converted into their monetary value and counted the same way.

58. Charity given to members of one's own clan or to people in misfortune is considered the same as above.

59. When one takes in poor people and feeds them, each day one does so counts as one merit.

60. To comfort a person who is burdened with worries successfully counts as one merit.

61. When one sells grain at a fair price in years of famine, each hundred cash lost will earn one merit. (Loss below what one would make if one were a profiteer.)

62. To give one meal to a hungry person counts as one merit.

63. To give ten drinks to a thirsty person counts as one merit.

64. To give a person who is cold a warm room for one night counts as one merit.

65. To give him a suit of padded cotton clothing counts as two merits.

66. To provide light for someone on a dark night counts as one merit.

67. To give one person raingear on a rainy day counts as one merit.

68. To give two feedings to domestic animals and fowl counts as one merit.

69. In canceling the debt others owe you, for each hundred cash thus canceled, count one merit.

70. If the debt has stood for many years and a great deal of interest has accumulated, and one knows that it is difficult to recover

the debt but cancels upon the debtor's piteous pleading, for each two hundred cash canceled count one merit.

71. But no merit is earned if one goes to the official first and, because the official does not agree to deal with it, only then is one forced to cancel the debt.

72. To relieve men or beasts for one hour because they suffer from fatigue counts as one merit. ("To relieve" means either to stop their work or to do the work for them.)

73. When giving coffins to families who have no money to bury their dead, for each hundred cash spent, count one merit.

74. To bury one abandoned corpse earns one merit.

75. To give land to a family that has no burial ground earns thirty merits.

76. No merit is earned if one charges land rent on it.

77. To set aside charitable burial ground (*i-chung*), each hundred cash spent counts as one merit.

78. To pave a road that is muddy, obstructed, and dangerous, for each one hundred cash spent, count one merit.

79. The same goes for digging charitable wells, building or repairing rest pavilions, bridges, ferries, and so on.

80. No merit is earned if it is done after receiving a bribe.

81. As a superior in office, be kind to subordinates. For each person thus treated, count one merit.

82. To keep a man in a post after he has comm'tted a pardonable mistake earns ten merits.

83. No merit is earned if it is done after receiving a bribe.

84. Also, no merit is earned if the superior does not mistreat his subordinates.

85. Treat the emperor's subjects as one's own children lest you hurt them; for each instance that so illustrates kindness, count one merit.

86. Make good [marriage] arrangements for one's concubines and maids after their dismissal. For each person thus taken care of, count ten merits.

87. For each hundred in cash so spent in giving them away, count one merit.

88. Return men or women servants to the person who sold them free and do not take the man's money in redemption. For each hundred cash of their original sale price thus annulled, count one merit.

89. The same applies if one spends one's own money to re-

deem men and women servants and return them to their original owners.

Deeds Beneficial to the Three Jewels
(san-pao kung-te lei)

90. When you pay for the making of Buddhist images, each hundred cash spent counts as one merit.

91. In having images made of devas *(chu-t'ien)*, former sages, orthodox gods who govern the world, and virtuous men and women,[10] each two hundred in cash spent earns one merit.

92. Each hundred cash spent in engraving Mahāyāna scriptures earns one merit.

93. Each two hundred cash spent engraving Hīnayāna and ethical texts[11] discussing karma and retribution, heaven and man *(jen-t'ien yin-kuo)* earns one merit.

94. No merit is earned if this is done under bribery. (That is, if one takes others' money for doing this or if one sells them for profit.)

95. Printing and distributing the scriptures are also considered the same as above.

96. Each hundred cash spent in building Buddhist temples, nunneries or monasteries or in buying beds, seats, and ritual utensils earns one merit.

97. In giving land to Buddhists, for each hundred in cash of its value, count one merit.

98. The same applies to the maintenance of [permanent] monastic property.

99. For each two hundred cash spent in building temples for devas, orthodox gods, and sages, count one merit.

100. No merit is earned if one uses animal meat in sacrifices.

101. Each hundred cash spent in offering incense, candles, lamps, and oil to Buddhist monasteries earns one merit.

102. Receiving the great bodhisattva precepts counts forty merits.

103. Receiving Hīnayāna precepts counts thirty merits.

104. Receiving the ten precepts counts twenty merits.

105. Receiving the five precepts earns ten merits.

106. Writing one volume of commentary on Mahāyāna sutras, shastras, and Vinayas counts as fifty merits. (If one writes many volumes, the maximum number of merits is fifteen hundred.)

107. Writing one volume of commentary on a Hīnayāna or ethi-

cal text counts as one merit. (If one writes many volumes, the maximum number of merits is three hundred.)

108. No merit is earned if the interpretation is biased or unfounded.

109. To compose or edit one volume of a religious nature counts as twenty-five merits. (If there are many volumes, the maximum number of merits is five hundred.)

110. If it is one volume of an ethical nature, count ten merits. (If there are many volumes, the maximum number of merits is one hundred.)

111. No merit is earned if the content is not beneficial.

112. When you find a forged sutra and persuade others not to study it, count one merit.

113. To recite one volume of a sutra for the benefit of one's emperor, parents, relatives, friends, and sentient beings in the Dharma realm counts as two merits.

114. To call on the Buddha's name a thousand times counts as two merits.

115. To prostrate oneself a hundred times in repentance counts as two merits.

116. No merit is earned if this is done under bribery.

117. For one's own benefit to recite one volume of a sutra, call on the Buddha's name a thousand times, and prostrate oneself a hundred times in repentance counts as one merit.

118. For every hundred cash spent in performing the ritual of "bestowing food" for the sake of one's emperor, parents, and sentient beings in the Dharma realm, count one merit.

119. To perform one ritual of "bestowing food" counts as three merits.

120. No merit is earned if this is done under bribery.

121. For each hundred in cash spent in performing one rite to avert disasters for the sake of the nation, count one merit.

122. No merit is earned if this is done under bribery.

123. In giving lectures on Mahāyāna sutras, shastras, or Vinaya, when five persons are present, count one merit. (When many people are present, the maximum number of merits is one hundred.)

124. In giving lectures on Hīnayāna or philosophical works, when ten persons are present, count one merit. (When many people are present, the maximum number of merits is eighty.)

125. No merit is earned if it is done under bribery or for fame, or if the content of the lecture is empty, unorthodox, and not beneficial to men.

126. Paying obeisance to Mahāyāna scriptures fifty times counts as one merit.

127. When lectures on the True Law are given, attend them with a sincere heart; each attendance counts one merit.

128. To feed three monks who ask for food counts as one merit.

129. To feed two monks after inviting them to one's home counts as one merit.

130. To feed one monk by donation to a monastery counts as one merit.

131. For each monk whom one feeds with utmost respect and sincerity, count five merits.

132. No merit is earned if one feeds monks only after their repeated begging.

133. In giving food to monks, do not refuse to give beggars food, but offer them the same amount. For two beggars fed, count one merit.

134. To protect one monk earns one merit.

135. No merit is earned if the monk is a criminal.

136. To ordain one person who later becomes a disciple of great virtue counts as fifty merits. (A disciple of great virtue is one who can glorify Buddhism and benefit mankind and the universe.)

137. To ordain one person who becomes a disciple of clear understanding and good discipline counts as ten merits. (If the disciple only has clear understanding or only observes discipline well, count five merits.)

138. No merit is earned if one ordains people indiscriminately *(lan-tu)*.

Miscellaneous Good Deeds
(tsa-shan lei)

139. For each hundred cash one refuses to accept because it is contrary to one's integrity, count one merit.

140. For each hundred cash one refuses to accept when one's integrity is not affected by accepting the money, count two merits.

141. For each one hundred cash one refuses to accept even when one is extremely poor, count three merits.

142. To remain chaste when faced with sexual temptation counts as fifty merits.

143. No merit is earned if one stops doing anything only because circumstances prevent it.

144. To return debts or borrowed articles on time counts as one merit.

145. For each hundred cash of someone else's debt that you pay for him, count one merit.

146. For ceding one hundred cash worth of land or real estate, count one merit.

147. Instruct children with lessons about justice *(i-fang);* each instruction so given earns one merit.

148. The same applies to the instruction given to members of the family and house guests *(men-k'o)* in an upper-class family *(ta-chia).*

149. Persuade others to donate money for philanthropy. For each one hundred cash donated as a result, count one merit.

150. No merit applies if the persuasion is carried out for one's own fame or profit.

151. Persuade people to stop lawsuits. One person thus saved, who would otherwise be sentenced to death,[12] counts as ten merits.

152. To save one person who would otherwise be sentenced to military exile or penal servitude counts as five merits.

153. To save one person from heavy bambooing counts as two merits.

154. To save one person from light bambooing counts as one merit.

155. To reconcile two parties who are quarreling counts as one merit.

156. No merit is earned if it is done under bribery.

157. To pronounce a lasting maxim of virtue counts as ten merits. (Maxims such as Duke Ching of Sung's three words or Yang Po-chi's four kinds of knowledge.)[13]

158. Do good whenever there is opportunity; each good deed counts as one merit.

159. Reform whenever you become aware of error; each error corrected counts as one merit.

160. To recommend one good person counts as ten merits.

161. To dismiss one evil person counts as ten merits.

162. Make known the good deeds of other people; for every deed so publicized, count one merit.

163. Conceal other people's shortcomings; for every shortcoming so concealed, count one merit.

164. To stop others from publicizing another person's shortcomings counts as five merits.

165. To pay respect and offer gifts to one virtuous man counts as five merits.

166. To stop others when they ill-treat or vilify a virtuous man counts as five merits.

167. To persuade one person to forsake evil and turn to good counts as ten merits.

168. To help one person become established in his family affairs counts as ten merits.

169. To help one person become established in scholastic accomplishment counts as twenty merits.

170. To help one person become established in moral cultivation counts as thirty merits.

171. If one has made a promise to a friend, to keep it counts as ten merits.

172. To keep a serious promise such as promise to the orphaned child of a friend or to respect the chastity of a friend's wife counts as one hundred merits.

173. To keep a promise regarding the safekeeping of money for the young son of a friend, each one hundred cash so taken care of counts as one merit.

174. For each favor returned, count one merit.

175. To return a favor with extra kindness counts ten merits.

176. To forego avenging a wrong counts as one merit.

177. No merit is earned if one returns a private favor by using public means.

178. To wear old clothes with patches counts two merits. To wear clothes made of coarse cloth counts one merit.

179. No merit is earned if they are worn because one has no good clothes, or if one wears them in order to invite praise.

180. For a meat-eater to do without one meal counts as one merit. [Because fasting is meritorious.]

181. For a vegetarian to do without one meal counts as two merits. [Because vegetarianism is already meritorious.]

182. No merit is earned if one does so because one cannot afford the meal.

183. For a meat-eater to refuse to eat the meat of an animal when he witnesses its killing counts as one merit.

184. To refuse to eat it because he hears the sound of the killing counts as one merit.

185. For a meat-eater to refuse to eat it when he knows that the killing is for his sake counts as one merit.

186. For each time one bears rude treatment by others, count one merit.

187. For everything worth one hundred cash that one returns to the person who lost it, count one merit.

188. For each time one bears blame oneself and leaves the praise to others, count two merits.

189. For each instance when one leaves fame, status, or profit to fate and refuses to scheme for them, count ten merits.

190. For every day in one's job when one always plans for the group and not for oneself, count one merit.

191. To cause other people to obtain their money and position even if one sacrifices one's own counts as fifty merits.

192. Do not blame other people or fate when you lose money or encounter various difficulties; for each time one avoids blaming, count three merits.

193. When one prays for blessings and the avoidance of disaster, to make only good vows and to refrain from sacrificing animals counts as five merits.

194. To transmit one volume on hygiene and the preservation of life counts as five merits.

195. To transmit five prescriptions that cure illness counts as one merit.

196. No merit is earned if this is done after receiving a bribe or if the treatment prescribed does not work.

197. Pick up papers with words on them in the street and burn them; for every hundred characters so burned, count one merit.

198. For each instance where a man with money and power refrains from exerting his own authority but acts reasonably, count ten merits.

199. To refrain from allying with the powerful counts as ten merits.

200. To refuse to accept instruction about the Taoist technique of making cinnabar *(lu-huo tan-shu)* counts as thirty merits.

201. When given finished cinnabar, refuse to use it as counterfeit silver *(tan-yin)*. For each hundred cash of value involved, count thirty merits.

Addition

202. To save one person's life counts as one hundred merits.

CATEGORY OF BAD DEEDS (<u>KUO-MEN</u>)
Disloyal and Unfilial Deeds *(pu-chung-hsiao lei)*

1. For each time one fails to respect one's parents or fails to take care of them, count one demerit.

2. For each time one disobeys their moral instructions, count one demerit.

3. For each time one becomes angry when scolded by one's parents, count one demerit.

4. When one talks back to one's parents, count ten demerits.

5. For each time one purposely neglects someone whom one's parents love, count one demerit.

6. For each religious service one omits to perform, but which ought to be performed after the death of one's parents, count ten demerits.

7. For each time one fails to use skill in remonstrating with one's parents for a fault, count one demerit.

8. For each time one is disrespectful or fails to take care of one's grandparents or stepmother, count one demerit.

9. For each time one fails to exhaust one's strength to serve one's emperor loyally, count one demerit.

10. When one fails to speak truthfully, a small matter counts as one demerit, a serious matter counts as ten demerits, an extremely serious matter counts as fifty demerits.

11. For each time one disobeys the laws and institutions of the land, count one demerit.

12. For each time one cheats one's emperor with false reports, count one demerit.

13. For every day one fails to respect or take care of one's teachers and elders, count one demerit.

14. For each instruction of the teacher one disobeys, count one demerit.

15. For every time one does exactly the opposite of what the teacher tells one to do, count thirty demerits.

16. No fault applies if one disobeys because the teacher is an evil man. (When Ch'en Hsiang imitated Hsü Hsing's behavior,[14] this was to do the exact opposite of what one should do. But when Mu-lien [Maudgalyāyana][15] left his teacher of an unorthodox sect, this was to forsake one's teacher because he was evil.)

17. For every time brothers hate each other, count two demerits.

18. For every time one ill-treats brothers born of a stepmother or one of the father's concubines, count three demerits.

Unaltruistic and Uncompassionate Deeds

19. To refuse to save a very sick person who asks for help counts as two demerits.

20. To refuse to save a slightly sick person who asks for help counts as one demerit.

21. No fault applies if the reason for not saving him is one's lack of money or skill.

22. Making poison counts as five demerits.

23. To make poison with the intention of harming people counts as ten demerits.

24. To poison one person to death counts as a hundred demerits.

25. If the person does not die but becomes sick, this counts fifty demerits.

26. To kill one animal or bird by poison counts as ten demerits.

27. If the creature does not die but becomes sick, count five demerits.

28. To cause one person's death by spells, prayers, and curses counts as one hundred demerits.

29. If he does not die but becomes ill, count fifty demerits.

30. To sentence one person by mistake to the death penalty counts as eighty demerits.

31. To sentence one person to the death penalty intentionally counts as one hundred demerits.

32. To sentence one person by mistake to military exile or penal servitude counts as thirty demerits.

33 To do so intentionally counts as forty demerits.

34. To sentence one person by mistake to heavy bambooing counts as eight demerits.

35. To do so intentionally counts as ten demerits.

36. To sentence one person by mistake to light bambooing counts as four demerits.

37. To do so intentionally counts as five demerits.

38. The same applies to punishment meted out to domestic servants in one's own household.

39. For illegal use of instruments of punishment, count ten demerits for every time they are used.

40. For beating an innocent person, each light stroke counts as one demerit.

41. As to plotting a person's death sentence, if successful, count one hundred demerits; if unsuccessful, count fifty demerits; a suggestion to this effect counts ten demerits.

42. As to plotting a person's military exile or his penal servitude, if successful, count forty demerits; if unsuccessful, count twenty demerits; a suggestion to this effect counts eight demerits.

43. As to plotting a person's heavy bambooing, if successful, count ten demerits; if unsuccessful, count eight demerits; a suggestion to this effect counts five demerits.

44. As to plotting a person's light bambooing, if successful, count five demerits; if unsuccessful, count four demerits; a suggestion to this effect counts three demerits.

45. If parents drown their newborn infant, it is fifty demerits. One abortion counts twenty demerits. (This is a serious crime because the Supreme Lord [Shang-ti] has instructed that for parents to kill their innocent children is the same as for them to kill people in general.)

46. One person killed in a surrendered city earns fifty demerits.

47. Taking an ordinary citizen prisoner of war earns fifty demerits.

48. To cause him to die counts as one hundred demerits.

49. A judge may clearly know that the defendant is innocent, yet either because of outside pressure or because the verdict has been given in a lower court or by a previous judge, he does not clear the person of guilt. Count eighty demerits if the death sentence results from this.

50. Military exile or penal servitude counts thirty demerits.

51. Heavy bambooing counts eight demerits.

52. Light bambooing counts four demerits.

53. If the judge receives a bribe and passes the death sentence, it is one hundred demerits. (The number of demerits is counted the same as above in regard to other sentences.)

54. To harbor evil thoughts against a person and desire to harm him counts as one demerit; to succeed in doing him harm counts ten demerits.

55. To kill a person intentionally counts as one hundred demerits.

56. To hurt a person without killing him counts as eighty demerits.

57. The same applies if one causes another to kill.

58. To kill intentionally one domestic animal that is capable of returning man's kindness counts ten demerits; if by mistake, two demerits.

59. To kill intentionally one domestic animal that is incapable of returning man's kindness counts ten demerits; if by mistake, two demerits.

60. To kill a small animal intentionally counts as one demerit. To kill ten small animals by mistake counts as one demerit.

61. To kill ten very small animals intentionally counts as one demerit.

62. To kill twenty very small animals by mistake counts as one demerit.

63. The same applies if one causes others to kill animals, helps others to kill them, kills them for food; or if one first raises them oneself and then sells them to a butcher; kills them because one believes in fate[16] and offers them to ghosts and gods as sacrifice; or kills them to make medicine. Keeping silkworms is the same as raising domestic animals and later having them butchered.

64. Intentionally to kill an animal harmful to men counts as one demerit.

65. Unintentionally to kill ten animals harmful to men counts as one demerit.

66. When one witnesses a killing and fails to prevent it, the demerits are half those listed above. (For instance, five demerits instead of ten in the case of allowing an animal capable of returning man's kindness to be killed.)

67. No fault applies if there is no way to prevent it.

68. If one does not feel compassion when one cannot prevent the killing, count two demerits.

69. When ploughing buffaloes, riding horses, domestic dogs, and so on, die of old age or sickness and one sells their meat, count ten demerits for a large animal.

70. Count five demerits for a small animal.

71. If one intentionally slaughters animals during the time when prohibition is appropriate, the demerit is increased to twice the above. (Since to kill an animal that is capable of serving men is twenty demerits, to kill it now will be forty demerits. The same rule applies to other cases.)

72. To buy meat secretly during the prohibition against slaughtering[17] is regarded as the same as above. (To buy the meat of an animal capable of serving men is forty demerits, and so on.)

73. If officials who occupy high posts give leave to common people who want to break the prohibition against slaughter, they receive the same demerits.

74. To cook living creatures in a strange way and make them suffer excruciating pain (boiling turtles or crabs alive or roasting a young lamb alive by fire, and so on) counts as twenty demerits.

75. In training hawks or dogs in fishing and in shooting birds, and so on, to harm one creature without killing it counts as five demerits.

76. Causing one creature's death is counted the same as killing it intentionally, and rule 58 applies.

77. In the case of disturbing a hibernating animal, surprising a nesting bird, filling up a hole in which animals live, upsetting a bird nest and breaking the eggs or harming a fetus, it is the same as killing animals with intent, and rule 58 applies.

78. No fault applies if one harms creatures unintentionally in these situations because one is engaged in some good activities (repairing bridges, paving roads, building temples, erecting pagodas, and so on). These are good activities done with good intentions. Therefore it is not demeritorious if one harms some creatures in the course of these activities. Even so, one ought to show repentance by performing a religious service for their salvation.

79. To keep birds in a cage or to bind animals with strings for one day counts as one demerit.

80. To feel no compassion when seeing people or animals die counts as one demerit.

81. To fail to help a widower, widow, orphan, childless person, or poor person who suffers from hunger, thirst, or cold counts as one demerit.

82. No fault goes to him who has no money to do anything about it.

83. To tease, cheat, or harm a blind person, a deaf person, a sick person, a fool, an old person, or a child counts as ten demerits.

84. To fail to comfort a person who has worries counts as one demerit.

85. To feel happy when one sees a person who has worries counts as two demerits.

86. To increase his worry counts as five demerits.

87. To take delight over someone's loss of profit or prestige counts as two demerits.

88. To wish that a rich and prestigious man become poor and lowly counts as five demerits.

89. To pile up one's store of rice in years of famine and ask exorbitant prices counts as fifty demerits.

90. The same applies to people who refuse to sell rice.

91. To press a poor person to repay his debt by resorting to physical violence and criminal charges counts as five demerits.

92. For every hundred cash of loans in either money or materials that one fails to return, count one demerit.

93. To make a domestic animal work to the point of physical exhaustion and, without any pity for its suffering, force it to continue working, for each hour count ten demerits.

94. For every stroke one whips it, count one demerit.

95. To set people's houses and forests on fire counts as fifty demerits.

96. If one man is killed in the resulting fire, count fifty demerits.

97. When animals are killed, the rule concerning the killing of animals (rule 58) applies.

98. If the original intent is to kill somebody, for every man thus killed count one hundred demerits.

99. To dig up a person's grave and expose the bones counts as fifty demerits.

100. To level a grave mound counts as ten demerits.

101. No fault applies if the grave is old and there are no bones in it.

102. If one takes over someone's fields, house, and so on, because one has the support of the powerful, for every hundred cash value of property thus taken count ten demerits.

103. If one forces others to sell property cheaply, for every hundred cash value involved count one demerit.

104. If one destroys roads and makes passers-by suffer inconvenience, each day they suffer counts as five demerits.

105. The same applies to the destruction of pavilions, wells, bridges, and ferryboats.

106. An official of high position who obstructs his surbordinate's future advancement earns thirty demerits.

107. If he obstructs it by illegal means, he earns fifty demerits.

108. The same applies to an official of high position who mistreats his subordinates.

109. To lock up a maid or a concubine[18] counts as one demerit.

110. To scheme for the possession of another man's wife or daughter counts as fifty dermerits.

Deeds Harmful to the Three Jewels

111. For the destruction of each hundred cash value of Buddhist images, count two demerits.

112. For the destruction of each hundred cash value of images of celestial beings, orthodox gods[19] who govern the world, saints, and good men, count one demerit.

113. No fault applies if the image is of a heretical god[20] who demands blood offerings and has deceived the world.

114. For every utterance that slanders the Buddha, bodhisattvas, and arhats, count five demerits.

115. For every utterance that slanders celestial beings, orthodox gods, saints, and good men, count one demerit.

116. No fault applies if the denunciation is aimed against heretical teachings, is meant to save the deluded, and issues from sincerity.

117. To fail to worship the Buddha at the right time counts as one demerit.

118. To fail to worship the Buddha at the right time because of indulging in wine, meat, and sexual acts counts as five demerits.

119. Double the number of demerits when one is guilty of negligence on the six fast days. [The 8th, 14th, 15th, 23rd, 29th, 30th of the month.]

120. If one destroys Buddhist buildings, beds, and seats, and various religious paraphernalia, for each hundred cash value of damage done, count one demerit.

121. The same applies if one teaches another person who originally had no intention of doing so to destroy them.

122. To fail to admonish and stop him when one sees another person doing the destruction counts as five demerits.

123. To help another destroy them counts as ten demerits.

124. In the case of a temple housing celestial beings, orthodox gods, and images of good men, for every two hundred cash value of damage caused, count one demerit.

125. No fault applies if the temple is a licentious shrine (yin-tz'u) belonging to a heretical sect that practices blood offerings and deceives people.

126. If one occupies by force the land of a Buddhist monastery, for every one hundred cash value (of the land occupied), count one demerit. The same applies to buildings.

127. Newly to erect a temple where blood offerings are accepted counts as fifty demerits (especially to set up a new temple where there was none before).

128. To cast an image of a deity to be so worshipped counts ten demerits.

129. One incurs half the demerit if the temple or image is already there and one does repairs on it.

130. If one destroys scriptures expounding the otherwordly true law [Mahāyāna Buddhism], for every one hundred cash value of damage, count two demerits.

131. If the scripture belongs to the Hīnayāna sect or if it is an ethical text discussing the causal relationship between heaven and man, for every one hundred cash value of damage, count one demerit.

132. For every word that slanders scriptures of the other-worldly true law, count ten demerits.

133. For every word that slanders a scripture of this-worldly morality [Confucian classics], count five demerits.

134. To be stingy about spreading the Dharma and to refuse to teach others counts as ten demerits.

135. No fault applies if the reason is because the recipient is unworthy of being taught.

136. To obstruct the spread of the good Dharma counts as ten demerits.

137. No fault applies if the obstructed teaching is heretical or unfounded. Also, no fault applies if, although it be good Dharma, one refrains from propagating it because objective conditions are unfavorable.

138. In chanting sutras, to misread one character counts one demerit, to omit one character counts one demerit.

139. To think all kinds of irrelevant thoughts while chanting a sutra counts five demerits.

140. To think evil thoughts while chanting a sutra counts ten demerits.

141. To say things that have no relation to sutra chanting counts five demerits.

142. To interrupt the sutra chanting to say good things [things beneficial to the hearer] counts one demerit.

143. To rise up to receive guest [while chanting the sutra] counts two demerits.

144. No fault applies if the guest is an imperial official.

145. To chant in a desultory manner and disregard the correct form counts as five demerits.

146. To become angry while chanting counts as ten demerits.

147. To scold people while chanting counts as twenty demerits.

148. To beat people while chanting counts as thirty demerits.

149. The same number is counted for making mistakes or leaving out characters in writing prayers and supplications.

150. If one teaches disciples unorthodox and evil ways, for every person taught, count twenty demerits.

151. To compose one *chüan* of forged scripture counts as ten demerits.

152. If one gives public lectures to propagate unorthodox teachings and mislead the people, for every person present at the lecture, count one demerit.

153. If one goes to such lectures and is a member of the audience, for each lecture attended, count one demerit.

154. If, in giving a lecture on the true Dharma, one gives his own biased views and departs from the teachings of the sutras and former sages, for every five persons in the audience who attend the lecture, count one demerit.

155. If one writes romantic rhymed verses, prose, tales, and so on, for every piece composed, count one demerit. (A "piece" here refers to one complete poem, one paragraph of prose, or one scene of a play.)

156. To transmit the piece to one person counts as two demerits. To memorize one such piece counts as one demerit.

157. In teaching people such evil skills as bringing harm to others through making a human image (*yen-mei*), abortion, and so on, for each skill passed on, count twenty demerits.

158. To refuse to give food to a begging monk counts as one demerit.

159. To refuse to give food to two ordinary persons counts as one demerit.

160. No fault applies if one refuses because one has no food.

161. Not only to refuse to give food but to scold and insult the beggar counts as three demerits.

162. When a monk refuses to give food to another monk, he earns two demerits. (This rule makes it clear that when lay people refuse to feed monks their demerit is not that grave, but when monks refuse it, their fault is indeed serious.)

163. To keep and care for bad disciples and refuse to send them away—in the case of one disciple, count fifty demerits.

164. If, when disciples make mistakes, one fails to instruct and correct them, for a small matter count one demerit; for a serious matter count ten demerits.

Miscellaneous Bad Deeds

165. For each hundred cash worth of property accepted that does not belong to one and is therefore unrighteous, count one demerit.

166. While one is already rich, for each hundred cash of such money accepted, count two demerits.

167. To have sexual intercourse with extremely close kin counts as fifty demerits.

168. To have sexual intercourse with a person of good family counts as ten demerits.

169. To have sexual intercourse with a prostitute counts as two demerits.

THE RECORD OF SELF-KNOWLEDGE

170. To have sexual intercourse with a nun or a chaste widow counts as fifty demerits.

171. If upon seeing a beautiful woman of a good family, one desires to make love to her, count two demerits. (This is for lay people. In the case of a monk, no matter whether the woman is related to oneself or not, of good family, or of lowly origin, to commit such an offense will be counted uniformly as fifty demerits, and to have the desire to make love to her will be uniformly counted as two demerits.)

172. If one steals money or goods, for each hundred cash they are worth, count one demerit.

173. When the stealing is done little by little, for each one hundred in cash worth accumulated, count one demerit.

174. The same applies in the case of concealing taxes from the government.

175. If one takes money from others either by force or by trickery, for each one hundred cash, count ten demerits.

176. When one takes charge of an affair and accepts a bribe to promote a person to become an official or charges him falsely with a crime, of which he is innocent, for each hundred cash of the bribe received, count one demerit.

177. If, because of receiving bribes, one obstructs somebody from becoming an official or foists a crime on him, for each hundred cash of the bribe received, count ten demerits.

178. To fail to return money or things to the lender, for each hundred cash involved count one demerit.

179. To wish the lender dead because one owes him debts counts as ten demerits.

180. If in using containers or weights one underweighs when measuring out to others and overweighs when receiving from others, for each one hundred cash worth of the commodity, count one demerit.

181. To fail to recommend a worthy person when one finds him counts as five demerits.

182. To persecute him counts as ten demerits.

183. To fail to dismiss a bad person when one finds him counts as five demerits.

184. To help him counts as ten demerits.

185. If one hides the good deeds of others, for every good deed count one demerit.

186. If one broadcasts the bad deeds of others, for every bad deed count one demerit.

187. No fault applies if one exposes another person's bad deed after having first admonished him.

188. It is also not demeritorious if one exposes another person's bad deeds for the sake of eliminating danger and saving people.

189. If one tries one's very best to seek out the shortcomings of former worthies and create one's own theory [in order to surpass them], for every pronouncement, count one demerit.

190. For every pronouncement that is in conflict with the truth, count ten demerits.

191. To write unofficial histories, novels, plays, or songs, to calumniate and defame good people counts as twenty demerits.

192. To broadcast others' secrets and family affairs without ascertaining if they are true counts as ten demerits.

193. To fabricate secrets out of nothing counts as fifty demerits.

194. If one distributes anonymous placards to reveal someone's infamous past, then when the accusation is half correct and half incorrect, count twenty demerits.

195. When it is completely untrue, count fifty demerits.

196. No fault applies if everything one says is true and one does it out of a sense of public duty to get rid of a public menace.

197. If, after asking for public donations to be used for some felicitous enterprise, one steals the money for oneself, for each hundred cash, count one demerit.

198. If one steals the money intended for religious equipment, for each ten cash, count one demerit.

199. In using the money, if one reverses cause and consequence, if one uses the money intended for one thing for something else, for each one hundred cash, count one demerit.

200. If one encourages or helps others to enter into a lawsuit and a death sentence results from it, count thirty demerits.

201. When military exile or penal servitude results, count twenty demerits.

202. When beating by heavy bamboo results, count ten demerits.

203. When beating by light bamboo results, count five demerits.

204. To encourage and help others to quarrel and fight counts as one demerit.

205. If one profits from encouraging and helping such lawsuits and death sentences result, count one hundred demerits.

206. When military exile or penal servitude results, count thirty demerits.

207. When beating with light bamboo results, count fifteen demerits.

208. To separate children from their parents counts as thirty demerits.

209. To destroy others' marriages counts as five demerits.

210. No fault applies if there is some reason why the parties should not be married.

211. If one pronounces utterances detrimental to morality, for each utterance, count ten demerits. (Such utterances as Ts'ao Ts'ao's [A.D. 155–220] "It is better for me to fail others than for others to fail me" belong to this category.)

212. For every lie one utters, count one demerit.

213. When the lie hurts people, count ten demerits.

214. For every time one fails to do good when there is an opportunity, count one demerit.

215. For each mistake one fails to correct, count one demerit.

216. When one is in the wrong and does not admit it but argues that one is right and contends with one's own generation, this counts as two demerits.

217. Arguing against parents, teachers, and elders counts ten demerits.

218. If, in argument, one persists in holding one's own opinion and refuses to acknowledge others' good points, for every point that one does not acknowledge, count one demerit.

219. For every time one fails to teach children but lets them do bad things, count one demerit.

220. The same applies if one shows indulgence toward servants and family retainers.

221. To fail to learn from a great worthy counts as five demerits.

222. To fail to befriend a superior counts as two demerits.

223. To defame and insult them counts as ten demerits.

224. To say vile things to one's superior counts as ten demerits.

225. To say vile things to one's contemporary counts as four demerits.

226. To say vile things to one's inferior and junior counts as one demerit.

227. To say vile things to a worthy or a gentleman counts as ten demerits; to say such things to a sage, one hundred demerits.

228. If a person teaches others to do bad things, one bad thing counts as two demerits.

229. To teach others great evils such as disloyalty and unfiliality counts as fifty demerits.

230. If one fails to advise and remonstrate when one sees someone do evil, count one demerit.

231. In great matters, the failure counts as thirty demerits.

232. It is no failing if the reason is that one knows the other person is obstinate and will not listen to advice.

233. To compose a ditty about a person or to give someone a nickname counts as five demerits.

234. To utter one untrue word counts as one demerit. If one proclaims that he has understood the true intention of sages and deludes people, for every such proclamation one makes, count fifty demerits.

235. If one fails to carry out a promise made to a friend in a small matter, count one demerit.

236. In a serious matter, it counts as ten demerits.

237. If one fails to return money or things one has accepted for safekeeping, for each one hundred cash involved, count one demerit.

238. Failure to return a kindness counts as one demerit.

239. Revenging a wrong counts as one demerit.

240. If, in revenging a wrong, one takes an excessive measure, count ten demerits.

241. Causing someone's death earns one hundred demerits.

242. To wish the person one has wronged to die counts as one demerit.

243. To feel joy upon hearing that a person one has wronged has died counts as one demerit.

244. For each time one eats meat, count one demerit.

245. For each time one eats such prohibited things as turtle or tortoise, count two demerits.

246. For each time one eats the meat of helpful animals such as water buffaloes, riding horses, or domestic dogs, count three demerits. (This refers to meat of animals one purchases at the market. If one kills them oneself and then eats, that will belong to the earlier category of killing with intent.)

247. If one drinks wine while discussing bad things, for every *sheng* [pint] consumed, count six demerits.

248. If one drinks with bad company, for every *sheng* consumed, count one demerit.

249. If one drinks with ordinary people for no particular reason, count one demerit.

250. No fault applies if one drinks in the course of serving parents, entertaining guests, or using wine as an accompaniment to medicine.

251. If one opens a wine shop and invites people to drink, for every person thus induced to drink, count one demerit.

252. To eat the five forbidden pungent roots[21] without any good reason counts as one demerit. No fault applies if one eats them to cure sickness.

253. To recite a sutra after eating the pungent roots counts as one demerit.

254. If one eats meat during the six fast days, for every time one does it, count two demerits.

255. To go to the great Buddha hall after eating meat counts as one demerit.

256. The same applies to people who go to the great Buddha hall after drinking wine or partaking of the five pungent roots.

257. To wear excessively fine clothes, for each article of clothing one wears, count one demerit.

258. To eat excessively fine food, for each meal one eats, count one demerit.

259. No fault applies if the food is for serving one's parent. (What do we mean by "excessive"? Rich people have the right to enjoy blessings because of their allotted share. But if they want luxury above and beyond their status, this is excessive. The exception is made for parents only and does not apply to sacrifice to gods or the entertainment of guests. This is because, as the *Chou-i*, the *Book of Changes*, says: "The grain which is contained in two square baskets of bamboo is sufficient for the enjoyment [of gods]." Or as Ma Jung[22] said: "Vegetarian food is not too humble for serving a guest.")

260. When a person who keeps a vegetarian diet seeks only to wear beautiful clothes and to eat fine food, for every article of clothing he wears, count one demerit; for every meal of fine food of which he partakes, count one demerit. (Since a person is already a vegetarian, he ought to know how to value blessings. If he uses beautiful clothes even though they be made of cotton cloth, or if he eats delicious food even though it be vegetable, this will reduce his blessings.)

261. If one despises and wastes the five grains, which are the products of heaven (*t'ien-wu*), for each hundred cash they are worth, count one demerit.

262. To sell butcher knives, fishing nets, and so on, for each hundred cash they are worth, count one demerit.

263. If one picks up something on the street and fails to return it to its original owner, for each hundred cash it is worth, count one demerit.

264. Every time one claims an achievement for oneself or puts the blame on others, count two demerits.

265. To plot and scheme by every possible means for status, prestige, and profit so that one goes to any length, even to do unrighteous things—for every time this happens, count ten demerits.

266. If, while occupying the position of a leader, one thinks about one's own good but not that of the rest of the people, for each day one occupies this position, count one demerit.

267. If, in order to preserve one's own position and property, one does not hesitate to make others lose their positions and property, count fifty demerits.

268. If, every time one meets with misfortune, one blames heaven or men, count three demerits.

269. If, in praying for blessing and to avoid disaster, one does not cultivate good deeds but promises to sacrifice animals or makes some other evil pledge, count ten demerits. To sacrifice an animal this way is the same as killing an animal gratuitously. (As soon as one makes such a promise, his heart is already devoid of goodness. Therefore the ten demerits apply. When later on the person slaughters the animal to fulfill his promise, his demerit is the same as that for killing an animal.)

270. If one is unwilling to pass on prescriptions that cure diseases, for five prescriptions refused, count one demerit.

271. For discarding paper with written characters on it, for every ten characters thrown away, count one demerit.

272. If, after leaving one's own parents to become a monk, one regards somebody else as one's godparent, count fifty demerits.

273. To accept someone's instruction in the Taoist technique of making cinnabar counts as thirty demerits.

274. In using silver transformed from cinnabar, for each hundred cash involved, count three demerits.

275. No fault applies if it is really silver and if it does not revert back to the original substance even after repeated boiling and burning.

Additions

276. To loiter in the Great Hall and climb to the pagoda without good reason counts as five demerits. (Burning incense, sweeping,

chanting sutras, and so on are good reasons for being at the Great Hall or the pagoda.)

277. To drink wine and eat meat and thus to pollute the hall and pagoda counts as ten demerits.

278. If one promotes a person to an official post or clears him of criminal charges because one has received a bribe, for every five hundred cash received, count one demerit.

279. To obstruct a person from becoming an official or to put a criminal charge against him because one receives a bribe, for each five hundred cash received, count ten demerits.

APPENDIX TWO

Personnel at Yün-ch'i and Their Duties

1. The abbot *(tang-chia)*. The abbot supervises everything. He must be alert and energetic.
2. The business prefect *(chih-k'o)*.
   a. He weighs grain together with the prior and the grounds prefect [the person in charge of the land in the surrounding mountains] on the third day after seasonal grain arrives. He seals its containers. Whenever he opens them, he has to report to the assembly and record it in the books. If he fails to do this, he receives the second degree of punishment *(chung-fa)*. If he uses it for other purposes, he has to repay its value at the rate of one to ten.
   b. The amount of rice used for meals, congees, and breakfast has to be decided in consultation with the proctor and the rice steward. It should be just right. If he wastes rice or if he serves spoiled food, he is to receive the second degree of punishment.
   c. He is responsible for supplying utensils such as lamps, candles, shoes, and the like on time and for buying vegetables, fruits, or condiments for sick people when they give him the money. To fail to do so will result in the third degree of punishment *(hsia-fa)*.
   d. Each season he audits the accounts once. To fail to do so results in the second degree of punishment.
3. The proctor *(chih-chung)*.
   a. He names people to various functionary posts when there is a vacancy and tells them their duties and responsibilities. Laziness in five instances yields the third degree of punishment.

Condensed from "Regulations Governing Various Functionaries," *YCFH* 32, 42a–56b.

b. He checks on the diligence and moral quality of the monks. Unfairness results in the second degree of punishment.

c. He takes care of tables and chairs in the Dharma Hall, the Great Shrine Hall, and the refectory. Disorder leads to the third degree of punishment.

d. He sees to it that bedding, mats, mosquito nets and so on are prepared ahead of time for the term of meditation (*an-ch'an*) and the summer retreat (*chieh-chih*) [the 16th of the 4th month to the 15th of the 7th month]. In the summer he makes the rooms cool, and for the winter, he has the windows papered and the stoves ready. To fail to do so five times results in the third degree of punishment.

e. He should often check on the infirmary and the old people's hall. He should have bedding, medicines, and lamps well stocked. Negligence results in the second degree of punishment.

4. The guest prefect (*chih-k'o;* two people occupy this post).

a. If anyone wishes to stay in the monastery or to receive the precepts [be ordained], the guest prefect investigates and takes care of the visitor. On the next day he takes him to see the prior. Carelessness results in the second degree of punishment.

b. Whoever desires to live in the monastery must be asked to read the *Rules and Agreements for Communal Living at Yün-ch'i.* If he agrees really to observe these, then the guest prefect together with other functionaries checks carefully on his credentials and his intentions. The guest prefect permits him to stay only when he is satisfied that the visitor is a genuinely good man. If by mistake he has admitted undesirable elements, then both he and the visitors have to be expelled.

c. If people want to see different parts of the monastery, he accompanies them.

d. At feast offerings (*chai-kung*) and light meals (*hsiao-shih*), monks from outside should be treated as our own. Partiality is punished by the second degree of punishment.

e. When a guest has just arrived, the guest prefect takes him first to the Meditation Hall to worship the Buddha if meditation is not in session. But if meditation has already started, then he asks the guest to withdraw or to look around. When the monks in the hall have finished silent meditation, he asks the guest to come in and questions him regarding how many are with him. He is not supposed to lose count.

f. He consults with the abbot, the clerk, and others concerning money, rice rent, interest, and feast offerings belonging to the monastery.

g. He reports to the abbot and the clerk in order that the latter may record the number of cows, deer, pigs, and sheep presented by lay donors to be released. He also records which animal keeper looks after which animal.

5. The secretary (shu-chi). When writing supplications (shu-wen) for donors, he should write with care. He must not do it hastily or perfunctorily.

6. The grounds prefect (chih-shan; two people occupy this post).

a. He should see to it that the boundaries of the monastic land are clear. They must not encroach on others' land so as to cause lawsuits. Every year he tours the land of the monastery with all the monks.

b. He discusses with the supervisor the interest on grain produced on monastery land.

c. When it is time to plant, he does so with the gardener on time.

d. When land has been cleared, he should follow a certain order as to which plot is to be cultivated first. Disobedience must be reported. Failure to take care of this results in the second degree of punishment.

7. The rooms prefect (chih-wu). The rooms prefect checks on the roofs of various halls and rooms. If there is a leak, he repairs it early. Whenever there is repairing or building to be done, he reports to the prior and he does it in good time. Failure to do this results in the second degree of punishment.

8. The meditation patrol (chih-pan).

a. He patrols the premises day and night. When he sees someone chattering and joking, he sounds the wooden board and recites the Buddha's name ten times. If the offenders do not collect themselves and think virtuous thoughts, he reports them for punishment.

b. At night he sounds the board in front of the Meditation Hall and the different rooms. If there are people who recite the Buddha's name in their sleep following the sounding of the board, he reports them for credit.

9. The chef (tien-tso; four persons occupy this post).

a. When there is fighting and quarreling in the kitchen, he first tells them to stop. If this has no effect, he strikes the wooden board five times. If they still do not stop, he beats the drum and reports to the persons in charge for the day, both inside and outside the Great Hall. If out of indulgence he fails to report, he gets the third degree of punishment. If the incident is grave, he gets the second degree of punishment.

b. He ought not to cook special food different from the rest for anyone. The giver and the receiver of such food receive the third degree of punishment. Food for the sick is an exception.

c. Before offering food to the Buddha, he should not give others any of it to eat. If he does so, both he and the receiver are to be punished in the third degree.

d. He must taste all food to be sure it has the right flavor.

10. The rice steward (*fang-t'ou;* two persons occupy this post).

a. Anyone who takes his own bowl to get food at the stove rather than receiving food at the Refectory must be reported. Failure to do this results in the third degree of punishment.

b. During the summer months water in the monastery pond [for fish, turtles, and other creatures which have been released by the faithful] has to be changed every day, and the bamboo water ducts [which carry water to the pond] have to be swept clean once every third day. In the winter the water in the pond has to be changed once every three days, and the water ducts swept clean once every seven days. Failure to do so results in the third degree of punishment.

11. The vegetable steward (*tsai-t'ou*). Vegetables have to be washed with clean water three times. Pickle jars must be covered with tops. Failure to do so results in the third degree of punishment.

12. The tea steward (*ch'a-t'ou;* three persons occupy this post).

a. At the fifth watch [6 A.M.] he lights the fire under the hot water caldron. But before pouring water on the ground, he first drives away insects and ants. Failure to do so results in the third degree of punishment.

b. In preparing breakfast for the fifth watch, he makes just enough. He sends it to their halls after the monks come back from their morning devotions.

c. He is charged with preparing hot water for washing, with making tea, regulating haircuts, and laundering clothes. There are days set for haircuts: the 7th, 14th, 22nd, 30th (or 29th of short months) of each month; and for washing and starching clothes, the 12th, 13th, 27th, and 28th of the month in spring, autumn, and winter (but the 2nd, 3rd, 12th, 13th, 22nd, and 23rd of the summer months). Failure to keep this regulation results in the third degree of punishment.

13. The firewood steward (*ch'ai-t'ou;* nine persons occupy this post).

The firewood steward piles up wood when the days are sunny in order to prepare for rainy days. He who neglects to do this is punished in the second degree.

14. The fire steward (*huo-t'ou;* five persons occupy this post). He does not leave too much firewood near the stove. He should clean the stove every evening. Failure to do so results in the third degree of punishment. He cleans the chimney once every month. When he forgets, he must pay a fine of ten cash.

15. The dish steward (*wan-t'ou;* two persons occupy this post).
    a. He searches everywhere for dishes and gathers them up. Failure to do so results in the third degree of punishment. Anyone who uses a dish should return it after using it. If not, the third degree of punishment applies. If the steward fails to check on the loss of dishes, he himself must repay the value.
    b. If someone breaks a dish, he has to pay double its value. If he breaks it out of anger, he has to repay ten times its value. If he refuses to pay, he is to be expelled from the monastery.

16. The mill steward (*mo-t'ou;* two persons occupy this post). He takes charge of all work having to do with the mill. He keeps it clean after use. If he fails to do so, he is punished in the third degree. If rice or other things become spoiled as a result of his carelessness, he must reimburse the monastery for them out of his own pocket.

17. The garden steward (*yüan-t'ou;* six persons occupy this post). He waters the garden at the right time. He plants seeds and harvests in season. When he makes mistakes, he is to be punished in the third degree. He must also make restitution. Except during very cold months, he is not to burn over the garden. Failure to follow this results in the second degree of punishment.

18. The bath steward (*ching-t'ou;* two persons occupy this post).
    a. He washes hand towels once every three days in winter, and once a day in summer. Failure to do so will lead to the third degree of punishment.
    b. He is responsible for the bath. The schedule for each month is the 7th, 14th, 22nd, 30th (29th of short months) for bathing the whole body; the 3rd, 10th, 18th, and 26th for partial bathing. On other days, unless they are workers with chits saying that they have exerted themselves for guests, no one is allowed to bathe. Laxity in carrying out this rule results in the third degree of punishment.

19. The carrier (*tan-li;* two persons occupy this post). He turns in the things he carries to the treasury. He must always give a clear

accounting. Failure to do so results in the third degree of punishment.

20. The alms gatherer (*hua-fan;* two persons occupy this post). When he arrives at the house of some laypeople, he does not talk with the womenfolk in a secluded place. He does not give gifts or carry on any communications. Minor violations are subject to the second degree of punishment. Serious violations should result in expulsion.

21. The dining-hall waiters (*p'u-t'ang;* eighteen persons occupy this post).
   a. They serve food and soup with respect.
   b. No one is allowed to make noise with dishes. A violation is punishable in the third degree.
   c. Talking while eating is prohibited. If after hearing the sounding of the wooden fish one still does not stop, the waiters should take away the offender's bowl and chopsticks. If the waiter excuses someone out of indulgence, the waiter himself must pay a fine of 20 cash.

22. The verger (*hsiang-teng;* two persons occupy this post).
   a. He keeps lamps and incense burners everywhere in good order. He frequently dusts the table with the offerings. He keeps the lampshades tightly closed lest creatures come and be harmed. He watches the lamps with care at night. To fail to do any of these things results in the third degree of punishment.
   b. He changes the water in the basins for washing hands and sweeps the floor of the Great Hall each morning. If the wooden clogs used in the toilet become worn out, he reports to the monk in charge that a new pair is needed. Failure to do so results in the third degree of punishment.
   c. He sounds the bell and drum at the appropriate times. Failure to do so results in the third degree of punishment. When striking the bell, he does not strike it too heavily lest it be damaged.

23. The acolyte (*shih-che;* four persons occupy this post).
   a. He must get up early. After finishing his own toilet, he snaps his fingers three times or coughs slightly outside the abbot's room. When he goes near the abbot's bed, he asks him if he has slept well the previous night. He prepares hot water for the abbot to wash his face. Dry towels must be kept in readiness.
   b. He folds the bedding, takes care of clothing, and remembers where it is all to be put.

c. Before meals he notifies the abbot. During meals he serves him with care.

d. When guests come to visit, he serves them tea. After they finish, he takes away the teacups.

e. He keeps track of letters and messages. If he forgets any, he is subject to the third degree of punishment.

24. The attendant to the sick *(k'an-ping)*.

a. If the patient's illness is serious, he asks the assembly for volunteers. If no one volunteers, turns are taken according to date of ordination. Attendants to the sick change over every three days.

b. In taking care of a patient, one must have a heart of compassion. Do not be angry if the patient says things that hurt. Do not be greedy for the patient's possessions, but only desire to create blessings for others with merit that arises from this work. Inattention results in the third degree of punishment.

25. The attendant to the aged *(k'an-lao)*.

a. He prepares water for them to wash their faces. He sees to it that their congee and vegetables are tasty and easy to digest.

b. He sweeps the floor, dusts the table, lights the incense, and changes the water in front of the Buddha.

c. He does not sit at ease or relax too much.

d. When he answers a question, he is patient and never loses his temper. He is always respectful.

e. He is careful about lamps and candles. He puts them out when he goes to sleep.

26. The instructor *(ching-ts'e)*.

a. Giving instruction to the infirm and the aged is done by turns. Each time two monks are assigned. Refusal to do the work is fined two cash.

b. The dates for giving instruction to the aged are the 15th, and 30th (29th in the short months) of each month. The procedure is: first recite the "Instructions to Old People" [*Ching-lao wen,* a short essay written by Chu-hung, YCFH 32, 33b]; then recite the Buddha's name 300 times, then call on Kuan-yin [Avalokiteśvara] Shih-chih [Mahāsthāmaprāpta], and the whole pure assembly of the sangha three times; and finally, transfer to the aged the marvelous merit of reciting the Buddha's name.

c. The dates for giving instruction to the infirm are the 8th, 15th, 23rd and 30th (29th in a short month). If the patient is seriously ill, instruction has to be given daily regardless of the date. After the recitation of the "Instruction to the Infirm" [*Ching-ping wen,* a short essay written by Chu-hung, *YCFH* 32, 34a], recite the Buddha's name as before and finally transfer the merit to the patient and pray for his early recovery.

27. The gatekeeper *(shan-men).*
   a. He takes itinerant monks to the kitchen, serves them tea, and accompanies them to the dormitory. If they act loosely, he restrains them with kind words. If there is any fighting, he calms them; otherwise he reports to the assembly and has them judged in accordance with the pure monastic rules. He who takes it upon himself to penalize the offenders gets the second degree of punishment. They should be allowed to walk around and look everywhere.
   b. When officials arrive, he reports to the guest prefect. Retired officials and local gentry should be treated the same way. Failure to do so results in the third degree of punishment.
   c. When a guest leaves, if there is no one to see him off, it is the duty of the gatekeeper to do so. Failure leads to the third degree of punishment.

28. The errand-runners *(ting-yung;* ten for heavy work and thirty for light work). When appointed by the abbot, they should not evade the work. But if there is reason to suspect unfair practices, it should be pointed out without fear *(chih-chü).*

29. The printer *(yin-fang).* He takes care of the printing blocks for scriptures so that they will not rot or become confused and out of order.

APPENDIX THREE

~~~~~~

Regulations Regarding Good Deeds and Punishments at Yün-ch'i

GOOD DEEDS

Good Deeds in the Category of Merit

1. In doing philanthropic acts, every two *fen* [.01 ounce] of silver spent is one good point.

2. No matter whether it is money or things, after picking it up return it to its owner. Each three *fen* thus returned counts as one good point. (It does not count if one does not put out a plaque announcing the discovery. This procedure is the rule to be followed.)

3. Taking care of patients suffering from slight illnesses for one day counts one good point; taking care of patients suffering from serious illnesses for one day counts three good points; taking care of patients suffering from extremely serious illnesses for one day counts five good points.

4. If when scolded one does not scold back, count five good points. If when hit one does not hit back, count ten good points.

5. If when not on duty one volunteers for work, count two good points. (If it is heavy labor, double the number of points.)

6. If when not on duty one runs errands for the monastery, for every forty *li*, count two good points; for every one hundred *li*, count five good points.

7. To carry out the duty of the meditation patrol conscientiously counts two good points.

Good Deeds in the Category of Wisdom

1. If one is capable of reciting from memory the Sutra of Brahma's Net, the *Kuan ching* [Amitāyurdhyāna Sutra], the chapter

YCFH 32, 36b–38a.

called "Hsing-yüan p'in" [in the Avataṁsaka Sutra], each constitutes eight good points. To be capable of reciting from memory the forty-eight vows [of the Amitābha Buddha] counts three good points. To be capable of reciting from memory *Kuei-shan's Instruction* counts three good points.

2. To perform prayer services on the first and fifteenth of each month counts two good points. To perform the services of reciting the five and the ten precepts counts two good points. To perform the service of reciting the complete precepts for the bhikshu counts two good points. To perform the service of reciting the bodhisattva precepts counts three good points.

3. To stop disputes counts one good point. To make a person change from evil to good counts ten good points.

4. To dismiss one bad member of the monastery counts two good points. To promote one good talent counts four good points.

5. To bring the defects of the monastery into open discussion, for each matter discussed count two points (for serious matters double the number of points).

6. When one gives lectures on the scriptures, one small volume of scripture counts three good points; one large volume counts six good points; one extremely small volume counts one good point. (If one accepts compensation, no points are counted.)

7. To be capable of explaining the meaning of a sutra when asked counts one good point. (A difficult sutra counts double.)

8. To be capable of handling an affair when consulted counts one good point. (Serious matters double the number of points.)

9. For each service of "bestowing food on the hungry ghosts" performed without accepting the fee, count four good points; for each volume of scripture recited for people without accepting a fee, count one good point.

Punishments

1. First-degree punishments. The fine is five hundred *wen*. If one does not have the money, one must "kneel for a hundred-inch incense" [kneel for the time it takes ten sticks of incense, each being ten inches in length, to burn down.] If one does not want to kneel, he is deprived of the one hundred good points. When one does not have any good points, he is dismissed from the monastery. This is applied to light offenses. If the offense is serious, then he must pay a fine. If the offense is even more serious, then besides paying a fine he still has to "kneel for one ten-inch incense."

2. Second-degree punishments. The fine is fifty *wen*. If one does not have the money, one has to "kneel for one ten-inch incense." If one does not want to kneel, he is deprived of ten good points. The treatment for light and serious offenses is the same as before.

3. Third-degree punishments. The fine is five *wen*. If one has no money, he has to "kneel for one ten-inch incense." If he does not want to kneel, he is deprived of one good point. The treatment for light and serious offenses is the same as before.

If a monk who has been demoted to a lower precept group *(t'ui-chieh jen)* because of misconduct is willing to pay double the fine and thus hopes to recover his previous status, he may be allowed to do so if his offense is light. But if his offense is serious, he must not be allowed to do so.

NOTES

~~~~~~

On the Illustrations

1. *Yün-ch'i fa-hui* (1897 ed.) 29, 31a (see ch. II, note 1).

2. *Ch'uan-ch'i* was probably another name for the southern drama *(nan-hsi)*, which was most popular in the Sung but was eclipsed by the northern drama *tsa-chü* in the Yüan. Colin P. Mackerras, *The Rise of the Peking Opera, 1770–1870* (Oxford: Clarendon Press, 1972), pp. 2–4.

3. These come from the fifteen rules *(kuei-yüeh)* the author lists in his preface. *Ching-tu ch'uan-teng kuei-yüan ching,* chüan 1, pp. 1a–2b.

4. Lin Ch'ing, *Hung-hsüen yin-yüan,* chüan 2, 67a–68a.

5. The edition is the *Hsin-k'o Wei Chung-hsüeh hsien-sheng pi-tien Hsi-hsiang chi* [The Romance of the Western Chamber, Newly Printed with Mr. Wei Chung-hsüeh's Comments and Punctuations], Tsun-ch'eng t'ang edition, late Ming. The wood-cut prints from this edition are found in *Ming-tai pan-hua hsüan ch'u-chi,* vol. II, pp. 226–227.

I. Introduction

1. For a thoughtful discussion of late Ming thought, see Wm. Theodore de Bary, "Individualism and Humanitarianism in Late Ming Thought," in his *Self and Society in Ming Thought,* pp. 145–225; also his "Neo-Confucian Cultivation and the Seventeenth-Century Englightenment," in his *The Unfolding of Neo-Confucianism,* pp. 141–216.

2. de Bary, *Self and Society in Ming Thought,* p. 22.

3. Yung-ming Yen-shou (904–975) was generally regarded as the first important advocate of the dual practice of Ch'an meditation and Pure Land recitation. Chu-hung referred to him for authority. See Mochizuki Shinkō, *Chūgoku Jōdo kyōrishi,* pp. 329–341.

4. See E. Zürcher, *The Buddhist Conquest of China,* especially his "Introductory Remarks" and "An Historical Survey from the First to the Beginning of the 4th Century A.D.," pp. 1–80.

5. The only in-depth studies of Ming Buddhism in English are one article on Chu-hung and one book on Te-ch'ing: Leon Hurvitz, "Chu-hung's One Mind of Pure Land and Ch'an Buddhism," in *Self and Society in Ming Thought,* pp. 451–482; Sung-peng Hsu, *A Buddhist Leader in Ming China: The*

Life and Thought of Han-shan Te-ch'ing, 1546–1623. Charles Luk makes frequent references to Te-ch'ing and quotes a great deal from the latter's autobiography in his *Ch'an and Zen Teaching*, Series 1 and 2. However, he does not examine Ming Buddhism as a whole, but only treats Te-ch'ing's ideas in isolation. Te-ch'ing's autobiography is the central theme for another article: Pei-yi Wu, "The Spiritual Autobiography of Te-ch'ing," in *The Unfolding of Neo-Confucianism*, pp. 67–92. Although in recent decades there has appeared only the article by Hurvitz mentioned above, nineteenth-century scholars may have paid more attention to Chu-hung. In 1831 the Oriental Translation Fund in London printed *The Catechism of the Shaman: Or the Laws and Regulations of the Priesthood of Buddha in China*, translated from the Chinese original with notes and illustrations by Charles Fried Neumann. This is a translation of the *Sha-mi lü-i yao-lüeh* (Essential Rules and Ceremonies for a Novice) which forms a part of the 13th *chüan* of Chu-hung's complete works.

6. The most authoritative historian of Chinese Buddhism, T'ang Yung-t'ung, ended his excellent study before the T'ang. See *Han Wei liang-Chin Nan-pei-ch'ao fo-chiao shih*. Fung Yu-lan, in his *History of Chinese Philosophy*, Vol. II, deals with the Buddhist schools of the T'ang. Ch'en Yüan's studies on Buddhism of more recent times still remain standard reference works. See *Ming-chi Tien-Ch'ien fo-chiao k'ao* and *Shih-shih i-nien lu* (Peking, 1964). There has been renewed interest in the study of Ming and Ch'ing Buddhism among Buddhist scholars in Taiwan in recent years. One example is the full-length study on the life and thought of Ou-i Chih-hsü by Chang Sheng-yen. He wrote the work as a Ph.D. dissertation and published it in Japanese as *Minmatsu Chūgoku Bukkyō no kenkyū*. Shih Tung-chu's *Chung-kuo chin-shih fo-chiao shih* is a survey of Chinese Buddhism up to the Republican era.

7. The exception is the treatment of contemporary (in contrast to recent) Chinese Buddhism. Some excellent books are: J. Prip-Møller, *Chinese Buddhist Monasteries;* Holmes Welch, *The Practice of Chinese Buddhism* and *The Buddhist Revival in China*.

II. CHU-HUNG'S LIFE AND MAJOR WORKS

1. The edition of *Yün-ch'i fa-hui* used here is the one reprinted by the Chin-ling K'o-ching Ch'u in the year 1897. *Yün-ch'i fa-hui* is hereafter abbreviated as *YCFH*. All these materials are found in *chüan* 34. Yü Ch'un-hsi's *Yün-ch'i Lien-ch'ih ta-shih chuan* is contained in *Huang-ming wen-hai, chüan* 169, which is quoted in full in Makita Tairyō's *Chūgoku kinsei Bukkyōshi kenkyū*, p. 208.

2. *YCFH* 29, 55a; *YCFH* 28, 50a–55a, 53a.

3. They are listed in the following: (1) Fei-yin, *Wu-teng yen-t'ung*, preface dated 1653, *chüan* 16, ZZ 2B, 12, 4, 368–369; (2) T'ung-wen, *Hsü-teng ts'un-kao* preface dated 1666, *chüan* 12, ZZ 2B, 18, 1, 142–143; (3) Ch'ao-yung, *Wu-teng ch'üan-shu*, preface dated 1693, *chüan* 120, ZZ 2B, 15, 1,

100–101; (4) Chou K'o-fu, *Ching-t'u ch'en-chung*, *chüan* 10, ZZ 2, 14, 2, 154;
(5) P'eng Shao-sheng, *Ching-t'u sheng-hsien lu*, *chüan* 5, ZZ 2B, 8, 4, 145–147;
(6) P'eng Shao-sheng, *Yi-hsing-chü chi*, *chüan* 6; (7) Ming-ho, *Pu-hsü kao-seng-chuan*, *chüan* 5, ZZ 2B, 7, 1, 55–56; (8) Hsü Ch'ang-chih, *Kao-seng chai-yao*, *chüan* 1, ZZ 2B, 21, 4; (9) Huan-lun, *Shih-shih chi-ku-lüeh hsü-chi*, *chüan* 3, T 49, 952; (10) Mei-yan, *Hsin-hsü kao-seng-chuan ssu-chi*, *chüan* 43; (11) Chao Shih-an, *Jen-ho-hsien chih*, preface dated 1690, *chüan* 28.

    4. *YCFH* 28, 52a, "Hsien k'ao-pi yi-hsing chi."
    5. *YCFH* 25, 43a, "Yüan kuan tze."
    6. *YCFH* 28, 53a, "Hsien k'ao-pi yi-hsing chi."
    7. *YCFH* 31, 68a–68b.
    8. *YCFH* 28, 57a, "Chang nei-jen chih-ming."
    9. *YCFH* 29, 55b, "Tzu-shang pu-hsiao wen."
    10. Yü Ch'un-hsi's *Yün-ch'i Lien-ch'ih ta-shih chuan* and *Pu-hsü kao-seng-chuan*.
    11. This is probably a work written by the Yüan monk Wen-ts'ai (1241–1302), whose biography appears in *Fo-tsu li-tai t'ung-tsai*, *chüan* 22. See Walter Liebenthal, *Chao Lun, The Treatises of Seng-chao* (Hong Kong, 1968), p. 14. However, according to Liebenthal, there was also a monk who was named either Hui-teng or Hui-ch'eng who wrote a commentary on *Chao Lun* in three *chüan* entitled "Chao-lun ch'ao." This was first listed in a catalogue of books Ennin brought back from China in 839. The exact identity of this Hui-teng (or Hui-ch'eng) is, however, unknown. Nor is it clear if he ever wrote a book bearing his own name.
    12. Te-ch'ing's inscription. A famous monk in this century, Hsü-yün, achieved enlightenment when he heard the sound of a teacup breaking. In his autobiography he described the incident: "In the last month of the year [1895], on the third night of the eighth week, during the recess after the sixth period, the attendants poured hot water according to the rule. It splashed on my hand. The teacup fell to the ground and broke to bits with a loud noise. Suddenly the roots of doubt were cut. In my whole life I had never felt such joy. It was like waking from a dream." Welch, *The Practice of Chinese Buddhism*, p. 82.
    13. *Jen-ho hsien-chih*, *chüan* 20.
    14. *YCFH* 29, 59b–60a, "Ch'u-chia pieh shih-jen T'ang."
    15. The monastery was built by King Yeh of Wu in 947 and was the first one in the western Chekiang area to erect the ordination platform in 978. The platform has continued to exist to the present, while neither of the platforms of the other two monasteries in the area, that of K'ai-yüan, erected in 1131, and that of Hsien-lin, erected in 1162, remain. For this reason, this monastery has always been held in esteem. See Prip-Møller, *Chinese Buddhist Monasteries*, p. 345. The government edict prohibiting the use of ordination platforms came in 1566, in the same year that Chu-hung received his ordination.
    16. *YCFH* 33, 79b.
    17. *YCFH* 33, 67a–68b.

18. *YCFH*, 76b–77a.

19. Their biographies are found in, among other sources, *Shih-shih chi-ku lüeh hsü-chi, chüan* 3, T 49, 95a.

20. *YCFH* 17, 60b. Chu-hung's biography of Hsiao-yen is contained in the *Huang-Ming ming-seng chi-lüeh.*

21. *YCFH* 17, 60b.

22. *YCFH* 25, 33a–33b, "Pien-jung."

23. Sources concerning the history of the Yün-ch'i monastery and its revival under Chu-hung: Tung Ch'i-ch'ang, *Ch'ung-chien Yün-ch'i ch'an-yüan pei chi, YCFH* 33, 18a–20a; T'ao Wang-ling, *Hang-chou Yün-ch'i ch'an-yüan fa-t'ang chi,* ibid., 20a–22b; Fen Meng-chen, *Yün-ch'i lan-jo chih,* ibid., 23a–24b; Chu-hung, *Ch'ung-hsiu Yü-ch'i ch'an-yüan chi,* ibid., 24b–26b; and his *Fu-ku Yün-ch'i lan-jo chi,* ibid., 26b–27a.

24. "Wu-t'ai Wu-yün Feng ch'an-shih," in *Wu-lin Hsi-hu kao-seng shih-lüeh,* compiled by Ma-nao Yüan-ching and Tung-chia Yüan-fu of the Sung, and reprinted by Chu-hung as part of *YCFH* 17, 14b–15a.

25. *YCFH* 24, 25b–26a, "Ch'ien-li tsung-ling."

26. *YCFH* 33, 25b, "Chu-hung hsiu Yün-ch'i Ch'an-yüan chi."

27. *YCFH* 28, 62b–63a, "Jang-hu shu."

28. *YCFH* 34, 3b, Te-ch'ing's *Ta-shih t'a-ming; YCFH* 33, 25b–26a, "Ch'ung-fu Yün-ch'i ch'an-yüan chi."

29. Wolfram Eberhard, "Temple-building Activities in Medieval and Modern China." See especially the section on "Temple Builders," pp. 312–317.

30. Ibid., p. 314.

31. Hsiang Shih-yüan, *Yün-ch'i chih.*

32. Sekino Tadashi and Tokiwa Daijō, *Shina Bukkyō shiseki.*

33. *YCFH* 28, 63a–64a, "Jang-tsai shu tai Yü t'ai-shou."

34. *YCFH* 28, 65a–66a, "Ch'ung-hsiu Chu-chiao yüan-shu"; *YCFH* 34, 4b; *Ta-shih t'a-ming.*

35. *YCFH* 34, 7a–7b, *Ta-shih t'a-ming.*

36. Ōura Masahiro, "Mindai Bukkyō ni kansuru ichi kōsatsu—Unsei Shukō to sono sōrin no shakai shisōshiteki kenkyū," pp. 36–49.

37. Kenneth Ch'en, *Buddhism in China: A Historical Survey,* pp. 263–267; also his *Chinese Transformation of Buddhism* (Princeton, 1973), pp. 125–178; Jacques Gernet, *Les Aspects Economiques du Bouddhisme dans la Societie Chinoise du Ve au Xe Siecle* (Saigon, 1956); Lien-sheng Yang, "Buddhist Monasteries and Four Money-Raising Institutions in Chinese History"; Dennis Twitchett, "Monastic Estates in T'ang China," *Asia Major,* N.S. 5 (1956), pp. 123–146; and "The Monasteries and China's Economy in Medieval Times," *Bulletin of the School of Oriental and African Studies,* 19, 3 (1957), pp. 526–549.

38. Kenneth Ch'en, *Buddhism in China,* p. 295.

39. This was formulated by Takao Giken in "Unsei Daishi Shukō ni tsuite," pp. 238–248. Later scholars followed this interpretation without any significant change. For instance, Mochizuki Shinkō, *Chūgoku Jōdo kyōrishi;* and Ogasawara Senshū, *Chūgoku kinsei Jōdokyōshi no kenkyū.*

40. Included in *YCFH* 22, 3–20.

41. P'eng Shao-sheng in *Ching-t'u sheng-hsien lu* gives Chu-hung's date of death as the sixth month of the fortieth year of Wan-li (1612). He gives the date of Chu-hung's birth as the tenth year of Chia-ching (1531). He, alone of all sources, gives this variant dating.

42. Te-ch'ing's *Ta-shih t'a-ming,* in *YCFH* 34, 8a–9a.

43. A detailed enumeration of the writings is given in the Bibliography.

III. CHU-HUNG AND THE JOINT PRACTICE OF PURE LAND AND CH'AN

1. *The Zen Master Hakuin: Selected Writings,* tr. Philip B. Yampolsky, pp. 147–148.

2. Ibid., pp. 170–171.

3. Holmes Welch, *The Practice of Chinese Buddhism,* p. 398. On the separate hall for reciting the Buddha's name, see pp. 89–104.

4. Ogasawara Senshū, *Chūgoku kinsei Jōdokyōshi no kenykū,* p. 213.

5. Details of the latter will be discussed in chapter VIII.

6. Or the ninth patriarch. The discrepancy as well as problems of patriarchal order in the Pure Land school are discussed in the section entitled "Chu-hung and the Pure Land School."

7. Concerning the early history of Ch'an Buddhism, see Philip B. Yampolsky, *The Platform Sutra of the Sixth Patriarch,* pp. 1–57.

8. Heinrich Dumoulin, S. J., *A History of Zen Buddhism* (Boston: Peacon Press, 1969), p. 106.

9. For a discussion of these Ch'an masters, see Yampolsky, *The Platform Sutra,* pp. 53–55; and Dumoulin, *The Development of Chinese Zen after the Sixth Patriarch,* pp. 4–6.

10. Yampolsky, pp. 54–55.

11. Chu-ting, *Hsü ch'uan-teng-lu.* Hui-tsung's preface, cited by Iwai Hirosato, *Nisshi Bukkyōski ronkō,* p. 460.

12. *Wu-teng hui-yüan hsü-lüeh,* cited by Iwai, p. 461.

13. Monk Hai-yün, who had close relationships with several Yüan emperors, including Genghis Khan, Ögödei, and Möngke Khan, belonged to Lin-chi; Chih-wen, who had influence during Qubilai's time, belonged to Ts'ao-tung. Ibid., pp. 462–534.

14 K'ung-ku Ching-lung's autobiography is found in *YCFH* 17, 21b.

15. Ibid., 23b.

16. *YCFH* 17, 25a.

17. *Han-shan lao-jen meng-yu chi, chüan* 53, p. 2885.

18. Ibid., *chüan* 46, p. 2525.

19. Ou-i Chih-hsü, *Tsung-lun,* Part 3, Vol. V. Quoted by Ch'en Yüan, *Ching-ch'u tseng-cheng chi,* pp. 14–15.

20. Ibid., p. 15.

21. Chu-hung is listed as the eighth patriarch in two widely read biogra-

phies of Pure Land patriarchs: Wu-k'ai, *Lien-tsung chiu-tsu lüeh-chuan*, and P'eng Shao-sheng, *Ching-t'u sheng-hsien lu.* See Ogasawara, *Chūgoku kinsei Jōdokyōshi no kenkyū*, pp. 182–183.

22. This is the version given by Yang Jen-shan in *Shih-tsung lüeh-shuo.* See Ogasawara, *Chūgoku kinsei Jōdokyōshi no kenkyū*, p. 183.

23. *Lo-pang wen-lei* (block printed by Chao Chin-ting, date unknown), *chüan* 3, 36–42.

24. This section constitutes *chüan* 26 of *Fo-tsu-t'ung chi*, T 49, 261–265.

25. P'eng-an Ta-yu, *Ching-t'u chih-kuei chi* (Yang-chou: Yang-chou ts'ang-ching-yüan, 1912), p. 86, "Lien-she li-tsu."

26. See Holmes Welch, "Dharma Scrolls and the Succession of Abbots in Chinese Monasteries," especially pp. 111, 116, 119, 121–123, 136–147.

27. Takao Giken, *Sōdai Bukkyōshi no kenkyū*, pp. 118–119.

28. Chih-p'an established the patriarchal transmission for the Pure Land tradition in "Ching-t'u li-chiao chih," which forms *chüan* 26 of his *Fo-tsu-t'ung chi*. Chih-p'an based much of his narrative on Tsung-hsiao's, but he frequently included far more material than did Tsung-hsiao.

29. *Lo-pang wen-lei, chüan* 3, 36–38. *Fo-tsu-t'ung chi, chüan* 26, T 49, 261–263.

30. *Lo-pang wen-lei, chüan* 3, 38–39. *Fo-tsu-t'ung chi, chüan* 26; T 49, 263.

31. Shan-tao advocated both the invocation of the Buddha's name and the contemplation of the Buddha in the hope of attaining a vision of Amitābha in this life. Most scholars have only emphasized the former in Shantao's teaching. Julian Pas, however, has rightly pointed out that the *Kuanching* contained different layers of doctrines and that Shan-tao was sensitive to these in his commentary on the sutra: "The present texts consist of different layers of composition in which two or three main tendencies are noticeable. The original tendency or the basic message of the text has to do with meditation only: it is a manual of Amida vision in *this* life. A secondary (and later) stratum emphasizes ethical and mental conditions in order to be reborn in Amida's Pure Land Sukhāvatī, and finally there is the almost casual recommendation to call the name of Amida Buddha at the moment of death in order to obtain remittance of one's past transgressions and—against all normal changes—to obtain rebirth in Sukhāvatī . . . Shan-tao, although in some places feeling the difficulties involved, tried to give an objective exegesis of the text and to harmonize various levels of doctrine. However, it appears that, after him, his views were gradually simplified even to the point of distortion. In modern works one very rarely finds his views on meditation explained. He seems to be known as the propagator of the *nien-fo* practice only, and in the very restricted meaning of the expression at that." See Pas, "Shan-tao's Interpretation of the Meditative Vision of Buddha Amitayus," p. 98.

32. *Fo-tsu-t'ung chi, chüan* 26; T 49, 263.

33. *Fo-tsu-t'ung chi, chüan* 26; T 49, 263–264.

34. This is explained in the section entitled "The Joint Practice of Ch'an and Pure Land."

35. *Fo-tsu-t'ung chi, chüan* 26; T 49, 264. *Lo-pang wen-lei, chüan* 3, 24–41.
36. *Fo-tsu-t'ung chi, chüan* 26; T 49, 264–265.
37. This is a ritual for confessing the sins committed by the six senses according to the work called *Fa-hua san-mei hsing-fa* (The Method of Practicing the Lotus Samadhi), written by the T'ien-t'ai master Chih-i. He created the ritual according to the Lotus Sutra and other Mahāyāna sutras. It was first used by Master Hui-ssu, the second T'ien-t'ai patriarch. See Oda, *Oda Bukkyō Daijiten,* p. 1050a.
38. *Fo-tsu-t'ung chi, chüan* 26; T 49, 265. *Lo-pang wen-lei, chüan* 3, 41.
39. *Lo-pang wen-lei, chüan* 3, 42.
40. Technically there are two kinds of *nien-fo* samadhi. The first kind is called the practice of causes (*yin-hsing*) and refers to three types of *nien-fo:* (1) visualize with a single mind the wonderful characteristics of the Buddha; (2) contemplate with a single mind the real nature of the *dharmakāya;* (3) call upon the name of the Buddha with a single mind. These three are all called the *nien-fo* samadhi of causes, and are also referred to as "cultivation" (*hsiu*). The second type of *nien-fo* samadhi is a higher stage. When the aforementioned practices are successful, either the practitioner's mind will enter samadhi, or the Buddha appears in front of him, or he understands truly the one nature of reality. When this happens, it is called the *nien-fo* samadhi of successful result (*kuo-ch'eng*). It is also referred to as "attainment" (*fa-te*). See Oda, *Bukkyō Daijiten,* p. 1381a.
41. Tsung-tse seems to have identified *nien-fo san-mei* (samadhi of Buddha contemplation) with the oral invocation of the Buddha's name. From this passage at least, he also seemed to have emphasized the quantitative aspect of *nien-fo:* the more one called the name, the more likely one was to achieve *nien-fo* samadhi.
42. See Leon Hurvitz, "Chu-hung's One Mind of Pure Land and Ch'an Buddhism," in de Bary, *Self and Society in Ming Thought,* p. 453.
43. Tsung-mi's theory is set forth in *chüan* 4 of his *P'u-hsien hsing-yüan p'in shu-ch'ao* (Commentary on the P'u-hsien hsing-yüan chapter of the Avataṁsaka Sutra). ZZ 1, 75, 457–458. See Mochizuki Shinkō, *Chūgoku Jōdo kyōri shi.*
44. *YCFH* 8, 66b–67a. Hurvitz, pp. 455–456. It is touched on by Welch, *The Practice of Buddhism,* pp. 90, 399.
45. In the case of Shan-tao, it is likely that he had put equal emphasis on the two aspects of *nien-fo,* Buddha contemplation and Buddha invocation, as Julian Pas in his recent studies on Shan-tao indicated ("Shan-tao's Interpretation of the Meditative Vision of Buddha Amitayus" and "The Significance of Shan-tao in the Pure Land Movement of China and Japan," paper delivered at AAR meeting in 1976). Commenting on Shan-tao's work the *Kuan-nien fa-men,* "The Dharma Door to Visualization and Contemplation of the Buddha," T. 1959, Pas pointed out that "He [Shan-tao] does not give any definition of its [*nien's*] meaning and content but uses the term as ambiguous, i.e., including both meditation on Amida and invocation of his name. . . . By using the term in its ambiguity he seems to stress the fact that

for him *nien-fo* is both meditation and recitation and should not be separated. In other words, meditation, aiming at the vision of Amida here and now, is always accompanied by worship, chanting the sutras, and reciting the name of Amida." See "The Significance of Shan-tao in the Pure Land Movement of China and Japan," p. 22. After discussing the passages in the Commentary of Shan-tao to the *Kuan-ching*, Pas disagreed with the views of K. Ch'en, R. Robinson, and S. Mochizuki and concluded: ". . . Shan-tao was not the one-tract-minded popular preacher that the Japanese Pure Land followers made him to appear. His approach to the Amida cult is many-sided; for everybody he recommends a suitable method to obtain rebirth: those of weak faith are attracted to Sukhāvatī by sincere invocation of Amida's name; however, the more fervent disciples are encouraged to perform better: both ethical conduct and meditation (according to the *kuan* method) are a higher and more perfect form of *nien-fo.*" Ibid., p. 39.

46. Yen-shou contrasted the two approaches in *Wan-shan t'ung-kuei chi, chüan* 21. The pursuit of contemplation leads to samadhi. This is what he called *ting-hsin* (mind of concentration), which he believed would result in rebirth in a superior category *(shang-p'in wang-sheng)*. Mere recitation of the Buddha's name, when accompanied by the performance of good deeds, leads to *chuan-hsin* (mind of single devotion). This will result in rebirth in an inferior category *(hsia-p'in wang-sheng)*. Mochizuki, p. 337.

47. On the White Lotus sect, see Mochizuki, pp. 411–425. Ogasawara, pp. 83–130; and Daniel L. Overmyer, *Folk Buddhist Religion: Dissenting Sects in Late Traditional China*, pp. 73–108.

48. According to P'u-tu, there were ten requirements a man had to fulfill if he wanted to achieve rebirth. P'u-tu called the ten "the orthodox practices of Buddha invocation." They were: (1) take care of one's parents with filial piety, (2) respect and serve one's teachers and elders, (3) take refuge in the Three Jewels, (4) raise the mind of enlightenment, (5) keep the five precepts, (6) practice compassion and nonkilling, (7) perform the ten good deeds, (8) believe in cause and effect (i.e., the law of karma), (9) recite the Mahāyāna scriptures, and (10) persuade others to practice the above. *Lien-tsung pao-chien, chüan* 1; T 49, 306a–309a.

49. See *YCFH* 16, *Wang-sheng chi*, 1, 27b–28c and 3, 5b, respectively.

50. It is possible that Chu-hung did not connect these two Pure Land Buddhists with the White Lotus sectarians of the Ming. Overmyer noted also that "In Ming Ching-t'u sources Mao appears as a pillar of the Pure Land tradition . . . in I-nien's *Hsi-fang chih-chih* (Pointing directly to the western land) Tz'u-chao is quoted in sharp criticism of ignorant folk who do not understand the proper way to seek rebirth in the Pure Land, who recite Amitābha's name to ward off illness and in times of difficulty call on gods and ancestors, burn paper money, and kill living beings for sacrifice. . . . After reading his material it is extremely difficult to conceive of Mao Tzu-yüan as the founder of a syncretic folk sect! If he had been involved in dubious or heretical activity, why would the Pure Land School have so venerated

him as an orthodox saint of the tradition, described alongside Hui-yüan and Shan-tao?" *Folk Buddhist Religion,* p. 93.

51. The White Lotus Society was first banned when Tzu-yüan was sent into exile. During the Yüan, the ban was reaffirmed by decrees in 1281, 1308, and 1322. Ch'en, *Buddhism in China,* p. 430.

52. Ogasawara, p. 90.

53. These include *Ch'an-kuan ts'e-chin (YCFH* 14), *Wang-sheng chi (YCFH* 16), *Huang-Ming ming-seng chi-lüeh (YCFH* 17) and *Chu-ch'uang erh-pi (YCFH* 25).

54. Mochizuki, p. 330.

55. Since the Sung, Chinese Ch'an monks have revered Pai-chang both as the originator of the Ch'an emphasis on manual labor ("no work, no food") and the Ch'an monastic code. The tradition credits him with the writing of the *Pure Rules of Pai-chang,* the first monastic code for Ch'an monks, who had until then lived in monasteries of the Vinaya (*lü*) school and observed basically Hīnayāna rules. This view was accepted by many scholars. Recent studies on the history of Zen codes, however, have questioned this view. Martin Collcutt in his dissertation, "The Zen Monastic Institutes in Medieval Japan" (Harvard, 1975) discussed the works of Japanese scholars such as Kondō Ryōichi ("Hajō shingi to Zen'on shingi"; "Hajō shingi no seiritsu to sono genkei"), Shiina Kōyū ("Shotō Zensha no Ritsuin kyojū ni tsuite"), Yanagida Seizan *(Shoki Zenshū shiso no kenkyū),* and Kagamishima Genryū ("Hajō koshingi henka katei no ichi-kōsatsu"). The consensus is that not only was Pai-chang not the originator of the Ch'an code, but he might not have compiled any code at all. Pai-chang himself, his disciples, and his biographers all failed to mention any code he might have compiled. The existing *Ch'ih-hsiu Pai-chang ch'ing-kuei* (Imperial Compilation of the Pai-chang Code) was a Yüan dynasty work which, according to Collcutt, was a synthesis of the best-known Sung dynasty codes and contained nothing that could be traced directly to Pai-chang. See Collcutt, pp. 189–190.

56. Mochizuki, p. 394.

57. *YCFH* 16, *Wang-sheng-chi fu,* 1b.

58. There are two versions of *Pan-chou san-mei ching* in the Taishō Tripitaka (T 417, T 418). One is in eight chapters, and the other in sixteen. Both are supposed to have been translated by Lokakṣema (Chih-lou-chia-ch'an) of the later Han. See Mochizuki, p. 12; E. Zürcher, *The Buddhist Conquest of China,* p. 35. The passages in the sutra dealing with *nien-fo san-mei* are gathered together in *Lo-pang wen-lei, chüan* 1.

59. Mochizuki, pp. 24–28; Zürcher, pp. 220–221.

60. *Lo-pang wen-lei, chüan* 1,29b.

61. Ibid., 29b–30a.

62. Mochizuki, p. 112. *Lo-pang wen-lei, chüan* 1,30–61.

63. Ui Hakuju, *Zenshūshi kenkyū,* pp. 169–174; Yampolsky, *Platform Sutra,* pp. 43–44. According to the *Leng-chia shih-tzu chi,* Chih-hsien was one of the ten great disciples of the Fifth Patriarch Hung-jen (T 85, 1289c).

However, it did not give much detailed material about either himself or the
school he was supposed to have established in Szechuan. The *Li-tai fa-pao
chi*, a later work centering on the thought of Wu-chu, who traced his lineage
to Chih-hsien, claimed that Chih-hsien passed the Dharma to Ch'u-chi. The
latter, in turn, passed it to Musang, who then passed it to Wu-chu. Moreover, the *Li-tai fa-pao chi* made them represent the Pao-t'ang school of early
Ch'an Buddhism, a separate tradition independent from the Northern and
Southern schools of Ch'an. Yanagida Seizan, *Shoki no zenshi II: Rekidai hōbō ki*,
pp. 14–15.

64. Ui, p. 180; Yampolsky, p. 44.
65. Ui, p. 190. *Na-mo* means "adoration of" or "homage to."
66. Mochizuki, p. 394.
67. Ibid., p. 332. Chu-hung used the same twofold distinction of "universal" *(li)* and "particular" *(shih)* to explain the two levels of *nien-fo*.
68. Mochizuki, p. 341.
69. *T'ien-mu Ming-pen Ch'an-shih tsu-lu*, ZZ 1, 2, 27, 4; 393b.
70. Ibid., 396a.
71. *Ch'an-kuan ts'e-chin*, YCFH 14, 21b–22a.
72. *YCFH* 17, 41b.
73. Ibid., 44a.
74. Ibid., 42b.
75. Ibid., 13a–14a.
76. Ibid., 55b.
77. *YCFH* 14, 22b.
78. *YCFH* 17, 19a.
79. *Han-shan lao-jen meng-yu chi*, *chüan* 9, 18.
80. *YCFH* 6, 18b.
81. Ibid., 22a.
82. Ibid., 28b–29a. The same idea was expressed by Te-ch'ing, who
characterized the method of Ch'an as no-thought and that of Pure Land as
thought. ". . . The Ch'an path teaches the method of no-thought, whereas
the Pure Land path teaches the method of thought. Since sentient beings
have fallen deeply into the ocean of delusions, it is difficult for them to get
rid of thoughts. If impure thoughts are transformed into pure thoughts, it is
like using one poison to counter another poison, playing a game of
exchange. Thus it is difficult to obtain enlightenment through the Ch'an
path, and easier to attain freedom through the Pure Land path." *Han-shan
lao-jen meng-yu chi*, *chüan* 8, 45–46.
83. *YCFH* 8, 58b.
84. Ibid., 59a; Hurvitz, p. 455.
85. Ibid., 66a–66b; Hurvitz, p. 463.
86. Ibid.
87. Ibid.
88. Ibid.
89. Ibid.

90. *YCFH* 6, 10a; Hurvitz, p. 461.

91. *YCFH* 8, 70b; Hurvitz, p. 464.

IV. Chu-hung and the Late Ming Lay Buddhist Movement

1. Kenneth Ch'en, *Buddhism in China*, p. 449.

2. For instance, Ch'en uses the subtitle "Decline" for his treatment of Buddhism from the Sung on. Arthur Wright calls the years ca. 900–1900 "the period of appropriation." Cf. Ch'en, chapter 14, and Wright, *Buddhism in Chinese History*, p. 86.

3. Chu-hung explains the meaning of these terms as follows: "When a thought arises in the mind that materializes into the intent to kill, this is the primary cause *(yin)*. The secondary causes are the various factors which lead to the killing *(yüan)*. The means and ways which the killing involves constitute the karma *(yeh)*." *YCFH* 2; *Chieh-shu fa-yin, chüan* 3, 8a.

4. *Fan-wang ching*, T 24, 1004b. This extremely important text has been translated from Chinese into French by J. J. M. DeGroot in *Le Code du Mahāyāna en Chine* (Amsterdam, 1893). This passage occurs on pp. 32–33. French is given on the left side of the page and the original Chinese text on the right.

5. *YCFH* 2; *Chieh-shu fa-yin, chüan* 3, 9a.

6. *Fan-wang ching*, T 24, 1006b.

7. *Chieh-shu fa-yin, chüan* 4, 47b–48a.

8. Ibid., 48b.

9. *Liang shu, chüan* 48, 7a–13a.

10. According to the notes supplied by Chu-hung, this refers to a passage in the Sūraṅgama Sutra *(Leng-yen ching):* "The Buddha says to Ananda, 'When a monk eats food, do you think the rest of the monks are also satisfied?' Ānanda answers, 'Although the monks are all arhats, since each of them has a different body, we cannot say that one person satisfies the rest.'" *YCFH* 5; *Chieh-shu shih-chien*, 27b.

11. Ibid., 28a. "The younger brother of Emperor T'ai-tsu of Sung, King Chin, was sick. The doctor applied cauterization by burning moxa. The king felt pain and the emperor cauterized himself with moxa in order to share the king's pain."

12. Ibid. "Ts'ai Shun lost his father at an early age and lived with his mother. One day he went out to gather firewood, and a visitor suddenly appeared. When he did not return quickly, his mother bit her finger. Shun felt something in his heart, and casting the firewood on the ground, rushed home."

13. Ibid. "In the T'ang dynasty there was an official who plotted rebellion with An Lu-shan. He was formerly the prefect of Szechwan, and a statue of him remained there. When Emperor Hsüan-tsung toured Shu and

saw it, he was very angry and he struck its head with a sword. At that time this official was living in Shansi, but his head suddenly fell to the ground."

14. *YCFH* 3; *Chieh-shu fa-yin, chüan* 4, 48b–49a.

15. *YCFH* 3, 49a–49b.

16. *YCFH* 3, 50a–50b.

17. *YCFH* 5; *Chieh-shu wen pien*, 1b.

18. Cf. Suzuki Chūsei, "Bukkyō no kinsatsu kairitsu ga Sōdai no minshu seikatsu ni oyoboseru eikyō ni tsuite," pp. 115–141.

19. *Fo-tsu-t'ung chi*, T 49, 359c.

20. *Fan-wang ching*, T 24, 1007b.

21. *T'ang ta-chao chüan-chi, chüan* 113.

22. "Liang Yüan-ti Ching-chou fang-sheng-t'ing pei," *I-wen lei chü, chüan* 77.

23. *Fo-tsu-t'ung chi*, T 49, 376a.

24. *Hsin T'ang shu, chüan* 153; *Chiu T'ang shu, chüan* 128.

25. "T'ien-hsia fang-sheng-ch'ih pei-ming," *Ch'üan T'ang wen, chüan* 339.

26. His biography is found in *Wu-teng hui-yüan, chüan* 10; *Fo-tsu-t'ung chi, chüan* 26; *Fo-tsu t'ung-tsai, chüan* 26; *Shih-shih chi ku lüeh, chüan* 3.

27. *Fo-tsu-t'ung chi*, T 49, 207a–209a.

28. *Fo-tsu-t'ung chi*, 208a.

29. *Sung shih, chüan* 8, "Chen-tsung pen-chi."

30. *Sung shih, chüan* 338; *Sung Yüan hsüeh-an, chüan* 99.

31. *Lin-an chih, chüan* 32.

32. T'ang Yung-t'ung, *Han Wei liang-Chin Nan-pei-ch'ao fo-chiao shih*, pp. 248–271.

33. Suzuki Chūsei, "Sōdai Bukkyō kessha no kenkyū," pp. 65–98, 205–241, 303–333.

34. For example: "Tung-p'o chü-shih yin shih shuo," 135b; "Yu-t'an tz'u-shih chieh-sha wen," 136a; "Fo-yin ch'an-shih chieh-sha wen," 136a; "Chen-hsieh ch'an-shih chieh-sha wen," 136a–b; "P'u-an tz'u-shih chieh-sha wen," 136b; all are included in *Kuei-yüan chih-chih chi, chüan* 2, the preface to which is dated 1570. ZZ 2, 13, 2.

35. "Tung-p'o chü-shih yin shih shuo," ZZ 2, 13, 2, 135b.

36. *YCFH* 22, 3–20.

37. Chu-hung's reply exhorting the empress to cultivate both wisdom and blessing is included in a verse entitled "Tz'u-sheng Huang-t'ai-hou ch'ien nei-ch'ih wen fa-yao chieh-sung," *YCFH* 29, 21a.

The story of the establishment of the ponds at the Shang-fang Ssu and Ch'ang-shou Ssu is found in *YCFH* 33, 27b–30a, 30a–32b.

38. Cf. Ogasawara Senshū, *Chūgoku kinsei Jōdokyō shi no kenkyū*, the section entitled "Byakurenshū no kenkyū," pp. 79–165; Suzuki, "Sōdai Bukkyō kessha no kenkyū," pp. 303–333; Li Shou-k'ung, "Ming-tai pai-liang-chiao k'ab-lüeh."

39. *Chu-ch'uang erh-pi*, YCFH 25, 23a–23b, "Lien she."

40. YCFH 25, 22a–22b, "Chieh she-hui."

41. YCFH 32, 16b–17a, "Fang-sheng wen."

42. YCFH 32, 17b.

43. The nine "untimely deaths" are: (1) death by suffering from a disease that is not attended to by a doctor; (2) death by doing evil and being punished by the law of the land; (3) death by indulging in excessive pleasure that causes one to become careless and thus to give ghosts and spirits the opportunity of stealing one's energy and breath away; (4) death by drowning; (5) death by burning; (6) death through being eaten by ferocious beasts in the forest; (7) death by falling off a cliff; (8) death through being killed by poison or a curse; (9) death from hunger and thirst. The reference is *Fo-hsüeh ta tzu-tien*, pp. 174b–c.

44. YCFH 31; *I-kao, chüan* 3, 78a, "Fang-sheng tu-shuo."

45. The main concepts of the work, those dealing with *nien-fo*, are discussed in chapter IV of this book. See also Leon Hurvitz, "Chu-hung's One Mind of Pure Land and Ch'an Buddhism," in de Bary, *Self and Society in Ming Thought*, pp. 451–476, esp. pp. 453–469.

46. Lo Chin-hsi gave Chou Ju-teng the Buddhist work *Fa-yüan chu-lin* (Cyclopedia of the Buddhist System). See *Ming-ju hsüeh-an, chüan* 36, 372.

47. YCFH 31; *I-kao, chüan* 3, 14b, "Ta Chou Hsi-meng shao-ts'an."

48. YCFH 22, 17b–19a, "Fang-sheng wen."

49. YCFH 32, 74a–75a, "Shang-fang shan-hui yüeh."

50. *Ming shih, chüan* 216; *Chü-shih chuan, chüan* 44.

51. *Ming shih, chüan* 283; *Ming-ju hsüeh-an, chüan* 35.

52. Preface to T'ao Wang-ling's "Fang-sheng pien huo" (Dispelling Doubts Concerning Releasing Life), in *Shuo-fu hsü-chi* (1647 reprint), *chüan* 30.

53. *Chü-shih chuan, chüan* 42.

54. YCFH 22, 3b–6b, "Chieh-sha wen." At points I have paraphrased the original in order to avoid unnecessary details.

55. YCFH 22, 6b–7a.

56. Cf. Ōchō Enichi, "Minmatsu Bukkyō to Kirisutokyō to no sōgo hihan," pp. 1–20; 18–38. See also Oyanagi Shigeta, "Rimatō to Minmatsu no shisōkai," pp. 83–109; Hou Wai-lu, *Chung-kuo ssu-hsiang t'ung-shih*, pp. 1189–1213; D. Lancashire, "Buddhist Reaction to Christianity in Late Ming China."

57. Included in *T'ien-hsüeh ch'u-han*, compiled by Li Chih-tsao (1964 Taipei reprint), pp. 351–635.

58. Ibid., pp. 501–502.

59. Ibid., p. 503.

60. Ibid., pp. 505–506.

61. Ibid., p. 509.

62. YCFH 26, 72a–75a.

63. YCFH 26, 73b–74a.

64. "Yü Teh-yüan ch'üan-pu yü Li Hsi-t'ai hsien-sheng shu," and "Li hsien-sheng fu Yü ch'üan-pu shu," in *Pien-hsüeh i-tu, T'ien-hsüeh ch'u-han, chüan* 2, 637–641, 641–650.

65. Ibid., "Li hsien-sheng fu Lien-ch'ih ta ho-shang chu-ch'uang t'ien-shuo ssu tuan," 651–684.

66. In the edition published in Fukien, there was a preface to *Pien-hsüeh i-tu* written by a Mi-ko-tzu [Michael], which was the religious name of Yang Ting-yün (1557–1627). Cf. Fang Hao, *Chung-kuo t'ien-chu-chiao jen-wu chuan*, pp. 126–138. Yang claimed that before Chu-hung died, the latter repented of his wrong faith in the Pure Land. This preface was missing from the Chekiang edition of the same book, and the fact was taken by many Buddhists as concrete proof that the book was a forgery, a shameless polemic against Chu-hung. Cf. "Cheng wang shuo" (Exposing the Wrong), by Chang Kuang-t'ien in *Ming-ch'ao p'o-hsieh chi, chüan* 7.

67. *YCFH* 2, 32b.

68. *YCFH* 2, 34a.

69. The work consists of 56 *chüan*, with 228 full biographies, in which 69 additional persons are also briefly mentioned. It was published in 1776.

70. The other two are *Chü-shih fen-teng lu* in 2 *chüan* by Chu Shih-en, published in 1632, and *Hsien-chüeh chi* in 2 *chüan* by T'ao Ming-ch'ien, published in 1672. P'eng's *Chü-shih chuan* was based on T'ao's work, but he added a great deal of new material. See Ogawa Kanichi, "Koji Bukkyō no kinsei hatten," pp. 51–52.

71. Five from Kiangsi, four from Fukien, two each from Hukuang (Hunan, Hupei) and Szechwan, and one from Shansi.

72. Sakai Tadao, *Chūgoku zensho no kenkyū*, pp. 303–304. Cf. Welch, *Practice*, pp. 126–128, 417, 500, note 12.

73. While there are as many definitions of the term "gentry" as there are studies about them, I find the classification into official-gentry and scholar-gentry, as outlined by Ch'ü T'ung-tsu in his *Local Government in China under the Ch'ing*, pp. 171–173, most helpful.

74. The titles (epistolary or literary) of these positions are: *chun-po* (prefect, 4B), *i-ling* (district magistrate, 7B), *chung-ch'eng* (governor, 2B), *t'ai-shih* (compiler, 5B). Besides these, the following titles are also found: *tsung-jung* (brigadier-general, 2A), *fang-po* (lieutenant-governor or financial commissioner, 2B), *tsung-po* (director of the court of sacrificial worship, 3A), *ching-chao* (prefect of the metropolitan prefecture, 3A), *tu-hsien* (first captain, 4A), *chih-chung* (subprefect of Shun-t'ien-fu, 5A), *chun-ch'eng* (first-class subprefect, 5A), *chu-cheng* (second-class secretary of a ministry, 6A), *chung-han* (secretary of the grand secretariat, 7B). The translations of the titles and their grades are made according to Charles O. Hucker, "An Index of Terms and Titles in the Governmental Organization of the Ming Dynasty," pp. 127–151; and H. S. Brunnert and V. V. Hagelstrom, *Present Day Political Organization of China*.

75. *Chü-shih chuan, chüan* 48.

76. Ibid., *chüan* 40.

77. Ibid., *chüan* 42.
78. Ibid., *chüan* 48.
79. Ibid., *chüan* 38.
80. Ibid., *chüan* 44.
81. Ibid., *chüan* 48.
82. Ibid.
83. Ibid., *chüan* 42.
84. Ibid., *chüan* 48.
85. Hsieh Kuo-chen, *Ming Ch'ing chih-chi tang-she yün-tung k'ao*, pp. 8–13.
86. Ibid., p. 10.
87. *Chü-shih chuan, chüan* 42.
88. Ibid., *chüan* 41.
89. Whom I cannot otherwise identify.
90. *YCFH* 30, *chüan* 2, 24a.
91. *YCFH* 30, 46b.
92. Ibid., 34b.
93. Ibid., 26b.
94. Ibid., 47a–47b.
95. Ibid., *chüan* 1, 45b.
96. Ibid., *chüan* 2, 24b.
97. *YCFH* 31, 17a.
98. One *chüan*. There are two versions. One was translated by T'an Wu-ch'an (d. 433) of the Northern Liang (T 24, 1107–1110). The other was translated by Hsüan-tsang (c. 596–664) of the T'ang (T 24, 1110–1115).
99. *YCFH* 2, 10a–10b.
100. *YCFH* 31, 17a.
101. *YCFH* 31, 26a.
102. *YCFH* 30, *chüan* 2, 22a.
103. *YCFH* 30, 35a–36b.
104. Ibid., 36a.
105. Ibid., 36b.

V. Syncretism in Action: Morality Books and The Record of Self-knowledge

1. Helmer Ringgren, "The Problems of Syncretism," in *Syncretism*, ed. Sven S. Hartman, p. 7.

2. Individual studies on gnosticism, Philo, and Hellenistic syncretism and George Widgren's studies of Syrian Christianity and ancient Near Eastern religions, of course, all bear on the subject matter of syncretism, but there has yet to appear a theoretical treatment of syncretism as a universal and perhaps even perennial human response to cultural and religious contact. In recent years, however, there has been some interest in the exploration of this area among Western scholars. Several colloquia and symposia have been held on the general topic of syncretism: at the Swedish University

of Abo, Finland, September 1966 and 1967; at the University of Strasbourg, June 1971; at the German Academy of Göttingen, October 1971; and at Santa Barbara campus, University of California, April 1972. The papers from the first colloquium were published as *Syncretism* and those of the last appear in *Religious Syncretism in Antiquity*, ed. Birger A. Pearson.

3. In *Religious Syncretism in Antiquity* both Raimundo Panikkar and Stanislav Segert went into the etymology of "syncretism" to show why the term might have acquired a pejorative connotation through the ages: "The traditional and, at the same time real, etymology of the word *synkretismos*, presented by Plutarch *(De fraterno amore*, 2, 490b), explains the word as the coming together of Cretans against an external enemy." See "Some Remarks Concerning Syncretism" in *Religious Syncretism in Antiquity*, p. 63. Raimundo Panikkar further analyzed this etymology and found four traits: (1) the joining of forces and interests; (2) from people who otherwise were neither united nor friendly to each other; (3) so that, forgetting internal rivalries, they became provisional allies; (4) in order to fight a common enemy or threat. Thus, according to the original etymology of syncretism, the union of elements is provisional or momentary; it lasts as long as the external menace remains and is therefore superficial. Panikkar continues: "No wonder, then, in point of fact, that the use of the word through the ages has almost constantly had a pejorative connotation, except when it began to be used as meaning a global and overall view, e.g., the 'syncretistic' perception of children or when it was used by the defenders of the respective 'syncretistic' doctrines of different periods in human thought." "Some Notes on Syncretism and Eclecticism Related to the Growth of Human Consciousness," *Religious Syncretism in Antiquity*, p. 49.

4. Panikkar uses the imagery of "growth" to characterize the syncretic process, which would agree with my view presented here: "Growth is neither immobility nor mere change; it is neither exclusive disrupture nor sheer continuity. . . . Growth implies assimilation of elements outside by virtue of a force inside. . . . Growth is endogenous, it comes from within and has an internal pattern, only disclosed in the growing process itself. But growth requires also an exogenous element, namely, the external materials, the food to be assimilated. . . . Growth is a holistic phenomenon; it has the paradigm of a *Gestalt*. We may know the elements needed for the growing process, but growth cannot be reduced to the increase of elementary particles forming independent configurations." See "Some Notes on Syncretism and Eclecticism Related to the Growth of Human Consciousness," *Religious Syncretism in Antiquity*, p. 57.

5. There is some uncertainty about the authorship and the date of this work. In the preface to *T'ai-shang kan-ying p'ien tu-shuo* (printed in 1893), it is stated: "This treatise was hidden in the *Tao-tsang*. Before the Sung dynasty, few knew of its existence." Takao Giken thinks it was written by a Taoist priest between the end of the T'ang and the beginning of the Sung, for two reasons: the *Treatise* was first mentioned in the *I wen chih* section of the *Sung shih* (History of the Sung); and Li Ch'ang-ling (fl. 1008) was the

first person to advocate the practice recommended in the *Treatise*. "Mindai ni taisei sareta kōkakaku shisō," p. 18. Sakai Tadao credited Li Chih-chi as the author of the *Treatise*. See *Chūgoku zensho no kenkyū,* p. 431.

   6. *Kao-tzu i-shu, chüan* 9, "T'ung-shan hui hsü," and "Ch'ung-k'o kan-ying p'ien hsü," cited by Sakai, p. 286.

   7. *Hung-pao chi, chüan* 42, "T'ai-shang kan-ying p'ien hsü," cited in Sakai, p. 261. Besides T'u, the two T'ao brothers were also interested in propagating morality books. T'ao Wang-ling wrote essays on the *Treatise*, and T'ao Shih-ling wrote on *The Ledger of Merits and Demerits*. See Sakai, p. 257.

   8. Tachibana Shiraki, *Shina shisō no kenkyū,* p. 37.

   9. Paul Carus, who together with D. T. Suzuki translated the work into English, said in his introduction: "If the popularity of books must be measured by either the number of copies in which they appear or the devotion of their reader, the *T'ai-Shang Kan-Ying P'ien,* i.e., *The Treatise of the Exalted One on Response and Retribution,* will probably have to be assigned the first place of all publications on the globe. Its editions exceed even those of the Bible and Shakespeare, which of all the books published in the Western world are most numerous, and many millions of devout Chinese believe that great merit is gained by the dissemination of the book." *The Treatise of the Exalted One on Response and Retribution,* tr. D. T. Suzuki and Paul Carus, p. 3.

   The popularity of morality books was not limited to imperial China, but to a certain extent carried over to modern China as well. Two Japanese authors attested to their popularity with eyewitness accounts. Tachibana Shiraki, who was in Manchuria in 1924, stated that even in the most dilapidated bookstores in Dairen and Lü-shun he saw a great many copies of the *Treatise* and *The Ledger of Merits and Demerits,* another important morality book to be dealt with in this chapter. *Shina shisō kenkyū,* p. 37. Another Japanese traveler, reporting from a small village in Hopei in 1942, saw peasant families venerating the *Chüeh-shih ching,* a late Ming morality book, as a family bible.

   10. The terms "great tradition" and "little tradition" were first proposed by Robert Redfield in *The Little Community, Peasant Society, and Culture*. Since then, this conceptual paradigm has been used by other cultural anthropologists who either refined it with modifications or questioned its basic assumptions and suggested alternate ways of assessing cultural contact and social change. Milton Singer suggested "text and context" ("Text and Context in the Study of Religion and Social Change in India," reprinted in *When a Great Tradition Modernizes*). M. N. Srinivas used "Sanskritization" (*Religion and Society among the Coorgs of South India*) in studying the process of the permeation of Hinduism into the local levels of Indian society. On the other hand, some scholars question the validity of treating the classical literary great tradition as a monolithic whole. Instead, they see the coexistence of various great traditions, the Sanskrit, Brahmanical, or Hindu being just one of the great traditions. In this case, instead of tracing the dichotomy between the great and the little traditions,

one tries to locate the dominant tradition in different localities and at different times. "I suggest that the structure of Indian culture is composed of multiple traditions, each tradition utilizing components (groups, centers, items, relationships) found through India. But I would insist that each tradition is of *equal* status on an all-India scale, and that our attention must be directed to the system which is dominant in any time, region or locality to assess which is the "Great Tradition" of the moment. . . . In a complex culture such as India represents . . . shared components are *not* the indicators of participation in a *single* system or tradition. It is the perceived relationship between components, the organization of the meaning of these relationships and components which give body to a 'tradition.'" See Robert Miller, "Button, Button—Great Tradition, Little Tradition, Whose Tradition?" pp. 40–41. In the case of late traditional China, it would be more appropriate to speak of a "great tradition" consisting of Confucian, Buddhist, and Taoist components than of three separate "great traditions."

11. Morality books represent the myths and values of the Chinese great tradition just as stories, songs, and sayings represent those of the Hindu tradition. Susan Snow Wadley collected and analyzed stories and songs of a North Indian village called Karimpur in *Shakti: Power in the Conceptual Structure of Karimpur Religion.* Both can tell us the belief and value systems of the common man, be he a Ming dynasty Chinese or a contemporary Indian villager. But there are some differences. Whereas the morality books were written by members of the elite, the Karimpur texts are strictly the work of often anonymous village storytellers and priests.

12. For instance, Holmes Welch, *The Parting of the Way,* p. 139. Welch used the term "religion of the masses" in the sense Wing-tsit Chan did in his *Religious Trends in Modern China,* pp. 139–185. Chan distinguished two levels of religion: the religion of the enlightened and the religion of the masses.

13. Tadao Sakai, "Confucianism and Popular Educational Works," in *Self and Society in Ming Thought,* p. 341.

14. *Hsü fen-shu, chüan* 1, "Ta Ma Li-shan," cited by Sakai, p. 242.

15. *Chiao-shih pi-ch'eng, chüan* 2, "Chih tan shen," cited by Sakai, p. 246.

16. Sakai, pp. 255–256.

17. In the *Record of Self-knowledge* Chu-hung used 100 cash *(wen)*, or 100 pieces of copper coin as the basic unit in counting money. In the Ming there were three kinds of currency: the paper note, copper coin, and silver. T'ai-tsu, following the practice of the Yüan, attempted to make paper currency the only official means of transaction. "The note was issued in six denominations, namely, 100, 200, 300, 400, 500 cash and one string. One string in paper currency was made the equivalent of 1,000 copper coins, one ounce of silver or one-fourth ounce of gold. Trading with gold and silver was forbidden." (Lien-sheng Yang, *Money and Credit in China, A Short History,* p. 67). However, the paper note never achieved this intended status. Instead, by the mid-fifteen century silver had become the preferred medium of exchange. James Geiss discusses the reasons for this development in his

dissertation, "Peking under the Ming (1368–1644)": "Since government paper currency had begun to inflate in value during the early reigns of the dynasty and since copper coins varied considerably in weight, metallic content and quality, people turned to silver. Silver had a stable value as a precious metal, and that value remained relatively unaffected by economic changes during the first two centuries of Ming rule. In the late sixteenth century, however, when silver from Mexico and Japan entered the Ming empire in great quantity, the value of silver began to decline and inflation set in, for as the metal became more abundant its buying power diminished" (p. 144). As one might expect, there was much fluctuation in the exchange rate between copper coins and silver. Geiss illustrated the wide range of fluctuations with the following examples. "In the early years of the Hung-wu reign (1368–1399) one thousand copper cash bought one ounce of silver. During the Ch'eng-hua reign (1465–1487) eight hundred copper coins bought an ounce, and in the early years of the Hung-chih reign (1488–1506) the figure stood at seven hundred. Although official prices in the Chia-ching reign (1522–66) indicate no change in this rate of exchange, the market prices tell another story. In the markets one ounce of fine silver could be had for three hundred good copper coins. In other words, the value of copper coins had increased threefold relative to silver in the course of two centuries. During the Lung-ch'ing reign (1567–72), when silver had become the currency of first choice throughout the empire, an ounce of silver could be had for 800 copper coins of good quality, or one thousand coins of inferior quality. The value of copper currency rose again slightly during the Wan-li reign (1573–1619), when an ounce of silver went for anywhere between five hundred to eight hundred copper coins" (pp. 153–54). Thus when Chu-hung wrote the *Record of Self-knowledge* in 1604, 100 copper coins would be worth somewhere between .20 to 0.125 ounces of silver. What would be the purchasing power of this sum of money? Geiss told us that in the 1590s, .07 ounces of silver could buy one picul *(tan)* of rice, or a fresh fish, or over two pounds of either beef, lamb, or pork, or two chickens, or considerably larger quantities of dates, vegetables, and wheat flour (p. 164). The urban poor in Peking got 30 copper cash for a day's work (p. 175). Porters, water carriers, and other day laborers earned slightly more than .01 ounces of silver *per diem* (p. 177). But a clerk at a government *yamen* could earn more than .03 ounces of silver *per diem* (p. 179). Geiss concluded that ".10 ounces of silver sufficed to get a bit of several things, enough to provide a varied and satisfying diet for many people" (p. 190). Another source, an account book dated from 1595 to 1615, tells us that .20 ounces of silver would buy two rolls of bleached cloth or pay the annual rent for a simple room occupied by a laborer. See Fang Hao, "Ming Wang-li nien-chien chih ke-chung chia-ke." Probably, then, 100 cash in Chu-hung's time would be the equivalent of $6 to $10 today.

18. When one sees in the street a piece of paper with characters written on it, one should pick it up and burn it so that it will not be trampled underfoot or be used as scrap paper. This attitude derives from the Chinese

reverence for learning and for the written language which is the concrete representation of it. As Stephen Feuchtwang observes, there was an incinerator for burning such paper with writings on it in most Wen-ch'ang temples (temples dedicated to the inventor of writing—the god of learning). In theory this is the only place where such paper could be destroyed. See his "School-Temple and City God" in *The City in Late Imperial China,* edited by G. William Skinner, p. 607.

19. A complete translation of the *Record* appears in Appendix I.

20. The exact number is 1,277, but later generations kept adding to the work explanations, commentaries, and case histories. By the late Ch'ing, when *T'ai-shang kan-ying p'ien tu-shuo,* the complete collection of materials relating to the *Treatise,* was published, it ran to eight *chüan.*

21. Suzuki and Carus, p. 51.

22. Already mentioned in *Shih chi* and *Fung-su t'ung.* See Takao, p. 18.

23. *Shih chi,* "T'ien-kuan shu." They are identified as *ssu-ming, ssu-chung, ssu-lu,* the fourth to the sixth stars of the seven stars included in the North Dipper group. Cf. Tachibana, pp. 46–47. Carus is mistaken when he regards these as the three body spirits or the Three Corpses. Suzuki and Carus, pp. 71–72.

24. *Pao-p'u-tzu* records the first appearance: "there are Three Corpses in our bodies, which, though not corporeal, actually are of a type with our inner, ethereal breaths, the powers, the ghosts, and the gods. They want us to die prematurely. (After death they become a man's ghost and move about at will to where sacrifices and libations are being offered.) Therefore, every fifty-seventh day of the sixty-day cycle they mount to heaven and personally report our misdeeds to the Director of Fates." *Alchemy, Medicine, Religion in the China of A.D. 320, The Nei P'ien of Ko Hung,* tr. James R. Ware, p. 115.

25. According to Takao, the God of the Stove first appears in *Feng-su t'ung,* p. 18. But the term already appears in the *Chan-kuo ts'e,* a collection of historical episodes of feudal times under the Chou dynasty, which was revised and rearranged by Liu Hsiang (80 B.C.–A.D. 9). Ssu-ma Ch'ien also mentioned it in the *Shih chi.* Both sources predate the *Fung-su t'ung,* which was a work of the Eastern Han dynasty. Morohashi, *Daikanwa jiten,* Vol. 8, p. 692b.

The God of the Stove is one of the great divinities of Taoism. Very early on he became identified with the Director of Destinies (Ssu-ming): "Under the title of Director of Destinies (Ssu-ming) he kept a register of men's good and bad deeds and determined the length of their lives through his recommendations to Heaven. By the third century A.D. he had acquired a niche in the house, and even today, as the kitchen god, he is worshiped in almost all Chinese families, who sacrifice and feast at New Year's on the occasion of his annual trip to report to the Jade Emperor." Welch, *Parting of the Way,* p. 100. Welch continues: "This title (Ssu-ming) originally may have represented a separate divinity and one which had had a long history. At least as early as the eighth century B.C. the *Book of Documents* tells us, 'Heaven, looking upon men below, keeps a record of their righteousness and accordingly bestows on them many years or few.' There is a bronze from the sixth century B.C. that records offering two jade goblets and eight tripods to Ta Ssu-ming, the great Director of Destinies. This bronze comes from Ch'i, the land of the shamans and magicians. In the fourth or third century B.C. Ssu-ming was a god with whom the shamans of Ch'u sought mystical dalliance. For them he was already the regulator of the length of human life."

In a recent article, Rolf A. Stein discusses the relationship between the God of the Stove, the Ssu-ming or the Controller of Destiny, and the Three Corpses: "It [the god of the stove] was identified with a stellar divinity, the Controller of Destiny, Ssu-ming. In both forms it was adopted by the Taoists, who regarded the Controller of Destiny as a quite important god and the stove as a minor one (a "demon," *kuei*, as it was often put). The two of them functioned separately at the same time: Ssu-ming received the reports of the Three Corpses *(san-shih)* and of the stove god. Yet when it is the stove who oversees good and bad deeds and keeps watch on the house, he is again associated with the soil god." See his "Religious Taoism and Popular Religion from the Second to Seventh Centuries" in *Facets of Taoism, Essays in Chinese Religion*, edited by Holmes Welch and Anna Seidel, pp. 76–77.

26. This is according to the *Pao-p'u-tzu:* "For the man who commits a wrong of great enormity, the Director of Fates will deduct a period of three hundred days; for lesser wrongs, a reckoning of three days. Deductions vary according to the degree of the transgression. In receiving his destiny each man is assigned a basic longevity. If this is large, it is not used up despite many deductions; so death arrives slowly. But if the assigned quantity is small and the wrongs are many, the deductions rapidly exhaust it and death arrives early." *Alchemy, Medicine, Religion*, p. 66.

27. Suzuki and Carus, pp. 64–65, with minor changes.

28. Tachibana's enumeration is followed here. Tachibana, pp. 49, 58–60.

29. Two of five classes of immortals, the others being aerial, human, and ghostly. See E. J. Eitel, *Handbook of Buddhism*, p. 130. "*Yu ch'ien ching* says, 'Those wishing to become earth genii must do three hundred consecutive good deeds; those wishing to be heavenly genii must acquire twelve hundred. If, after acquiring 1199, one commits a single bad deed, all the ones previously acquired are lost, and one must begin anew.' Therefore, there is no question of the good merely outweighing the evil. Even though no wrong has been committed, if one merely speaks of one's own deeds and demands a reward for alms, the merit from the one vaunted deed will be lost immediately; but the whole series of merits will not be lost. It further says, 'No benefit is to be derived from taking geniehood medicine before the full quota of merits has been acquired.' If the medicine is not taken but the good deeds are performed, geniehood may not be acquired, but one can at least avoid the misfortune of sudden death." *Alchemy, Medicine, Religion*, pp. 66–67. A major difference between this and the *Treatise* is that the latter requires 1,300, not 1,200, good deeds.

30. Welch, *Taoism, The Parting of the Way*, p. 127. The *Pao-p'u-tzu* contains two parts, the *Nei-p'ien* (Inner chapters) and the *Wai-p'ien* (Outer chapters). The *Nei-p'ien* has been translated into English by James R. Ware *(Alchemy, Medicine, Religion in the China of A.D. 320: The Nei P'ien of Ko Hung)*. The *Wai-p'ien* has now been translated into English by Jay Sailey as well. It is called, *The Master Who Embraces Simplicity; A Study of the Philosopher Ko Hung; A.D. 283–343.*

31. Suzuki and Carus, pp. 65–66.

32. Suzuki and Carus, pp. 65–66, with minor changes. The correct original for "thinks what is good" is *ssu-shan* and not *shih-shan;* i.e., sees or looks at what is good.

33. *T'ai-p'ing ching, chüan* 110, cited in T'ang Yung-t'ung, *Han Wei Nan-pei-ch'ao fo-chiao shih*, Vol. 2, p. 283.

34. For instance, the *Fo-shuo chieh tsui fu ching*, and the *Miao-fa lien-hua ching Ma-ming p'u-sa p'in*. Both were found in Tun-huang. See T'ang, Vol. 2, pp. 283–284.

35. T'ang, Vol. 2, p. 284. The sutra is included in the Chinese Tripitaka. See T 15 (No. 590).

36. The reason why "fast" should be kept in the first, fifth, and ninth months and the six days of each month *(san-chai, liu-chai)* was supplied by Chih-i in his commentary on the 30th precept of the Sutra of Brahma's Net. He said that since these were the days when supernatural beings were in ascendance, one should do good and the merits accrued on these days would surpass those of other times. Chu-hung, in the subcommentary, added that during the three months (first, fifth, and ninth) the heavenly king Vaiśravana, Guardian of the North, would personally oversee the affairs of Jambudvīpa. Each month on the 8th and the 23rd the messengers of the king, on the 14th and 29th the prince, and on the 1st and the 15th the king himself would come down to the world to inspect the good and evil deeds of men. *YCFH* 4, 76a.

37. T'ang, Vol. 2, p. 284. The *Ta-chih-tu lun, chüan* 13, contains the same passage, but the phrase "increase lifespan" is missing. Therefore, T'ang maintains that the *Ssu-t'ien-wang ching*, as it now stands, was not a translation from the original Indian source made by Chih-yen (602–668), but a product of Chinese monks who believed in Taoism.

38. Such as "to receive favors as if surprised"; "to accuse heaven and find fault with men"; "to take up the new and forget the old"; "to assert with the mouth what the heart denies"; "to be greedy and covetous without satiety."

39. For instance, the protection of animals during the period of their procreation. Tachibana, p. 63.

40. Shimizu Taiji, "Mindai ni okeru shūkyo yūgō to kōkakaku," pp. 29—55.

41. For Hui Tung's explanation of "shooting at the flying birds and chasing after the running animals," and so on, see *Tai-shang-kan-ying p'ien tu-shuo*. It is quoted in Tachibana, p. 63.

42. *YCFH*, 15, 3a.

43. *Hui-ts'uan kung-kuo-ko* (printed in 1858 by the Chin-hua ching-hsin-hui), "Yü Ching-i yü tso-shen chi," *chüan* 13, 9a–11a.

44. Ibid., 9a.

45. Cf. Wm. Theodore de Bary, "Neo-Confucian Cultivation and the Seventeenth-Century 'Enlightenment'," in *The Unfolding of Neo-Confucianism*, pp. 141–216, esp. pp. 153–188.

46. *YCFH* 15, 1b.

47. The following anecdote, found in *Hui-ts'uan kung-kuo-ko*, "Yin-kuo san-shih shuo," *chüan* 13, 16b, further illustrates the same point: "In former times someone asked a monk if there was heaven and the monk said yes. He then asked if there was hell and the monk also said yes. The man said, 'Master Ching-shan [d. 1160] said that there was neither heaven nor hell. Now why do you say there is?' The monk asked him, 'Did Ching-shan have a wife or eat meat?' To which the questioner answered no. Thereupon the monk said, 'It is all right only for Master Ching-shan to deny the existence of heaven and hell. Generally speaking, men of superior virtue may regard the theory of retribution or cause and effect as nonexistent, while men of supreme evil definitely do not believe in it. However, since under heaven men of middle range occupy the majority, this theory of retribution is most effective in teaching them. Its success is also the greatest."

48. *Hui-ts'uan kung-kuo-ko*, "Yao Lung-huai yin-kuo san-shih shuo," *chüan* 13, 17a.

49. *Tao-tsang*, "Tung-chen pu, Chieh-lu lei."

50. Sakai, p. 372. Yoshioka Yoshitoyo, "Shoki no kōkakaku ni tsuite," pp. 119–125.

51. Yoshioka, pp. 119–120.

52. Ibid., pp. 120–123.

53. Ibid., p. 123.

54. Preface to *Tzu-chih-lu*, *YCFH* 15, 2b.

55. Ibid., 1a.

56. *Hui-ts'uan kung-kuo-ko*, "Li-ming p'ien," *chüan* 13, 5a.

57. Cited by Yoshioka, p. 116.

58. *YCFH* 15, 1a, preface to *Tzu-chih-lu*.

59. Sakai, p. 358.

60. Merit-making in Sri Lanka is described by Michael Ames in *Religious Syncretism in Buddhist Ceylon*, Chapters VI, VII. Melford E. Spiro discusses the practice of merit-making in Burma in *Buddhism and Society: Its Burmese Vicissitudes*, Chapters 3, 4, 5.

61. Spiro, p. 119.

62. Ibid., p. 111. These "merit account books" contain much useful information about the financial aspects of Burmese Buddhism. "Where merit account books are kept, each case of *dāna* is entered in the following details: the date, the occasion, the number of persons involved, and the total cost." Ibid., p. 112. The merit account books, however, do not quantify acts of *dāna* (donation) on a sliding scale. This is a very important difference be-

tween the Theravāda Buddhist and the Chinese case—that is, there is in Burma and Sri Lanka no similar document giving the precise number of merits or demerits associated with particular acts. Likewise, Michael Ames says certain "unit acts" of merit always occur in Ceylonese merit-making ceremonies. Each unit act is worth a certain amount of merit, *"although the amount itself is never concretely specified for that would be an expression of greed"* [emphasis added], p. 111. I think this difference is significant. It proves that while the *Record* shares the "karma/merit" ideology of popular Buddhism, it must also owe its quantitive and legalistic approach toward morality to other sources, a point to be taken up in detail later in this chapter.

63. *Hui-ts'uan kung-kuo-ko,* "Li-ming p'ien." *chüan* 13, 5a.

64. Ibid., 7b.

65. Ibid.

66. Chu Kuo-chen, *Yung-ch'uang hsiao-p'in, chüan* 10, 223. "Nowadays people who do good all hope to receive rewards. There is even such a saying that one can expect one thousand pieces of gold when one does ten thousand good deeds. I think this belief must have been created for ignorant men and women. Educated people should realize that we ought to be concerned only with doing our own duty, that we do good for its own sake, but do not expect rewards. Take the man who saved the ants or the man who returned the belt. They did these things spontaneously, just like the man mentioned in the *Mencius* who saved the child who was about to fall into a well. If the two men had had the mind to seek for reward, the god would not have rewarded them."

67. *Hui-ts'uan kung-kuo-ko, chüan* 13, 21b.

68. Sakai, pp. 359–361.

69. On the correspondence between actualities and names, the *Han Fei Tzu* says: "When a ruler wishes to prevent wickedness, he examines the correspondence between actualities and names, words and work. When a subject makes claims, the ruler gives him work according to what he has claimed, but holds him wholly responsible for accomplishment corresponding to this work. When the accomplishment corresponds to the work, and the work corresponds to what the man has claimed he could do, he is rewarded. If the accomplishment does not correspond to the work, nor the work correspond to what the man has claimed for himself, he is punished." *Han Fei Tzu, chüan* 7, as quoted in Fung Yu-lan, *A History of Chinese Philosophy,* p. 324. On the "two handles": "The way in which the intelligent ruler leads and governs his subjects is by means of two handles. These two handles are penalty and benevolence. What are penalty and benevolence? By penalty is meant capital punishment, and [by] benevolence is meant the giving of rewards. Then subjects will stand in fear of punishment and will receive benefit from rewards. Therefore when the ruler uses penalty and benevolence, his multitude of subjects stand in fear of his majesty and rally around what is beneficial to them." *Chüan* 7, in Fung, p. 326.

70. *Hsü Han-shu, chüan* 24, "Pai kuan chih" (photoprint copy of the Ching-yu-ch'ien pen of North Sung), 3a, 5a, 6a. Sakai, p. 360.

71. Sakai, p. 360.

72. "Cheng K'ang-ch'eng [A.D. 127–200] said, "A gentleman has a hundred different acts. He may cancel his demerits with merits. In the *Cheng-i* to the *Odes*, we read that when a gentleman performs a great merit, it can cancel his slight demerit. Therefore merit and demerit may cancel each other out.'" *Shih-chia-chai yang hsin lu, chüan* 18, cited in Sakai, p. 401.

73. Charles O. Hucker, *The Censorial System of Ming China*, pp. 4–29, esp. pp. 12–13.

74. *San-kuo chih, chüan* 22, 3a–9a.

75. Chao I. *Nien-erh-shih ta chi*, p. 148, "Chiu-p'in chung-cheng." The defect of this system is also pointed out by Etienne Balázs in *Chinese Civilization and Bureaucracy*, pp. 231–232.

76. Even though the sutra was supposed to have been translated from Sanskrit into Chinese by Kālayaśas in A.D. 424, no Sanskrit text has been discovered. In fact, the title of the sutra, Amitāyurdhyāna Sutra, was a reconstruction made by J. Takakusu based on the Chinese title, *Kuan Wu-liang-shou ching*. Attribution of a Buddhist sutra to an Indian or central Asian origin is not uncommon. There is strong possibility that the sutra was composed in Central Asia or even in China. Detailed discussion on this question is found in Fujita Kōtatsu, *Genshi Jōdo shisō no kenkyū*.

I owe this information to Professor Masatoshi Nagatomi through a personal communication. If the sutra is indeed a Chinese forgery, the nine-grade classification of rebirth was probably influenced by secular bureaucratic practices. However, since the sutra was regarded as canonical by faithful Buddhists, this classificatory approach might have served to reinforce the native tradition and give it spiritual sanction.

77. T 12 (No. 365), 344c. The Amitāyurdhyāna Sutra, tr. J. Takakusu, in *Buddhist Mahāyāna Texts*, ed. F. Max Müller, The Sacred Books of the East, Vol. XLIX, p. 188.

78. Amitāyurdhyāna Sutra, p. 189.

79. Amitāyurdhyāna Sutra, p. 198. The technical length of a kalpa is 4,200 million earthly years, which constitute a "day of Brahma." According to Indian cosmology, to which Buddhism basically conforms, the cosmos passes through cycles within cycles through eternity. A kalpa is the basic cycle.

80. *Hsü kao-seng chuan, chüan* 20, See also the biography of Tao-ch'o contained in Chia-ts'ai's *Ching-t'u lun* (T 47, 98b).

81. In fact, the rosary was supposed to have been invented by Tao-ch'o. See Mochizuki Shinkō, *Chūgoku Jōdo kyōri shi*, pp. 137–138.

82. *YCFH* 26, 60b–70a, "Nien-tou fo."

83. *YCFH* 26, 5b–6a, "Chou-yeh mi-t'o shih-wan sheng."

84. Ch'ü T'ung-tsu, *Law and Society in Traditional China*, esp. the section on magic, religion, and the law. Derk Bodde and Clarence Morris, *Law in Imperial China*, chapter 1, "Basic Concepts," esp. pp. 43–48.

85. Bodde and Morris, pp. 45–46.

86. Ibid., p. 46. The specific dates are then listed: (1) an unbroken

period from the beginning of spring (ca. February 4 in the western calendar) to the autumn equinox (ca. September 23); (2) the first, fifth, and ninth lunar months, these being Buddhist months of fasting; (3) the twenty-four days that were "breaths" or "joints" of the year; (4) other annual sacrifice days and holidays; (5) days one, eight, fourteen/fifteen, twenty-three/twenty-four, and twenty-eight/thirty of each lunar month, these being Buddhist fast days. Connecting with some of them, but separately listed, are the four days in each lunar month of new and full moon and the first and last lunar quarters; (6) rainy days and nighttime. Cf. Ch'ü T'ung-tsu, p. 219.

87. Ibid., p. 47.

88. Bodde and Morris, p. 47.

89. Ch'ü T'ung-tsu, p. 219.

90. Ibid., pp. 217–218.

91. Bodde and Morris, p. 99.

92. On the nature and function of diffused religion in China, Yang says: "Diffused religion . . . lacks any independent ethical position of its own, for its chief function lies in furnishing supernatural support for the ethical values in the basic concepts of the secular institutions. Diffused religion itself is not the source of ethical values for the operation of the secular institutions . . ." C. K. Yang, *Religion in Chinese Society*, p. 285.

93. Ibid., p. 291.

94. Bodde and Morris, p. 100.

95. Ibid., p. 30.

96. Ibid., pp. 30–31.

97. In the category of good deeds, the new entries are 1–18, 21, 36, 38–40, 41, 45–51, 54, 58–61, 65–68, 70–71, 81–89, 91, 96–105, 112, 127–135, 138–148, 157–159, 164–177, 180–202. In the category of bad deeds, the new entries are 1–18, 30–40, 45–54, 62–64, 70–84, 86–111, 113–114, 120, 127–138, 151–165, 167, 170, 171, 174–244, 258–279. The text of the *Ledger,* on which the comparison is based, is the one reproduced in Yoshioka's article, "Shoki no kōkakaku ni tsuite," pp. 130–160. According to the author, it is identical to the one contained in the *Tao-tsang.* Sakai also made a comparison between the entries in the *Ledger* and those in the *Record.* His enumeration of the entries, being less detailed, is different from that of Yoshioka, but his conclusion is similar. See "Shukō no jichiroku ni tsuite," pp. 471–478.

98. Sakai, "Shukō no jichiroku ni tsuite," p. 480. These two entries are interesting, as they reflect a contemporary social problem. Citing an account in the *T'ien-kung k'ai-wu,* Sakai says that some people used *ch'ien-kung* or *ch'ien-tan,* which was a substance produced by combining mercury *(shui-yin)* and lead *(ch'ien),* to extract the content of silver. As a result, although the silver thus extracted resembled silver in its external shape, it was in fact counterfeit and worth nothing. It was called *chu-sha-yin.*

99. Nos. 107–110 of the *Ledger;* Yoshioka, p. 135.

100. Nos. 148–160 of the *Ledger;* Yoshioka, p. 137.

101. Chu-hung's view on the relationship of Buddhism, Confucianism,

and Taoism is best summarized by himself in a short essay: "People always say, 'The three teachings are one.' But it would be a mistake if one took this to mean that there is no distinction among them. The three teachings indeed belong to one family. However, among members of a family, is there no difference between the senior and the junior, the exalted and the humble, and the intimate and the distant? Buddhism makes clear what happened before the dissolution of the cosmos and is therefore most senior, whereas Confucianism and Taoism expound what is near in time. The Buddha is the most heavenly of the heavens, and he is the most saintly of the saints and is therefore the most exalted, whereas Confucians and Taoists occupy the position of ordinary men. Buddhism enables all beings to realize their original selfhood and is therefore closest [to our life], whereas Confucianism and Taoism want us to serve the external. Even though the three religions agree in principle, yet they differ most clearly in their profundity and shallowness. However, although there is the difference in profundity and shallowness, they nevertheless lead to the same principles. Only in this sense can we say that the three teachings are one. It certainly does not mean that there is therefore no difference among them." "San-chiao i-chia," in *Cheng-o chi, YCFH* 27, 15b.

VI. THE CONDITION OF THE MONASTIC ORDER IN THE LATE MING

1. A world cycle *(chieh)* is called *kalpa* in Sanskrit and *kappa* in Pali. It is of almost infinite length in time and is divided into a variable number of "incalculables" *(asaṃkhyeya* in Sanskrit; *asankheyya* in Pali). Buddhaghosa, the Ceylonese Buddhist scholar who lived in the fifth century A.D., spoke of four phases of the destruction, the continuance of destruction, the renovation and the continuance of renovation of a world cycle. He also discussed three kinds of destruction at the end of each world cycle: by fire, by water, and by wind. *Visuddhi-magga,* chapter xiii, in Warren, *Buddhism in Translations,* pp. 315–330. However, the process of deterioration and the final destruction of the world as depicted by Buddhaghosa are not the only tradition; in the twenty-sixth sutta of the *Dīgha Nikāya* we see a somewhat different version. Here there is not a total destruction of the earth consequent on its corruption, but only deterioration to an unbelievably low point before the ensuing improvement sets in: "At this lowest point human life is only ten years long and a woman is married at five years. Food is coarse and scarce. The good old customs are neglected. Sexual promiscuity abounds, including the sexual use of animals. But seeing the evil of their ways, human beings repent and amend their conduct. As they begin to practice the virtues again, life, health, and wealth increase. The life span doubles to twenty years, twenty years to forty, until 'at the apex among humans living 80,000 years, brethren, maidens are marriageable at 500 years of age!' And there arise then the Maitreya Buddha and his fitting companion, a wise, 'wheel-turning,' i.e.,

Buddhist, universal monarch who rule in peace and plenty." Winston L. King, *A Thousand Lives Away*, pp. 105–106.

2. Both King and Gombrich (*Precept and Practice*, pp. 287–293) were told by their respective Burmese and Ceylonese informants that the gradual decay of Buddhism would last for about 5,000 years. King further reports that according to Theravāda Buddhists, the influence of Buddhism will disappear in five stages: "There are five stages of the disappearance of Buddhist influence in certain epochs, taking place roughly every thousand years in succession. First, there is the disappearance of spiritual attainment above the grade of Sotapanna or Stream-Enterer. (The Once-Returner to human life, the Non-Returner, and the Arhat who goes directly to Nibbana upon death, no more appear). Then, good Buddhist conduct disappears from the earth; then Buddhist learning itself beginning with the *Abhidhamma*, proceeding "downward" through the *Anguttara, Samyutta, Majjhima, Dīgha, Kuddaka Nikāyas,* and lastly through the *Jātaka Tales* and the *Vinaya Pitaka* (or monk's rules portion of the scriptures). And in the fourth period there are not even any monks left. Finally, the last and greatest Buddhist treasure, the relics of the Buddha and his saints, all come together to form one Buddha image, but this can be seen only by the devas, and finally disappears altogether. Thus is the universe in five thousand years bereft of all Buddha influence, and thus it becomes impossible for any living being to make any progress toward Nibbana, even though the universe itself may not immediately disintegrate. Currently, it is held that the teaching of the Gotama Buddha is half-way (2,500 years) towards its ultimate disappearance. Hence Buddhists must now exert themselves individually to escape the catastrophe of its total disappearance on this planet, to be born in a more fortunate one." King, *A Thousand Lives Away*, p. 106.

3. (1) True, five hundred years; counterfeit, five hundred years; (2) true, five hundred years, counterfeit, one thousand years; (3) true, one thousand years; counterfeit, five hundred years; and (4) true, one thousand years; counterfeit, one thousand years. See Ch'en, *Buddhism in China*, p. 298.

4. Ibid., pp. 298–300. Yabuki Keiki, *Sankaikyō no kenkyū.*

5. Chung-feng Ming-pen (1286–1323) was a native of Ch'ien-t'ang (in present-day Chekiang). He studied under Kao-feng Miao of Mt. T'ien-mu and attained great enlightenment. Emperor Ayurbarwada honored him with the title of Ch'an Master Fo-tz'u Yüan-chao Kuang-hui. Among his works are the *Chung-feng kuang-lu* and the *Chung-feng tsa-lu*. The views on Ch'an and the Pure Land of Ming-pen and the following two monks were discussed in chapter III.

6. T'ien-ju Wei-tse (fl. 1341), a native of Yung-hsin, Chi-an (in present-day Kiangsi) was a disciple of Chung-feng and lived in the Lion's Grove of Ku-su. He wrote the *Ching-t'u huo-wen*, in which he argued for the dual practice of Ch'an and Pure Land. He also left behind nine volumes of collected sayings, *T'ien-ju Wei-tse ch'an-shih yü-lu*.

7. Ch'u-shih Fan-chi (1295–1370) was a native of Ming-chou, Hsiang-shan (in present-day Chekiang). His collected sayings, in 20 *chüan*, are con-

tained in *Zoku-zōkyō*. His biography, sayings, and ten excerpts from his *Poetry on the Pure Land* are found in Chu-hung's *Huang-Ming ming-seng chi-lüeh*, YCFH 17, 2a–12a.

8. YCFH 24, 30a, "Ku-chin jen pu hsiang chi."

9. YCFH 24, 26a, "Seng-su hsin-hsin."

10. According to Wu Han, the novel was written between the tenth and the thirtieth year of Wan-li (1582–1602). He states that the earliest date would have been the second year of Lung-ch'ing (1568), and the latest could not have been the thirty-fourth year of Wan-li (1606). *Chin-p'ing-mei yü Wang Shih-chen chih chu-tso shih-tai chi ch'i she-hui pei-ching*, pp. 72–73. Cheng Chen-to did not give the exact date but felt that it was clearly a work of the Wan-li period, not of the Chia-ching. Wu denied that the author was Wang Shih-chen; Cheng did not go into the problem of authorship. See Cheng Chen-to, *Ch'a-tu-pen Chung-kuo wen-hsüeh shih*, p. 921.

11. Discussion of this novel is based on the Wan-li edition of the work entitled *Chin-p'ing-mei tz'u-hua* (the preface is dated 1617, the forty-fifth year of Wan-li). The copy used here is in five *chüan*, reprinted by Daian Bookstore, Tokyo, 1963. See *Chin-p'ing-mei tz'u-hua*, *chüan* 1, 20, 487. The translation is mine, although there is an English translation made by Clement Edgerton, *The Golden Lotus*.

12. Cf. Norman Cohn, *The Pursuit of the Millennium: Revolutionary Millennarians and Mystical Anarchists of the Middle Ages*.

13. Vincent Y. C. Shih, "Some Chinese Rebel Ideologies"; Shigematsu Shunshō, "Tō Sō jidai no Mirokukyō hi"; T'ao Hsi-sheng, "Yüan-tai Mi-le Pao-lien-chiao-hui ti pao-tung"; Ogasawara Senshū, "Gendai Byakurenshū kyōdan no shōchō"; Li Shou-k'ung, "Ming-tai pai-liang-chiao k'ao-lüeh"; Daniel L. Overmyer, *Folk Buddhist Religion: Dissenting Sects in Late Traditional China*.

14. See above, chapter IV.

15. The so-called soul mass or *shui-lu* ceremony was different from the funeral service proper, which was performed before it. Wu Ta, for instance, was buried three days after he died. Another service was performed on the hundredth day after Wu Ta's death. It was called "water and land" *(shui-lu)* and was supposed to help release the dead man's soul from hell. After the ceremony, which lasted for a day, the soul tablet of the dead was buried, and only then were the rites connected with a death considered complete. The ceremony which is called *shui-lu-hui* in its complete form was originally a Tantric rite. Tradition dates it as early as the time of Emperor Wu of Liang. It was performed for the sake of "universal salvation" *(p'u-tu)*. The term *shui-lu* refers to the lost souls of people who have died in water and on land. These are the souls that are not taken care of by anyone. For this reason, the ceremony is also connected with the rite of "bestowing food on hungry ghosts," and during the *shui-lu* ceremony, which lasts seven days, the rite for bestowing food is also performed. Chu-hung revised the text for performing the ceremony, and the revised version, which is entitled *Shui-lu i-kuei* (YCFH 18, 19) has been the authoritative text in China ever since. For a

detailed study of the history and evolution of this rite, see Makita Tairyō, *Chūgoku kinsei Bukkyō shi kenkyū*, pp. 169–193. Holmes Welch, in his *Practice of Chinese Buddhism*, translates the term "plenary mass," and on pp. 190–191, 198–199, 231–233, 296–297 gives a description of it as it was performed during the Republican period. According to the description in *chüan* 8 of *Chin-p'ing-mei*, the *shui-lu* service lasted only one day. But it does contain the ritual elements of reciting the "Confessional of Emperor Liang" (*Liang huang ch'an*), the invocation of deities from all regions, and the offering of food to the hungry ghosts. The author may have been describing a variant of the service current at that time. It is also possible, of course, that the standard procedure for performing the rite as outlined in Chu-hung's text was not then in use.

16. *Shih-shih chi-ku-lüeh hsü-chi, chüan* 2, T 49, 936a–b, "Shen-ming fo-chiao pang-ts'e."

17. *Huang-chao pen-chi,* quoted in Wu Han, *Chu Yüan-chang chuan,* pp. 8–18.

18. Wu Han, "Chu Yüan-chang nien-piao," in ibid., p. 236. He puts Chu's age at seventeen (1344).

19. The *Huang-ch'ao pen-chi* says: "The Master had a wife and dependents. Therefore the resources were not adequate." Quoted by Wu Han in *Chu Yüan-chang chuan,* p. 18.

20. Wu Han, *Chu Yüan-chang chuan,* p. 10.

21. The primary sources for this summary are *Ming shih-lu* (Veritable Record of the Ming Dynasty), *Ta Ming lü* (Code of the Great Ming Dynasty), *Ta Ming hui-tien* (Collected Institutions of the Great Ming Dynasty), *Ming hui-yao* (Essential Institutes of the Ming Dynasty), and *Shih-shih chi-ku-lüeh hsü-chi* (Continuation of a Brief Compilation of Buddhist History). I have also drawn upon the findings of several excellent studies by Japanese Buddhist historians.

22. *Ming shih-lu,* T'ai-tsu, Hung-wu sixth year, twelfth month, *chüan* 86, 4/1537; *Ming hui-yao, chüan* 39; *Ta Ming hui-tien, chüan* 226, 2979.

23. Ryūchi Kiyoshi, "Minsho no jiin."

24. Ibid., p. 15.

25. Ibid., pp. 15–16. See the chart of nine monasteries with the dates of their reestablishment provided by Ryūchi.

26. Some monks, it would appear, not only lived away from monasteries, but also got married. A proclamation of Hung-wu 27 says: "If a monk has a wife, he can be beaten and insulted. People can also demand money from him. If he has no money, people can kill him." Cf. *Shih-shih chi-ku-lüeh hsü-chi,* T 49, 938b.

27. *Ta Ming hui-tien,* p. 2979.

28. *Ch'ih-hsiu P'ai-chang ch'ing-kuei, chüan* 3, ZZ 2, 16, 3; p. 251b.

29. See the entry "T'u-ti-yüan," Dōchū, *Zenrin shōki sen,* p. 8.

30. Ryūchi, p. 10. For a modern way of classification, see Welch, *Practice of Chinese Buddhism,* pp. 395–408.

31. *Ming shih-lu*, T'ai-ts'u, Hung-wu fifteenth year, twelfth month, *chüan* 150, 6/2368.

32. *Shih-shih chi-ku lüeh hsü-chi*, T 49, 932a.

33. For instance, in the edict dated the twenty-fourth year of Hung-wu.

34. Welch, in *The Practice of Chinese Buddhism*, p. 492, notes that the term *ying-fu seng* appeared as early as 1735 in an edict of Ch'ien-lung, which forced monks who had married to return to monasteries. But the term had already appeared in *Ch'i-hsiu lei-kao*, a *pi-chi* written by Lang Ying of the Ming dynasty. See the entry on "Monks' Clothes," where after the term *yü-chia seng* the author explained it by putting the following sentence in parentheses: "They are what we call 'monks responding to call' today." Lang Ying, *Ch'i-hsiu lei-kao*, Vol. 1, p. 360.

35. *Shih-shih chi-ku lüeh hsü-chi*, T49, 936c. The document was the "Shen-ming fo-chiao pang-ts'e," issued on the first day of the sixth month in the twenty-fourth year of Hung-wu.

36. Fa-fang, "Chin-jih Chung-kuo fo-chiao hsien-chuang," *Hai-ch'ao yin*, October 1934. Quoted by Makita Tairyō in his *Chūgoku kinsei Bukkyō shi kenkyū*, p. 169.

37. *Ming shih-lu*, Hung-wu fifteenth year, twelfth month, ch. 150, 6/2368. But from the *Ch'i-hsiu lei-kao* we get a somewhat different description concerning the colors of monks' robes: "The present rule provides that Ch'an monks should wear brown, monks specializing in doctrine red, and yoga monks [i.e., monks responding to calls] greenish white" (Vol. 1, p. 360, "Seng i").

38. Ryūchi, "Minsho no jiin," p. 28.

39. *Ch'in lu chi*, twenty-seventh year edict, quoted by Ryūchi, p. 27.

40. *Shih-shih chi-ku lüeh hsü-chi*, T 49, 938b–c. The edict was issued on the eighth day of the first month in the twenty-seventh year of Hung-wu (1394). The argument that begging would "corrupt the Buddhist tradition" is of course ironic and shows the lawmaker's apparent ignorance of the Buddhist tradition. Daily begging was practiced by the Buddha and is still practiced in Theravāda countries, though in a somewhat formalized fashion. Begging has been regarded not only as a right livelihood for monks, but as a spiritual exercise in humility and nonattachment.

41. *Ta Ming lü, chüan* 11, "Li lü," 33b.

42. *Hang-chou Shang-t'ien-chu-chiang-ssu chih, chüan* 11, quoted in Ryūchi, p. 27.

43. Hsüan-tsung's "Chin seng-su wang-huan chao" and "Chin pai-kuan yü seng-tao wang-huan chih," *Ch'üan T'ang wen, chüan* 30.

44. *Shih-shih chi-ku lüeh hsü-chi*, T 49, 938c. Edict of the twenty-seventh year of Hung-wu, which would be the year 1394.

45. Mano Senryū, "Mindai chūki no Bukkyō taisaku—Eisō chō o chūshin to shite."

46. Ibid., p. 23.

47. *Ming shih-lu*, Ying-tsung, Cheng-t'ung thirteenth year, second month, *chüan* 171, 29/3290.

48. *Ming shih-lu*, Ching-ti, Ching-t'ai fourth year, tenth month, *chüan* 234, 34/5104.

49. Shen Te-fu, *Wan-li yeh-huo pien*, in *Yüan Ming shih-liao pi-chi ts'ung-kan* (Shanghai, n.d.), Vol. II, p. 686.

50. The brief survey is based primarily on *Wan-li yeh-huo pien*, p. 679, "Shih-chiao sheng-shuai," p. 684, "Seng-tao i-en," and pp. 683–684, "Chu-shang chung i-chiao."

51. Ibid., p. 683.

52. Ibid., p. 686.

53. Wu Han, *Chin-p'ing-mei yü Wang Shih-chen chih chu-tso shih-tai chi ch'i she-hui pei-ching*, pp. 58–59.

54. Kenneth Ch'en, *Buddhism in China*, pp. 242–243.

55. This is found in *Ku T'ang shu-i*, *chüan* 12, as cited by Ogawa Kan-ichi, "Sōgen Minshin ni okeru kyōdan no kōzō," hereafter abbreviated as *Kyō-dan*, p. 290.

56. A decree issued in the first year of Chien-yüan (758) during the reign of Hsüan-tsung. *Shih-shih chi-ku lüeh hsü-chi*, T 49, 827c. However, the system of testing the postulant's understanding of sutras before granting him the certificate was started earlier by Chung-tsung, who in the eighth month of the second year of Shen-lung (706) issued a decree which stated that a postulant must be well versed in the meaning of sutras in order to be ordained. *Kyōdan*, p. 822c.

57. Quoted in full in Tsukamoto Zenryū's "Sō jidai no zunan shikyō tokudo no seido," p. 52.

58. The regulation was found in *Ch'ing-yuan tiao-fa shih-lei*, cited by Tsukamoto, p. 61.

59. Ch'en, *Buddhism in China*, pp. 247–248; See also *Kyōdan*, p. 295; Tsukamoto, p. 57.

60. *Shih-shih chi-ku lüeh hsü-chi*, T 49, 827c; *Kyōdan*, p. 822c.

61. Ch'en, *Buddhism in China*, pp. 391–393; See also Tsukamoto, pp. 59–63.

62. *Ming shih-lu*, Hung-wu fifth year, twelfth month, *chüan*, 77, 4/1415–16. The "money of leisure" was first instituted by Kao-tsung of the Southern Sung in 1146. It was levied on all Buddhist and Taoist monks. It was divided into nine categories ranging from three hundred to one thousand strings of cash. Only those over sixty or the disabled were exempted. Cf. *Fo-tsu-t'ung chi*, *chüan* 47.

63. *Ta Ming hui-tien*, *chüan* 226, 2979.

64. *Ming hui-yao*, *chüan* 39, 696. The purpose of raising the age limit was undoubtedly to prevent losing young men and women from the labor force.

65. *Ta Ming hui-tien*, 2979.

66. *Ming hui-yao*, 695.

67. *Ming shih-lu,* Yung-lo sixteenth year, tenth month, *chüan* 205, 14/2109.

68. *Ming shih-lu,* Hsüan-te tenth year.

69. *Ming shih-lu,* Cheng-t'ung first year, *chüan* 23, 23/0462.

70. *Ming hui-yao, chüan* 39, 696.

71. *Ming shih-lu,* Ching-t'ai second year, seventh month, *chüan* 206, 32/4422. The 1453 sale was to supply grain to soldiers sent out to put down bandits in Szechuan. The price was five piculs of rice. The 1454 sale was to furnish military granaries in Wan-chüan. The price rose to twenty piculs. See Ryūchi, "Mindai ni okeru baichō," p. 282.

72. *Ming shih-lu,* Ch'eng-hua twentieth year. The official's remark was found in *Shih-lu,* Hung-chih ninth year, fifth month, cited by Ryūchi, p. 285. This was obviously an overstatement. According to Ping-ti Ho, "The actual population of China toward the end of the fourteenth century was probably over 65,000,000. . . . The later Ming population returns, however, indicate a mildly falling population during the first half of the fifteenth century and then a stationary population fluctuating slightly around the 60,000,000 level." See *Studies on the Population of China, 1368–1953,* p. 9, and Welch, *Practice,* Appendix I.

73. *Ta Ming hui-tien,* cited by Ryūchi, p. 288.

74. Ibid.

75. Ibid.

76. Ch'i-sung, *Tan-ching wen-chi* (Nanking: Chin-ling ke-ching-chu edition), Vol. II, 17a–17b, "Fo-chiao p'ien."

77. Hattori Shungai, "Shina sōkan no enkaku," pp. 399–400, where he gives the date monk-officials were first mentioned as 398 and their formal appointment as 405. Kenneth Ch'en notes that "as far as is known, the earliest government organ established to exercise such control was the *chien-fu-ts'ao* (Office to Oversee Blessings), set up by the Northern Wei ruler, probably in 396." Following the record of the *Shih-Lao-chih* (Treatise on Buddhism and Taoism), Ch'en also identifies the first monk-official as Fa-kuo, who was given the title Chief of Monks *(sha-men-t'ung).* See Ch'en, *Buddhism in China,* p. 253.

78. Ch'i-sung, p. 16a.

79. Hattori, p. 404.

80. Takao Giken, "Sōdai sōkan seido no kenkyū," p. 14. In the Ming dynasty, monk-officials were specifically ordered to pass judgment on cases relating to monastic irregularities, but not civil offenses. "The Buddhist and Taoist Bureaus both inside and outside the capital are to restrain and supervise Buddhist monks and Taoist monks and priests in the land. They must keep the rule of purity. Whoever commits infractions against this rule must be dealt with by the Bureau involved. The authorities should not interfere with this. If the nature of the offense has to do with the military and civilian population, only then are the civilian authorities allowed to pass sentence." *Ming shih-lu,* Hung-wu fifteenth year (1380) fourth month, *chüan* 144, 5/2262–3.

81. Hattori, p. 400. Tsan-ning, *Ta-Sung seng-shih lüeh*, T 54, 245b.

82. Hattori, p. 403. Welch translates the titles differently. He translates *shang-tso* as "rector" and *ssu-chu* as "prior." See *Practice of Chinese Buddhism*, p. 35.

83. Tsan-ning, *Ta-Sung seng-shih lüeh*, T 54, 243c.

84. Ibid., 245b–c. For instance, in 727 Hsüan-tsung listened to the suggestion submitted by the Imperial Secretariat and the Imperial Chancellery and put the monastic order under the Bureau of Ceremonies for Foreigners. But this was reversed in the following year, and the Bureau of Sacrifice became the controlling agency. In 846, during the persecution of Buddhism by Wu-tsung, the monastic order was again put under the Bureau of Ceremonies for Foreigners.

85. Takao Giken, "Sōdai sōkan seido no kenkyū," pp. 2–3, 5–7.

86. Tsan-ning, *Ta-Sung seng-shih lüeh*, T 54, 245c.

87. Ibid., 246a. Kenneth Ch'en states in *Buddhism in China*, p. 256, that the commissioners "were usually not monks but powerful eunuchs, who utilized the posts to amass great fortunes for themselves."

88. *Ta-Sung seng-shih lüeh*, T 54, 243c.

89. This is borne out by the description Takao Giken gives in regard to the monk-officials in the Sung. He states that from 960 to 1078, the monastic order was under the commissioner of good works. However, the position was often simultaneously occupied by the governor of K'ai-feng, the seat of the capital. Their original duty was to supervise the Central Buddhist Registry in matters relating to ordination certificates, the appointment of monk-officials on all levels, the handing out of purple robes and honorary titles to distinguished monks, and so on. During the Sung, however, the post became almost just a name. At most it had jurisdiction over monks in the prefecture of K'ai-feng, but could not claim to have control of the entire monastic order. On the other hand, the Buddhist Registry for the Left and Right, which was also situated in K'ai-feng, dealt with the real workaday problems of the monasteries. "Sōdai sōkan seido no kenkyū," p. 3.

90. *Ennin's Diary: The Record of a Pilgrimage to China in Search of the Law*, tr. Edwin O. Reischauer, p. 75 (hereinafter abbreviated as *Ennin*). Reischauer translates the titles of monk-officials somewhat differently.

91. The Central Buddhist Registry in K'ai-feng has the following officials: left and right directors (*tso-yu seng-lu*), vice-director (*fu-seng-lu*), chief lecturer on sutras and shastras (*chiang-ching-lun shou-tso*), and the general manager (*chien-i*). On the local level, there was the prefectural Buddhist Registry (*seng-cheng-ssu*), which was headed by the *seng-cheng*, who in turn was assisted by one deputy (*fu-seng-cheng*) and one judge (*seng-pan*). See Takao, pp. 8–9, and Tsan-ning, *Ta-Sung seng-shih lüeh*, T 54, 242c.

92. *Ennin*, pp. 74–95. "The Minister of State recently invited Kuang-i, a Reverend of the Vinaya of the Hao-lin-ssu of Jun-chou, to stay temporarily at the Hui-chao-ssu. Since the Minister of State intends to make this monk the Bishop of this prefecture, he is now having him at the K'ai-yüan-ssu." The Minister of State, as identified by Ennin, was Li Te-yü (787–849).

93. Takao, p. 3.

94. *Ming shih-lu*, Hung-wu first year, first month, *chüan* 29, 2/0500.

95. The titles of these officers, in descending order, were *t'ung-ling*, *fu-t'ung-ling*, *tsan-chiao*, and *chi-hua*. Ryūchi Kiyoshi, "Mindai no sōkan," p. 35.

96. Shimizu Taiji, quoting an entry in the *Ta-cheng tsuan-yao*, affirmed that the *shan-shih-yüan* was abolished in 1371. "Mindai ni okeru Butsudō no torishimari," p. 263. Ryūchi Kiyoshi suggested that it might have been left inactive around that year, but that it was not formally abolished before 1381. He quotes the entry in 1388 in the *Shih-lu* as his proof. "Mindai no sōkan," p. 37.

97. Appointment to the office of *tso-chüeh-i*, one of the offices in the Central Buddhist Registry, had already been made in 1379. *Shih-shih chi-ku lüeh hsü-chi*, T 49, 930a. It then must have been in existence before 1382.

98. Ryūchi, "Mindai no sōkan," p. 42.

99. Ibid., p. 43, quoting an edict in the *Ch'in lu chi*.

100. Ibid., p. 44.

101. It was instituted either in 1386 according to *Shih-shih chi-ku lüeh hsü-chi*, *chüan* 2, T 49, 930c, or 1394 according to the *Ming shih-lu*, Hung-wu twenty-seventh year, first month, *chüan* 231, 8/3372.

102. *Shih-shih chi-ku lüeh hsü-chi*, T 49, 935.

103. Ryūchi, "Minsho no jiin," p. 15.

104. Ryūchi, "Mindai no sōkan," p. 45.

105. *Shih shih chi-ku lüeh hsü-chi*, T 49, 935b.

106. *Wan-li yeh-huo-pien*, pp. 687–688, "Seng-chiao k'ao ke."

VII. Internal Causes of Monastic Decline in the Ming Dynasty

1. The *Pi-yen lu* consists of 100 *kung-an* selected from the *Transmission of the Lamp*. The selection was made by Hsüeh-tou (980–1053), who also wrote poetic comments on these cases. Yüan-wu (1063–1135) wrote additional notes. Each case was preceded by an introductory remark and the case as well as Hsüeh-tou's poems were then annotated. The book came out in print in 1125, edited by Kuan-yu Wu-tang. Later, because he regarded the book as harmful to a true understanding of Ch'an, Ta-hui (1088–1163) burned it. It was about two hundred years later that Chang Ming-yüan found a good copy in 1302 at Ch'eng-tu. He collated this with other copies obtained in the south, and the resulting version is the one handed down. D. T. Suzuki, *Essays in Zen Buddhism*, pp. 239–240. The *Wu-men kuan* is shorter than the *Pi-yen lu*, consisting of forty-eight cases. It was compiled by Wu-men Hui-k'ai (1183–1260) of the Sung, who also wrote comments on the cases. Ting Fu-pao, *Fo-chiao ta-tz'u-tien*, p. 2166a. *Pi-yen lu* has been translated into English as *The Blue Cliff Records: the Hekigan Roku*. The text of *Wu-men kuan*, together with the comments made by Shibayama Zenkei, a former

Zen master of the Nanzenji of Kyoto, has been translated into English by
Sumiko Kudo as *Zen Comments on the Mumonkan* (New York: Harper & Row,
1974).

2. *YCFH* 26, 10b, "Chiang tsung."

3. When a student monk was asked by the master, he gives a sentence
that does not answer the question directly but indicates his level of awareness.

4. *YCFH* 25, 9a, "I chuan-yü."

5. Ibid., 18b, "Tsung-men-yu pu-ke luan-ni."

6. *YCFH* 15, 53a, "Wan-li chueh-i."

7. Ibid., 54b, "Tsun lun."

8. Ibid., 55a.

9. *YCFH* 24, 42a, "Seng Hsing-k'ung."

10. Ibid., 42b, "Hsing chiao."

11. Ibid., "Seng Hsing-k'ung."

12. *YCFH* 17, 26a–26b, "Shih tso-kuan."

13. *YCFH* 25, 15a, "Tsan-fang hsü chü yen."

14. *YCFH* 15, la, preface to *Tzu-men ch'ung-hsing lu*.

15. *YCFH* 25, 33b, "Ch'an chiang lü."

16. *YCFH* 31, 55b, "Shih Ssu-k'ung kuang-shen." "In this epoch of the
Degenerate Law there is no great Dharma teacher comparable to those of
ancient times. This is because while there are many monks who would respond to the invitation to perform funeral services and give lectures on sutras, there are very few who study sutras with conscientiousness. Therefore
these are all Dharma teachers of worldly truth."

17. *YCFH* 24, 29b–30a, "Seng hsi."

18. *YCFH* 26, 16a–16b, "Seng wu wai-hsüeh."

19. Ibid., 39a–39b, "Chiang fa-shih."

20. Ibid., 36a–36b, "Hsüeh kuei ch'uan ching."

21. Ibid., 38a–38b, "Shih-shih shih."

22. Ibid., 16b, "Seng wu tsa-shu."

23. *YCFH* 31, 58a–58b, "Shih Ssu-chuan P'eng chün."

24. *YCFH* 26, 44b–45a, "Shao lien."

25. Ibid., 64b–65a, "Hsiu fu."

26. Ibid., 54a–54b, "Tao chi shih."

27. *YCFH* 31, 47b, "Chuan-chieh kuo-wei ku-hsing hsien-i huo-chung
che."

28. Ibid., 55b, "Shih Ssu-kung Kuang-sheng."

29. *YCFH* 26, 22b, "Seng ch'u t'ung p'u."

30. *YCFH* 25, 53b, "Ch'u-chia, II."

31. Ibid., 28a, "Lai-sheng, II."

32. *YCFH* 26, 42a–42b, "Hu fa."

VIII. CHU-HUNG'S MONASTIC REFORM:
THE YÜN-CH'I MONASTERY

1. Heinrich Dumoulin, S. J. *The Development of Chinese Zen after the Sixth Patriarch in the Light of Mumonkan*, p. 14. The title of Pai-chang's work, or rather the code attributed to him, is called *Chih-hsiu Pai-chang ch'ing-kuei ch'ung-pien* (Revised Edition of the Pure Rule of Pai-chang Compiled by Imperial Decree). It is now T 2025.

2. Kondō Ryōichi, "Hajō shingi no seiritsu to sono genkei."

3. *YCFH* 26, 76b–77a, "Pai-chang ch'ing-kuei."

4. *YCFH* 32, 39b–40a, "Ch'u-chia shih."

5. Ibid., 40a–40b, "T'i-fa shih."

6. The sutras for the morning and evening devotional services refer to the Heart Sutra and the Lesser Sukhāvatīvyūha Sutra, which are included in *Various Sutras for Daily Recitation (YCFH* 12), a work Chu-hung compiled for the use of his followers at Yün-ch'i.

7. Ch'en, *Buddhism in China*, p. 247.

8. *YCFH* 32, 68b, "Shou-chieh shih."

9. The complete list together with the full texts can be found in the *Various Sutras for Daily Recitation (YCFH* 12), 5a–39b. The sutras are the Heart Sutra and the Lesser Sukhāvatīvyūha Sutra. The rest are mantras of various kinds and short devotional psalms.

10. This work in one volume was written by Kuei-shan Ling-yu (d. 853), a disciple of Pai-chang Huai-hai. He was the founder of the Kuei-yang school, one of the five Ch'an schools.

11. *YCFH* 32, 66b, "Hsüeh-ching hao-tz'u."

12. Ibid., 67a.

13. Sukumar Dutt, *Early Buddhist Manachism, 600 B.C.–100 B.C.*, p. 99. Charles S. Prebish, *Buddhist Monastic Discipline*, pp. 1–33.

14. *YCFH* 15, 56b–57a.

15. Ibid., 57a.

16. *Pan-yüeh sung-chieh i-shih, YCFH* 13, la.

17. Ibid., 3b.

18. Henry Clarke Warren, *Buddhism in Translations*, p. 405.

19. *YCFH* 32, 27a–29b.

20. They are a group of works written by Lo Tsu or Lo Ch'ing (fl. 1509–1522) in the fourth year of Cheng-te (1506): *K'u-kung wu-tao chüan, Tan-shih wu-wei chüan, P'o-hsieh hsien-cheng yao-shih chüan* (2 vols.), *Cheng-hsin chü-i wu-hsiu-cheng tzu-tsai pao-chüan* and *Wei-wei pu-tung t'ai-shan shen-ken chieh-kuo pao-chüan*. These works are arranged in the order they were written in. Altogether they comprise five titles and six volumes, thus the name. Lo Tsu was the founder of a heretical sect, the Wu-wei Chiao, and these works were condemned by the government as heretical and were suppressed. They were burned in Wan-li 46 (1618). Besides Chu-hung, Te-ch'ing also condemned the sect. The texts for these works are highly syncretic, drawing materials from all three traditions. They belong to the group of popular

religious literature called *pao-chüan*. See Sakai Tadao, *Chūgoku zensho no kenkyū*, pp. 440, 469–480; and Overmyer, *Folk Buddhist Religion*, pp. 113–129.

21. *YCFH* 32, 29b–31b.

22. *YCFH* 15, 1a–2a.

23. *Liu-ho* refers to bodily unity in form of worship, oral unity in chanting, mental unity in faith, moral unity in observing the commandments, doctrinal unity in views and explanations, and economic unity in community of goods, deeds, studies or clarity. Soothill, *A Dictionary of Chinese Buddhist Terms*, pp. 133a–b.

24. *Smṛtyupasthāna*, the fourfold stages of mindfulness. It consists of contemplating the body as impure and utterly filthy; sensation or consciousness as always resulting in suffering; mind as impermanent, merely one sensation after another; things as dependent and without a nature of their own. Soothill, p. 175.

25. *YCFH* 32, 40a, "Chin-t'ang shih."

26. *YCFH* 25, 21b–22a, "Seng t'ang."

27. *YCFH* 32, 3a–6a.

28. A period covers a complete set of activities (meditation, recitation of Buddha's name, or devotions), which is measured by sticks of incense. Welch described a period in the modern Pure Land temple of Ling-yen Ssu; it lasted one and one-half hours. *The Practice of Chinese Buddhism*, pp. 92–98.

29. *Chih-ching, k'ai-ching* are terms also used in Ch'an meditation halls, where they signify the beginning and the end of a meditation cycle (sitting and running in circumambulation, respectively.) But I believe that here it means silent Buddha recollection (in contrast to the oral invocation of the name).

30. This was written by Tz'u-yün Tsun-shih (963–1032) and is found in Chu-hung's *Chu-ching jih-sung* (*YCFH* 12, 23b).

31. There is usually a brief formula in which the merit generated by the recitation of Buddha's name and scriptures would be credited to three accounts. Welch lists them: "First, it was transferred to the benefit of others so that they too might go to the Western Paradise *(hui-tzu hsiang-t'a)*. Second, it was transferred to one's own credit in the Western Paradise so that one might have a higher position there *(hui-yin hsiang-kuo)*. Third, it was transferred to one's credit in the absolute *(hui-shih hsiang-li)*." *Practice of Chinese Buddhism*, p. 99.

32. The *Ch'an-hui wen* is included in *Various Sutras for Daily Recitation* (*YCFH* 12), 30a–35b.

33. It is an abbreviation for *ch'u chung-sheng shih* (to put out food for sentient beings). Chu-hung set down the proper way of performing this as follows: "One should offer no more than seven grains of cooked rice, no more than one inch of a noodle, and no more than one pinch of a cooked bun. To offer more is to be greedy, but to offer less is to be stingy. Vegetables and bean curd are not offered. When one offers the food, one puts it in

the palm of one's left hand and silently recites this verse (*YCFH* 13, 11a–11b):

> To the assembly of gods and ghosts,
> I now present this as an offering.
> May it prevail in the ten directions,
> And be shared by gods and ghosts alike.

Welch describes the way it is done in the twentieth century. "An acolyte (*chih-che*) takes seven grains of rice from a bowl before the Buddha image and places them on a low pillar in the courtyard. He snaps his fingers to notify the ghosts that they have not been forgotten." *Practice of Chinese Buddhism*, p. 59.

34. *YCFH* 12, 22b–23a.

35. This was written by Chu-hung himself and is included in *Various Sutras for Daily Recitation (YCFH* 12), 24b–35b.

36. *YCFH* 32, 7a–9a.

37. There are various things a monk could do at Yün-ch'i to accumulate good points. A list of good deeds and punishments is furnished in Appendix III.

38. *YCFH* 32, 10a–12a.

Appendix One

1. Chu-hung supplies a note on the value of "one hundred cash." He says: "A hundred cash always refers to a hundred *wen* of copper money and equals ten *fen* of silver. This rate holds even if the value of the copper money fluctuates." In this translation, a passage enclosed in parentheses indicates Chu-hung's own explanation, but that enclosed in brackets is the translator's gloss.

2. Military exile (*chün*). This was more severe than the ordinary form of exile. It is the fourth of the traditional five punishments. "Military exile began to be clearly distinguishable from ordinary exile during Sung times, was further elaborated under the Yüan dynasty, and became really systematized and accepted as a major punishment during the Ming. During the early Ming, military exile was primarily a substitute for ordinary exile in the case of military officers or soldiers guilty of crime; as such, it consisted of lifetime military service at some distant frontier military post or military colony (of which there were many facilitating the opening up of new lands). . . . Increasingly, with the passage of time, military exile apparently became a punishment for civilians as well as for military personnel. At the same time, its scope was broadened to include service at military posts within, as well as along, the national frontiers." Derk Bodde and Clarence Morris, *Law in Imperial China*, p. 88.

3. Penal servitude (*t'u*), the third of the traditional five punishments. It consists of five degrees, ranging from one to three years. ". . . The pun-

ishment included hard labor for the offender as well as his removal from his place of origin to another area for a fixed term of years. In Ming times persons thus sentenced were sent from the province of their conviction to another province where, during the term specified, they worked in an iron or salt works. In these establishments the daily quotas required of them consisted either of the smelting of three catties [about four English pounds] of iron or the production, through boiling, of the same amount of salt. Persons sentenced to penal servitude were not sent from their own province to another province haphazardly. On the contrary, for each province of origin there was a specific counterpart province to which its convicts were always to be sent. According to the account and table in *Ta Ming hui-tien*, 61:27b–28, convicts from Fukien, for example, were to be sent to salt works in Kiangsu, and convicts from Kiangsi to iron works in Shantung." Ibid., pp. 81–82.

4. Light *(ch'ih)* and heavy *(chang)* bamboo were the first and second of the traditional five punishments in imperial China. Each consisted of five degrees: from ten to fifty blows of light bamboo and from sixty to one hundred blows of heavy bamboo. "Beating was administered on the buttocks—bared for men, covered with underpants for women. During the Han dynasty and for several centuries thereafter, the sticks used for beating had been made of bamboo. Beginning probably in the Liang dynasty (502–556), however, they were instead made of a special kind of wood known as *ch'u*. The diameters of these *ch'u* sticks, as fixed by law from the T'ang through the Ming dynasty, were, for the small stick, 0.2 Chinese inches at the large end and 0.15 inches at the small end; for the large stick, 0.27 inches at the large end, 0.17 inches at the small end." Bodde and Morris, p. 88. The reader will notice that Chu-hung assigns more merit points to a person who reduces another's sentence as a judge (M 27–35) than to one who succeeds in convincing another person not to file a lawsuit, thus saving a person from receiving such a sentence (M 151–155).

5. See the preceding note.

6. Chu-hung supplies an explanation for the various terms used. He says: "To save, *chiu*, means that when one is not in charge of the case, one tries his best to help. To pardon, *mien*, means that when one is in charge of the case, one specifically pardons the offender. Biased judgment refers to a situation in which one does not investigate the case carefully and according to fact, but makes a wanton judgment and thereby lets the real criminal get away."

7. Chu-hung explains the different types of animals: "Animals capable of returning people's kindness are domesticated water buffaloes, draft horses, watchdogs, and so on. Animals incapable of returning people's kindness are pigs, sheep, geese, ducks, deer, and so on; small creatures are those such as fish, sparrows, and so on; extremely small creatures are those such as small fish, shrimp, snails, even including flies, ants, mosquitoes, bedbugs, and so on. In saving them, one may buy them and release them, or prohibit their being killed or dissuade others from killing them. If one saves only small creatures but not large one, it signifies a greed for one's own bles-

sings, and not a compassionate heart toward sentient beings. Therefore it is of no merit."

8. Chu-hung supplies a note which says: "Harmful animals are those such as snakes, rats, and so on. Before a snake bites people, it does not commit a crime worthy of death. As for rats, although they may do harm, it is not a crime serious enough to warrant the death penalty."

9. One must kill the silkworms in order to make silk; therefore taking care of silkworms, like fishing and hunting, is not a proper profession for a good Buddhist. It is thus meritorious when one refuses to continue this line of work. Related to this is the prohibition against monks' wearing silk. At the best monasteries in China, even in this century, the wearing of silk was forbidden.

10. Chu-hung's commentary makes clear who these gods and people are: "Devas refers to Brahma, Indra, and so on, of the three worlds of desire, of form and of formlessness, as well as Taoist gods and saints. Former sages refers to Kings Yao and Shun, to the Duke of Chou, and to Confucius, and so on; orthodox gods are the city god and mountain gods; virtuous men and women are the people who are loyal subjects, filial sons, righteous husbands, and faithful wives, and so on."

11. According to Chu-hung, the "ethical texts" are the following: "The Five Precepts and Ten Virtues preached by the Buddha and bodhisattvas; the Six Classics, *Analects,* and *Mencius,* as well as instructions and acts of former sages, are all considered ethical texts relating to heaven and man."

12. The death penalty *(ssu-hsing)* is the last of the traditional five punishments. In the Sui Code of 581–583 (the prototype of the surviving T'ang Code of 653), the death penalty consisted of two degrees: strangulation and decapitation. Besides these two standard forms of death, there was another, *ling-ch'ih,* or "death by slicing," which was the severest of all. "The dynastic history of the Liao records at least six instances of rebels against Liao rule who underwent execution by *ling-ch'ih.* From Liao the punishment was then apparently transmitted to the contemporary Chinese Sung empire in the south, where references to it appear in 1028, 1075, and later. Although it was used sporadically during the Sung as an extra-legal punishment, death by slicing achieved legal status only in the Yüan and Ming Codes, from which it passed to that of the Ch'ing." Bodde and Morris, pp. 94–95.

13. Their sayings cannot be identified.

14. Hsü Hsing was a native of Ch'u and lived during the period of the Warring States. He advocated that everybody ought to plough the fields and work for food. He also advocated an extremely austere and simple style of life. He is mentioned by Mencius (*Mencius,* III A, 4.)

15. (Mahā) Maudgalyāyana. One of the ten chief disciples of Śākyamuni noted for his miraculous powers. Formerly an ascetic, he agreed with Śāriputra that whoever first found the truth would reveal it to the other. Śāriputra found the Buddha and brought Maudgalyāyana to him. Both became the Buddha's disciples. Soothill and Hodous, *A Dictionary of Chinese Buddhist Terms,* p. 199a.

16. People killed animals to placate ghosts by their sacrifice. Ghosts were thought to affect one's fate supernaturally.

17. The period during which slaughter (together with fishing and hunting) was prohibited by law included the so-called long fasting month: the 1st, 5th, and 9th months, as well as the ten fast days in each month: the 1st, 8th, 14th, 15th, 18th, 23rd, 24th, 28th, 29th, and 30th in T'ang and Sung times. See Ch'ü T'ung-tsu, *Law and Society in Traditional China*, p. 219. This practice was continued in the Ming. Moreover, not only was slaughtering prohibited, but the execution of criminals was also prohibited. Ch'ü cites the *Ming lü li* (28, 52a), where any official who failed to observe this rule was subjected to a punishment of forty strokes (p. 219).

From contemporary reports, some Ming emperors ate vegetarian food on such fast days, which all together numbered more than one hundred days. See Chu Kuo-chen, *Yung-chung hsiao-p'in.*

18. Chu-hung uses the terms *yu* (to put someone in isolated confinement) and *chi* (to tie someone up in ropes). Both refer to the inhuman treatment of a man's concubine or maid for the purpose of preventing the latter from having a normal social life and thus an opportunity of committing sexual misconduct.

19. Orthodox gods are the gods recognized by the imperial government, whose worship is permitted by the state. Gods such as the city god, Kuan-ti (god of war), and T'ai-shan (Mt. T'ai) belong to this category.

20. Heretical gods are the gods who are not recognized by the imperial government and whose worship is not sanctioned by the state. The shrines housing them are called *yin-tz'u* (licentious shrines), mentioned in no. 125.

21. According to Soothill and Hodous, garlic, three kinds of onions, and leeks are the five forbidden pungent roots. "If eaten raw, they are said to cause irritability of temper, and if eaten cooked, to act as an aphrodisiac; moreover, the breath of the eater, if reading the sutras, will drive away the good spirits." See Soothill and Hodous, p. 128.

22. Ma Jung (d. 166) served as prefect of Nan-chün during the reign of Emperor Huan. He was noted for his broad learning and literary talent. He had disciples by the thousands, among them Cheng Hsüan and Lu Chih. He wrote commentaries on the *Classic of Filial Piety*, the *Analects*, the *Book of Changes*, the *Book of Poetry*, and other classics.

GLOSSARY

an-ch'an 安禪

ch'a-t'ou 茶頭
chai-chiao 齋醮
chai-kung 齋供
ch'ai-t'ou 柴頭
ch'an-chiao 闡教
ch'an-t'ang 禪堂
chang-chiao 章醮
chang-hsing 扙刑
ch'ang nien hsiang-chi 唱念相繼
chao 照
chao-ch'ing 招請
Chao-ch'ing Ssu 昭慶寺
ch'ang-hsing san-mei 常行三昧
Ch'ang-shou 長壽
Che-ke nien-fo-te pi-ching shih shui 這個念佛的畢竟是誰
chen-ch'eng hsin 眞誠心
chen-chi-pu 砧基簿
chen-chi-tao-jen 砧基道人
cheng-fa 正法
cheng-hsin 正信
Cheng-hsin chü-i wu-hsiu cheng tzu-tsai pao-chüan 正信除疑無修證自在寶卷
Ch'eng-Chu 程朱
ch'eng-i 誠意
ch'eng-ming nien-fo 稱名念佛
chi 記
chi 寂
chi 繫
chi-hua 紀化
chi-ming tu-tieh 記名度牒

chi-tsu 繼祖
ch'i-shih 乞士
chiang 講
chiang-ching 講經
chiang-ching-lun shuo-tso 講經論首座
chiao 敎
chiao-jen sha 敎人殺
Chiao-shan 焦山
chiao-tien men 敎典門
chieh 戒
chien-i 鑒義
chieh-hsiang 戒相
chieh-in 結印
Chieh sha wen 戒殺文
chien-fu-ts'ao 監福曹
chien-k'u chih hsing 堅苦之行
ch'ien-kung 鉛汞
chien-ssu 監寺
ch'ien-tan 鉛丹
chien-tso sui-hsi 見作隨喜
chih 智
chih-chung 知衆
chih-ch'ih 執持
chih-ching 止靜
chih-chung 治中
ch'ih-chung chih hsing 持重之行
chih-chü 直舉
ch'ih-hsing 筈刑
chih-k'o 知客
Chih-lou-chia-ch'an (Lokakṣema) 支婁迦讖
Chih-men Tso 智門祚
chih-pan 值板
chih-shan 知山
Chih-shun 智舜
Chih-tsang 智藏
Chih-wen 至溫
chih-wu 知屋
Chih-yen 智儼
chih-yüan 知院
ch'ih-ts'ai shih-mo 吃菜事魔
chin-na 進納
Ch'in lu chi 欽錄記

ching 敬
ching-ch'an 經懺
ching-ch'an shih 經懺師
ching-ch'an t'ang 經懺堂
ching-chao 京兆
Ching-ming Chung-hsiao Tao 淨明忠孝道
Ching-shan 徑山
ching-shih 經事
ching-t'ou 淨頭
ching-ts'e 警策
ching t'u 淨土
ching-t'u chung-hsing 淨土中興
ching-t'u tao-ch'ang 淨土道場
ching-yeh 淨業
Ch'ing-chiang 清江
Ch'ing-hsiu 慶修
ch'ing-li shih-tao 清理釋道
ch'ing-su chih hsing 清素之行
ch'ing-yüan tiao-fa shih-lei 慶元條法事類
chiu-e 舊額
ch'iu 救
chou 州
chou 咒
chou-sha 咒殺
chu-cheng 主政
chu-ch'ing 主磬
Chu Pai-min 朱白民
chu-sha-yin 硃砂銀
chu-t'ien 諸天
ch'u-chia 出家
ch'u chung-sheng shih 出眾生食
ch'u-sheng 出生
ch'u-shih-chien shan tao 出世間善道
chuan-hsin 專心
chuan-nien pu-wang 專念不忘
chuan-yü 轉語
ch'uan-ch'i 傳奇
ch'üan-chiao 權教
Chuang Fu-chen 莊復眞
chüeh-i 覺義
chun-ch'eng 郡丞
chun-po 郡伯

chung 中

chung-ch'eng 中丞

chung-ching-chin che 中精進者

chung-chün chih hsing 忠君之行

chung-fa 中罰

chung-han 中翰

chung-hsiao lei 忠孝類

chung-p'in 中品

chung-shih 中士

chü-chieh 具戒

chü-shih 居士

chüeh-i 覺義

Chüeh-shih ching 覺世經

chün-hsing 軍刑

chün-ming tzu-ti 軍民子弟

Fa-hua ch'an 法華懺

Fa-hua san-mei hsing-fa 法華三昧行法

fa-shih 法施

fa-t'ang 法堂

fa-te 發得

Fa-yü 法遇

Fan-wang ch'ing hsin-ti p'in p'u-sa chieh i-shu fa-yin
    梵網經心地品菩薩戒義疏發隱

fang-pien 方便

fang-pien sha 方便殺

fang-po 方伯

fang-sheng-so 放生所

Fang sheng wen 放生文

Fang Ta-chih 方大湜

fang-teng 方等

fang-t'ou 飯頭

fei-jen 非人

fen 分

fen-hsiu men 焚修門

Feng tai ch'ü 馮泰衢

fo-ch'ü 佛曲

Fo-shuo A-mi-t'o ching shu ch'ao 佛說阿彌陀經疏鈔

Fo-shuo chieh tsui fu ching 佛說解罪福經

fu 福

fu-seng-lu 副僧錄

Fu-shang 富上

fu-shui 符水
fu-tu-kang 副都綱
fu-wang 伏妄

Hai-yün 海雲
hao chih 號紙
ho-ho 合和
Hsi-t'ang 西堂
Hsi-t'ien fo-tzu 西天佛子
hsia 下
hsia-ching-chin che 下精進者
hsia-fa 下罰
hsia-p'in 下品
hsia-shih 下士
hsiang 相
hsiang-fa 像法
hsiang-teng 香燈
hsiang-teng liao 香燈寮
hsiao-ch'in chih hsing 孝親之行
Hsiao ching-t'u wen 小淨土文
hsiao chung-cheng 小中正
hsiao-shun hsin 孝順心
hsiao kuo 小過
hsiao-shih 小食
hsieh-shu 寫疏
hsien 縣
Hsien-lin Ssu 僊林寺
hsien-tsai fo hsi tsai chien-li san-mei 現在佛悉在前立三昧
hsin 心
hsin chieh 心戒
hsin-yüan hsiang 心緣相
hsing-chiao 行腳
hsing-e 行惡
hsing-shan 行善
hsing-shan chih-e 行善止惡
hsing-wu-che 行務者
hsiu-fu 修福
hsiu-hui 修慧
hsiu-shen 修身
Hsiu-sheng shih-shih 修身十事
hsiu-ts'ai 秀才
Hsü Ko-ju 許戈如

hsün-hsiang 巡香
Hu-chieh Shen 護戒神
hu-shen 護神
hua-fan 化飯
hua-fo 化佛
Huang-ch'ao pen-chi 皇朝本記
Huang P'ing-ch'ing 黃平倩
Huang Yüan-fu 黃元孚
hui 會
hui 慧
Hui-ch'en 會眞
hui-hsiang 迴向
hui-hsiang fa-yüan hsin 迴向發願心
hui-ming 慧命
hui-shih hsiang-li 迴事向理
hui-tzu hsiang-t'a 迴自向他
hui-yin hsiang-kuo 迴因向果
hun 魂
Hua-yen 華嚴

i-ch'ing 疑情
i-fang 義方
i-hsin ch'ih-ming 一心持名
i-hsin nien-fo 一心念佛
i-hsin pu-luan 一心不亂
i-ling 邑令
i-nien wu-chien 一念無間
i-t'i san-pao 一體三寶
i-t'uan 疑團

ju 如
ju-kuan 入觀
jen-t'ien yin-kuo 人天因果
jen-tz'u lei 仁慈類

k'ai-ching 開靜
K'ai-yüan Ssu 開元寺
kan-ying chih hsing 感應之行
k'an-lao 看老
k'an-ping 看病
kao-ming chih-jen 高明之人
kao-shang chih hsing 高尚之行

Kao Yün 高允
ko 格
Ko I-an 戈以安
K'u-kung wu-tao chüan 苦功悟道卷
kuan-hsiang nien-fo 觀像念佛
kuan-hsiang nien-fo 觀想念佛
Kuan-nien fa-men 觀念法門
kuang 廣
Kuang-yün 廣闊
Kuei-shan Ling-yu 溈山靈祐
Kuei-yang 溈仰
k'un 坤
kung 功
k'ung-ming tu-tieh 空名度牒
k'ung san-mei 空三昧
k'ung-t'ou tu-tieh 空頭度牒
k'ung-yu hsiang-ch'eng 空有相成
kuo 過
kuo-ch'eng 果成

Lan-jung 嬾融
Leng-chia shih-tzu chi 楞伽師資記
li 理
li-ch'ih 理持
Li Hsiu 李繡
li i-hsin 理一心
li-shih wu-ai 理事無礙
li-sung 禮誦
Li-tai fa-pao chi 歷代法寶記
li-ti i-sheng 团地一聲
Lin-chi 臨濟
ling-chih 凌遲
Ling-ku Ssu 靈谷寺
Ling-pao ching-ming-yüan hsing-ch'ien-shih 靈寶淨明院行遣式
liu-ho 六和
lu-huo 爐火
lu-huo tan-shu 爐火丹術
lü 律
Lü-t'ang 律堂

mai-tieh 賣牒
men-k'o 門客

Miao-fa lien-hua ching Ma-ming p'u-sa p'in 妙法蓮華經馬鳴菩薩品
mien 免
mien-ting ch'ien 免丁錢
ming-ch'ih 明持
ming-tzu hsiang 名字相
mo-ch'ih 默持
mo-t'ou 磨頭

na-mo A-mi-t'o-fo 南無阿彌陀佛
nan-hsi 南戲
neng-nien 能念
neng-so 能所
nien 念
nien-fo kung-an 念佛公案
nien-fo t'ang 念佛堂
nien-hsin 念心
nien-nien pu-wang, hsin-hsin wu-chien 念念不忘，心心無間

pa-chieh hsing-hsing 八節行刑
pai-ch'an 拜懺
pai-hao 白毫
pai-huai tsu-feng 敗壞祖風
pai-i 白衣
pai-min 百緡
Pan-chou tao-ch'ang 般舟道場
pan-ming pan-mo-ch'ih 半明半默持
pan-tao-che 辦道者
pan-yüeh sung-chieh shih 半月誦戒式
pao-chüan 寶卷
Pao-en Ssu 報恩寺
pao-jang tao-ch'ang 保禳道場
pen-hsin 本心
pen-lai mien-mu 本來面目
pi-chi 筆記
pi-ch'i 閉氣
pi-ch'iu 比丘
pi-yin 敝寅
p'ing-shang-sheng 平上聲
p'ing sheng 平聲
p'o 魄
P'o-hsieh hsien-cheng yao-shih chüan 破邪顯正鑰匙卷
p'o wang 破妄

pu-chung-hsiao lei 不忠孝類

pu-hsing fang-chiu chieh 不行放救戒

pu-pu sheng-sheng nien-nien, wei tsai Mi-t'o 步步聲聲念念唯在彌陀

pu-sa 布薩

pu-sha 不殺

pu-t'ui 不退

pu yüeh i-nien, tun cheng p'u-t'i 不越一念，頓證菩提

p'u-sa chieh 菩薩戒

p'u-t'ang 舖堂

p'u-tu 普度

P'u-yüan 普願

san-chai, liu-chai 三齋，六齋

san-kang 三綱

san-shih 三世

se-shen 色身

seng-cheng 僧正

Seng-cheng-ssu 僧正司

seng chi ts'e 僧籍册

Seng-ch'ou 僧稠

seng-hui 僧會

Seng-hui-ssu 僧會司

Seng-kang-ssu 僧綱司

Seng-lu-ssu 僧錄司

Seng-min 僧旻

seng-p'an 僧判

seng-t'ung 僧統

sha-fa 殺法

sha-men-t'ung 沙門統

sha-yeh 殺業

sha-yin 殺因

sha-yüan 殺緣

shan-fa chieh 殺法戒

shan-men 善門

shan-men 山門

shan-shih 善世

shang 上

shang-ching-chin che 上精進者

shang-chung 上中

Shang-fang 上方

shang-p'in 上品

shang-p'in chung-sheng 上品中生

shang-p'in hsia-sheng 上品下生
shang p'in shang-sheng 上品上生
shang-shih 上士
shang-shu 尙書
shang-tso 上座
she-sheng chieh 攝生戒
shen chieh 身戒
shen hsin 深心
shen-tsu 神足
shen-tu 愼獨
sheng 升
sheng-mieh 生滅
sheng-t'ai 聖胎
Shi-chia-chai yang hsiu lu 十駕齋養心錄
shi-chung 侍中
shih 事
shih-che 侍者
shih-chiao 實教
shih-chien san-pao 世間三寶
shih-chien shan-tao 世間善道
shih-chih 事執
shih-chung 十重
shih-e 視惡
shih-hsiang 實相
shih-hsiang nien-fo 實相念佛
shih i-hsin 事一心
Shih Lao chih 釋老志
shih-lu 實錄
shih-shan 視善
shih-shih 施食
shih-t'ao 事道
shih-tsu 始祖
shou-chieh 受戒
shou-tso 首座
shu-chi 書記
shu-wen 疏文
shui-lu nei-t'an 水陸內壇
shui-yin 水銀
so-nien 所念
ssu-chu 寺主
ssu-ch'i 四期
ssu-chung 司中

ssu-fa 死法
Ssu-fen-chieh pen 四分戒本
ssu-hsing 死刑
ssu-kuan 死關
ssu-k'ung 司空
ssu-liao chien 四料簡
ssu-lu 司錄
ssu-ming 司命
Ssu-nien-ch'u-fa 四念處法
ssu-shan shih-ch'i tsui 四善十七最
ssu-shih-pa ch'ing 四十八輕
Ssu-t'ien-wang ching 四天王經
ssu-t'u 司徒
ssu-tzu tsan-t'i 私自簪剃
su-ken 宿根
suan 算
sung-ching 誦經
sung-chou 誦咒

ta 大
Ta-cheng tsuan-yao 大政纂要
ta-chia 大家
Ta-chih-tu lun 大智度論
Ta-ch'ing fa-wang 大慶法王
ta chung-cheng 大中正
Ta-hsing-lung Ssu 大興隆寺
Ta-lung-fu Ssu 大隆福寺
Ta-pao-en Ssu 大報恩寺
ta-shih 大事
Ta-t'ang 大堂
tai-t'i ch'u-chia 代替出家
T'ai-chou 泰州
T'ai-hsing 太行
T'ai-shang 太上
T'ai-shang kan-ying p'ien 太上感應篇
T'ai-shang ling-pao ching-ming fei-t'ien tu-jen ching 太上靈寶淨明飛天度人經
t'ai-shih 太史
t'ai-wei 太尉
T'ai-wei Hsien-chün kung-kuo-ko 太尉仙君功過格
T'an-i 曇一
tan-li 担力
Tan-shih wu-wei chüan 嘆世無爲卷

tan yin 丹銀

T'an-yün 曇韻

tang-chia 當家

Tao-chi 道積

Tao-lin 道琳

te-hsing 德行

t'i-chiu wu-chien 體究無間

t'i-chiu 體究

tien-tso 典座

T'ien-chieh Ssu 天界寺

T'ien-chu shih-i 天主實義

T'ien-kung k'ai-wu 天工開物

T'ien-t'ai 天台

t'ien wu 天物

ting 定

Ting Chien-hung 丁劍虹

ting-hsin 定心

ting-yung 聽用

To-fo-ko 多佛閣

tou-erh-fo shih-fu 荳兒佛師父

t'ou-t'o 頭陀

tsa-chü 雜劇

Ts'ai Huai-t'ing 蔡槐庭

ts'ai-shih 財施

ts'ai-t'ou 菜頭

tsan-chiao 贊教

ts'an-chiu nien-fo 參究念佛

ts'an-fang 參方

tsan-t'an sha 讚嘆殺

ts'an-tao 參道

tsang-ching-t'ang 藏經堂

Ts'ao-tung 曹洞

tso-ch'an 坐禪

tso-kuan 作觀

tso-kung 坐功

tso-shih 座師

tso-yu-chieh seng-lu 左右街僧錄

tso-yu seng-lu 左右僧錄

Tsou K'uang-ming 鄒匡明

tsun-shih chih hsing 尊師之行

Ts'ung-chien 從諫

tsung-jung 總戎

tsung-po 宗伯
tsung-lin 叢林
tu-hsien 都閫
t'u-hsing 徒刑
tu-kang 都綱
tuan-shih sha-men 斷事沙門
t'ui-chieh jen 退戒人
Tung-lin 東林
t'ung-ling 統領
T'ung-shan hui 同善會
Tzu-lin 子鄰
tzu-sha 自殺
tz'u-pei hsin 慈悲心
Tz'u-shou Ssu 慈壽寺
tz'u-wu chih hsing 慈物之行

Wa-kuan Ssu 瓦官寺
Wan-shou Ssu 萬壽寺
wan-t'ou 碗頭
Wang Chen 王震
Wang Jo-sheng 王弱生
Wang Meng-su 王孟夙
Wang Tao-an 王道安
Wang Yü-ch'un 王宇春
wei-chi hsing-ming 爲己性命
wei-fa chih chung 未發之中
wei-hsiang fa-ssu 未詳法嗣
wei ju-liu 未入流
wei-no 維那
Wei-shih 唯識
wen 文
Wen-ch'ang 文昌
Wen Tsai 文才
Wei-wei pu-tung t'ai-shan shen-ken chieh-kuo pao-chüan
   巍巍不動泰山深根結果寶卷
Wen Tzu-yu 聞子與
wu 悟
wu 無
wu-li pao-jen 無力報人
Wu-men Hui-k'ai 無門慧開
wu-sheng 無生
wu-tsung 五宗

Wu-yu 無憂

Yang Ting-yün 楊廷筠
yeh-chü hsiao-san 夜聚曉散
yen-cheng 嚴正
yen-cheng chih hsing 嚴正之行
yen-li 嚴厲
yen-mei 厭魅
Yen Min-ch'ing 嚴敏卿
yen-shuo hsiang 言說相
yin-fang 印房
yin-hsing 因行
yin-kuo san-shih 因果三世
yin-sheng nien-fo 引聲念佛
yin-tz'u 淫祠
yin-yang 陰陽
yu 幽
yu-fang wen-tao 遊方問道
yu i-lu 有義路
yu-k'ung 有空
yu-li pao-jen 有力報人
yü-chia 瑜伽
yü-chia yen-k'ou 瑜伽熖口
yü-e 語惡
yü-shan 語善
Yüan Pin 袁濱
yüan-t'ou 園頭
yüeh-chung 悅衆
Yün-men 雲門

BIBLIOGRAPHY

COLLECTIONS OF BUDDHIST WORKS

Taishō shinshū daizōkyō 大正新修大藏経 [The Buddhist Canon Published in the Taishō Era]. Eds. Takakusu Junjirō 高楠順次郎 and Watanabe Kaikyoku 渡辺海旭. 85 vols. Tokyo, 1924–1934. Abbreviated as T.

Dainihon zokuzōkyō 大日本續藏経 [Supplement to the Japanese Edition of the Buddhist Canon]. 150 cases 帙. 750 fasicules 冊. Kyoto, 1905–1912. Abbreviated as ZZ.

DICTIONARIES

Dōchū 道忠 *Zenrin shōki sen* 禪林象器箋. [Symbols and Implements of Zen Monasteries]. Tokyo, 1909.

Mochizuki Shinkō 望月信亨. *Bukkyō daijiten* 佛教大辞典. [Great Buddhist Dictionary]. 10 vols. Tokyo, 1955–1963.

Morohashi Tetsuji 諸橋轍次 *Daikanwa jiten* 大漢和辞典 [Great Sino-Japanese Dictionary]. 13 vols. Tokyo, 1955–1959.

Oda Tokunō 織田得能 *Oda Bukkyō daijiten* 織田佛教大辞典. [Oda's Great Buddhist Dictionary]. Tokyo, 1965 edition.

Ting, Fu-pao 丁福保. *Fo-hsüeh ta-tz'u-tien* 佛學大辭典. [Great Buddhist Dictionary]. Taipei, 1961 edition.

PRIMARY SOURCES

Chao Shih-an et al. 趙世安. *Jen-ho hsien-chih* 仁和縣志. [Gazetteer of Jen-ho County]. 28 *chüan*. Blockprint edition, 1687.

Chih-ta 智達. *Ching-t'u ch'uan-teng kuei-yüan-ching* 淨土傳燈歸元鏡. [Transmission of the Lamp in the Pure Land Tradition: Mirror of the Return to the Origin]. 2 *chüan*. Hangchow, 1710.

Chin-lin fan-ch'a chih 金陵梵利志 [Record of Buddhist Monasteries in

Nanking]. Comp. Ko Yin-liang 葛寅亮 53 *chüan*. 1607 (1936 reprinted by Chin-shan Chiang-t'ien Monastery).

Chin-p'ing-mei tz'u-hua 金瓶梅詞話. [The Story of the Golden Lotus with *Tz'u* or Rhymed Songs]. 5 *chüan*. Tokyo: Daian Bookstore, 1963 reprint of the Wan-li edition with a preface dated the forty-fifth year of Wan-li (1617).

Chou Ts'ung 周淙. *Lin-an chih* 臨安志. [Gazetteer of Lin-an Prefecture]. 3 *chüan*. Taipei: Shih-chieh Bookstore, 1963.

Chu-hung 袾宏. *Yün-ch'i fa-hui* 雲棲法彙 [Collected Works of Master Yün-ch'i]. 34 *ts'e*. Nanking: Ching-ling k'e-ching ch'u, 1897. Hereinafter *YCFH*. The following is an enumeration of the contents. The dates of the individual works are indicated when they were given by Chu-hung in his prefaces.

Chieh-shu fa-yin 戒疏發隱 [Elucidation of the Commentary on the Precepts Contained in the Sutra of Brahma's Net]. Wan-li 15 or 1587, *YCFH* 1–4.

Shih-i 事義 [Notes on Terminology]; *Wen-pien* 問辯 [Questions and Answers]. *YCFH* 5.

A-mi-t'o ching shu-ch'ao 阿彌陀經疏鈔 [Phrase-by-Phrase Commentary on the Smaller Sukhāvatīvyūha Sutra]. Wan-li 12 or 1584, *YCFH* 6–9.

Shih-i, Wen-pien, Ssu-shih-pa wen-ta 四十八問答 [Forty-eight Questions and Answers]; *Ching-t'u i-pien* 淨土疑辯 [Dispelling Doubts on Pure Land]. *YCFH* 10.

Fo-i-chiao-ching lün chieh-yao 佛遺教經論節要 [A Summary of Commentaries on the *Fo-i-chiao ching*]. Wan-li 24 or 1596, *YCFH* 11.

Chu-ching jih-sung 諸經日誦 [Various Sutras for Daily Recitation]. Wan-li 28 or 1600, *YCFH* 12.

Chü-chieh pien-meng 具戒便蒙 [Primer of Precepts for Monks]; *Sha-mi lü-i yao-lüeh* 沙彌律儀要略 [Essential Rules and Ceremonies for a Novice]; *Sha-mi-ni pi-ch'iu-ni chieh lu-yao* 沙彌尼比丘尼戒錄要. [Selection of Main Precepts for a Female Religious Novice and Nun]; *Sung chieh shih* 誦戒式 [Rite for Reciting the Prātimokṣa]. *YCFH* 13.

Ch'an-kuan ts'e-chin 禪關策進 [Progress in the Path of Ch'an]. Wan-li 28 or 1600. *Seng-hsün jih-chi* 僧訓日記 [Diary of Instructions to Monks]. *YCFH* 14.

Tzu-men ch'ung-hsing lu 緇門崇行錄 [Record of the Exalted Acts of Buddhist Monks]. Wan-li 13 or 1585. *Tzu-chih lu* [The Record of Self-knowledge]. Wan-li 32 or 1604, *YCFH* 15.

Wang-sheng chi 往生集 [Biographies of People Who Achieved Rebirth in the Pure Land]. Wan-li 12 or 1584, *YCFH* 16.

Huang-Ming ming-seng chi-lüeh 皇明名僧輯略 [Selected Biographies of Famous Monks of the Ming Dynasty]; *Wu-lin Hsi-hu kao-seng shih-lüeh* 武林西湖高僧事略 [Selected Biographies of Eminent Monks of the Hangchow Area]. *YCFH* 17.

Shui-lu i-kuei 水陸儀軌 [Direction for the Ritual of the Plenary Mass of Water and Land]. *YCFH* 18–19.

Shih-shih i-kuei 施食儀軌 [Direction for the Ritual of Bestowing Food on Hungry Ghosts]. Wan-li 34 or 1606, *YCFH* 20.

Shih-shih pu-chu 施食補註 [Supplementary Explanation on the Ritual of Bestowing Food on Hungry Ghosts]. *YCFH* 21.

Hua-yen kan-ying lüeh-chi 華嚴感應略記 [Miraculous Responses from Worshipping the Avataṁsaka Sutra]; *Fang-sheng-i* 放生儀 [Ritual for Releasing Life]. *YCFH* 22.

Leng-yen mo-hsiang chi 楞嚴摸象記 [Record of Models Contained in the Sūraṅgama Sutra]. Wan-li 30 or 1602, *YCFH* 23.

Chu-ch'uang sui-pi 竹窗隨筆 [Jottings under a Bamboo Window]. *YCFH* 24.

Chu-ch'uang erh-pi 竹窗二筆 [Further Jottings under a Bamboo Window]. *YCFH* 25.

Chu-ch'uang san-pi 竹窗三筆 [Final Jottings under a Bamboo Window]. *YCFH* 26.

Cheng-e chi 正訛集 [Refutation of Mistaken Views]; *Chih-tao lu* 直道錄 [Clarification of the Way]. Wan-li 42 or 1614, *YCFH* 27.

Shang-fang tsa-lu 山房雜錄 [Miscellaneous Writings at a Mountain Hut]. *YCFH* 28–29.

I-kao 遺稿 [Remaining Papers]. *YCFH* 30–31.

Yün-ch'i kung-chu kuei-yüeh 雲棲共住規約 [Rules and Agreements for Communal Life at Yün-ch'i], *YCFH* 32.

Yün-ch'i chi-shih 雲棲記事 [Notes about the Yün-ch'i Monastery], *YCFH* 33.

Yün-ch'i ta-shih t'a-ming 雲棲大師塔銘 [Stupa Inscription of Master Yün-ch'i], *YCFH* 34.

Chu Kuo-chen 朱國禎. *Yung-ch'uang hsiao-p'in* 湧幢小品. [Essays Written at the Spring-sprung Pavilion]. 2 *chüan*. Peking: Chung-hua Shu-chü, 1959.

Erh-shih-ssu shih 二十四史 [Twenty-four Histories]. Shanghai: T'ung-wen Shu-chü, 1884.

Fan Tsu-shu 范祖述. *Hang-su i-feng* 杭俗遺風. [Traditional Customs of Hangchow]. 1 *chüan*. Blockprint edition, 1867.

Han-shan Te-ch'ing 憨山德清. *Han-shan lao-jen meng-yu-chi* 憨山老人夢遊集. [Record of Dream Wanderings of Old Man Han-shan]. 55 *chüan*. Hong Kong: Hong Kong Buddhist Book Distributors, 1965.

Hsiang Shih-yüan 項士元. *Yün-ch'i chih* 雲棲志. [Record of Yün-ch'i]. 10 *chüan*. Nanking: Hsin-kuang Printing Press, 1934.

Huang Tsung-hsi 黃宗羲. *Ming-ju hsüeh-an* 明儒學案. [Biographies of Ming Confucianists]. Ed. Li Hsin-chuang 李心莊. Taipei: Chang-chung Shu-chü, 1964.

Hui-ts'uan kung-kuo-ko chu-shih 彙纂功過格註釋. [Comprehensive Edition of the Ledger of Merits and Demerits with Commentaries and Explanatory Notes]. Nanking: Chin-hua Ching-hsin-hui, 1858.

Hung-hsüeh yin-yüan t'u-chi 鴻雪因緣圖記. [Illustrated Record of Causes and Conditions of Bright Snow]. 3 *chüan*. Comp. Lin Ch'ing 麟慶. Shanghai: T'ung-wen Shu-chü, 1886. Lithograph edition.

Lang Ying 郎瑛. *Ch'i-hsiu lei-kao* 七修類稿. [Essays Classified under Seven Topics]. Peking: Chung-hua Shu-chü, 1959.

Ming hui-yao 明會要. [Essential Institutes of the Ming Dynasty]. Taipei: Tung-nan Shu-pao-she, 1963. Reprint of 1887 edition.

Ming shih-lu 明實錄. [Veritable Record of the Ming Dynasty]. Taipei: Institute of History and Language, Academia Sinica, 1961–.

Ming-tai pan-hua hsüan ch'u-chi 明代版畫選初輯. [The First Selections from Woodblock Prints of the Ming]. Ed. Ch'ang Pi-te 昌彼得. Taipei: National Central Library, 1969.

Ou-yang Hsün 歐陽詢. *I-wen lei-chü* 藝文類聚. [Literary Writings Grouped According to Categories]. 100 *chüan*. Shanghai: Chung-hua Shu-chü, 1965.

P'eng Shao-sheng 彭紹升. *I-hsing-chü chi* 一行居集. [Essays Composed at the One Act Retreat]. Blockprint edition, 1927.

P'eng-an Ta-yu 蓬庵大祐. *Ching-t'u chih-kuei chi* 淨土指歸集. [Pointing to the Return to the Pure Land]. Yang-chou: Yang-chou Ts'ang-ching-yüan, 1912 edition.

Ricci, Matteo 利瑪竇. *Pien-hsüeh i-tu* 辯學遺牘. [Remaining Letters Concerning the Elucidation of Learning] in *T'ien-hsüeh ch'u-han* 天學初函 [The First Collection of Letters Discussing the Knowledge of Heaven]. Comp. Li Chih-tsao 李之藻. *Chüan* 2. Taipei: Taiwan Hsüeh-sheng Shu-chü, 1965.

Shen Te-fu 沈德符. *Wan-li yeh-huo-pien* 萬曆野獲編. [Literary Acquisitions of a Rustic Scholar of the Wan-li Era]. 2 *chüan*. Peking: Chung-hua Shu-chü, 1959.

Ta Ming hui-tien 大明會典 [Complete Institutions of the Great Ming]. Taipei: Tung-nan Shu-pao-she, 1963. Reprint of 1587 edition.

Ta Ming lü chi-chieh fu-li 大明律集解附例. [Code of the Great Ming, with Collected Commentaries and Cases]. 30 *chüan*. Taipei, 1970. Fascimile reproduction of the Wan-li edition kept at the National Central Library.

T'ai-shang kan-ying p'ien t'u-shuo 太上感應篇圖說. [The Treatise of the Exalted One on Response and Retribution with Illustrations]. Comp. Huang Cheng-yüan 黃正元. Blockprint edition, 1893.

T'ao Wang-ling 陶望齡. "Fang-sheng pien-huo" 放生辯惑 [Dispelling Doubts about Releasing Life], in *Shuo-fu hsü-chi* 說郛續集 [Further Collections of the City of Tales]. *Chüan* 30. Blockprint edition, 1647.

Tung Kao 董誥. *Ch'üan T'ang wen* 全唐文 [Complete Literary Writings of the T'ang Dynasty]. 100 *chüan*. Taipei: Ching-wen Shu-chü, 1965.

WORKS IN TRIPITAKA COLLECTIONS BY TITLE

A-mi-t'o ching 阿彌陀經 [Smaller Sukhāvatīvyūha Sutra]. T12 (no. 336), pp. 346–348.

Chen-hsieh Ch'ing-liao ch'an-shih yü-lu 眞歇淸了禪師語錄 [Recorded Conversations of the Ch'an Teacher Chen-hsieh Ch'ing-liao]. ZZ 2, 29, 3.

Ch'ih-hsiu Pai-chang ch'ing-kuei 勅修百丈淸規. Pai-chang Huai-hai 百丈懷海. [Pure Rules of Pai-chang Compiled under the Imperial Order]. Revised and enlarged by Tung-yang Te-hui 東陽德輝. T48 (no. 2025), pp. 1109–1160.

Ching-te ch'uan-teng lu 景德傳燈錄. [Record of the Transmission of the Lamp]. Tao-yüan 道原. T51 (no. 2076), pp. 196–467.

Chung-feng Ming-pen ch'an-shih tsa-lu 中峰明本禪師雜錄 [Miscellaneous Records of the Ch'an Teacher Chung-feng Ming-pen]. ZZ 2, 27, 4.

Ching-t'u ch'en-chung 淨土晨鐘 [Morning Bells of the Pure Land]. Chou K'e-fu 周克復. ZZ 2, 14, 2.

Ching-t'u sheng-hsien lu 淨土聖賢錄 [Record of Sages and Worthies of the Pure Land]. P'eng Shao-sheng 彭紹升. ZZ 2B, 8, 2.

Chü-shih chuan 居士傳 [Biographies of Lay Devotees]. P'eng Shao-sheng 彭紹升. ZZ 2, 22, 5.

Chü-shih fen-teng chuan 居士分燈傳 [Biographies of Lay Devotees Who Shared the Lamp]. Chu Shih-en 朱時恩. ZZ 2, 20, 5.

Ch'u-shih Fan-ch'i ch'an-shih yü-lu 楚石梵琦禪師語錄 [Recorded Conversations of the Ch'an Teacher Ch'u-shih Fan-ch'i]. ZZ 2, 29, 1–2.

Fan-wang ching 梵網經 [Sutra of Brahma's Net]. T24 (no. 1484).

Fo-tsu li-tai t'ung-tsai 佛祖歷代通載 [A Comprehensive Record of Buddhas and Patriarchs in Successive Generations]. Nien-ch'ang 念常. T. 49 (no. 2036).

Fo-tsu-t'ung chi 佛祖統記 [Record of the Lineage of the Buddhas and Patriarchs]. Chih-p'an 志磐. T. 49 (no. 2035).

Hsin-chin wen-chi 鐔津文集 [Collected Writings of Ch'i-sung]. Ch'i-sung 契嵩. T 52 (no. 2115).

Hsü ch'uan-teng lu 續傳燈錄 [Continuation of the Record of the Transmission of the Lamp]. Hsüan-chi 玄極. T 51 (no. 2077).

Hsü-teng tsun-kao 續燈存稿 [Remaining Documents from the Continuation of the Transmission of the Lamp]. T'ung-wen 通問. ZZ 2B, 18, 1.

Kao-seng chai-yao 高僧摘要 [Essential Selections from the Biographies of Eminent Monks]. Hsü Ch'ang-chih 徐昌治. ZZ 2B, 21, 4.

Kuan-wu-liang-shou ching 觀無量壽經 [Amitayurdhyāna Sutra]. T 12 (no. 365).

Kuei-yüan chih-chih chi 歸元直指集 [Pointing Directly to the Return to the Origin]. Tsung-pen 宗本. ZZ 2, 13, 2.

Lo-pang wen-lei 樂邦文類 [Essays on the Land of Bliss]. Tsung-hsiao 宗曉. T 47 (no. 1969A).

Lu-shan lien-tsung pao-chien 蘆山蓮宗寶鑑 [The Precious Mirror of the Lotus School of Mount Lu]. P'u-tu 普度. T. 47 (no. 1973).

Mo-ho chih-kuan 摩訶止觀 [Great Concentration and Insight]. Chih-i 智顗. T 46 (no. 1911).

Pan-(Po-)chou san-mei ching 般舟三昧經 [Pratyutpannasamādhi Sutra]. T 13 (no. 417); T. 13 (no. 408).

Pu hsü kao-seng chuan 補續高僧傳 [Supplement to the Continuation of the Biography of Eminent Monks]. Ming-ho 明河. ZZ 2B, 7, 1–2.

Shih-men cheng-t'ung 釋門正統 [Orthodox Lineage of Buddhist Schools]. Tsung-chien 宗鑑. ZZ 2B, 3, 5.

Shih-shih chi-ku lüeh hsü-chi 釋氏稽古略續集 [Continuation of the Brief Compilation of Buddhist History]. Huan-lun 幻輪. T 49 (no. 2038).

Ta-Sung seng-shih lüeh 大宋僧史略 [Sung Compilation of a Brief History of the Sangha]. Tsan-ning 贊寧. T 54 (no. 2126).

T'ien-ju Wei-tse ch'an-shih yü-lu 天如惟則禪師語錄 [Recorded Conversations of the Ch'an Teacher T'ien-ju Wei-tse]. ZZ 2, 27, 5.

Wan-shan t'ung-kuei chi 萬善同歸集 [Myriad Virtues Return to the Same Source]. Yen-shou 延壽. ZZ 2, 15, 5.

Wu-liang-shou ching 無量壽經 [The Larger Sukhāvatīvyūha Sutra). T 12 (no. 363).

Wu-teng ch'üan-shu 五燈全書 [Compendium to the Five Lamps]. Ch'ao-yung 超永. ZZ 2B, 13, 1–15, 1.

Wu-teng yen-t'ung 五燈嚴統 [Strict Lineage of the Five Lamps]. Fei-yin 費隱. ZZ 2B, 12, 1–5.

BOOKS AND ARTICLES IN CHINESE AND JAPANESE

Araki Kengo 荒木見悟. *Bukkyō to Jukyō* 仏教と儒教 [Buddhism and Confucianism]. Kyoto, 1966.

——"Minmatsu ni okeru Ju Butsu chōwaron no seikaku" 明末に於ける儒仏調和論の性格 [The Nature of the Late Ming dispute on the

Comptibility of Confucianism and Buddhism]. *Nihon Chūgoku gakkaihō* 日本中国学会報 XV (October 1966), 210–224.

Chao I 趙翼. *Nien-erh-shih cha chi* 廿二史劄記. [Notes on the Twenty-two Histories]. Peking: Commercial Press, 1958.

Chang Sheng-yen 張聖嚴. *Minmatsu Chūgoku Bukkyō no kenkyū* 明末中国佛教 の研究 [Studies on Chinese Buddhism at the End of the Ming]. Tokyo, 1975.

Chang Wei-ch'iao 張維喬. *Chung-kuo fo-chiao shih* 中國佛敎史 [History of Chinese Buddhism]. Shanghai: Commercial Press, 1929.

Chang Wei-hua 張維華. "Ming-Ch'ing chien Chung-hsi ssu-hsiang chih ch'ung-t'u yü ying-hsiang" 明清間中西思想之衝突與影響 [Conflict and Influence between Chinese and Western Thought during the Transition from the Ming to the Ch'ing]. *Hsüeh ssu* 學思 vol. 1, no. 1 (1942).

——"Ming-Ch'ing chien fo-yeh chih cheng-pien" 明清間佛耶之爭辯 [Controversies between Buddhists and Christians during the Transition from the Ming to the Ch'ing]. *Hsüeh ssu* 學思 vol. 1, no. 1 (1942).

Ch'en Yüan 陳垣. *Ming-chi Tien-Ch'ien fo-chiao k'ao* 明季滇黔佛敎考 [Investigations into Buddhism of Yün-nan and Kuei-chou at the End of the Ming]. Peking, 1940.

——*Ch'ing-ch'u seng-cheng chi* 清初僧諍記 [Controversies within the Sangha at the Beginning of the Ch'ing Dynasty]. Peking: Chung-hua Shu-chü, 1962.

Cheng Chen-to 鄭振鐸. *Ch'a-t'u-pen Chung-kuo wen-hsüeh shih* 插圖本中國文 學史 [The Illustrated History of Chinese Literature]. Hong Kong: Commercial Press, 1961.

Chi Wen-fu 嵇文甫. *Wan-Ming ssu-hsiang shih-lun* 晚明思想史論 [On the History of Thought of the Late Ming]. Chungking: Commercial Press, 1944.

Fa-fang 法舫. "Chin-shih Chung-kuo fo-chiao hsien-chuang" 近世佛敎現 狀. [Conditions of Chinese Buddhism in Contemporary Times]. *Hai-ch'ao yin* 海潮音 October 1934.

Fang Hao 方豪. *Chung-kuo t'ien-chu-chiao jen-wu chuan* 中國天主敎人物傳. [Biographies of Famous Chinese Catholics]. Vol. 1. Hong Kong, 1967.

——"Ming Wan-li nien-chien chih ko-chung chia-ko" 明萬曆年間之各種 價格 [Prices of Various Objects during the Wan-li Reign of the Ming]. *Shih-huo* 食貨 vol. 1, no. 3 (June 1971), pp. 18–20.

Fujita Kōtatsu 藤田宏達. *Genshi Jōdo shisō no kenkyū* 原始浄土思想の研究 [Studies on the Original Pure Land Thought]. Tokyo: Iwanami, 1970.

Hattori Shungai 服部俊崖. "Shina sōkan no enkaku" 支那僧官の沿革 [Evolution of Chinese Monk Officials]. *Bukkyō shigaku* 佛教史学 II (1912), 375–460.

Hirano Yoshitarō 平野義太郎. "Shina ni okeru kyōtō no shakai kyōdō sei-katsu o kiritsu suru minzoku dōtoku—Kōkakaku o chūshin to shite" 支那における郷党の社会協同生活を規律する民衆道徳 ——功過格を中心として [Popular Morality Regulates the Social Cooperative Life of the Community in China—A Study Centering around the *Ledger of Merits and Demerits*]. *Hōritsu jihō* 法律時報 vol. XV, no. 11 (1943), pp. 7–14.

Hou Wai-lu 侯外盧. *Chung-kuo ssu-hsiang t'ung-shih* 中国思想通史 [A General History of Chinese Thought]. Vol. 4B. Peking, 1963.

Hsieh Kuo-chen 謝國楨. *Ming Ch'ing chih-chi tang-she yün-tung k'ao* 明清之際黨社運動考. [Investigation into the Movement of Organizing Parties and Associations during the Period between the Ming and the Ch'ing]. Shanghai: Commercial Press, 1935.

Iwai Hirosato 岩井大慧. "Gensho ni okeru teishitsu to Zensō to no kankei ni tsuite" 元初に於ける帝室と禅僧との関係について. [On the Relationship between the Imperial Household and Ch'an Monks at the Beginning of the Yüan Dynasty]. In *Nisshi Bukkyō shi ronkō* 日支仏教史論考 [Researches into Sino-Japanese Buddhist History]. Tokyo: Toyo Bunko, 1957; pp. 451–544.

Kagamishima Genryū 鏡島元隆. "Hajō koshingi henka katei no ichi-kōsatsu" 百丈古清規変化過程の一考察 [Changes in the *Pai-chang ch'ing-kuei*]. *Komazawa Daigaku Bungakubu kenkyū kiyō*, XXV (March 1967), 1–13.

Kondō Ryōichi 近藤良一. "Hajō shingi to Zen'on shingi" 百丈清規と禅苑清規 [The *Pai-chang ch'ing kuei* and the *Ch'an-yüan ch'ing-kuei*]. *Indogaku Bukkyōgaku kenkyū* 印度学佛教学研究, vol. XVII, no. 2 (1969), pp. 328–330.

——"Hajō shingi no seiritsu to sono genkei" 百丈清規の成立とその原形 [The establishment and original form of the *Pai-chang ch'ing-kuei*]. *Hokkaidō Komazawa Daigaku kenkyū kiyō* 北海道駒沢大学研究紀要, III (November 1968), 19–48.

Li Shou-k'ung 李守孔. "Ming-tai pai-lien-chiao k'ao-lüeh" 明代白蓮教考略 [A Brief Investigation into the White Lotus Sect of the Ming]. *Wen-shih che-hsüeh pao* 文史哲学報 IV (1952), 151–177.

Makita Tairyō 牧田諦亮. *Chūgoku kinsei Bukkyō shi kenkyū* 中国近世佛教史研究 [Studies in the History of Chinese Buddhism of Recent Times]. Kyoto, 1957.

——*Sakugen nyūminki no kenkyū* 策彦入明記の研究 [Studies of the Record of Sakugen's Entry into Ming China]. Vol. II. Kyoto, 1959.

Mano Senryū 間野潜龍. "Mindai chūki no Bukkyō taisaku—Eisō chō o chūshin to shite" 明代中期の仏教対策 ——英宗朝を中心として [Mid-Ming Policies toward Buddhism—Using the Reign of Yin-tsung as the Center of Study]. *Ōtani shigaku* 大谷史学 IV (March 1955), 14–23.

——"Mindai ni okeru sankyō shisō—Rin Chōon o chūshin to shite" 明代に於ける三教思想—林兆恩を中心として [The Thought of Three Teachings in One in the Ming—A Study Centering about Lin Chao-en]. *Tōyōshi kenkyū* 東洋史研究, vol. XII, no. 1 (1952), pp. 18–34.

Masunaga Reihō 増永霊鳳. "Unsei Shukō no kyōgaku" 雲棲袾宏の教学 [The Teaching and Learning of Chu-hung of Yün-ch'i]. *Komazawa daigaku Bukkyō gakkai gakuhō* 駒澤大学仏教学会学報 VIII (April 1938), 52–71.

Mizuno Baigyō 水野梅暁. *Shina Bukkyō kinsei shi no kenkyū* 支那仏教近世史の研究 [Studies in the Recent History of Chinese Buddhism]. Tokyo, 1925.

Mochizuki Shinkō 望月信亨. *Chūgoku Jōdo kyōrishi* 中国浄土教理史 [History of Chinese Pure Land Doctrine]. Kyoto, 1964.

Nan Huai-chin 南懷瑾. *Ch'an-tsung ts'ung-lin chih-tu yü Chung-kuo she-hui* 禪宗叢林制度與中國社會 [The Institution of Ch'an Public Monasteries and Chinese Society]. Taiwan: Tzu-yu chu-pan-she, 1962.

Nukariya Kaiten 忽滑谷快天. *Zengaku shisōshi* 禅学思想史 [History of Zen Buddhist Thought]. Vol. II. Tokyo, 1925.

Ōchō Enichi 横超慧日. "Minmatsu Bukkyō to Kirisutokyō to no sōgo hihan" 明末仏教と基督教との相互批判 [The Mutual Criticisms of Buddhism and Christianity at the End of the Ming]. *Ōtani gakuhō* 大谷学報 vol. XXIX, no. 2 (1949), pp. 1–20; vol. XXIX, nos. 3, 4 (1950), pp. 18–38.

Ogasawara Senshū 小笠原宣秀. *Chūgoku kinsei Jōdokyō shi no kenkyū* 中国近世浄土教史の研究 [Studies in the History of Chinese Pure Land School of Recent Times]. Kyoto, 1963.

——"Chūgoku kindai ni okeru Bukkyō kessha no mondai" 中国近代の於ける仏教結社の問題 [The Problem of Buddhist Associations in China of Recent Times]. *Ryūkoku daigaku ronsō* 龍谷大学論叢 no. 336 (February 1949), pp. 23–35.

——"Gendai Byakurenshū kyōdan no shōchō" 元代白蓮宗教団の消長 [The Growth and Decline of the White Lotus Religious Community in the Yüan Dynasty]. *Ryūkoku daigaku ronsō* 龍谷大学論叢 no. 344 (1952), pp. 1–12.

Ogawa Kan'ichi 小川貫弌. "Sōgen Minshin ni okeru kyōdan no kōzō" 宋元明清に於ける教団の構造 [The Structure of the Sangha during the Sung, Yüan, Ming, and Ch'ing Dynasties]. In *Bukkyō kyōdan no kenkyū* 仏教教団の研究 [Studies on the Buddhist Sangha]. Ed. Yoshimura Shūki 芳村修基. Kyoto, 1968.

——"Koji Bukkyō no kinsei hatten" 居士仏教の近世発展 [Development of Lay Buddhism in Recent Times]. *Ryūkoku daigaku ronsō* 龍谷大学論

叢 no. 339 (1950).

——*Bukkyō bunkashi kenkyū* 仏教文化史研究 [Studies in the History of Buddhist Culture]. Kyoto, 1975.

Ōura Masahiro 大浦正弘. "Mindai Bukkyō ni kansuru ichi kōsatsu—Unsei Shukō to sono sōrin no shakai shisō shi no kenkyū" 明代仏教に関する一考察―雲棲袾宏とその叢林の社会思想史の研究 [A Case Study of Ming Buddhism—The Study in the History of Social Thought of Chu-hung of Yün-ch'i and His Community]. *Hokuriku shigaku* 北陸史学 VII (December 1958), 36–49.

Oyanagi Shigeta 小柳司気太. *Rōsō no shisō to Dōkyō* 老荘の思想と道教 [The Thought of Lao Tzu and Chuang Tzu and Taoism]. Tokyo, 1935.

——"Rimatō to Minmatsu no shisōkai" 利瑪竇と明末の思想界 [Matteo Ricci and the Intellectual Circles of the Late Ming]. In *Zoku Tōyō shisō no kenkyū* 續東洋思想の研究 [Further Studies in Oriental Thought]. Tokyo, 1943; pp. 83–109.

——"Minmatsu no sankyō kankei" 明末の三教関係 [Relationships among the Three Teachings at the End of the Ming]. In *Takase Hakushi kanreki kinen Shinagaku ronsō* 高瀬博士還暦紀念支那学論叢 [Collection of Essays in Chinese Studies Honoring the Sixty-First Birthday of Dr. Takase]. Kyoto, 1928; pp. 349–370.

Ryūchi Kiyoshi 龍池清. "Mindai ni okeru baichō" 明代に於ける賣牒 [The Sale of Ordination Certificates in the Ming]. *Tōhō gakuhō* 東方学報 vol. XI, no. 2 (1940), pp. 279–290.

——"Mindai no sōkan" 明代の僧官 [Monk Officials of the Ming]. *Shina Bukkyō shigaku* 支那仏教史学, vol. IV, no. 3 (1940), pp. 35–46.

——"Minsho no jiin" 明初の寺院 [Buddhist Monasteries in the Early Ming]. *Shina Bukkyō shigaku* 支那仏教史学 vol. II, no. 4 (December 1938), pp. 9–29.

——"Mindai no Yūga kyōsō" 明代の瑜伽教僧 [Monks Specializing in Tantric Rites in the Ming Dynasty]. *Tōhō gakuhō* 東方学報 vol. XI, no. 1 (1940), pp. 405–413.

——"Mindai Pekin ni okeru Rama kyōdan" 明代北京に於ける喇嘛教団 [The Lamaist Monastic Community in Peking during the Ming Dynasty]. *Bukkyō kenkyū* 仏教研究 vol. IV, no. 6 (1941), pp. 65–76.

Sakai Tadao 酒井忠夫. *Chūgoku zensho no kenkyu* 中国善書の研究 [Studies on the Morality Books of China]. Tokyo, 1960.

——"Shukō no Jichiroku ni tsuite" 袾宏の自知録について [Concerning the Record of Self-Knowledge of Chu-hung]. In *Fukui Hakushi shōju kinen Tōyō bunka ronshū* 福井博士頌寿紀念東洋文化論集 [Collection of Essays in Oriental Thought Honoring the Birthday of Dr. Fukui]. Tokyo: Waseda Daigaku, 1969; pp. 467–482.

Sakakibara Tokusō 榊原徳草. "Unsei Shukō no Nembutsu Zen" 雲棲株宏の念佛禅 [The Zen of Buddha-Recitation of Yün-ch'i Chu-hung]. *Zenshū* 禅宗 vol. XXXVIII, no. 1, (1931), p. 3.

Sasaki Senshō 佐々木宣正. "Unsei Shukō to sono chosaku" 雲棲株宏と其著作 [Yün-ch'i Chu-hung and His Writings]. *Rokujō gakuhō* 六条学報 nos. 102, 103 (April 1910), pp. 41–46, 35–40.

Sekino Tadashi 関野貞 and Tokiwa Daijō 常盤大定. *Shina Bukkyō shiseki* 支那仏教史蹟 [Chinese Buddhist Historical Sites]. Tokyo, 1925–1929.

Shigematsu Shunshō 重松俊章. "Tō Sō jidai no Mirokukyō hi" 唐宋時代の弥勒教匪 [The Maitreya Rebels of the T'ang and Sung Times]. *Shien* 史淵 III (1931), 68–103.

Shih Tung-ch'u 釋東初. *Chung-kuo chin-shih fo-chiao shih* 中国近世佛教史 [History of Chinese Buddhism in Recent Times]. Taipei: Chung-hua fo-chiao wen-hua-kuan, 1974.

Shiina Kōyū 椎名宏雄. "Shotō Zensha no Ritsuin kyojū ni tsuite 初唐禅者の律院居住について [Zen Monks Living in Vinaya Temples in the Early T'ang Dynasty]. *Indogaku Bukkyōgaku kenkyū* 印度学仏教学研究, vol. XVII, no. 2 (1969), pp. 325–327.

Shimizu Taiji 清水泰次. "Mindai ni okeru Butsudō no torishimari" 明代に於ける仏道の取締 [Government Restrictions on Buddhism and Taoism during the Ming]. *Shigaku zasshi* 史学雑誌 vol. XL, no. 3 (1929), pp. 1–48.

——"Mindai ni okeru shūkyō yūgō to Kōkakaku" 明代に於ける宗教融合と功過格 [Religious Syncretism and the *Ledger of Merits and Demerits* in the Ming]. *Shichō* 史潮 vol. VI, no. 3 (1936), pp. 29–55.

Suzuki Chūsei 鈴木中正. "Bukkyō no kinsatsu kairitsu ga Sōdai no minshu seikatsu ni oyoboseru eikyō ni tsuite" 仏教の禁殺戒律ガ宋代民衆生活に及せる影響について [The Buddhist Precept Against Killing and Its Influence on the Life of the Common People in the Sung Dynasty]. *Shūkyō kenkyū* 宗教研究 vol. 3/1, no. 107 (1941), pp. 115–141.

——"Sōdai Bukkyō kessha no kenkyū" 宋代仏教結社の研究 [Studies on the Buddhist Associations of the Sung Dynasty]. *Shigaku zasshi* 史学雑誌 vol. LII (1941), pp. 65–98, 205–241, 303–333.

Tachibana Shiraki 橘樸. *Shina shisō no kenkyū* 支那思想の研究 [Studies in Chinese Thought]. Tokyo, 1936.

Takao Giken 高雄義堅. "Unsei Daishi Shukō ni tsuite" 雲棲大師株宏について [On Chu-hung, the Great Master of Yün-ch'i]. In *Naitō Hakushi shōju kinen shigaku ronsō* 内藤博士頌寿紀念史学論叢 [Collection of Essays in Historical Studies Honoring the Birthday of Dr. Naitō]. Kyoto, 1930; pp. 215–272.

——"Sōdai sōkan seido no kenkyū" 宋代僧官制度の研究 [Studies of Monk Officials of the Sung]. *Shina Bukkyō shigaku* 支那仏教史学,

vol. IV, no. 4 (1941).

——"Mindai ni taisei sareta Kōkakaku shisō" 明代に大成された功過格思想 [The Thought of the *Ledger of Merits and Demerits* Which Reached Its Completion in the Ming]. *Ryūkoku daigaku ronsō* 龍谷大学論叢 no. 244, pp. 324–337.

——*Sōdai Bukkyōshi no kenkyū* 宋代仏教史の研究 [Studies in the History of Buddhism of the Sung Dynasty]. Kyoto, 1975.

T'ang Yung-t'ung 湯用彤. *Han Wei liang-Chin Nan-pei-ch'ao fo-chiao shih* 漢魏兩晉南北朝佛教史 [History of Buddhism in the Han, Wei, Western and Eastern Chin, and North and South Dynasties]. Taipei: Commercial Press, 1962 reprint.

T'ao Hsi-sheng 陶希聖. "Yüan-tai Mi-le Pai-lien-chiao-hui ti pao-tung" 元代彌勒白蓮教會的暴動 [Riots of Maitreya and White Lotus Sectarians in the Yüan]. *Shih-huo* 食貨 vol. I, no. 4 (1935), pp. 36–39, 152–155.

Tokiwa Daijō 常盤大定. *Shina ni okeru Bukkyō to Jukyō Dōkyō* 支那に於ける仏教と儒教道教 [Buddhism and Confucianism, Taoism in China]. Tokyo: Toyo Bunko, 1966.

Tsukamoto Zenryū 塚本善隆. "Sō jidai no zun'an shikyō tokudo no seido" 宋時代の童行試経得度の制度 [The Sung Practice of Initiating Novices after Testing Their Scriptural Knowledge]. *Shina Bukkyō shigaku* 支那仏教史学 III (1941), 42–64.

——*Tō chūki no Jōdokyō* 唐中期の浄土教 [Pure Land School of the Mid-T'ang]. *Tōhō Bunka Gakuin Kyōto Kenkyūjo kenkyū hōkoku* 東方文化学院京都研究所研究報告 vol. IV. Kyoto, 1933.

Ui Hakuju 宇井伯寿. *Zenshūshi kenkyū* 禅宗史研究 [Studies in the History of the Ch'an School]. Vol. II. Tokyo, 1941.

Wang Te-chao 王德昭. *Ming-chi chih cheng-chih yü she-hui* 明季之政治與社會 [Politics and Society at the End of the Ming]. Chungking, 1942.

Wu Han 吳晗. *Chin-p'ing-mei yü Wang Shih-chen chih chu-tso shih-tai chi ch'i she-hui pei-ching* 金瓶梅與王世貞之著作時代及其社會背景 [The Golden Lotus and Its Time of Writing as Well as the Social Background of Wang Shih-chen]. Hong Kong: Nan-t'ien shu-yeh kung-ssu, 1967 reprint.

——*Chu Yüan-chang chuan* 朱元璋傳 [Biography of Chu Yüan-chang]. Hong Kong: Chuan-chi wen-hsüeh-she reprint, n.d.

Yajima Genryō 矢島玄亮. *Shina Butsudō nempu* 支那仏道年譜 [Year by Year Account of the Main Events in Chinese Buddhism and Taoism]. Tokyo, 1937.

Yabuki Keiki 矢吹慶輝. *Sankaikyō no kenkyū* 三階教の研究 [Studies in the Three-Stage Sect]. Tokyo: Iwanami Shoten, 1927.

Yanagida Seizan 柳田聖山. *Shoki no zenshi II: Rekidai hōbō ki* 初期の禅史II:

歴代法宝記 [History of Early Ch'an, vol. II: Record of the Dharma Treasure in Successive Generations]. In *Zen no goroku* 禅の語録 [Recorded Conversations of Ch'an Masters], vol. 3. Tokyo: Chikuma Shobo, 1976.

——*Shoki Zenshū shisho no kenkyū* 初期禅宗史書の研究 [Studies in Early Ch'an Historical Texts]. Kyoto, 1967.

Yoshioka Yoshitoyo 吉岡義豊. "Shoki no Kōkakaku ni tsuite" 初期の功過格について [On the *Ledger of Merits and Demerits* in the Early Period]. *Tōyō Bunka Kenkyūjo kiyō* 東洋文化研究所記要 no. 27 (1962), pp. 107–186.

——"Chūgoku minshū no rinrisho Kōkakaku ni tsuite" 中国民衆の倫理書功過格について [On the *Ledger of Merits and Demerits*, A Book of Ethics for the Chinese Common People]. *Shūkyō kenkyū* 宗教研究 no. 127 (October 1951), pp. 72–74.

BOOKS AND ARTICLES IN ENGLISH

Alchemy, Medicine, Religion in the China of A.D. 320: The Nei P'ien of Ko Hung. Tr. James R. Ware. Cambridge, Mass.: MIT Press, 1966.

Ames, Michael. *Religious Syncreticism in Buddhist Ceylon.* Unpublished PhD dissertation, Harvard University, 1962.

The Amitāyur-dhyāna-sūtra. Tr. J. Takakusu. In *Buddhist Mahāyāna Texts.* Ed. F. Max Müller. *The Sacred Books of the East,* vol. XLIX. New York: Dover Publications, 1969; pp. 161–201.

The Blue Cliff Records, The Hekigan Roku: Containing One-Hundred Stories of Zen Masters of Ancient China. Tr. and ed. with commentary by R. D. M. Shaw. London: Joseph, 1961.

Balazs, Etienne. *Chinese Civilization and Bureaucracy.* New Haven, Conn.: Yale University Press, 1964.

Bodde, Derk, and Clarence Morris. *Law in Imperial China.* Cambridge, Mass.: Harvard University Press, 1967.

Brunnert, H. S., and V. V. Hagelstrom. *Present-Day Political Organization of China.* Taipei: Book World Company, undated reprint of the 1910 edition.

The Catechism of the Shaman: or, The Laws and Regulations of the Priesthood of Buddha in China. Tr. Charles Fried Neumann. London: Oriental Translation Fund, 1831.

Chan, Wing-tsit. *Religious Trends in Modern China.* New York, Columbia University Press, 1953.

Ch'en, Kenneth. *Buddhism in China: A Historical Survey.* Princeton, N. J.: Princeton University Press, 1964.

Ch'oe Pu's (1454–1504) Diary: A Record of Drifting across the Sea. Tr., with introduction and notes, by John Meskill. Tuscon: Published for the Association for Asian Studies by the University of Arizona Press, 1965.

Ch'ü, T'ung-tsu. *Law and Society in Traditional China.* Paris and the Hague: Mouton, 1961.

——*Local Government in China under the Ch'ing.* Cambridge, Mass.: Harvard University Press, 1962.

The City in Late Imperial China. Ed. G. William Skinner. Stanford: Stanford University Press, 1977.

Cohn, Norman. *The Pursuit of the Millennium: Revolutionary Millenarians and Mystical Anarchists of the Middle Ages.* Rev. and enlarged edition. New York: Oxford University Press, 1970.

Collcutt, Martin. *The Zen Monastic Institutes in Medieval Japan.* Unpublished Ph.D. dissertation, Harvard University, 1975.

de Bary, Wm. Theodore. "Individualism and Humanitarianism in Late Ming Thought." In *Self and Society in Ming Thought,* by Wm. Theodore de Bary and the Conference on Ming Thought. New York: Columbia University Press, 1970; pp. 145–225.

"Neo-Confucian Cultivation and the Seventeenth-Century 'Enlightenment.'" In *The Unfolding of Neo-Confucianism.* Ed. Wm. Theodore de Bary. New York: Columbia University Press, 1975; 141–216.

DeGroot, J. J. M. *Le Code du Mahayana en Chine: Son Influence sur la vie monacale et sur le monde laïque.* Amsterdam: Johannes Müller, 1893.

Dumoulin, Heinrich, S. J. *The Development of Chinese Zen after the Sixth Patriarch in the Light of Mumonkan.* Tr. Ruth Fuller Sasaki. New York: The First Zen Institute of America, Inc., 1953.

Dutt, Sukumar. *Early Buddhist Manachism, 600 B.C.–100 B.C.* London: Kegan Paul, 1924.

Eberhard, Wolfram. *Guilt and Sin in Traditional China.* Berkeley: University of California Press, 1967.

——"Temple-Building Activities in Medieval and Modern China," *Monumenta Serica,* XXIII (1964), 264–318.

Eitel, E. J. *Handbook of Buddhism.* 2d rev. ed. Tokyo: Sanshusha, 1904.

Ennin's Diary. The Record of a Pilgrimage to China in Search of the Law. Tr. Edwin O. Reischauer. New York: Ronald Press, 1955.

Erikson, Erik H. *Young Man Luther.* New York: W. W. Norton, 1962.

Facets of Taoism. Ed. Homes Welch and Anna Seidel. New Haven: Yale University Press, 1979.

Fonti Ricciane. Ed. P. M. d'Elia. 3 vols. Rome, 1924–1949.

Fung, Yu-lan. *A History of Chinese Philosophy.* Tr. by Derk Bodde Vol. I. Princeton, N.J.: Princeton University Press, 1952.

Gallagher, Louis J. *China in the 16th Century: The Journal of Matteo Ricci, 1583–1610.* New York: Random House, 1953.

Geiss, James. *Peking Under the Ming (1368–1644)*. Unpublished Ph.D. dissertation, Princeton University, 1979.

Hackmann, H. "Buddhist Monastery Life in China." *East of Asia Magazine*, vol. I, no. 3 (September 1902), pp. 239–261.

Ho, Ping-ti. *The Ladder of Success in Imperial China*. New York: John Wiley and Sons, 1964.

——*Studies on the Population of China, 1368–1953*. Cambridge, Mass.: Harvard University Press, 1959.

Hsu, Sung-peng. *A Buddhist Leader in Ming China: The Life and Thought of Han-shan Te-ch'ing*. University Park: Pennsylvania State University Press, 1979.

Hucker, Charles O. *The Censorial System of Ming China*. Stanford, Calif.: Stanford University Press, 1966.

——"An Index of Terms and Titles in Governmental Organization of the Ming Dynasty." *Harvard Journal of Asiatic Studies*, XXIII (1960–1961), 127–151.

Hurvitz, Leon. "Chu-hung's One Mind of Pure Land and Ch'an Buddhism." In *Self and Society in Ming Thought*, by Wm. Theodore de Bary and the Conference on Ming Thought. New York: Columbia University Press, 1970; pp. 451–476.

The Golden Lotus. Tr. Clement Edgerton. New York: Grove Press, 1954.

Gombrich, Richard F. *Precept and Practice: Traditional Buddhism in the Rural Highlands of Ceylon*. Oxford: Clarendon Press, 1971.

Johnston, Reginald F. *Buddhist China*. London: Murray 1913.

King, Winston, *A Thousand Lives Away*. Oxford: Cassirer, 1964.

Lancashire, D. "Buddhist Reaction to Christianity in Late Ming China." *The Journal of the Oriental Society of Australia*, VI, nos. 1, 2 (1968–1969), 82–103.

Liu, Ts'un-yan. "Yuan Huang and His 'Four Admonitions.'" *The Journal of the Oriental Society of Australia*, vol. V, nos. 1, 2 (1967), 108–132.

The Master Who Embraces Simplicity: A Study of the Philosopher Ko Hung, A.D. 283–343. Tr. Jay Sailey. San Francisco: Chinese Materials Center, 1978.

Miller, Robert, "Button, Button—Great Tradition, Little Tradition, Whose Tradition?" *Anthropological Quarterly*, 39 (1966), 26–42.

Overmyer, Daniel L. "Folk Buddhist Religion: Creation and Eschatology in Medieval China." *History of Religions*, vol. XII, no. 1 (August 1972), 42–70.

——*Folk Buddhist Religion: Dissenting Sects in Late Traditional China*. Cambridge, Mass.: Harvard University Press, 1976.

Pas, Julian. "Shan-tao's Interpretation of the Meditative Vision of Buddha Amitayus." *History of Religion*, vol. 14, no. 2 (1974), pp. 96–116.

Prebish, Charles S. *Buddhist Monastic Discipline: The Sanskrit Prātimokṣa Sūtras of the Mahāsāṃghikas and Mūlasarvāstivādins.* University Park. Pennsylvania State University Press, 1975.

Prip-Møller, J. *Chinese Buddhist Monasteries.* Copenhagen: G.E.C. Gad; London: Oxford University Press, 1937.

Redfield, Robert. *The Little Community, Peasant Society, and Culture.* Chicago: Chicago University Press, 1962.

Reischauer, Edwin O. *Ennin's Travels in T'ang China.* New York: Ronald Press, 1955.

Religion and Ritual in Chinese Society. Ed. Arthur Wolf. Stanford: Stanford University Press, 1974.

Religious Syncretism in Antiquity. Ed. Birger A. Pearson. Montana: Scholars' Press 1975.

Sakai, Tadao. "Confucianism and Popular Educational Works." In *Self and Society in Ming Thought,* by Wm. Theodore de Bary and the Conference on Ming Thought. New York: Columbia University Press, 1976; pp. 331–366.

Shih, Vincent Y. C. "Some Chinese Rebel Ideologies," *T'oung Pao,* 44 (1956), 151–226.

Singer, Milton. *When a Great Tradition Modernizes: An Anthropological Approach to Indian Civilization.* New York: Praeger, 1972.

——"Text and Context in the Study of Religion and Social Change in India." *Adyar Library Bulletin,* 15 (1961), 274–303.

Spiro, Melford E. *Buddhism and Society: Its Burmese Vicissitudes.* New York: Ronald Press, 1955.

——*Burmese Supernaturalism.* Englewood Cliffs, N.J.: Prentice-Hall, 1967.

Srinivas, Mysore N. *Religion and Society among the Coorgs of South India.* London and New York: Oxford University Press, 1952.

Staal, J. F. "Sanskrit and Sanskritization." *Journal of Asian Studies,* 22 (1963), 261–276.

Suzuki, D. T. *Essays in Zen Buddhism.* 2d. ser. London: Rider, 1958.

Syncretism. Ed. Sven S. Hartman. Stockholm: Almqvist, 1969.

Tambiah, S. J. *Buddhism and the Spirit Cults in Northeast Thailand.* Cambridge: Cambridge University Press, 1970.

——*World Conqueror and World Renouncer.* Cambridge: Cambridge University Press, 1977.

——"The Ideology of Merit and the Social Correlates of Buddhism in a Thai Village." In *Dialectic in Practical Religion.* Ed. E. R. Leach. Cambridge: Cambridge University Press, 1968.

Traditional Chinese Stories: Themes and Variations. Ed. Y. W. Ma and Joseph S. M. Lau. New York: Columbia University Press, 1978.

Treatise of the Exalted One on Response and Retribution. Tr. D. T. Suzuki and

Paul Carus. La Salle, Ill.: The Open Court Publishing Company, 1944.

Wadley, Susan Snow. *Shakti: Power in the Conceptual Structure of Karimpur Religion.* Chicago: University of Chicago Department of Anthropology, 1975.

Warren, Henry Clarke. *Buddhism in Translations.* New York: Atheneum, 1963.

Welch, Holmes. *The Parting of the Way.* Boston: Beacon Press, 1966.

——*The Practice of Chinese Buddhism.* Cambridge, Mass.: Harvard University Press, 1967.

——*The Buddhist Revival in China.* Cambridge, Mass.: Harvard University Press, 1968.

——*Buddhism under Mao.* Cambridge, Mass.: Harvard University Press, 1972.

——"Dharma Scrolls and the Succession of Abbots in Chinese Monasteries," *T'oung Pao,* 50 (1963), 93–149.

Wright, Arthur. *Buddhism in Chinese History.* Stanford, Calif.: Stanford University Press, 1970.

Wu, Pei-i, "Self-Examination and Confession of Sins in Traditional China," *Harvard Journal of Asiatic Studies,* Vol. 39, no. 1 (June 1979), 5–38.

Yampolsky, Philip B. *The Platform Sūtra of the Sixth Patriarch.* New York: Columbia University Press, 1967.

——Tr. *The Zen Master Hakuin: Selected Writings.* New York: Columbia University Press, 1971.

Yang, C. K. *Religion in Chinese Society.* Berkeley and Los Angeles: University of California Press, 1967.

Yang, Lien-sheng. *Money and Credit in China: A Short History.* Cambridge, Mass.: Harvard University Press, 1952.

——"Buddhist Monasteries and Four Money-Raising Institutions in Chinese History," in *Studies in Chinese Institutional History.* Cambridge, Mass.: Harvard University Press, 1961.

Yü, Chün-fang. "Ta-hui Tsung-kao and *Kung-an* Ch'an," *Journal of Chinese Philosophy,* 6 (1979), 211–235.

Zen Comments on the Mumonkan. Tr. Sumiko Kudo. New York: Harper & Row, 1974.

Zürcher, E. *The Buddhist Conquest of China.* Leiden: E. J. Brill, 1959.

INDEX

NEO-CONFUCIAN STUDIES

TRANSLATIONS FROM THE ORIENTAL CLASSICS

MODERN ASIAN LITERATURE SERIES

STUDIES IN ORIENTAL CULTURE

COMPANIONS TO ASIAN STUDIES

INTRODUCTION TO ORIENTAL CIVILIZATIONS
Wm. Theodore de Bary, *Editor*